American Voting Behavior

EDITED BY EUGENE BURDICK

AND ARTHUR J. BRODBECK

The Free Press, New York
Collier-Macmillan Limited, London

Printed in the United States of America

Collier-Macmillan Canada, Ltd., Toronto, Ontario

Library of Congress Catalog Card Number: 57-12634

Second printing March 1968

Contents

lished in 1928, is the first noteworthy attempt to connect quantitative research on voting behavior with more general social science problems, such as the study of social change and the determinants of attitudes.

The second work appeared sixteen years later. *The People's Choice*, by Paul F. Lazarsfeld, Bernard Berelson, and Hazel Gaudet, was first published in 1944, with a second edition in 1948.[4] The book reports on the first sophisticated application of survey techniques to a presidential election, the 1940 contest between Franklin D. Roosevelt and Wendell Willkie. Although public opinion polling agencies had been in operation since 1934 and had correctly forecast the 1936 presidential contest, it remained for Lazarsfeld and his associates, in their study of the 1940 election in Erie County, Ohio, to exploit thoroughly the possibilities of the interview technique as a means of studying voting.

Directly linked with the previous study by authorship, the third major work to be considered is *Voting*, by Bernard Berelson, Paul F. Lazarsfeld, and William N. McPhee.[5] Employing much the same technique of repeated interviews with a sample of respondents, this is a study of the surprising 1948 contest between Harry S. Truman and Thomas E. Dewey. The setting for the study was the small industrial city of Elmira, New York.

The final work examined is another interview study, this time of the 1952 presidential election, based on a nationwide sample. *The Voter Decides*,[6] by Angus Campbell, Gerald Gurin, and Warren E. Miller, represents the most sophisticated nationwide study of a presidential election yet reported. The continuity between this and previous works is less direct than between *The People's Choice* and *Voting*. In large part, this report stems from a different research tradition and will provide, therefore, a useful contrast to the previous two works.

Procedure. Our investigation into continuity takes us in two directions—back into the past and forward into the future. To begin with, the threads of continuity which link together the four researches will be traced. Here three major concerns are involved: First, what are the continuities and discontinuities over time in substantive interests? What do they all have in common beyond a general concern with voting behavior? What are the common problems which they touch upon? What does each have as its particular contribution?

Second, what are the modifications over time in explanatory interpretations? What are the different "models" of voting behavior explicitly or implicitly held?

Third, what is the impact of changes in research techniques upon substantive interests and explanatory schemes? What sorts of substantive questions are particularly suited to the techniques employed, and which substantive questions have been by-passed as a consequence of the employment of a particular technique?

Looking forward into the future is almost a necessary consequence of assessing the past. An attempt will be made to suggest new questions and to reactivate old ones which have been by-passed. In addition, the new research designs which appear to me to be most appropriate in providing continuity into the future will be given in rough outline.

In the sections that follow, the procedure is to present brief descriptions of each research, stressing continuity with its immediate predecessor. Then a small number of crucial substantive topics are discussed in detail, using the same treatment of each topic through the several researches. Finally, my assessment of the future is presented.

"QUANTITATIVE METHODS IN POLITICS." In retrospect, it seems almost inevitable that some of the earliest work on voting behavior began within Columbia University's Department of Sociology in the period of the dominance of Franklin H. Giddings (1910-30). His strong emphasis on quantitative research, in a period when original data collection methods were only crudely developed, led a generation of graduate students to exploit available forms of quantitative data in a variety of published sources. Official election statistics were one source of data to which those students turned. Among the voting researches which were carried out by this group were Rice's own dissertation and a number of smaller studies by William F. Ogburn.[7]

Topical Summary. In writing *Quantitative Methods in Politics*, it was Rice's primary purpose to present the case for an empirical, value-free political science. Accordingly, a long prefatory section[8] sets forth general arguments for his point of view, followed by the presentation of eighteen small researches, each illustrating the utility of the quantitative approach to the study of politics. The following discussion is concerned primarily with these empirical studies.[9]

The eighteen studies cover a wide range of topics, and the data used are drawn from diverse sources. Looked at in a larger perspective, each study can be subsumed under one or another of four major topics. Each topic, or theme, is reviewed briefly below.

The first theme expressed by Rice is concerned with political behavior as the manifestation of political attitudes. Ultimately, all political events are the resultants of the attitudes of individuals. The citizen expresses his political attitudes in his voting pattern; officials, in their decisions; and so on. Rice develops three major ideas concerning the political attitudes which underlie political behavior. Taken together, these form his more or less explicit model of political behavior.

He shows first of all that attitudes are only partly determined by objective reality; they serve largely to screen objects in the social world. Rice describes a small study in which students were asked to match occupations to a set of photographs of prominent persons. He found that the students were guided in their matching primarily by their stereotyped notions of what a labor leader, senator, Bolshevik, etc., look like.

Rice's second point on attitudes is to propose the hypothesis that they are distributed normally. Being the outcome of an infinite number of causes, political beliefs should therefore show the same tendencies to normality that are shown by other traits with the same causal patterning, such as body weight or height. However, upon examining a number of distributions obtained from administering attitude tests to student populations, he found that normality is not typical. Anormality is then interpreted as indicating the presence of "disturbing factors," such as the activity of propagandists. Rice suggests that one way of studying the conditions under which attitudes are changed is to investigate those cases in which their distributions depart from normality. Thus, the highly skewed distribution of the proportions of the vote obtained by the Republican party in Philadelphia's precincts can be regarded as a measure of the success of the Republican machine.

His third point concerning political attitudes is implied rather than well articulated. For Rice, political attitudes are primarily variants of one basic continuum, radicalism-liberalism-conservatism. Parties, candidates and issues, and voters are all distributed along this single continuum, the outcome of elections being the end product of interactions between voters' positions and those of candidates and parties. The major practical problem of the politician is how to draw the lines between himself and his opponent so that he attracts to himself a majority of voters from his own end of the distribution and from the middle segments.

Rice's second theme concerns the detection and analysis of political differences among various subgroups. Using official election statistics, he shows that urban and rural areas, as well as working-class and white-collar districts, differ in their voting patterns for candidates and referenda; this illustrates the use of official election statistics along with characteristics of small areas, a technique foreshadowing the "ecological" voting studies. Turning to legislative groups, he devises ways of analyzing roll call votes in order to detect differences within legislative bodies. An "index of cohesion" is proposed as a measure of the degree of consensus within subgroups of the legislature, e.g., farmers, workers, Republicans, or Democrats. Another index, measuring the amount of agreement between pairs of legislators, is proposed as a technique for inductively identifying blocs.

None of the other researches to be reviewed here either use official election statistics or study the behavior of legislative bodies. Only Rice's concern with the sources of political differentiation among voters survives in the later studies. His concerns with voting statistics and legislative behavior find their contemporary expressions in another tradition of political behavior research, which will not be considered in this chapter.[10] This should not be taken to mean that such studies do not form a significant line of research; indeed, prominent works clearly in this tradition, such as V. O. Key's *Southern Politics* or Samuel A. Lubell's *The Future of American Politics*, testify to both the vitality and fruitfulness of endeavors along these lines.

Rice's third major concern is with the spatial distribution of political attitudes, as brought about through the diffusion of political beliefs. In a very ingenious way, he shows that "progressive" attitudes (votes for LaFollette) in a number of western states cluster in fairly definite subregions within each state. Adjacent counties are more like each other than like those farther removed. Furthermore, when adjacent counties are connected by well-traveled transportation routes—main roads, railroads, or mail routes—they tend to resemble each other even more closely. Political attitudes, concludes Rice, diffuse along the main lines of communication, opposed only when the character of one area differs radically from that of its neighbor—e.g., open country versus urban areas—or when state boundaries intervene.

The fourth topic Rice takes up is perhaps the most interesting to the present-day reader. A group of six studies is presented, each concerned with the description and analysis of changes in political preference over time. Four of the studies are of long-term trends in vote turnout or party preference. Attention here will be given mainly to the remaining pair of studies of short-term changes.

In brief, Rice's long-term researches are concerned primarily with fitting curves to time-series trends in voter turnout and party preference. For example, he finds that the average length of tenure of office for congressmen increased from the end of the Civil War to the early twenties.

The two studies of major interest are researches on changes in attitudes in student populations. The first is appropriately considered as a sort of "proto-panel," and the second as perhaps the first panel study of changes in voting intentions of individuals. Rice correctly saw that the methods he employed in these two studies were of considerable importance, presenting a close approximation to controlled experiments in field situations.

The design of the "proto-panel" was as follows: William Jennings Bryan visited and spoke to Dartmouth undergraduates on evolution. After his speech, which had been preceded by a considerable amount of discussion on the campus, Rice administered a questionnaire to his students, asking them to report their opinions on evolution before and after Bryan's speech. Rice compares the differences in marginal distributions of attitudes toward evolution before and after the speech for different subgroups of the population, and attributes such differences as may be found to the stimulation of Bryan's visit and the accompanying discussion among students.

Rice's panel study also involved Dartmouth undergraduates. During the 1924 presidential election, Rice and his colleagues administered two waves of questionnaires, one in October and the other in November, to some 400 students. The first-wave questionnaire contained a graphic scale of radicalism-conservatism, on which the student marked his own position, and a question concerning the student's choice for president. The November questionnaire, administered on or about election day, repeated the candidate preference question, but not the radicalism-conservatism scale, Rice's assumption being that such generalized attitudes would not be subject to short-term shifts.

The analysis made by Rice centered around the relationship between the attitude scale and candidate preference. He also noted the turnover in preference between waves, relating the amount of turnover to position on the attitude scale. Contrary to his expectations, he found that the minority radicals shifted more than the majority conservatives, a phenomenon which was later to be noted by the authors of *Voting* and attributed to the effects of the predominant tone of opinion.

Although Rice's analysis was severely limited by the extremely small number of variables for which he had measures, his handling of what he had was very much along the lines of analysis pursued in both *The People's Choice* and *Voting.*

This brief summary obviously cannot do justice to what must be regarded as a thorough-going exploration of a number of avenues of research on political behavior. Many of Rice's most valuable comments are contained in his parenthetical remarks and footnotes.

Style. Reading *Quantitative Methods in Politics*, one cannot help being impressed at many points by its modernity. Many of the questions with which Rice was concerned still interest the reader of today, as is indicated by their persistence in the other researches to be reviewed. Attention is still focused on the topics of political participation, the effects of political campaigns, how political attitudes diffuse through a population, and so on. Nor does the book's modernity rest on the continuity of substance alone. Rice's formulations of the problems of research on these topics and his methodological reasoning are clearly and correctly phrased.

Only one of Rice's preoccupations would strike the reader of today as old-fashioned—his use of the normal curve as his model of the distribution of political attitudes. Rice wrote at the time when attitude measurement was at its earliest beginnings. The normal curve was a model which had been of much utility in the area of intelligence and aptitude testing, and it seems plausible to suppose that Rice and other persons working in the new field of attitude testing were influenced by the success of this model in the area of mental tests.

Despite the seeming modernity of *Quantitative Methods in Politics*, its predominant style is journalistic. Along with historians, journalists then dominated the field of interpretation of voting behavior (even as they do today). Their topical concerns were picked up by Rice and tend to incline his interpretations to historical particulars rather than to general statements. To the extent that he does depart from this predominant style, he seems to be led to do so by his techniques. For example, he starts out with the problem of how the enfranchisement of women affected the balance of support for political parties. His analysis leads him to classify issues into a more general framework of "moral" versus "economic" issues, which differ in their ability to generate differences between the sexes.

There are several reasons for the style Rice used. First of all, it must be remembered that he did his research at a period when social psychology was just beginning to turn to empirical research.[11] Attitude measurement had barely begun. Public opinion polls were to appear some six years later, although "straw votes" and polls of other types were being used by journalists.[12] Experimental work in social psychology, which was to receive such an impetus in the thirties, had just gotten under way, primarily with students as subjects.[13]

Rice's notions about attitudes are as naïve as was the field of social psychology of his time. The simplicity of his approach can be seen in the implicit model of political behavior which underlies his treatment. Political attitudes are viewed mainly as lying along a single continuum of radicalism-conservatism. Their distribution is normal, except when "disturbed" by such processes as the operation of a political machine or a presidential campaign. Another example of simple mechanisms is the culture trait diffusion mechanism, originating in anthropology and applied by Rice to the distribution of political preferences through space.

It must also be recalled that Rice was pioneering in an area where little empirical research had been undertaken before his time. Political science, although long established, had been more concerned with normative political theory, public administration, and public law than with the empirical study of politics. Rice, along with Harold F. Gosnell and William F. Ogburn, who were his contemporaries, was breaking new trails, and no large body of empirical generalizations was available to him.[14]

Another reason for the book's style lies in the primitive state of research technology in Rice's time. Direct attitude measurements could be made only with school or other "captive" populations, and then only with crude and abbreviated instruments. In this connection, it may be noted that only within recent years have such survey organizations as the National Opinion Research Center been bold enough to try interviews lasting more than fifteen to thirty minutes.

Official election statistics were available in the twenties for small political units, but the ecological analyses which were to come later in the history of voting researches had to wait until the census presented detailed breakdowns for comparable areas. It was not until the 1930 census that detailed data on small areas became generally available, especially for cities. The *County Data Book*, presenting complete data by counties for the United States, was published for the first time following the 1940 census.

The restriction imposed by techniques meant that Rice's analyses were necessarily reduced to simple paired relationships, as compared with the complex multivariate analyses which are attempted in the later voting studies. With simple analyses, only questions of relatively low generality can be put to test. Furthermore, the "feedback" from empirical findings is necessarily restricted.

Given these limitations, it must nevertheless be said that Rice managed to lay out, in one form or another, the major problems to which the later voting studies are primarily addressed. It is to Rice's great credit that he saw his book as constituting mainly a prolegomenon to an empirical approach in the study of political behavior, as its last paragraph, quoted below, indicates:

> In conclusion, then, I can express little more than the hope, already indicated repeatedly in preceding pages, that this book will contribute to a genuine development of a science of politics by finding employment in the labor of other investigators. A working philosophy, a few hypotheses, a few evidences more or less successfully bearing upon verification, not a little 'raw' and undigested statistical data, and some samples of technical devices which may suggest analogous procedures to others, are

to be found in the foregoing pages. Whoever can put any of these ingredients to use and in doing so discover the errors, shortcomings and unseen possibilities which are contained, is more than welcome. He will share in the creative enterprise to which the book aspires, the limited realization of which is to no one more apparent than the author.[15]

"THE PEOPLE'S CHOICE." Between the publication of Rice's classic work and the start of the research reported in *The People's Choice* lies a gap of twelve years. An additional four years were to pass until publication of the volume itself in 1944. The gap between these two books is large not only in time, but in many other respects. Lazarsfeld and his associates entered upon the study of voting from an entirely different direction, using techniques unknown to Rice and without any knowledge of his previous work. Despite these disparities, however, there is considerable continuity in substance and some in method, as will be documented below.

The Intellectual Background. The historical roots of *The People's Choice* stem mainly from two sources, neither of which is directly related to voting behavior or to the other concerns of political science.[16] One main impetus stems from the senior author's long-standing interest in the "psychology of choice." Early in his career, while still in Vienna, he was concerned with the occupational choices of youth.[17] Finding that such choices were exceedingly difficult to unravel, he then turned to the study of simpler decisions—consumer market preferences, radio program popularity, etc.

The second main historical root derives from research on effects of advertising and propaganda, and thus on effects of the mass media. During the thirties, the Office of Radio Research, of which Lazarsfeld was director, conducted much of the pioneer research on both consumer preferences and mass-media effects. A few years before the 1940 presidential election, Lazarsfeld became convinced that the research design best suited to joint study of consumer preference and mass-media effects would be a panel study[18] of consumer purchases. A sample of households would be repeatedly surveyed over time and their changes in brands of consumer goods could be related to their exposure to advertising in the mass media.

Despairing of obtaining financial support for a panel study of consumer preferences, Lazarsfeld hit upon the idea of studying the impact of a presidential campaign upon a panel of voters, who would be interviewed repeatedly during the course of the campaign. With this less commercial focus, financial support was obtained from the Rockefeller Foundation for a panel study of the 1940 presidential campaign. Later Time, Inc., was to contribute additional funds.

As finally laid out, the Erie County study was to have two main goals. The first was to study how voters made up their minds during a presidential campaign, with primary emphasis on how they were affected by exposure to the mass media of communication. An elaborate analysis of content of the mass media in Erie County during the campaign was to be undertaken, along with lengthy interviews with a panel of voters concerning their exposure to the media.

The second major concern was methodological. Little was known at that time about effects of repeated interviewing, or about characteristics of persons who dropped out of panels in the later interviews—hence the elaborate sampling design, consisting of a main panel of 600 respondents interviewed seven times, plus four matched control groups who were each interviewed twice.

Explicit in the goals of the study and built into the design was a model of voting behavior which subsequently turned out to be far from the mark. The view incorporated in the study was an analogy drawn from the senior author's work in consumer behavior in a highly competitive consumer goods market. The prospective voter, like the new shopper in a supermarket, is confronted after the conventions with an array of candidates, similar to the array of brands in a store. Each candidate has his own particular qualities, some superficial like the packaging of food products, others more intrinsic like his opinions on issues. The predispositions (attitudes) of the voter are acted upon by the mass media, just as advertising acts upon the shopper. The voter vacillates between one and the other candidate as propaganda from both sides filters down to him. Finally he comes to a decision, perhaps at the last moment before he enters the polling booth, just as the undecided shopper makes her choice at the food bins in the supermarket.

In other words, voting, like buying, was considered an individualistic act, affected mainly by the voter's personality and his exposure to the mass media. Hence, the emphasis in the study design was on the mass media. The choice of a single community as the study's setting was dictated largely by the desire to keep the diverse exposures of the individuals studied to a minimum.

The model turned out to be wrong at several crucial points. First, it was discovered that on the electoral "market" there are a large number of voters with strong "brand loyalties"; most of them had long-standing attachments to one or the other political party. Second, most voters had made up their minds very early in the campaign and remained steadfast in their choices throughout the period of study. Out of 600 respondents in the main panel, only 54 persons were found who changed preferences during the study. Third, in the absence of changes in voting preference, effects of the mass media and the campaign could not be clearly discerned. Finally, of the several "personality" measures used—e.g., "extroversion-introversion"—none were found to be variables which carried any weight in the analysis.[19]

Perhaps the most serious failure of the model was the heavy weight it gave to the anticipated effects of the mass media. Considerable labor went into content analyses of newspapers and radio broadcasts, and much interviewing time was spent in obtaining careful measures of the exposure of voters to campaign news.

So few of the initial expectations of the study were borne out in the findings that it would be difficult for the reader to reconstruct the study's original aims from the report alone. The analysis[20] as finally presented is organized along lines very different from what the original emphasis in the design would seem to indicate.

A word of caution must be inserted at this point: It is easy for present-day readers to judge *The People's Choice* as perhaps an elaboration of the obvious, and to marvel that these researchers were so naïve in employing the simple model described above as a starting point. From the vantage point of current knowledge of voting behavior, much of it stemming from this work and other survey researches following it, these findings may appear much more obvious than they did to readers at the time of the first appearance of the study.

Topical Outline. In view of the breakdown of the original focus of the Erie County study, much of what was finally published must be judged to be unanticipated findings that emerged primarily in the course of the analysis. Three of the four major themes may be considered largely as examples of emergent findings.

To begin with, it was discovered early in the analysis phase that the two "background variables," socioeconomic status and religion, along with rural-urban residence, played a very heavy role in determining which candidate the respondent would prefer. Particularly puzzling[21] to the researchers was the strong difference in party preference between Catholics and Protestants, which was maintained regardless of what third variable was employed as a control. Here was a variable only remotely related to the 1940 presidential election or to politics in general, which nevertheless played at least as important a role as many seemingly more politically relevant factors. The weak interpretation offered by the authors for this finding is evidence of their inability to assimilate its implications properly.

So strong were the relationships of religion, socioeconomic status, and rural-urban residence that the index of political predispositions —a combined measure of the three—was able to account for more of the variation in the vote than any other measure included in the survey.

The second major set of findings concerned amount and character of voter changes during the campaign. Contrary to the researchers' expectations, few respondents actually came to their final decision during the campaign period, and an even smaller number was found to change from one to the other candidate. Far from conforming to the portrait of the "rational independent voter," the favorite of the political seer, changers were characterized by a relatively low interest in the election contest and a low level of exposure to campaign propaganda; they were closer in characteristics to the apathetic citizen. The most important finding was the discovery of the role of "cross-pressures." Voters having some characteristics predisposing them to vote in one direction and other characteristics with opposite implications were most likely to show a pattern of vacillation and indecision. The "independent voter" was seen to be a voter in conflict, who reacted to the conflict by withdrawal and indecision.

The third major set of findings concerned the social character of voting, although the initial model of the vote decision process had viewed voting as an individual act. The homogeneity of political preference within the respondents' families, and the frequent mention of personal contacts as reasons for their changes in voting preference led to the realization that the electoral choice was more of a "group decision" than an individual one. Furthermore, there was more evidence of the effectiveness of personal influence on voters than there was evidence for the effectiveness of mass media. The data from which these conclusions arose were fragmentary, and most of the treatment of this area must be considered speculative rather than empirical, yet this was to constitute one of the most widely disseminated findings of *The People's Choice.* The wholly speculative last chapter, "The Nature of Personal Influence," became the most frequently reprinted and referred-to section of the book.

Finally, the selective attention of the voter to the content of the campaign was to force a revision of the researchers' conceptions of the role of mass media. Far from serving to convert the undecided, convince the independent, and seduce the antagonist, the campaign of each party reached primarily the most partisan within each camp. The major function of the mass media was to reinforce already formed preferences, with the minor function of reactivating dormant predispositions. If the campaign was to be thought of as having any effect, it would have to be through the highly partisan within each camp. The "two-step flow of influence"—from the mass media, to the opinion leaders, to the rank and file—was therefore advanced as a hypothesis which would tie together these findings and the social character of the voting decision.

If these findings were so largely unanticipated, as suggested here, how did Lazarsfeld and his associates arrive at them? This question breaks down into two subquestions: Why were measurements made on the variables which turned out to be crucial, but which were not anticipated to play such roles? And, how did the analysts hit on the correlations upon which the final interpretation rested? While there is no direct evidence about how the analysts came to their final conclusions, an attempt can be made to reconstruct the process from our general knowledge of the research "tradition" underlying the study.

Many of the variables were included in the study because they were standard items in the usual public opinion poll or market research study: socioeconomic status, religious preference, education, or age, are ordinarily included as a matter of course in any survey research. These are the so-called "background" or "demographic" variables, so useful as checks on the representativeness of one's sample and as probable correlates of the phenomenon under study. It is almost standard operating procedure in the usual survey to investigate their relationships to the major dependent variables early in the analysis.

Other items were included for purposes other than the final uses to which they were put. Perhaps the most dramatic example of this sort is one of the questions used to define opinion leadership: "Have you tried to convince anyone of your political ideas recently?" This item was originally included as part of a battery designed to measure "extroversion." Although the entire battery of items turned out to be rather unfruitful in the analysis, this one item became one of the bases for the extremely important conception of opinion leadership.

Still other items were probably included on the vague hunch that they might turn out to be useful. A seven-wave panel contains room for a large enough number of items so that rather vague hunches may be indulged without sacrificing items believed to be of central importance at the design stage.

Given the relevant measurements of the crucial variables, the very procedures of multivariate analysis maximize the chances of inductively arrived-at relationships. In the analysis tradition which has arisen in survey research, there is a large premium on the continuous testing of relationships by the introduction of possibly intervening variables,[22] a process which, when successful, builds the interpretation into a more or less connected set of empirical generalizations. For example, the extremely important findings concerning the role of cross-pressures probably stemmed from the search for additional correlates of voting preference.

Thus, it may be judged that the final version of the Erie County monograph represents an interpretation of voting behavior which is largely inductive, arising from a process in which an initial model of behavior was progressively modified and transformed when tested against empirical data.

Continuity with "Quantitative Methods in Politics." Despite the lack of direct influence of Rice upon the work of Lazarsfeld and his associates, and the considerably different interests which motivated the latter in their entry into the field of voting behavior, there is nevertheless some continuity between their books in terms of topics covered and even in method. Many of the major topics touched upon by Rice appear also in the later study, although usually transformed by the research techniques employed. It must also be recalled that Rice was very much aware of the utility of the panel design, even though his research technology was not developed enough to take full advantage of it.

The transformation in the treatment of topics in *The People's Choice*, as compared with Rice's work, arises mainly from the employment of the survey technique. Rice's concern with attitudes could only be indirectly satisfied, because direct measurement on a large scale was not available to him. Hence, many of the processes about which Rice could only speculate were directly accessible to Lazarsfeld and his associates. A few examples of this transformation follow.

In *Quantitative Methods in Politics*, the treatment of participation is severely handicapped by a serious measurement problem. Rice had available to him the numbers of citizens voting in national elections over a period of time, but he was not able to relate these data to satisfactory measures of the total eligible electorate. The size of the population varied through time, along with the eligibility rules. His treatment of the historical trends in participation, based on ingenious estimates of the eligible electorate, still had to remain primarily descriptive. In *The People's Choice*, where the eligibility of each individual respondent could be easily ascertained, turnout (and participation in general) could be handled on a more analytic basis. Voters and nonvoters could be contrasted according to a large number of variables.

In his study of the bases for support for different candidates, Rice was unable to make definitive statements concerning which social groups were allied with each of the candidates. Rural-urban differences were studied, but official election statistics, even in combination with census data, did not give him the breakdowns of the electorate necessary to study the different voting patterns of ethnic groups and socioeconomic classes. Rice's method limited him to a study primarily of regional patterns of voting.[23] The survey technique, by providing direct measurements of both vote and individual characteristics, was able to compare the support for the two parties in terms of variables in which Rice indicated an interest, but had expressed despair at being able to study. Note, however, that because *The People's Choice* deals with only one county, regional patterns could not be studied. Urban-rural differences are treated as social structural variations, rather than as spatial distributions of voting patterns as in the earlier study.

Rice treated "social density" or political consensus in terms of spatial units. Lazarsfeld's concern with the political homogeneity of social groups is the direct translation of social density in the framework of personal interviews. His "groups," however, were given greater specificity: The respondent was asked about his family, and the social density in the interpersonal environment immediately about him was ascertained in a very direct way.

The diffusion of political attitudes which Rice treated as an explanation for the similarity in voting between contiguous counties is also picked up and transformed within the framework of the personal interview. In *The People's Choice*, the diffusion becomes personal influence, the spread of political preferences from persons with more than average competence and interest in politics. In Rice's study, the spatial arrangements of individuals were indices of paths of contact and communication; in Lazarsfeld's, contact among persons could be studied more directly.

The one element of continuity in method between the two works is provided by the common use of the panel design. However, as between the two the use of repeated observations really received its first important mass application in the Erie County study.[24]

Style. In technical sophistication, *The People's Choice* represents a considerable advance over its predecessors, either voting behavior studies or researches employing the survey method. The panel design and the large number of measurements made, plus the complicated multivariate analysis approach, gave rise to a number of fairly sophisticated empirical generalizations. In addition, the study still stands as a model for the analysis of survey data, presenting a standard which contemporary surveys all too often do not attain.

Despite these advances, however, the book's style is quite journalistic. The questions pursued are particularistic rather than general, topical rather than universal. The concepts employed are *ad hoc* constructions and have little continuity with the literature of either sociology or social psychology. The interpretations drawn are limited in character and do not provide an easy basis for generalizations about other elections or similar forms of human behavior. A concern for description rather than generalization dominates the treatment of each topic.

In style, the book strongly resembles the reports of other researches conducted around the same time by the Office of Radio Research.[25] Often stimulated by a client's interest in a directly practical problem, the published accounts[26] of these researches are written primarily for a nonacademic audience, heavily stressing the sorts of questions in which the sponsors were interested. Undoubtedly there is some carry-over of this style of research reporting to the treatment of the findings of the Erie County study.

However, the style cannot be attributed entirely to carry-over of a mode of research reporting from other research interests. Some large degree of responsibility for the descriptive emphases used must be laid at the doors of the academic disciplines of sociology and social psychology. Relevant concepts in these fields were not highly developed, especially in application to empirical work. For example, empirical work on "social stratification" had its beginnings in the late thirties. The pioneer work of W. Lloyd Warner began to appear in published form in the early forties. Research on leadership and interaction processes within small groups was not to get under way until after World War II. At the time of the Erie County study, research on attitudes had been conducted primarily with student populations, and in style was probably more descriptive and less analytic than the work of Lazarsfeld and his associates.

In summary, *The People's Choice* represents a considerable advance over the research of its time in both political behavior and social psychology. Judged in absolute terms, however, it leaves much to be desired.

Transition to the Elmira study. When the second edition of *The People's Choice* was issued in 1948, the senior author, Lazarsfeld, added a preface evaluating the work and presenting suggestions for future research in voting behavior. Because this statement provides the bridge between *The People's Choice* and *Voting*, it is worth while to present a brief summary.

Lazarsfeld saw the shortcomings of his original report as being of three types: First, at certain points the panel technique itself could not be successfully exploited. Second, analysis of the report pointed to several large gaps in data. Finally, he felt it was necessary to tie the analysis of voting closer to more theoretical interests.

The panel technique broke down at two crucial points. As noted before, too few changers were obtained to make maximum use of the virtues of the panel. In addition, interviewing of changers left much to be desired. Analysis of reasons given for change by respondents could not be successfully undertaken because the interviewers were not skillful enough to follow through the elaborate instructions prepared for them.[27]

Perhaps more serious were the "sins of omission." Lazarsfeld felt that more information on the community itself—particularly the activities of the political party organizations—would have been desirable. The institutional structure of the community should be related to voting behavior in any future study. A second omission was that of extensive data on voters' social environments. In the Erie County study, only information on the voting preferences of the respondents' families was obtained. Similar data on friends and co-workers should help to give a firmer empirical footing to the findings on the importance of primary social groups. Finally, opinion leadership, the most dramatic of the findings, also rested on relatively inadequate measures. Lazarsfeld suggested an elaboration of the treatment of this phenomenon in the next study.

The third general item in Lazarsfeld's critique was dissatisfaction with the lack of connection between *The People's Choice* and more general treatments of the stability and change of attitudes. Unfortunately, he did not specify which theoretical schemes appeared to be most relevant.

In general, Lazarsfeld's evaluations express satisfaction with the design of the study but some discontent with the way in which it was carried out. The panel study of a single community was the right idea, but, for one reason or another, it did not live up to his fullest expectations. His suggestions for the future are along the lines of bolstering the design and filling in the most obvious gaps in data.

"VOTING." Early in 1948, soon after publication of the second edition of *The People's Choice*, planning was begun for a repeat study, centering on the presidential election of that year. Berelson and Lazarsfeld, the senior researchers, envisaged the research primarily as an opportunity to replicate the older Erie County study in a different community and under different historical conditions. Although some obvious gaps were to be filled, no radical changes were to be made in the design itself.

Financial support for the new research was obtained from a variety of sources, and the study itself was undertaken as a joint venture of three universities and the research divisions of several private organizations. The joint sponsorship of the project was to be reflected in the final design through the inclusion of problems of specific interest to each of the sponsors.

Elmira, New York, a small upstate industrial city, was selected as the setting for the research. The sociology department of Cornell University, one of the participating schools, had begun studies of Elmira. Their activities showed promise of adding to this new study data on the community setting which, in retrospect, seemed so lacking in the earlier report.

The early stages of the task of analysis were carried out primarily by a generation of Columbia graduate students working under Lazarsfeld's direction. The final report, building upon and extending earlier work, appeared finally in late 1954, some six years after the research team had entered Elmira.

Design of the Elmira Study. Like its predecessor, the Elmira study employed a panel design. The size of the panel was considerably larger, 1,000 instead of 600, but the respondents were interviewed only four times, as compared with seven in the earlier study. Control groups, which were such a prominent methodological feature of the Erie County study, were not employed. The Elmira study was to be primarily substantive in its interests.

Besides the panel, two other research operations were conducted. Content analyses were made of local newspapers and of radio speeches made by the two candidates. This subproject, however, did not approach the scale reached in the prior report. In addition, field workers from Cornell University observed the activities of the political party organizations and the political efforts of other groups throughout the campaign.

The questionnaires used in the panel interviews (fortunately reproduced as an appendix to *Voting*) contained several "new" variables. Particularly important were items obtaining data on political preferences of respondents' friends, co-workers, and families. As compared with the Erie County study, more and better data were obtained on respondents' opinions on issues. In addition, their perceptions were obtained of the candidates' stands on the same issues. These new data on the voters' social environments and on the role of issues were to play an important part in the analysis.

Several variables were added mainly to serve the interests of one or another of the sponsors—a short "authoritarian personality" scale, measures of intergroup prejudice, attitudes toward large corporations, etc. Some of these items were later to be of use in the analysis.

Some of the topics which were important concerns of *The People's Choice* received only scant attention in the Elmira questionnaires. Elaborate measures of exposure to campaign materials were not made, nor was much attention paid to respondents' anticipation of the winner—the "band-wagon" effect. Surprisingly, no serious attempt was made to extend the prior concern with opinion leadership, the two relevant items in the Elmira questionnaires being little improvement over the items in the earlier study.

In one serious respect, the design of the Elmira study fell far short of expectations. In order to exploit the full advantages of the panel design, repeated measurements must be made of variables which are expected to vary concomitantly over time. Only in this way would it be possible to unravel the intricate web of cause and effect. However, aside from items on vote preference and interest in the election, few questions were repeated once, and none in more than two waves. Considering the stress which Lazarsfeld places on the panel technique, it is hard to understand this serious design defect. The effect of this gap in the data is particularly noticeable in the analysis of the role of issues, where interpretation of the interaction between issues and votes could easily have been given considerably more substantial empirical foundations.

In other respects, the Elmira study design maintained a strong resemblance to the Erie County research. The underlying model is still one of the individual making a choice among alternatives, his final decision being a resolution of a number of "forces" arising from within himself and from his environment. Different "forces" were postulated in the later study, but the general model was the same. As we shall see, the major differences between *The People's Choice* and *Voting* do not arise so much from differences in design as from the way in which the data were analyzed and interpreted.

Topical Outline. The wealth of topics discussed and data presented in *Voting* can be only inadequately summarized in a few pages. The careful reader of the volume itself will find that this summary touches only the highlights and major themes, ignoring some of the very suggestive treatments of minor topics.

Voting is organized into four sections, each developing a major theme of the book. An introductory section describes the Elmira community and presents a summary of the course of the 1948 election in that city. Data are also presented on interest in the election and on turnout.

The second section, entitled "Social Processes," describes the social factors in voting, starting with the activities of formal organizations, going on to effects on voting of such social structural features as class and ethnicity, and ending with an analysis of the role of primary groups. A final chapter in this section examines the consequences of these processes for the stability and change of the votes of individuals and social units.

The third section of *Voting*, entitled "Political Processes," contains chapters paralleling those of the previous section but focusing on the political aspects. From observers' reports, activities of the political parties are described. The role of issues is treated next, primarily as the interaction between respondents' opinions, the weights they give to particular issues, and their perceptions of the candidates' stands on these matters. A primarily descriptive chapter presents a content analysis of the campaign as reflected in the local mass media. The final chapter is devoted to an analysis of the ebb and flow of support for Truman, showing how his campaign brought back into the party fold persons who had earlier deserted to the opposite camp.

The final section of *Voting* attempts to tie in findings of the study to more academic interests. One chapter is devoted to showing how these findings fit into the concerns of social psychology and sociology. The last chapter draws implications for a theory of the functioning of a political democracy.

Cutting across the organization of the book is the major attention given to three topics: the group context of voting behavior, the role of issues, and the part played by the community and its institutions.

The social context of voting behavior received perhaps the most attention in *Voting*. The basic data are relatively simple, but the authors, through skillful analysis and interpretation, build a model of how patterns of interpersonal association in Elmira produced cleavages within the population on election day.

Starting with respondents' accounts of the political preferences of their families, friends, and co-workers, the authors show that, by and large, Elmira is composed of a large number of politically homogeneous families, cliques, and work groups. Furthermore, the accounts given by respondents of the political discussions in which they engaged indicates that interchanges of opinion within these circles were mostly exchanges of mutually agreeable commentaries on the campaign rather than vigorous debates among antagonists. The few respondents who held views at variance with their social environments tended over time to adjust their political choices in the direction of conformity. Those whose environments were not uniform tended to withdraw from the contest and vacillate in their political choices. Thus, as the campaign progressed, bringing about a rise in popular interest and discussion, the primary groups of Elmira became more and more homogeneous.

However, homogeneity does not extend through the entire community. There are discontinuities in the web of interlocking cliques, families, and work groups. Homogeneity characterized the tendency *within* segregated segments of social structure, while heterogeneity increased *between* segments. Since interpersonal association takes place primarily within class and ethnic lines, the traditional political allegiances of these groups become intensified, producing as an end result the main political cleavages within Elmira. Note that this interpretation assumes enduring class and ethnic political allegiances and accounts only for their persistence, not for their origin.

This line of interpretation was, of course, first advanced in *The People's Choice*. The contributions of *Voting* are to add data going beyond that of the earlier study and to stress the aggregate effects of the interaction process. In the former, the authors saw the individual as conforming to his environment; in the latter, the individual and his environment are viewed as a mutually influencing system. As a consequence, the role of opinion leadership receives less emphasis in the Elmira study.

The second major focus of *Voting* is on the role of issues. In the earlier Erie County study, issues were studied primarily through the content of the mass media. Little attention was paid to issues as reflected in the opinions of respondents; the major sets of data on this topic related to content of the mass media and measures of respondents' exposure to campaign material.

While the Elmira study did not drop altogether the concern for content of the mass media, the attention given is considerably less. The results of a content analysis of local newspapers are presented in a short section (pp. 235-40), and are not integrated closely into the body of the study. Much more attention is paid to attitudinal reflections of the campaign.

Three types of attitudinal data are presented: First, there are the opinions of respondents on a variety of political questions, ranging in content from the Taft-Hartley Act to minority group rights. Second, the importance of issues to the respondents is measured, allowing subjective weight to be attached to their opinions. Finally, perceptions of the candidates' stands on a small number of issues are obtained.

The direct relationship between opinion on issues and vote is not very large in the aggregate. In part, this is because only some issues were at stake in the campaign. In the 1948 election, economic issues (or "position issues," as they were called in *Voting*) discriminated between the two parties, while such matters as minority discrimination and international affairs (called "style issues") received the same degree of endorsement from the supporters of both parties. In addition, voters tended to place different emphases on one or another issue, and those which they considered to be important counted more as correlates of their vote.

Furthermore, voters tended to be relatively inconsistent in their opinions on issues. Their inconsistency was solved in two ways: First, as mentioned above, some issues were given a stronger emphasis. Second, they denied that their candidate disagreed with them on a particular issue. Thus, the Truman supporter who opposed price control tended to perceive Truman as agreeing with him on this issue.

The general impression which emerges from the analysis of the role of issues in voting behavior is that the data define a set of mutually interacting variables. The voter tends toward self-consistency, but he seems to be as likely to do so by changing his view of his candidate's opinions as by changing his candidate.

Unfortunately, since the opinion items were not repeated from wave to wave, it is not possible to pursue the analysis of mutual interaction with as much detail as might be desired.[28]

Going considerably beyond their data, the authors speculate on the career of issues over long-time periods. Confronted by data which show that some issues are points of cleavage between the two parties, whereas others are endorsed by supporters of both sides, *Voting* suggests that issues vary in this way because they are at different points in their careers across the political arena. Typically, innovations are proposed first by the extremists of the left and are endorsed initially only by the far left wing. Gradually, such issues get to be the major points of contention between the parties, as illustrated in 1948 by the Taft-Hartley Act. Finally, when a decision is made to accept an innovation, it gradually attains acceptance from all except the extreme right—e.g., Social Security in 1948. In other words, innovations are first suggested by the left and are gradually accepted in a wave moving from left to right.

Compared to *The People's Choice*, the treatment of issues in *Voting* has both psychological and historical depth. The sense of historical continuity is provided by the discussion of issue careers, and the psychological sophistication by their ingenious analysis of opinions on issues. As will be seen in the next section, the authors handle this topic with much more sensitivity than do the authors of *The Voter Decides*.

In line with what the authors felt to be a major gap in the data of the Erie County study, the 1948 research made provision for the collection of materials on the "community context" of the election. The treatment of the role of community and its institutions became the third major theme in *Voting*.

During the campaign, observers from Cornell's department of sociology kept running accounts of the political activities of organizations. They attended party meetings and interviewed labor-union presidents and the heads of other organizations. In addition, the panel interviews contained questions on respondents' contacts with party organizations and their membership in labor unions and other associations.

The community context data thus come partly from observers' accounts and partly from the panel interviews. The observers' reports produced running accounts of organizational activities, e.g., what the several labor unions did, what the Republican party did, who the party workers were, and so on. The panel interviews present the "reflections" of the organizational activities, e.g., how union members voted as compared with other persons, who was contacted by party workers, etc.

Interpretation and analysis of these data are weaker than for other topics treated. There is a strong tendency to play down activity of organizations, even though the survey indicates some effectiveness. Thus, the observers report that labor unions were, by and large, inactive during the campaign, but the survey data indicate that union members were more Democratic in their vote than were nonunion members. Furthermore, the more a union member associated with his fellow workers, the more likely he was to vote Democratic. Similarly, the political parties were discovered to be staffed by persons who were not the leading businessmen and/or professionals in Elmira. The party workers were found to be largely persons unmotivated by ideological concerns or ideals of civic duty or welfare. The parties engaged in little that might be considered proselytizing, but were mainly concerned with "administrative" matters—conducting canvasses, etc. The panel interviews, however, indicated that one-fourth of the respondents were contacted by a party worker. Furthermore, there is some evidence that these contacts were at least effective in bringing the less interested out to the polls on election day. In other words, one set of data is interpreted in a way which plays down the political effects of organizations, while the other set shows that such effects were at least as great as those attributable to the mass media.

Why do the authors treat the organizations so begrudgingly in assessing their roles in the election? In large part, this treatment seems to be a function of their implicit model of the well functioning political organization. Labor unions and other organizations, when functioning properly, should be highly politicized, making strong efforts to convert both the opponents within their ranks and outsiders. The political parties, according to this ideal model, are staffed by ideologically committed people, serving, at best, their cause, and, at least, committed to better civic welfare.

Apparently the model was so far from reality that the most the observers could do was to document the activities in which the organizations were not engaged. Differences between parties and between organizations, or changes in the rate and tempo of activity over time, were lost sight of in the face of the discovery that the organizations were active at a much lower level than anticipated. As a consequence, the observers' reports, as summarized in the volume, are only poorly integrated with the main body of *Voting*.

The community context finds its way into *Voting* on another level besides the discussion of organizations. Because Elmira went so heavily Republican, and its media showed the same bias, it can be looked upon as supplying each voter with a sort of political "atmosphere." The predominant tone of political discussion was Republican, and presumably the individual voter had more of a chance to come into contact with Republicans and Republican influences than he had to feel Democratic influence.

The authors use the Republican atmosphere of Elmira as an explanation at several points. Given the same conditions affecting the individual, Republicans appeared to pick up more votes than Democrats. Thus, voters who were in conflict in their group memberships tended to go Republican rather than Democratic. Where the choice in political transactions could go equally one way or the other, the Republicans were seen to get the breaks. Implicit in this sort of explanation is a hierarchy of influences: Where the voter's choice was clearly indicated by his social characteristics, the tone of his immediate interpersonal environment, or his ideology, the influence of the tone of the community was hardly felt; where such directives were not present, or where they pressured the voter in contradictory directions, the influence of the community made itself felt.

Style. As compared with any of its predecessors, *Voting* represents the most thorough-going attempt to present a generalized interpretation of voting behavior. The traces of topical, journalistic concerns which characterize *The People's Choice* are no longer present. At almost every point, the authors go beyond Elmira and the 1948 political contest to discuss the American political system and American social structure. They also go beyond voting behavior to establish links with the more general concerns of sociology, social psychology, and political science. If the audience for the earlier work could be said to be the intelligent layman interested in current politics, the reader for whose eyes *Voting* was written is the academic social scientist.

The change is manifested at many points: in the organization of the book itself, in the problems tackled, and in the vocabulary used. But the "new look" is especially apparent in the concluding section of the book, where the authors make very self-conscious attempts to draw out the implications of their work for the three academic fields. To catch the full flavor of this academic orientation, a brief summary of the last two chapters is presented below.

In Chapter 13, Lazarsfeld presents a case for considering the research as a contribution to the fields of social psychology and sociology. Here he returns to his early interest in the "psychology of choice" and shows that the study of voting behavior can be fitted into the field of psychology as an example of "implementation"—the process intervening between predisposition and act. The laboratory experimenter in psychology has focused his attention on the relationships between stimuli and the organism through studies of cognition and perception. Field studies like the Elmira research add to the total picture by studying the way in which predispositions are implemented in action.

In answer to critics who claimed that *The People's Choice* had failed to specify the "mechanisms" by which the individual's attributes were related to his vote, Lazarsfeld shows that the process of "reactivation" may be regarded as such a mechanism. "Reactivation" describes the way in which Truman's campaign brought persons with Democratic predispositions back into the Democratic fold by playing on economic issues.

To the sociologist, Lazarsfeld points out that the interpretation of group voting patterns in the study treats social groups as systems of interaction, illustrating that the concept of social system may be given an empirical definition.

Finally, he points to the panel design as a methodological contribution to the fields of both sociology and psychology. The "process analysis" which panels make possible provides a way to study the complex sets of mutually interacting variables so characteristic of these two fields.

Berelson's Chapter 14 is directed primarily to the political "theorist." He takes as his point of departure a normative "theory" of democracy, which specifies that, for the proper functioning of a democratic system, each and every citizen should be highly politically informed and active. Berelson points out that the data of the Elmira study show that the individual hardly conforms to this ideal, and yet democracy is far from collapse in America. He suggests that the apathy of the individual and his vulnerability to the influence of his social environment have several positive consequences for the functioning of society. For one thing, apathy keeps political conflict from becoming too acute and makes possible the acceptance in good grace of defeat at the polls. Also, the persistence of group voting patterns and their seeming invulnerability to political discussion insure that political change will proceed slowly, providing continuity over time. In other words, there is enough flexibility to allow ordered change and enough stability to provide for the necessary social cohesion.

As one reads through *Voting*, one cannot help but admire the ability of the authors to maintain a high level of generality and their successful attempts to establish the validity of their endeavors as social science. The handling of the data is always highly imaginative, extracting the last bit of meaning from each table. Their interpretations are ingenious, and, whatever their worth as valid inferences from the data at hand, they still deserve serious consideration. The implications which the authors draw for our democratic system are also serious and worth-while attempts to understand the viability of our political system. Unfortunately, when placed against the limitations of the design of the study, the analyses and interpretations appear as a case of too much, too late. Instead of the impression of a theoretically oriented piece of empirical research in which data and problems are closely related, one receives the impression of a superstructure of interpretation only shakily supported by its empirical base. Furthermore, and this is perhaps the most serious criticism, one cannot help but conclude that the builders of this edifice have not properly warned the prospective tenants of the dangers involved.

To be more specific, three serious criticisms may be directed at the manner in which the authors have handled their materials: To begin with, generalizations are offered which go considerably beyond what any study of one community during one election could support. To be sure, the authors point out the tentative character of their interpretations in the preface, but the tone is more self-assured in the text.

Second, the data are treated all too often without proper regard for their inherent limitations. For example, much is made of the intercampaign changes at several points in the analysis. The data are the differences between respondents' reports of their 1944 votes and their 1948 preferences. Interpolations concerning the intervening four years are treated with as much confidence as the better measured intracampaign changes. Another serious defect is the way in which data on political preferences of friends and co-workers are handled. The data relate only the respondents' *perceptions* of these preferences; the analysis treats the data as if they were the preferences themselves. The question of how much the congruencies between the respondents and their social environments are due to familiar tendencies toward perceptual distortion is not considered in the text. Perceptual distortion *is* introduced, however, in the interpretation of respondents' perceptions of candidates' stands on issues. Apparently, when reference to these mechanisms would seriously undermine their interpretations, the authors do not choose to mention them. As another example, many of the results on which the analysis of changes heavily depends are possibly statistical artifacts of the kind familiar to any statistician. [See Chapter 3 below for a discussion of the regression effect as an alternative explanation of some of the data in *Voting*.]

Third, speculation and findings are not segregated clearly enough in the text. For example, much is made of the effects on changes of the predominantly Republican character of Elmira. While the data are consistent with this interpretation, only comparisons with other communities of predominantly Democratic complexion can buttress it. As it stands, this interpretation has only the lowest kind of proof, but the discussion gives the impression that the data unequivocally support it. Another example is found in the discussion of the career of issues over time. The data indicate only that the parties disagree over some issues and agree over others. The interpretation offered is that the issues are all in different stages of passing through the political arena, some being completely accepted by all partisans, others being at the center of contemporary controversy, and others only entering as issues onto the political scene.

The authors' treatment of their data is all the more unfortunate because of their great ingenuity in developing coherent speculative explanations. Their interpretations are so intelligent that it is easy to lose sight of the loose fit to the data. The total effect is to give a spurious sense of closure to many problems. The impression is left that problems are solved, when in reality they have only been raised. Responsibility to the future of research in voting behavior would have been served much better by a cautious and skeptical attitude toward their own work.

Why is there this discrepancy between data and interpretation in the Elmira study? In part, this characteristic must be ascribed to the general nature of survey research. In this approach, a premium is placed on *post hoc* interpretations. Analysis looms greater as a skill to the survey researcher than does the ability to design studies.

But there is a more specific reason for the defects of *Voting*. Basically, this is a failure in design. The Elmira study was not designed to sustain the analysis to which it was subjected; its purpose was to carry the study begun in *The People's Choice* a little further. The authors, in their laudable zeal to take giant steps forward, apparently departed too far from their original intentions. One cannot help but wish that the great ingenuity expended on the analysis of the Elmira data had been used earlier in designing the study or in making preparatory studies. Perhaps the authors would have had less to write about a number of topics, but what they might have said would have been more clearly backed up by their research.

"THE VOTER DECIDES." Although *The Voter Decides* was published a few months before *Voting*, the research reported on was conducted in 1952 and hence forms the last point in this review of researches on voting behavior.[29] The main body of data treats the presidential contest of that year between Eisenhower and Stevenson, and is based on a nationwide sample survey.

The research tradition behind the book is somewhat different from that of the previous two studies considered. The Survey Research Center traces back to the Program Surveys Division of the U. S. Department of Agriculture. After World War II, when the federal government cut back its expenditures, a number of researchers from the Division moved to the University of Michigan to set up the Survey Research Center, at first under the direction of Rensis Likert. Engaging in contract research for private organizations and governmental agencies, as well as in basic research supported by foundations, the Center has become one of the foremost social research organizations. Through the Center, the University of Michigan has become a leader in the training of social researchers.

Academically, the Center's roots lie more in social psychology than in sociology, although recently closer relations have been established with Michigan's sociology and political science departments. The research of the Center is largely socio-psychological in orientation,[30] being guided by the philosophy that the immediate determinants of an individual's behavior lie more clearly in his attitudes and his perceptual organization of his environment than in either his social position or other "objective" situational factors.

Compared to other survey organizations, the Center prefers to rely more heavily on less structured interviewing procedures. A person's attitude is better measured by his spontaneous remarks about general questions than by his answers to highly structured items. The questionnaires used by the Center tend to have many open-ended items, the answers to which are handled by rather detailed and often ingenious classification.

The Survey Research Center entered upon the study of voting behavior almost by accident. In October, 1948, its staff was conducting a survey for a government agency on attitudes toward certain public policies. An item was included asking what the candidate preferences of respondents were in the 1948 election. After the debacle of the commercial polls, the Center was quick to use this opportunity to conduct valuable research on what had upset the expectations of the polling agencies. The sample for the October study was reinterviewed after the election. The analysis of these data was of considerable aid in the assessment of the 1948 presidential polls by the Social Science Research Council.[31]

Following the 1948 election, the Council's Committee on Political Behavior held a series of conferences on voting behavior, in which staff members of the Center participated. Partly as an outgrowth of these conferences, the Carnegie Corporation early in 1952 gave the Center a grant to undertake the research reported in *The Voter Decides.*

The research staff of the Center was, of course, familiar with the Erie County study. The authors acknowledge the influence which the early work of Lazarsfeld had upon their own research. In addition, the staff was familiar with some of the earlier reports arising out of the later Elmira study.

Design. The design of *The Voter Decides* differs in several important respects from those of the preceding studies. To begin with, the research is based on a national probability sample of some 2,000 respondents. Also, although respondents were interviewed twice, it is a panel only in a very truncated sense. Interviews took place immediately before and directly after the November election date.

With such a short time span between interviews, little attention was paid to the analysis of changes. Finally, the study places its major emphasis on topics and variables which were only tangentially touched upon in either of the two previously listed books. In line with the Center's emphasis on studying the psychological intervening variables, little attention is given to "social" factors such as socioeconomic status or interpersonal contacts. In the section following, where *Voting* and *The Voter Decides* will be compared in detail it will be shown how these differences in design affect the treatment of voting behavior.

Topical outline. The Voter Decides is organized around four major themes or questions. To begin with, because it is based on a national sample, the report can interpret the outcome of the election itself. A good part of the analysis is devoted to showing the sources from which the support for Eisenhower was drawn. Unlike *Voting,* whose results, strictly speaking, can only be used to interpret the victory of Dewey in Elmira, *The Voter Decides* performs a greater service to the historian of the future by providing national projections of its sample findings.

The second theme is a comparative one. The Survey Research Center's adventitious study of the 1948 presidential election provides a comparative frame which increases considerably the value of the 1952 study. Some of the most interesting findings of the study arise from tables comparing the correlations of variables to vote in 1948 and in 1952 (see, for example, their Table 5.1, pp. 70-73).

The third theme concerns participation as a dependent variable. An index of political participation was constructed, composed of items concerning respondents' electioneering, campaign contributions, and turnout at the polls. Participation, so defined, is related to the absence of conflicting motivation for voting for one or the other side of the contest. Conversely, the more the voter's motivation is in conflict, the less is his participation. For example, the more clearly partisan the voter is on issues, the more likely he is to be a heavy participant.

The fourth theme, on which the authors place the most emphasis, concerns the "motivation" for candidate preference. Motivation is seen as composed of three basic variables: party identification, issue partisanship, and candidate partisanship. The more clearly these motivational variables all pressure the voter in one direction, the more likely he is to vote for that candidate.

Style. Perhaps the best way to characterize *The Voter Decides* is to compare its treatment of voting behavior with that of *Voting*. The two works present strong contrasts at many points, both in the form of analysis presented and in the interpretations offered.

Part of the contrast stems from difference in design. Because *Voting* is based on a single community, it can only suggest an explanation for Truman's victory, although, as mentioned earlier, the authors are often guilty of leaving out the necessary qualifications on their findings. *The Voter Decides*, in contrast, can deal with the Eisenhower victory with confidence in its statistical basis. In addition, the comparative frame of reference afforded by the Center's previous survey of the 1948 election lends an historical depth to the data.

Different emphases on substantive matters also form part of the differences between the two works. The authors of *Voting* pay little attention to the problem of participation, devoting only a small section of one chapter to the topic. The authors of *The Voter Decides* made participation one of its major preoccupations.

Correspondingly, themes which are given heavy emphasis in the former receive only light treatment in the latter. Prominent among these are the political preferences of the respondents' social groups, the role of socioeconomic variables, and the analysis of changes in vote preferences. The lack of emphasis on the latter topic is, of course, in large part due to differences in design.

However, the major contrasts between the two researches are only in small part due to "matters of taste" in the substantive themes pursued. More basic are the differences in the explanatory models employed and in the forms of data analysis.

The authors of *The Voter Decides* show a strong preference for explanatory variables of a psychological sort, and are not concerned to raise the question of how these variables are in their turn determined. The implicit model is of the individual being moved to vote for a candidate primarily in response to psychological forces from within himself. For example, considerable attention is paid to the variable "party identification"—roughly, the voter's conception of himself as either a Republican or a Democrat; little attention is given to the role of socioeconomic status. For the authors, socioeconomic status could only operate on the voter's candidate preferences through the effect it might have on such motivataional variables as party identification. Hence, the relationship which socioeconomic status might have to voting is regarded as a spurious correlation which would disappear once the proper motivational variables were held constant.

Roughly, the model operates as follows: Events impinge upon the individual's attitudes, built up in part out of past experience and in part from his contemporary needs. His attitudes serve to screen outside events—the evaluations often producing modifications in the initial attitudes. The attitudes are the major immediate determinants of behavior; they intervene between the outside world and the resultant vote behavior. Hence, reason the authors, attitudes are the only important determinants of vote behavior. To understand and predict how a person is to vote, his attitudes are the most important information to have (see particularly their pages 7 and 8).

Consequently, the main variables treated in detail are the three "motivational" indices—party identification, issue partisanship, and candidate partisanship. These three variables are shown to be strongly and independently related to both candidate preference and political participation. Phrased in another way, the more strongly a voter considers himself to be a Democrat—the more he takes Democratic stands on the issues of the campaign and the more he likes the Democratic candidate—the more likely he is to vote for the Democratic candidate. The more equivocal his stand is on any combination of these variables, the less likely he is to participate in the campaign and to vote clearly for one or the other candidate.

How useful explanations in terms of variables all on the same "level" are is open to question.[32] It helps us little to know that voters tend to select candidates of whom they have high opinions. Voting for a candidate and holding a favorable opinion of him may be regarded as alternative definitions of the same variable. The more interesting problems start where the author's analysis ends. Why does a voter develop a favorable opinion of a candidate? What are the conditions under which his opinion and his vote do or do not coincide?

By contrast, the model of explanation employed in *Voting* transcends several levels of data. The voter's opinions on issues are considered a determinant of his vote, but, in turn his opinions are considered as dependent variables. The individual is located in the social structure of Elmira and within primary groups—conditions of experience which transform attitudes. Furthermore, candidate preference is considered as an attitude not very different from other attitudes, which are all part of a mutually interacting system tending toward self-consistency and congruency with the immediate social environment.

Another contrast between the two studies lies in the form of analysis presented. Few complicated cross-tabulations are presented in *The Voter Decides.* Most of the tables present zero-order relationships between pairs of variables. Rarely are third variables held constant, although many of the interpretations could be tested directly by doing so. For example, the heavier Democratic vote of Catholics is interpreted as a function of their greater concentration in urban areas, but residence is not held constant in pursuing this interpretation.

The authors at several points assert that the relationships of "demographic" variables to the vote are not as important as the pursuit of "intervening" relationships. However, the reader is not given an opportunity to judge whether the "motivational" variables *in fact* serve as efficient explanations of the relationships of demographic variables to either voting or participation. Very few tables are shown in the text which hold occupation, age, or education constant. Especially lacking in the analysis of participation are tables in which educational attainment is considered along with the "intervening" variables.

Another difference in analysis stems from the static character of the design of *The Voter Decides.* Candidate preference is viewed as the outcome of a process in which it is affected by other variables. The possibility that the individual may pick his candidate and then bring his other attitudes, such as position on issues, into line with his choice, is not considered. *The People's Choice* demonstrated how this type of adjustment frequently occurred.

These considerations cast some doubt on the usefulness of the approach to voting behavior offered by the explanatory model and the form of analysis employed in *The Voter Decides.* Because, as has been indicated, the major explanatory variables and voting are roughly on the same level, it is difficult to understand how changes over time come about. For example, the data show that in the 1952 election candidate partisanship was closely related to the vote. However, from the analysis and interpretations one cannot be sure that this is a peculiar characteristic of this election or common to elections of this historical period. While it is quite likely that the three motivational factors play a role in every election, without knowing why and how they do so one cannot use the model as a basis for prediction.

In order to use the explanatory model, more information is needed than is presented by the authors. For one thing, it is necessary to know how the political sphere—the character of issues and candidates—is related to motivational patterns. Second, in view of the large role played by social factors, it seems necessary to understand how social events and social factors affect the motivational pattern. (Analyses undertaken since 1954 have filled in this gap to some extent.[33]) Third, the interrelationships of variables which are on the same level are hard to unravel without some knowledge of the time relationships obtaining among them. The appropriate design for a motivational study would be a panel. From the information given, one cannot tell whether voters bring their views on issues into line with their choice of a candidate or vice versa.

In evaluating *Voting*, it was pointed out that the authors had gone too far in the interpretation of their data. In the case of *The Voter*

Decides, it is my opinion that the data were not sufficiently analyzed and that fruitful ideas were lacking.

A NEW STRATEGY FOR VOTING BEHAVIOR RESEARCH. Continuity in research leads forward into the future as well as back into the past. The studies reviewed in the preceding pages will soon be joined by others, some of which are perhaps even now being planned or under way. Their progress will be made easier by evaluating the successes and failures of the past.

This excursion into the continuity of voting research had as one of its major purposes to present some guideposts for the future. Obviously, the presentation of new research directions is much more of a "risk operation" than the evaluation of the past: only actual trials can prove the worth of whatever suggestions are made here.

The objective of this section is to make a more positive contribution by suggesting a new strategy for research. This will be done by pointing out major gaps in the researches reviewed earlier, and at the same time suggesting research designs which could adequately fulfill the needs created by these deficiencies.

New Designs for Old. In beginning research on a new problem, there is considerable justification for a strategy of the "shotgun approach," in which a large number of measurements are made in the hope of finding one or two correlates of the dependent variable. In the absence of many empirical generalizations about a phenomenon, the best move is to include in its study as many variables as are suggested by common sense and knowledge of analogous or related phenomena.

In field studies, the research design most appropriate to the earliest stages is the survey method applied to a representative sample. Thus, if nothing were known about voting behavior, the best strategy would be to conduct a sample survey in which representative voters were asked a large number of questions concerning themselves, their views of the election, etc. The employment of a representative sample insures that each element of the population which is of any significant size would be included and, theoretically, that it could be isolated for study by cross-tabulation. The survey interview, because of its adaptability to a host of problems which can be defined socio-psychologically, generally yields better measurements for a large number of variables than most techniques.

As research findings accumulate from sample surveys, knowledge about the major correlates of the phenomenon grows at the same time that the problems from research become more specific. In short, as more is learned the questions to be put to empirical test tend to become more pointed. Enough is learned about the topic to identify both the crucial problems to be studied and the crucial populations most suitable for settling such problems. The representative sample survey at this stage often becomes an inefficient design. What may be needed most at such stages in the history of research on a given problem are a number of small, pointedly designed studies of crucial populations, rather than "shotgun" designs.

Voting behavior research is fast reaching the point where limited purpose designs may be most profitably employed. To crowd into a representative sample survey adequate measures of everything of interest, and at the same time enlarge the sample size to obtain sufficient case bases for the desired crucial subgroup comparisons, may lead to a cumbersome, expensive, and inefficient study. *Voting* is an instance. Throughout the volume, the small number of cases for the authors' most interesting tables detracts considerably from the plausibility of their analyses and interpretations. For example, the number of party shifters, the case bases for "cross-pressured" groups, etc., are all too small to establish reliable differences. In addition, the study was designed to serve a large number of interests, some determined by implicit hypotheses concerning voting behavior, the others perhaps included to serve specific interests of one or another sponsor. The Elmira study was designed to serve too many purposes; hence, it serves few well.

In other words, the strategy suggested for the future researcher is to limit his research interests and build the design which would optimally serve those interests. This may mean a design concerned entirely with the study of small groups, or of issues, etc. While the scope of inquiry would be limited, compensation would accrue in the more definitive character of the findings. Measurements would be more adequate, subjects more appropriate, analysis more definitive. Several ways in which this might be accomplished are suggested below.

"Factorial" Sampling Designs. The first suggestion offered is that the researcher of the future abandon representative in favor of "factorial" sampling designs.[34] In descriptive surveys—the objective of which is to estimate population parameters—representative samples are a highly valued desideratum, but in analytic studies—centering around the relationships between variables—little advantage accrues from the representativeness, as such, of the samples studied. For example, it would make little difference in the evaluation of either the Elmira or the earlier Erie County studies if it were discovered that the samples interviewed were "unrepresentative" (but unbiased). The major interest of the analyst and the reader is not in whether the results hold for Erie County or Elmira, but in whether the differences between subgroups would hold up under replication. The same is true, to some extent, of *The Voter Decides*. The farther behind him the 1952 election lies, the less interested the reader of the future will be in the particulars of that contest and the more he will be concerned with the analytic findings of the study.

In fact, a good case can be made that the representativeness of the surveys involved in all three studies actually hindered the analysis at many points. For example, the number of changers found in both the Erie County and the Elmira study was extremely small, the variance of stability (or change) being correspondingly slight in the universes involved. How much more soundly based would be findings drawn from a larger number of changers! Similarly, in the Elmira study, where the major social characteristics of ethnicity and socioeconomic status were found to be necessary controls on so many cross-tabulations, the small number of Catholics and the largely working-class character of Elmira meant that most such tabulations contained too few cases in crucial cells.

"Factorial" or stratified sampling designs are sampling plans in which the objective is to obtain specified types of individuals in given proportions without regard to their actual proportion in the total population under study. For example, a more useful factorial design in the Elmira study would have been one which obtained equal numbers of Catholics and Protestants, each divided equally into industrial and white-collar workers. Cross-tabulations which held these two factors constant could then go on more easily to explore relationships within each of the four groups. Note that it is not suggested here that the sample drawn be a "biased" one, but only that it be composed in such a way that maximum use may be made of it for analytic purposes. The Catholics, Protestants, etc., to be found in the sample should be selected without bias but sampled more heavily (or more lightly, as the case may be) than their proportions in the total population.

At least two kinds of factorial designs are suggested by the weaknesses of the researches reviewed here: First, for future panel studies, sampling designs which would maximize the number of changers. Enough is probably known about the demographic characteristics of changers to build up those cells in a sample which would produce large numbers of such crucial cases. For example, such samples might be designed to contain large numbers of marginal, cross-pressured individuals, etc.

Second, in general studies of voting behavior, rectangular rather than skewed distributions of the basic demographic variables should be sought for. More equal distributions of the major occupational and ethnic groups would be desirable in general, although for different purposes different factors might be employed in the sampling design.

In short, what is suggested here is that the sample used be tailor-made for the research problem. If the researcher is interested in change, the design should maximize the probability of obtaining changers; if he is concerned with socioeconomic status, the design should obtain sufficient cases from each of the status levels he wishes to distinguish, and so on. As a corollary, the suggestion implies that the researcher will have to restrict the scope of his interests.

"Sociometric" Designs. In both *The People's Choice* and *Voting*, where much of the analysis was concerned with the group character of voting behavior, the data displayed a crucial weakness. Information on political preferences of friends, co-workers, and family members was obtained from the respondent himself. While there is no reason to suspect that the persons interviewed deliberately distorted their reports in the direction of greater-than-actual agreement with their friends and family, there *is* reason to believe that there may be a good amount of selective perception and unconscious projection at work. If respondents can misperceive the stands

of candidates on prominently debated issues, how much more blatant must be their mistakes about persons whose political beliefs are not so well articulated? Furthermore, in the two studies, respondents were left free to choose those friends and co-workers on whom they would report. The homogeneity of their social environments might be partially a function of that part of the environment on which respondents chose to report. There is some evidence that this is the case. In a study conducted by this writer, the correspondence in candidate preference between the respondent and his friends declined with each additional friend or co-worker discussed.

In short, more needs to be known about the relationships between the actual preferences of members of social groups than can be obtained from respondents alone. While the general finding of group homogeneity is not likely to be contradicted, one can anticipate a larger number of deviants than studies have revealed so far.

Two types of design modifications seem indicated: First, it should be possible to obtain independently the political preferences of at least the household groups of respondents, and, at best, the members of their social circles. A recently reported study[35] indicates that it is possible to obtain names and addresses of persons with whom respondents had exchanged advice on a variety of topics. This experience indicates that it may be feasible to try a design which starts with a sample of respondents and, through their sociometric choices, ends up with a sample of small informal groups.

A second type of design might consist of the direct sampling of groups. Because they have a definite location in space and fairly definable boundaries, work groups would be easier to study than friendship groups. All indications, however, point to the lesser importance of work groups as compared to friendship cliques in the area of political behavior. Ingenuity expended in locating groups initially heterogeneous in political preference and composed of persons brought into close contact with each other over a period of time would be highly rewarded in terms of findings. Several type situations[36] easily come to mind: newly formed military units, composed of recruits drawn from various regions and social backgrounds; newly married couples; members of newly established housing developments; students in beginning classes of schools; etc. The criteria to be sought in locating such groups for study are three in number: the members should be drawn from heterogeneous backgrounds, preferably brought together in a non-self-selected fashion, and in fairly close contact with each other over time. While few situations are normally available to the researcher which would fulfill all three criteria, approximations are still worth studying.

Extension of the Panel Design. It seems somewhat ironic that all the resources of the panel technique have not yet been fully exploited in the studies reviewed here. The value of this technique stems from its ability to detect and interrelate changes in a set of mutually interacting variables. Its use, then, depends to a large extent on two empirical characteristics of the phenomena to which it may be applied: First, changes must occur in the dependent variable—in this case, candidate preference; and second, the independent variables—e.g., opinion on issues—must also be changing at the same time. In both *The People's Choice* and *Voting*, the data could not fulfill these requirements. Changes were small in number, and either parallel measurements were not available for independent variables or such changes were also slight.

It has already been suggested that one method of insuring that sufficient changes are obtained for study would be to concentrate on types of individuals most likely to change. Several other ways of accomplishing the same end should also be considered. First, there are identifiable regions or communities which can be expected to contribute more than their share of changes in a given campaign. For example, it may be that in the 1960 election, the wheat belt area of the midwestern states will make significant shifts toward the Democratic column. The southern states, now wrestling with the problem of integration, would be another area where a number of cross-pressures are likely to produce changes.

Second, there is at least some evidence that the campaign period might not be the best time to study change. Data from both *The People's Choice* and *Voting* suggest that the major changes in the electorate occur during the interelection period. For example, defectors from the Democratic fold in 1948 had already left by the time the national conventions were held. The extension of the panel to interelection periods may provide documentation for the ebb-and-flow hypothesis advanced in *Voting* (discussed above). Obviously, interelection studies will have to be centered about a different dependent variable—perhaps opinion of the performance of the incumbent official.

Another modification, partly suggested earlier, would be to employ the panel in study of processes of conformity in natural groups. What happens to the new dwellers of America's mushrooming suburbs, or to the political consensus within military units composed of draftees from varied social backgrounds?

Finally, any panel study must contain a sufficient number of repeated measurements of possibly independent variables to make a panel analysis possible. As pointed out above, some of the failure of the panel to realize its promise stems from the neglect to include in the Erie County and Elmira studies a sufficient number of repeated measurements. The mutual interaction between opinion on issues, vote intentions, small group references, etc., studied in this fashion, might yield much more valuable information on the ebb and flow of political fortunes than is now available.

Comparative Community and Institutional Designs. None of the studies reviewed here has contributed much to the understanding of the role of political parties and other organizations, or of the local community context in which voters are embedded. The only serious attempt, the Elmira study, must be judged as falling far short of the mark. The descriptions presented of the political activities of organizations appear by and large irrelevant to our understanding of the election. The speculations concerning the effect of Elmira's heavily Republican "atmosphere" are highly suggestive, but cannot be regarded as anything more than a possible fruitful hypothesis.

There appear to be two reasons for the failure of the Elmira study to make more progress in the study of organizations: First, at least in Elmira, it appears that the effects of the political activities of organizations are long run rather than short run in character. Thus, we noted that, while the labor unions were not particularly active politically, members voted Democratic more often than nonmembers. Similarly, the parties were in contact with the more partisan of their adherents, and the data can be interpreted to mean that contact increases partisanship, or that partisans are more likely to be contacted (or to remember being contacted). Whether the effects of organizational efforts are always of a long-run character is something which would require more comparative data than the Elmira study can supply. At any rate, the researcher should be prepared to find that the campaign activities of organizations have little discernible effect on the course of any particular election.

Second, at the point where the Elmira study might have made a contribution, the data were lacking. Within a given community, the only analysis possible would be to compare the relative effectiveness of different types of organizations. In *Voting*, the authors concern themselves so much with showing how inactive organizations were, that it is not possible to tell how the parties or labor unions compared with each other in activity, or whether organizations of certain types were more effective than other types, etc.

The effect of community context has been explored only along the dimension of the effects of consensus. The tendency of the "breakage" in Elmira to go to the Republicans was attributed in *Voting* to the predominantly Republican "tone" of the community. Obviously, without being able to show that the "breakage" would go to the Democrats when that party set the tone for a community, this interpretation can only remain suggestive. It may be, for example, that the advantage always goes to the high-status party in the community—to the Democrats in the South and to the Republicans in the North. Whatever the case may be, only the comparison between communities with different tones will settle the issue.

Other dimensions of the community—its class system, ethnic mixture, general economic welfare, etc.—have not yet been systematically studied. In general, are one-class, homogeneous ethnic communities characterized by consensus? What provides the basis for political differentiation in the mining town, the middle-class suburb, the farming community?

Three community dimensions seem worth while building into comparative community studies: First, it would be desirable to study communities which vary in the level of activity of political parties and other organizations. Second, the communities should present a range in political consensus, from predominantly Republican through an even division to predominantly Democratic. Finally, since social status plays such an important role in voting, communities should be studied which vary in ethnic and socioeconomic homogeneity.

Many of the problems which can be defined in connection with the community can be studied at least in a preliminary way by the use of existing election statistics in combination with census data. For example, some inkling of the effects of status homogeneity on political consensus can be gained in this fashion. In any event, electoral statistics and census data provide the means for selecting the types of communities which would be called for in the comparative design suggested above.

Comparative Politics. Voting behavior research using survey methods has paid almost exclusive attention to presidential elections. In large part, this has been due to the intrinsically dramatic character of the contest. To some degree, however, this emphasis stems from the greater ease with which these contests can be studied and the findings generalized to the United States as a whole.

Presidential elections have a fairly standardized form. Ordinarily two candidates contend for the presidency. Knowledge of the candidates and the issues of the election are widespread due to the attention given by the mass media to the campaign. The contest is roughly the same in New York as it is in Podunk, in Oregon as it is in Mississippi. The volume published on Erie County interests the reader in Florida as much as the reader in Ohio.

In contrast, congressional, state, and local elections appear to have a much more diverse character. The candidates differ from locality to locality; the election system may include "nonpartisanship," or a multi-party system, or a two-party contest similar to the presidential election. Often there are no discernible issues, the campaign may be desultory and may reach few voters, and the candidates may be known to only a minute proportion of the electorate. Each election appears unique and so noncomparable that the researcher despairs at making studies which would add much to the general stock of knowledge concerning either human behavior or politics.

The diversity of nonpresidential elections, however, need not be looked upon primarily as a source of bafflement. This very variety may be employed positively, as providing a set of comparative frames which may illuminate processes which cannot be studied in the presidential contests. For example, in many local contests, candidates run without party affiliation. The continuity from election to election is provided only by individual candidates. Without enduring parties, what provides the voter with cues for identifying how he should express his political predispositions? In other elections, no discernible issues enter into the campaign: What are the grounds for the voter's choice in the absence of discernible political platforms distinguishing among the candidates? By their very difference from presidential contests, local and, to some extent, state and congressional elections provide the means for examining electoral choice in the absence of some of the strong features of a presidential election. A comparison among different types of electoral contests may help to illuminate the roles played by the more prominent features of the presidential elections.

Substantive Problems. The suggestions given above for future research have been mainly along the lines of new types of research designs. Implicitly, what appear to be the more strategic substantive problems have also been suggested. "Sociometric" sampling implies that group influences on voting behavior deserve additional research; the comparative community designs presuppose that the influence of the community context is worth investigating; and so on.

There are, of course, crucial problems for future research which are not touched on in a treatment of design. Considerable improvement can be made in the measurement of basic variables, a task in which the new scaling techniques should play a role. The measurement, for example, of opinion on issues might be made more elaborate. In addition, new variables, perhaps suggested by research in related areas, may be profitably investigated. For example, the subjective aspects of social stratification and reference group measures might add to our understanding of the role of both ethnicity and socioeconomic status.

CONCLUSIONS. To account for some of the major developments in research on voting behavior has been the first goal of this chapter. In a sense, the above review is an exercise in the sociology of knowledge. Four outstanding monographs on voting behavior have been considered. These points in the history of the field are not selected as representative ones; on the contrary, they are among the best. Obviously, work of considerable stature has been neglected and research employing the survey method has perhaps been overemphasized. Nevertheless, the four monographs reviewed collectively represent a research tradition of primary importance.

Each work was seen to make its special contribution. The review of the pioneer work of Stuart A. Rice indicated that his most important contributions were to lay out the major problems in voting behavior and to present research fragments, each of which was, by and large, an ingenious use of scanty empirical materials.

The earlier work of Lazarsfeld and his associates on the 1940 election came next under review. Although initially drawn into voting research through methodological concerns, the authors made a substantial contribution to the growth of knowledge about voting behavior. Most of all, they showed that the survey method could serve as an important research device in this area. Judged by present-day standards, *The People's Choice* falls short primarily in its conceptualization.

Voting, based on a follow-up of the earlier Erie County study, was seen to have a mixed character. On the one hand, it represents a high level of maturity in conceptualization. Skillful analysis and imaginative interpretation were used in linking its findings to the study of politics, social psychology, and sociology. The questions posed for the analysis bore on the concern of the sociologist for small groups, on the social psychologist's interest in the connections between attitudes and behavior, and on the political implications of the social characteristics of voting behavior. On the other hand, the fact that the Elmira study was designed primarily as a replication of the earlier Erie County study meant that the empirical bases for the analysis provided only limited support for the intellectual ambitions of the authors. At too many points, the proper data were either missing or too fragmentary. *Voting* thus points the way voting behavior studies should go in their orientation to problems, but sets a bad precedent as far as design and proof are concerned.

The last monograph in the series under review, *The Voter Decides*, was based on a national study of the 1952 presidential election. In many ways, it represents the opposite of *Voting*. It emphasizes "psychological" variables as opposed to the more sociological interests of the latter; the data are much more adequate to its problems, but the analysis is less thorough; its conceptualization is less rich, but the authors' conclusions are more firmly supported by their data.

The reader of this chapter may have noted that later works were judged against much higher standards than earlier ones. This differential treatment stems from the conviction that a research should use the best in technique and conceptualization available in its time. Hence, what was Rice's virtue becomes his successor's vice. Lest the impression be given that no headway has been made in this field because of this tendency to employ ever higher standards in evaluating each successive work, let it be said that not even the most careless reader of the four works reviewed could fail to note how each one has added to our knowledge and understanding of both politics and human behavior.

The other major purpose of this chapter was to extrapolate beyond the present into the future of research in voting behavior. Method rather than substance received the primary emphasis in suggesting a new strategy for future research. Research designs tailor-made to the study of limited substantive questions were at the heart of the strategy proposed. It is my hope that the suggestions given here will prove of value.

CHAPTER 2

Early Socialization of Attitudes

H. H. REMMERS

In October, 1952, Poll No. 33 of the Purdue Opinion Panel[1] included the following question: "If you were going to take part in this year's election, for which of the following candidates would you vote: Eisenhower-Nixon, Stevenson-Sparkman, Some Other?"

The response to this question predicted the Eisenhower popular vote with less than one-half of 1 per cent error—considerably more accurately than the results achieved by professional pre-election pollsters of the adult population. That teen-agers in high school should so accurately reflect adult attitudes and voting behavior raises many questions of interest to the social scientist.

The purpose of this chapter is to present data related to the problem of early socialization of attitudes so far as this can be done within the range of senior high school students—grades 9-12 inclusive. The source of these data will be chiefly the results of polling the Purdue Opinion Panel and the studies that these polls have generated by my students, associates, and myself, although attitude studies carried on by myself and under my direction began more than twenty years ago and some of these earlier studies are also relevant for this chapter. Of particular interest, of course, are data related to the generalizations developed in the Erie County, Ohio, study of voting behavior,[2] and I shall present data bearing especially upon these generalizations.

Since methodological problems of social science are of prime importance as related to validity of results, a brief explanation of the mode of operation of the Purdue Opinion Panel is in order. Polls of the Panel are given by participating high schools to several thousand students in high schools all over the nation. The numbers in the total sample have fluctuated from approximately 7,000 to 18,000 from one year to another. Students record their answers anonymously on a special ballot (mark-sensing) card using an electrographic pencil. When the cards are returned to Purdue University, a machine converts these marks into punched holes, making it possible to process all the data on IBM equipment. Each school is sent a report of its own results in addition to a national report.

From the total number of students responding to the poll, a working sample is selected so that the proportion of students from each region in the country is the same as the proportion in the total population of high school students. Because absolute control cannot be exercised over how many pupils participate in the polls in various parts of the country, the proportion of the total returns from one region may be different from the proportion of teen-agers actually residing in that region. The stratification of the sample corrects for this bias.

The working sample, usually 3,000, is stratified on a number of characteristics, including sex, grade, and rural-urban residence. We have found that the total returns are not far from the national teen-age population characteristics with respect to all factors except grade and region of the country. Table 2-1 shows the composition of the sample in Poll 33 concerning the 1952 election.

Table 2-1—Composition of Stratified Random Sample of 3,000 High School Students Used in Making the Analysis of the 1952 Pre-election Poll

Subpopulations	*Number*	*Percentage*	*Subpopulations*	*Number*	*Percentage*
Boys	1,535	51	Rural	1,213	40
Girls	1,465	49	Urban	1,787	60
9th graders	870	29	Protestant	1,941	65
10th graders	810	27	Catholic	565	19
11th graders	690	23	Jewish	58	2
12th graders	630	21	Other	320	10
			None	116	4
East	840	28			
Midwest	960	32	Mothers' education:		
South	750	25	Grade school	1,546	52
Mountain-Pacific	450	15	High school	1,080	36
			College	374	12
Democrat	1,209	40			
Republican	1,335	45	Low income	859	29
Other	33	1	Middle income	1,827	61
None	423	14	High income	314	10

In keeping with the purpose of this chapter, the concept of *family homogeneity* in attitudes and voting behavior developed in the Erie County study is particularly relevant. For example, the authors of that study say: "In August . . . 78% of these [family members] eligible voters intended to vote for the same candidate as did the respondent, 20% were uncertain, and 2% disagreed with the respondent in his choice of a candidate. . . . After the election, only 4% of the 413 panel members who voted claimed that someone in their families had voted differently from themselves."[3]

With respect to various family members, they found as follows: "Among husbands and wives, both of whom had decided to vote, only one pair in 22 disagreed. Among parents and children, one pair in 12 disagreed. . . . Agreement was least . . . among 'in-laws' living in the same household. One pair in five showed disagreement on party alignment."[4]

With respect to change of voting intentions they found: "Less than 3% of voters in families homogeneous in August changed their vote intention during the rest of the campaign. But if there were some relatives who were undecided . . . almost 10% of the respondents shifted between August and October. And in the small group of families in which there was definite disagreement, 29% of the respondents went through at least one change in position. . . . And when the people in families not homogeneous in their vote intentions did change their minds, they changed toward the party favored by the rest of the family."[5] They also found that fully 81 per cent of the Republican families and 71 per cent of the Democratic families, originally undecided, shifted to their families' candidates in October.

And finally, to the question "Do you consider that your family (parents, grandparents) have always been predominantly Democratic or predominantly Republican?" fully three-fourths of the respondents with voting intentions in September answered that they followed the political lead of their families.[6]

While, of course, we made no study in the 1952 pre-election poll of the direct relationship between voting intentions of parents and children, the accuracy in predicting the Eisenhower popular vote mentioned above is highly persuasive with reference to the inference that this relationship must be very high.[7]

Very few of our many attitude studies, obviously, are concerned with voting interests directly. Family homogeneity with respect to a wide variety of attitudes, however, can be demonstrated from our results. Table 2-2, for example, presents correlation data for attitudes of fathers, mothers, and their children for attitude objects studied in the middle thirties when most of these topics were of considerable public interest.[8] The median correlations when corrected for unreliability of the attitude scale indicate relationships between mothers and fathers and between parents and children of the same general sort as reported by Lazarsfeld and his associates.

Table 2-2—Correlations—Mothers vs. Fathers, Mothers vs. Children, and Fathers vs. Children

Attitude object	Mothers vs. Fathers N	r	r ∞	Mothers vs. Children N	r	r ∞	Fathers vs. Children N	r	r ∞
Capital punishment	36	0.63	0.98±.1	43	0.57	0.90±.1	40	0.43	0.70±.1
Labor unions	34	.84	1.05±.0	41	.74	1.07±.1	37	.47	.65±.1
Social insurance	37	.70	1.33±.1	44	.71	1.28±.1	43	.51	.98±.1
Unemployment relief	38	.69	.98±.1	46	.58	.80±.1	41	.74	1.07±.1
Negro	28	.31	.46±.2	37	.58	.97±.1	33	.42	.70±.1
Negro*	89	.57	.80±.1	76	.27	.37±.1	64	.26	.36±.1
Attending movies	78	.61	.95±.1	67	.24	.37±.1	58	.20	.31±.1
Government ownership of railroads*	58	.73	.89±.0	54	.36	.44±.1	49	.43	.52±.1
New Deal*	72	.80	.95±.0	62	.70	.83±.0	57	.57	.68±.1
Control liquor sales in Indiana	75	.60	.76±.1	63	.22	.28±.1	55	.25	.31±.1
CCC*	77	.54	.75±.1	64	.27	.38±.1	56	.35	.49±.1
AAA*	84	.75	.94±.0	69	.57	.71±.1	63	.55	.68±.1
Old Age Pension*	89	.54	.67±.1	72	.46	.58±.1	65	.08	.10±.1
Median		.63	.94		.57	.71		.43	.65

*Indicates a study done in 1934-35 when the attitude objects studied were of considerable public interest.

In another study[9] the poll reproduced in Figure 2-1 was administered to approximately 4,500 high school students in five states—Indiana, Illinois, Kentucky, Michigan, and Ohio. The face sheet of the poll asked for the usual personal data including political party preference. Tetrachoric correlations based on the dichotomy of preference for the Republican party and preference for the

Fig. 2-1.—Poll questionnaire used by the Purdue Opinion Panel in determining attitudes of high school students. (Reproduced by permission of the Division of Educational Reference, Purdue University.)

This is not a test. Your grades will not be influenced by the way you mark this poll.

There is no time limit, but you should finish in about 20 minutes.

After you have read each question, decide how you feel about it. Then record your feeling by placing a check (√) in the appropriate box. If you are uncertain check the question mark.

	a	?	d
1. Should or should not some military training of all able-bodied young men be continued after the war?	Should	?	Should not
2. Would or would not most high-school students like to discuss their personal problems with a sympathetic adult who would tell no one?	Would	?	Would not
3. Would or would not high-school youth like to have a program of genuine self-government in school?	Would	?	Would not
4. Do you or do you not favor a federal sales tax?	Do	?	Do not
5. Should or should not the schools put chief emphasis upon training in the "Three R's"—reading, writing, and arithmetic?	Should	?	Should not
6. Should or should not the schools put chief emphasis upon training in character and citizenship?	Should	?	Should not
7. Should or should not the schools put chief emphasis upon training for earning a living?	Should	?	Should not
8. Should or should not more be taught in school concerning the way people live in other countries?	Should	?	Should not
9. In order to have a more varied educational offering, should or should not most small high schools consolidate?	Should	?	Should not
10. Do you or do you not approve of the Political Action Committee of the C. I. O.?	Do	?	Do not
11. Should or should not the schools give instruction in detecting propaganda?	Should	?	Should not
12. Do you or do you not favor polls such as this one?	Do	?	Do not
13. As compared with other subjects, do you or do you not think social studies worthwhile?	Do	?	Do not
14. Should or should not the United Nations require defeated enemy countries to pay our war costs?	Should	?	Should not
15. After the war will Negroes and white people get along with each other better or worse than before the war?	Better	?	Worse
16. If you could vote in the November, 1944, election, would you vote for Dewey, Roosevelt, or some other person?	Dewey	Other or ?	Roosevelt

Democratic party were obtained for children and their parents as follows:

Mothers-Sons	+0.94
Mothers-Daughters	+ .91
Fathers-Sons	+ .80
Fathers-Daughters	+ .93
Mothers-Fathers	+ .89

Obviously, members of the same family, for the most part, prefer the same political party, amply supporting the findings of the Erie County study.

This kind of family homogeneity is demonstrated in a wider context when we consider the sixteen items in the poll as a sample of attitude objects and obtain the rank order correlations of the proportions of fathers, mothers, daughters, and sons agreeing with each item. These correlations were:

Mothers vs. Fathers	+0.96
Daughters vs. Sons	+ .93
Daughters vs. Mothers	+ .87
Daughters vs. Fathers	+ .80
Sons vs. Mothers	+ .80
Sons vs. Fathers	+ .82

When similar correlations were computed separately for Democratic parents vs. their children and for Republican parents vs. their children, the rank order correlations were:

Democratic Parents vs. Democratic Children	+0.84
Republican Parents vs. Republican Children	+ .89

In the same study the teachers of the children polled also completed the questionnaire. There is a substantial functional relationship between teachers' and children's attitudes and also between teachers' and parents' attitudes as shown by the following rank order correlations:

Teachers vs. Children	+0.65
Teachers vs. Parents	+ .65

On October 16, 1950, *Life* magazine published a report[10] of the findings of a survey conducted by Elmer Roper on a national sample of adults. The survey was concerned with such attitudes as those toward satisfaction with the public school system as a whole, segregation in the schools, teachers' pay, federal support, etc. The same questions were administered to the Purdue Opinion Panel.[11]

The doctoral dissertation of R. Bruce Kirk analyzed the results of our poll much beyond those reported in Poll Report No. 29. In the interest of conserving space, I quote his conclusion relevant to the present discussion: "There is substantial agreement between the opinions of high school students and adults as reflected by their responses to this questionnaire on the public schools."[12]

In summary, it is evident, directly from the correlational studies of attitudes of parents and their children and inferentially from the agreement between adults and children in general that the concept of family homogeneity is amply supported and the literary fancy of the inevitable and ineluctable conflict between "crabbed age and youth" is emphatically denied. It appears that Robert Louis Stevenson indicts a whole nation when he says, "To hold the same view at forty as we held at twenty is to have been stupefied for a score of years, and to take rank, not as a prophet, but as an unteachable brat, well birched and none the wiser."[13] A cynic viewing the foregoing evidence might comment that the myth that man is rational dies hard.

The old saw, "a man convinced against his will will hold the same opinion still," is given point and scientific support in much relatively recent research in social perception and group processes. The individual's need to retain his attitudes intact and thus to minimize conflicts and disagreements with persons in his social environment entail to a marked degree *selective perception* and a kind of *self-insulation* against conflicting and therefore disturbing attitudes. It is a well-known fact that people tend strongly to read those newspapers and to listen to those news commentators who most support their own attitudes.

Probably religious attitudes are among the more stable attitude systems of the individual. For them the modern world provides many possible conflicts; hence selective perception and "self-insulation" should be demonstrable in this area. This was done in a relatively recent study.[14] In this study Myers developed a six-item unidimensional orthodoxy-secularism scale à la Guttman.[15]

In Poll No. 27, on whose data Myers' study was based, a paired comparison-choice list was included with the instructions, "From each pair choose the one subject which you think you would like best." Myers then related the Orthodoxy Scale to the choices made. The relevant conclusion from this part of his study is: "Orthodox students protect their dogmas by choosing courses that do not force them to examine and evaluate them . . . in that the more secular than orthodox chose psychology, sociology, philosophy, biology, and physics as their favored courses."[16]

That the kind of college education fathers have affects the citizenship attitudes of their children was demonstrated in a study by Drucker and Remmers.[17] This study was undertaken because of the following background.

In 1947, the Research Department of *Time* magazine began a nationwide survey of college graduates to discover, if possible, the kind of citizens our college graduates had become. Replies from a group of nearly 10,000 individuals, believed to be a good cross-section of American college graduates, were received on a thirteen-page questionnaire. Analyzing some of the results on four opinion scales labeled Politics, Government, Civic Relations, and The World, Pace[18] found sharp disagreement between college graduates and a group of experts on the six-item Government Scale—especially with regard to items dealing with an understanding of the concepts of democracy, communism, and fascism—a disagreement that led him to the tentative conclusion: "If the experts [thirty to forty professors of history, economics, political science, sociology, public administration, and education] are right in these opinions, we need much better teaching in our colleges about the role of government in the modern world."[19]

He also found that the pattern of response of college graduates who had said that their college work had been "mostly generalized education"—presumably liberal arts—on all four opinion scales was closer to that of the experts than was that of the college graduates who said their college work had been "mostly specific training for an occupation," i.e., technical-professional education.

Responses to the above-mentioned questionnaire and Pace's findings led me to hypothesize that since the family is a primary institution of cultural transmission, the children of such differing groups of fathers would show the same kind of differences. Hence we polled our national panel of teen-agers on a number of the same items used in the *Time* survey. On twelve of the same item responses which Pace had analyzed, the students whose fathers had attended college tended to agree more with the social scientists than did the other students. The major hypothesis that students whose fathers had taken liberal arts courses would be significantly closer in opinion to the social scientists and differ significantly from their fellow students whose fathers had taken technical-professional training was confirmed.[20]

The concept of *cross-pressures*, originated by Lazarsfeld and his associates, to the extent that it is functional, is analogous to the concepts of selective perception and self-insulation, but attitudes do change. That in the realm of political ideology such potential cross-pressures are adjudged to be effective is easily inferred from the "guilt by association and kinship" notions prevalent at mid-century.

Obviously, to the extent that homogeneity of attitudes is greater in the family than in the school community, it follows necessarily that youngsters will be subjected to cross-pressures as they move out of the home psychologically into the neighborhood and school. And as they are increasingly subjected to the mass media of communication, these cross-pressures will increase. The correlations between the attitudes of teachers and pupils and those of teachers and parents cited earlier[21] bear directly on the problem.

One somewhat controlled experiment on a national scale tested the effectiveness in gross terms of one kind of "cross-pressure" in our Purdue Opinion Panel—the effect on attitude scale responses over a six-month period related to the presence or absence of features typically found in intergroup education programs, programs in which high schools differ to a very marked extent.

Polls 33, 34, and 35, administered in the school year 1952-53, were concerned—along with pre-election and postelection attitudes toward candidates—with attitude toward social discrimination. To enable each student to be traced through the year while guaranteeing anonymity, an envelope containing four ballot cards was prepared for each pupil at the beginning of the year. The four cards in each envelope were pre-punched with a code number differentiating that set from the sets used by other pupils. The schools were instructed to have each pupil place his name on an envelope containing a set of ballot cards and to instruct him to use only cards from that envelope in responding to all the polls of the year. In this way a pupil's ballot card could not be associated easily with him once it was removed from the envelope and yet his ballot cards for the year could be reassembled at Purdue University to compare his responses on the various polls.

One variable included in the study was the number of features, if any, in the school's intergroup education program. Administrators of the polls in the high schools were sent a check list of features typically found in intergroup programs. They were asked to indicate which features were employed in their school, if any, and to mention any other features not listed that were also included. The number of features checked or mentioned was taken as an index of the breadth of the intergroup education program in the school. Complete usable data at the end of the year were available for 1,480 pupils in the study. The conclusions from this study by Mainer are cited below.

"1. The D [discrimination] Scale appears to provide a reliable measure of attitude toward social discrimination.

"2. Changes in attitude as measured by repeated administration of the D [discrimination] Scale after a five month interval, while very unreliable in this study, nonetheless are related to other socio-psychological variables. Specifically:

"a. Upper grade pupils maintain their attitudes or change in the direction of greater opposition to discrimination, while pupils from lower high school grades change in the direction of greater endorsement of discrimination.

"b. Students with higher vocabulary levels change more in the direction of opposition to discrimination than do pupils with lower vocabulary levels.

"c. Geographic region and religion both are related to attitude change, but their interactions with other variables have more clear cut effects upon attitude change. These are discussed below.

"3. Intergroup education programs are successful in producing greater opposition to social discrimination.

"4. Certain socio-psychological variables interact with intergroup education programs to produce attitude changes, as follows:

"a. In schools with intergroup programs, Catholic pupils shift more in the direction of opposition to discrimination than do Protestants. However, in schools without intergroup programs, Protestant pupils tend either to maintain their attitudes or to shift toward opposition to discrimination, while Catholic pupils tend to change toward greater endorsement of discrimination.

"b. Differences in attitude change between pupils exposed to intergroup programs and those not exposed are much greater among Southern pupils than among Easterners.

"c. An interaction may exist between intergroup education and authoritarianism. If confirmed in future investigations, it may be concluded that highly authoritarian pupils become more opposed to discrimination in schools with intergroup programs, but become more in favor of discrimination in schools without such programs."[22]

These conclusions obviously raise many questions, but limitations of space preclude consideration of them here. They are ably discussed in Chapter 5 of Mainer's study.

The concept of a *hierarchy of stability* of attitudes appears in the research literature with increasing frequency. Two or three examples from our researches can be briefly mentiond by way of illustration. Attitudes concerning race are highly stable over time. Over the period of a decade the question "Is or is not race prejudice inborn?" was included five times in our polls with percentage results as follows:

	March 1944	*Nov. 1946*	*Oct. 1948*	*March 1950*	*Oct. 1954*
It is	29	26	26	20	18
It is not	41	42	49	47	55
Uncertain	30	32	25	33	24

Over a period of only six years in answer to the question, "Do you or do you not think that the U. S. will be able to settle its differences with Russia by peaceable means?" the affirmative response (in per cent) changed in the same amount as the preceding question on race prejudice.

	Oct. 1948	*March 1950*	*Oct. 1954*
Do	31	23	21
Do not	49	40	54
Undecided	20	37	25

In three different polls over a three-year period we asked two questions: "Have you heard or read about Senator McCarthy and his actions, which led to the Senate hearings?" and "In general, do you approve or disapprove of the methods used by McCarthy?"

The percentages given below are based only on those answering "yes" to the first question.

	Nov. 1951	*March 1954*	*Oct. 1954*
Approve	45	33	25
Disapprove	24	31	59
Uncertain	31	36	16

Of particular interest beyond the sharply increasing disapproval of Senator McCarthy's methods is the sharp decrease in uncertainty in October, 1954, compared to the two preceding polls, indicating a definite "crystallization" process.

A final illustration of fairly rapid change is the percentage response to the question "Do you or do you not think that the age for voting should be lowered from 21 to 18?" Here the change in attitude in a four-year period is almost 100 per cent from the figures in the original poll.

	March 1950	*March 1953*	*Oct. 1953*	*March 1954*
Should	34	56	58	63
Should not	54	32	32	26
Undecided	12	12	10	8

The relationship of social and personal characteristics to attitudes —the ecology of attitudes—is a growing and fascinating area of research. Scientific interest and attention has been focused on the extent of the existence of *social class* and attitude variables related to it. In one of our polls[23] both an objective criterion (father's occupation) and a subjective criterion (self-class identification) were used. Table 2-3 summarizes the results. Evidence for the psychological reality of social class is clear. In the entire sample, 94 per cent of the students believed that social classes exist in America and 37 per cent of these students said that differences among the classes are large. Moreover, attitudes toward deferred gratification, choice of friends, educational and vocational goals, violence and aggression, and a number of school activities as well as political party preference were all related to social class position. Parents' education, region of the country, and religious affiliation are also related to social class position.

The technically sophisticated reader will before this have wondered, no doubt, what various cross-tabulations and more intensive statistical analyses such as multiple correlation, analysis of variance, and factor analysis might provide by way of additional light on various aspects of the problem discussed in this chapter. In some of the doctoral dissertations cited such techniques have, of course, been applied and the interested reader can consult these studies.

In summary, the studies cited in this chapter have corroborated the findings of other studies, particularly *The People's Choice*, with reference to the attitudinal concepts of family homogeneity, selective perception, self-insulation, hierarchy of stability, cross-pressures, and social class.

Table 2-3—Social Class Identification of 2,500 High School Students, Grades 9 to 12, Related to Father's Occupational Grouping (Percentage)

	SELF-IDENTIFICATION			
Father's occupation	*Upper class*	*Middle class*	*Working class*	*Totals**
Professional and managerial	12	68	19	99
Middle-level job dealing with people	6	69	24	99
Middle-level job dealing with tools	4	59	35	98
Unskilled labor	3	47	48	98

*Not an even 100 per cent because a few students failed to answer.

CHAPTER 3

Measurement Problems in Panel Studies

ELEANOR E. MACCOBY AND RAY HYMAN

The problem of how to measure change is important for all the social sciences. At first thought it might seem that, relative to other measurements, the measurement of change presents no new problems. But, in fact, the simple questions "Has a change occurred?" and "Has group A changed more than group B?" stir up many difficulties. Many of these difficulties cannot be resolved with current measurement procedures.

The major advantage of a "panel" design over a series of cross-section surveys is presumed to be that it is more sensitive to change —that it can give more information about *who* changed, how much, in what direction, and why. It is especially important, therefore, to consider the measurement problems inherent in "change analysis" in any effort to evaluate the panel method in general or any selected panel study in particular.

A first difficulty seems to be one of scale units. At best, scaling in the social sciences, especially attitude scaling, gives us ordinal scales. To answer many questions of attitude change, it seems at least an equal-interval scale is needed. Let us look at a typical problem. We want to see whether a certain instructional film has a greater effect upon an extreme group than it has upon a moderate group on some attitude continuum. We observe changes on the attitude scale for each group. We want to be able to say that group A changed by a different amount than did group B. But this assumes that a change of x scale units at the high end of the scale is equivalent to a change of x scale units at the lower end of the scale. Clearly we cannot say this unless we have an equal-interval scale.

A further limitation in comparing changes between groups who are at different initial levels is imposed by ceiling effects. An individual who is at the top of the scale has little room to improve relative to someone who is much lower on the scale. Hovland *et al.* (**3**) discuss and illustrate the different approaches toward handling such a problem and the different results obtainable in the same data with different measures. Any of the techniques that they suggest for evaluating the effectiveness of a change must necessarily be arbitrary until the problem of scale units is solved. An equal-interval scale is necessary if we are to compare the differential change between two groups; a ratio scale is necessary if we are to have an index of amount of change which is to have any absolute meaning.

A second kind of measurement problem is introduced by errors of measurement—by unreliability in the measuring instruments. Perhaps we should raise first the question of what kinds of response variability are to be regarded as error. If a child's I.Q. is measured once, and then measured again a week later with a parallel form of the test, and the two scores differ by ten points, we say that the difference is due to measurement errors. We do not believe that the I.Q. has actually changed ten points in a week. Our reason for calling the change "error" arises partly out of our definition of I.Q.—we are trying to measure something stable enough, something basic enough, that it could not change so much in such a short period. (Of course, those who define I.Q. simply as what I.Q. tests test, can regard the change as *real* change—as real as any other change.)

In studying changes in voting intentions, response instability is the very center of our interest. We would obviously be throwing out the baby with the bath water if we labeled all changes in response, from one measurement to another, as "error." Kendall, in her book *Conflict and Mood* (**4**), has focused her attention on the characteristics of people who change their minds on public opinion issues, and for her this group is of interest not because it includes the cases concerning which an interviewer or a coder made a mistake, but because the members of this group demonstrably have something in common in their life situations and in their personalities which leads them to vacillate. Let us attempt, then, to classify the different sources of response instability, and point out which ones we propose to consider "error" and which ones are the kinds of changes that we feel deserve study in their own right.

Let us assume that interview questions concerning an individual's candidate preferences are intended to tell us how the individual would actually vote if the election were held the day of the interview. The ballot he would cast if he actually went into a voting booth we shall call the criterion. If we interview the individual repeatedly over time, the criterion itself may be unstable. That is, we interview some people who would actually vote differently at Time 1 than they would at Time 2. Some of this "criterion instability" is predictable, in that it is related to specific characteristics of the individual or his environment which are subject to study by a social scientist. These specific characteristics may be dealt with as *variables* and are assumed to have comparable effects on the different people who share a similar score on the variable. Thus, people who are subject to persuasive efforts from proponents of both candidates during a campaign share a high score on the "cross-pressures" variable, and one can ask whether they are more alike in their "criterion instability" than people who share a low score.

There is criterion instability that is highly idiosyncratic, however. The writers know of an instance of a young wife, reared in a Republican family, who was persuaded to her husband's Democratic views and voted as a Democrat in several elections. Then her father, to whom she was very close, died just before a presidential election. She voted Republican because she knew how much her father had wanted to cast a Republican vote in this particular election, and she decided to cast her vote in his place, as a kind of last gesture of loyalty. The fact that this young woman had a Republican father and a Democratic husband meant, of course, that she was subject to cross-pressures, and her voting instability might be predicted on that basis. The fact that the cross-pressures showed up in her voting behavior only upon her father's death, however, was more idiosyncratic. Another woman, under similar cross-pressures, might vote with her father while he was alive and feel freer to vote with her husband after her father's death. For purposes of studying the effects of cross-pressures alone (without reference to interaction with personality variables), these individual situational factors which determine whether cross-pressures will be effective may be regarded as a source of error. So may the momentary headache, the recovery of a loved one from sickness, the arrival in the mail of a heavy insurance bill—any one of which, occurring on the day before rather than on the day after the casting of a vote, may make a difference in the vote, and a difference which varies from one individual to another.

In addition to what we have called "criterion instability," there is instability in voting intentions owing to measurement errors. By measurement error we mean any deviation of our measurement from the criterion. Such deviations could arise from deliberate misstatements by the respondents. In addition, they may occur when the interviewer makes a mistake in reading the question or recording the respondent's answer, or when the coder in the home office miscodes, or when the IBM clerk punches the wrong number in a punch card. Occasionally such errors are systematic (as when an interviewer anticipates that most respondents in a particular part of town will belong to the same party, and therefore over-records the votes for that party). More often, they have as great a probability of occurring in one direction as in the other. When such errors are made on one measurement and no error is made on an earlier or later measurement, then the respondent is recorded as a person who changed his mind, even though his voting intentions were actually stable.

To summarize, then, instability in response to a question about voting intentions may be classified as follows:

Type A. Criterion instability

1. Idiosyncratic—uncorrelated with other variables of interest
2. Systematic—related to a variable which affects numbers of people alike

Type B. Instability due to measurement errors

1. Systematic (biased)
2. Random

Berelson *et al.* (**2**) are interested primarily in Type A-2 instability. The problem is to sort out this variety of instability from the rest. There are instances in which errors of Type B-2 could produce the kinds of shifts in response which are reported in *Voting*, and there are of course serious difficulties, when this is the case, in attributing the changes to anything other than measurement error. Specifically, this is true when statistical regression is involved. When errors of measurement exist, then on remeasurement the extreme groups will be less extreme. Hovland *et al.* (**3**) in their Appendix illustrate such effects and how they may mislead the unwary into unwarranted conclusions.

Maccoby (**5**) in her review of *Voting* illustrates how errors of Type B-2 might vitiate some of the conclusions made by Berelson *et al.* Let us examine the reconstruction of Chart LVIII which she presents. We will deal only with those people who state they are going to vote the same as, or opposite to, their families. The measurements are taken at two different times—intentions in June are compared with how respondents said they actually voted in November. We are interested in the kind of shifts that take place in voting intentions as illustrated by Table 3-1.

Table 3-1—Respondents' Voting Intentions in June in Relation to Family Preference Compared to November Vote* (Number)

	VOTING INTENTIONS IN JUNE		
	Same as Family	*Opposite to Family*	*Marginals*
November vote:			
Same as intention in June	273	25	298
Changed to other party	22	13	35
Total	295	38	333

*Data from Berelson *et al.*, *Voting*, Chart LVIII, p. 121.

Before we proceed to discuss the implications of this table, we should carefully note two features of the data. The proportion of people who intend to vote the same as their families is overwhelmingly large both in June and in November, being approximately 89 per cent and 86 per cent respectively. Secondly, the proportion of people who show any shift in voting intention from June to November is slightly more than 10 per cent of the total. In evaluating marginal changes, it is only these 35 individuals who can provide us with useful information.

Now what kinds of inferences do we want to make from the data in such a table? We will follow Berelson *et al.* and arbitrarily assume that these 333 people constitute the complete population concerning which we want to make conclusions about attitude shifts. Such a restriction eliminates the problem of sampling error. For the moment we are only concerned with the question: Did these 333 people show a shift in either direction? Such a question, however, is trivial. It is obvious that we would ask such a question only because we are interested in generalizing to a larger population from which these 333 people are only a sample. But for the sake of simplicity, we will start by assuming no sampling error.

But the removal of sampling errors does not remove all the sources of error in the table. If there were no errors in the table, we could look at it and say whether a change took place and in what direction. And we could say this with probability 1.00. But we can expect that we will have mistakes, errors of recording, and other errors which we can classify as errors of measurement. The existence of such errors of measurement means that we are still dealing with a sampling problem. We can imagine that our table is one of a large set of possible tables that we could have obtained on these 333 panelists. If we assume that these errors are random and nonsystematic, then this one table can be used as an unbiased estimate of what the "true" population table looks like. Because our one table is one sample of an indefinitely large number of possible tables, any inferences must be of a statistical nature. This means, contrary to the position of Berelson *et al.*, that we cannot avoid making statistical inferences, even if we wish to restrict our inferences to changes exhibited by only these 333 people.

Berelson *et al.* want to use such a table to say something about the direction of shifts in voting intentions. Let us construct a dummy table (Table 3-2) to correspond to Table 3-1 to illustrate their argument.

Table 3-2—Voting Intentions in June in Relation to Family Preference Compared to November Vote (Generalized Form)

	VOTING INTENTIONS IN JUNE		
	Same as Family	*Opposite to Family*	*Marginals*
November vote:			
Same as intention in June	a	b	$a + b$
Changed to other party	c	d	$c + d$
Total	$a + c$	$b + d$	N

Berelson *et al.* point out that only 7 per cent of those who intended to vote the same as their families in June defected from this position in November; whereas 34 per cent of those who intended to vote differently from their families in June returned to the fold. Such a result is interpreted as implying a greater shift toward conforming with the family than toward defecting. The comparisons are based on the proportions *c*/(*a* plus *c*) vs. *d*/(*b* plus *d*).

But, as Maccoby points out **(5)**, such a comparison is misleading if errors of measurement exist. The first thing to note in Table 3-1 is that if we look at the total proportion who tend to vote with their families in June as compared with the same proportion in November, there is a slight decrease in the proportion of people who stick with family intentions (89 per cent in June vs. 86 per cent in November). And we should further note that we have a statistical test by which we can detect whether a systematic shift has taken place in either direction (we can use either the chi-square test for correlated proportions, or its equivalent, the sign test). The test is based only on the number of people who change in either direction; therefore its sensitivity is proportional to the total number who shift and not to the total number in the panel. For the 35 cases in Table 3-1 who show a change, the probability of finding a deviation this great or greater from a hypothetical split of 0.50 is between 0.25 and 0.10. This would not lead us to conclude that a change has taken place, but note that if we did conclude a change had taken place, we would have concluded that it took place in a direction opposite to that suggested by Berelson *et al.*

Note that we have suggested that the appropriate comparison is between the frequencies *d* vs. *c* rather than the proportions *c*/(*a* plus *c*) vs. *d*/(*b* plus *d*). And note further that two procedures tend to give opposite results for this table. Why is this so? And why do we maintain that the appropriate comparison is between *d* and *c*? We can illustrate our point with a hypothetical example. Let *P* equal the proportion of results which are accurately reported and let *Q* equal 1-*P* or the probability of making an error in measurement. Further, let us assume a dichotomous scale and that *P* and *Q* are the same for all the individuals.

Now let us imagine a situation wherein the "true" number of people who intend to vote the same way as their family is *S* and the "true" number who intend to vote opposite their family is *O*. We will assume that *S* and *O* do not change, i.e., remain constant over the time period in which we are interested. To make our illustration concrete, let us assign the following numbers to P, Q, S and O.

Let P equal 0.90
Q equal 0.10
S equal 200
O equal 100. N equals S plus O equals 300.

In other words, the probability of misclassifying each of our panelists is 0.10. We assume that the probability of misclassifying an individual is independent of how another individual was classified. Now imagine that we measure these 300 individuals at time $t1$ and again at time $t2$. The observed number of Sames and Opposites at time $t1$ will be:

Observed number of Sames equals PS plus QO equals
0.9(200) plus 0.1(100) equals 190.
Observed number of Opposites equals QS plus PO equals
0.1(200) plus 0.9(100) equals 110.

Note that the errors of measurement tend to make us underestimate the number of panelists who are Sames (in the majority) and overestimate the number of panelists who are Opposites (in the minority). As unreliability increases the estimates of the proportions of Sames and Opposites will regress to toward 0.50 regardless of the true split. This is one effect of unreliability.

Now let us examine the effect of regression as we study the changes on remeasurement at time $t2$. We can predict the following numbers of observations in each of our four categories:

Observed number of Sames who stay Same on second measurement equals
P^2S plus Q^2O equals 0.81(200) plus 0.01(100) equals 163
Observed number of Sames who change to Opposite equals
PQS plus PQO equals 0.09(200) plus 0.09(100) equals 27
Observed number of Opposites who change to Same equals
PQS plus PQO equals 0.09(200) plus 0.09(100) equals 27
Observed number of Opposites who stay Opposites equals
Q^2S plus P^2O equals 0.01(200) plus 0.81(100) equals 83

Table 3-3—Hypothetical Observations on Respondents at Time 1 Compared to Those at Time 2 (Number)

	OBSERVATIONS AT *t1*		
	Same as Family	*Opposite to Family*	*Marginals*
Observations at *t2*:			
Same as at *t1*	163	83	246
Opposite to those at *t1*	27	27	54
Total	190	110	300

These observations can be placed into a 2 by 2 table analogous to Table 3-1 and Table 3-2. Note that Table 3-3 is what we would expect the observations to look like on times *t*1 and *t*2 under the assumptions that no change has taken place, but that errors of measurement which are equally probable for all individuals have occurred.

Note that if we estimate the proportion of each group that has changed from *t*1 to *t*2, as do Berelson *et al.*, we find that 27/190 or approximately 14 per cent of those who originally intended to vote the same as their families have defected and now intend to vote opposite to their families. But 27/110 or approximately 24 per cent of these who intended to vote opposite to their families have come back into the fold. If we followed Berelson *et al.*, we would use such information to conclude that pressures are stronger to change toward voting with family than vice versa. But we have constructed our problem so that this is not the case. We have estimated changes on the basis of unreliability of measurement alone.

If we wish to find out whether this sample is becoming more homogeneous (more voters agreeing with their families' political positions), the correct procedure is to compare the marginals. We note that the proportion of Sames is exactly the same at *t*1 as it is at *t*2. The correct statistical comparison is between the frequencies of those who changed from Same to Opposite vs. those who changed from Opposite to Same. We see that these are identical as we would expect them to be if only errors in measurement are involved. The differences in the *proportions* of changers in each group are due to the fact that the groups are unequal in size to begin with.

So far we have considered only whether a systematic change has occurred over the whole sample in a particular direction. There is another question. It is possible that although the marginals remain the same at *t*1 and *t*2, a large number of counterbalancing "real" changes have taken place. In other words, is the total of 54/300 changers greater than we should expect on the basis of unreliability of measurement alone? Clearly, we cannot answer such a question unless we have a control comparison or independent knowledge of the reliability of measurement. One possible way in which such a question might be answered is in terms of the model for attitude change developed by Anderson (**1**). Here we would measure our panelists at times *t*1, *t*2, *t*3. Times *t*1 and *t*2 would be separated by a very short interval in time, say one day or a week, whereas *t*2 and *t*3 might be separated by a much longer period–say several months. Following Anderson's model we would test the hypothesis that the same matrix of transitional probabilities fits changes from *t*1 to *t*2 and those from *t*2 to *t*3. If such an hypothesis were rejected it might suggest that a real change occurred between times *t*2 and *t*3 which could not be explained by changes occurring due to unreliability between times *t*1 and *t*2. One difficulty with this procedure would be the acceptability of using the changes from *t*1 to *t*2 as a measure of unreliability. Also the memory factor and the effects of a recently preceding measurement may produce a spurious stability.

The primary concern in most panel studies is not to detect whether a change in marginals has occurred over the whole sample. This question could be answered by comparing the marginals of two successive cross-section studies. A panel design is employed in the hope that it will permit the study of *internal* changes within the sample–showing how some groups change differently from other groups. Even some of these questions can be answered without reinterviewing the same respondents. Using two successive cross-section studies, one can see, within the limits of sampling error, whether white-collar union members have changed more than blue-collar union people, for example. A panel design is primarily useful to determine whether people change differentially who have different initial positions on a variable (such as an attitude variable) which is itself subject to change.

A panel analysis often involves the comparison of two or more groups in the direction and amount of their shift. Let us take for illustration a reconstruction of Chart LXII from *Voting*. The "don't knows" have been omitted from both groups in Table 3-4.

Table 3-4—Comparison Between Shifts in Voting Intentions of Two Groups at Two Times* (Number)

	NONUNION WHITE COLLAR			UNION LABOR		
	Voting Intentions in June			Voting Intentions in June		
	Rep	Dem	Marginals	Rep	Dem	Marginals
August intention:						
Same as intention in June	174	28	202	104	69	173
Changed to opposite party	7	7	14	13	11	24
Total	181	35	216	117	80	197

*Data from Berelson *et al.*, *Voting*, Chart LXII, p. 125.

Looking at the marginals, we see that neither group showed an over-all shift in political preference. And on the basis of our earlier analysis, it is evident that one can *not* conclude (as Berelson *et al.* did) that "within social strata with unambiguous political preferences, the political majority is more stable than the political minority." This conclusion was derived from the fact that, among nonunion white-collar people, a higher *proportion* of June Democrats changed party by August than was true among June Republicans. But as we have seen, if equal numbers changed in the two white-collar groups (as they did), this fact could be explained on the basis of Type B-2 errors alone, and cannot therefore be attributed to the "criterion instability" in which the authors of *Voting* are interested.

There is another interesting question which may be asked of the data in Table 3-4, however. This question concerns whether there was more instability among union labor than among nonunion white-collar people. We have seen that the number of shifts from one position to another upon remeasurement that can be attributed to measurement error depends on (*a*) the error rate and (*b*) the total number of cases to whom this error rate is applied. If measurement errors are random, there is no reason to expect that more errors would be made in measuring the political preferences of union people than in measuring nonunion white-collar people. Table 3-4 shows that among the nonunion white-collar group, there were 14 "changers" out of a total of 216 people. Among union labor, there were 24 "changers" out of 197 people—a somewhat higher proportion. There should be no difference in these proportions if errors of measurement alone were involved, so that if the difference between the proportions is greater than we would expect by chance, there is evidence for greater criterion instability among union labor.

We believe that there are a number of questions that may be answered by comparing groups such as the two groups described in Table 3-4, questions which are not made indeterminate by the problem of errors of Type B-2. One can determine, on the basis of the reasoning above, whether there is a greater total amount of counterbalancing changes (not reflected in marginal change) in one group than in the other. One can also determine whether the marginal changes of the two groups differ in amount or direction. What one cannot determine without a control group (or some other source of an estimate of the amount of measurement error) is how much of the internal shifts within any one group may be attributed to Type B error and how much to the "real" Type A changes which the panel analyst would like to study.

CHAPTER 4

"Voting" and the Equilibrium of the American Political System

TALCOTT PARSONS

This chapter[1] concerns certain *theoretical* issues raised by the research studies that this volume as a whole discusses in a broader framework. There are two broad types of problem involved in the studies as a whole, namely (1) why a given *individual* votes as he does, and (2) how the voting process functions as part of the *social system* in which it operates. I shall focus my attention on the latter, the sociological as distinct from the psychological problem. The two are, however, so closely interwoven in the studies that some discussion of the relation between the two problems will prove necessary. I shall also, like the studies themselves, be concerned with recent presidential elections in the United States.

Because of the compactness with which *Voting*[2] presents a set of findings and interpretations that throw a great deal of light on political process in a society like ours and fit on the whole very well with a generalized analysis in terms of the theory of social systems, I shall concentrate my attention on it. To show the relation between such an analysis and the findings will be my main theme. Naturally critical questions will be raised at certain points, but I shall not anticipate them.

A framework of broad analysis of certain aspects of the structure, processes, and functional problems of the American political system will be developed, and then applied to the principal findings of the study.

A THEORETICAL MODEL OF A TWO-PARTY SYSTEM. The political aspect of a social system may be thought of as centered on the generation and distribution of power. Power may, for the present purposes, be conceived as the capacity of the society to mobilize its resources in the interest of goals, defined as positively rather than permissively sanctioned by the system as a whole —goals that are "affected with a public interest." The amount of its power is an attribute of the total system and is a function of several variables. These, as I conceive them, are the *support* that can be mobilized by those exercising power, the *facilities* they have access to (notably the control of the productivity of the economy), the *legitimation* that can be accorded to the positions of the holders of power, and the relatively *unconditional loyalties* of the population to the society in its politically organized aspects. It is above all the factor of support which will be the center of concern here. In a modern, differentiated society the most important "producers" of power on the collectivity level, though by no means the sole ones, are those who hold responsible positions in what we call the structure of government—here, of course, the federal government.

An old question about power needs to be mentioned. One school of thought emphasizes power as power *over* others, with the implication that in a larger system the power held by different units must cancel out. My own emphasis is on power as capacity to get things done. Whether there is opposition or not is an empirically very important but theoretically secondary matter. My point of reference will be the *capacity of a social system to get things done in its collective interest.* Hence power involves a special problem of the *integration* of the system, including the binding of its units, individual and collective, to the necessary commitments.

Looked at in this way, the capacity to act focuses on the capacity for an agency or system of organization to make decisions responsibly, i.e., with relative assurance that they can be effectively carried out. Power is essentially the basis of responsible action in this sense. The variables just mentioned are the "ingredients" of power—which can vary in quantity and combination; on them capacity for responsible action depends.

I have defined power as the capacity of a social system to mobilize resources to attain collective goals. A total society's paramount "goal" must be conceived on a very high level of abstraction.

It is a function primarily of two sets of factors, the institutionalized value system of the society and the exigencies of the situation. Together they define states of affairs that need to be changed in the interest of a higher level of value-implementation. The specificity of a societal goal will vary greatly for different societies, but in any case there will be many subgoals that vary as functions of a societal development and the manifold relations of the society to the situation.

The value system of the contemporary United States centers on what may be called "instrumental activism." It is oriented to control the action situation in the interest of range and quality of adaptation, but with more economic than political emphasis. In goal definition it is highly indefinite and pluralistic, being committed to a rather general direction of progress or improvement, without any clearly defined terminal goal. Economic production is highly valued as the most immediate focus of adaptive capacity. Beyond that, however, we value particularly technology and science as means to productivity, and the maximization of opportunity for individuals and subcollectivities (manifested above all in concern with health and education). Moreover, we have a special set of attitudes toward organization and authority which might be summed up as involving, on the one hand, a pragmatic acceptance of authority in the interest of limited specifically approved goals, but, on the other hand, an objection to any pretensions of generalized superiority of status.

The over-all goal of American society (in a special technical sense) may then be tentatively defined as the *facilitation* of effective adaptive development of the society and of the societal conditions associated with it. It centers on economic development, but definitely includes the integrative conditions which are relevant. At the next lower level of specifications, American society stresses the more immediate facilitation of production and the development of productivity, the effective ordering of political organization itself, the furthering of effective integration of the social system, and the promoting of conditions on the level of opportunity for operation of the system and adjustment of personalities.

The generation and allocation of power in a society occurs through a set of structures and processes, a subsystem parallel to the economy which we may call the "polity." It is essentially a functional-relational system, controlled by institutional patterns and controlling collectivities and roles.[3] The relevant institutional patterns are those governing the hierarchical ordering of social statuses, authority, and the compulsory regulation of "private" activities. The focus of the collectivity structure is clearly government, though there is a political as well as economic component in all collectivities in the society. Government is that complex of collectivities which have political *primacy*. This means that governmental organizations primarily, in their relations to the rest of the society, generate power and make it available to the rest of the society.

Like the economy, the polity is an analytically distinct subsystem of the society. It too is conceived to stand in relations to other parts of the society which involve the interchange of inputs and outputs over its boundaries. Of these interchanges, one is of primary importance for present purposes. It may be characterized through a comparison between the functions of government and those of the polity. On the federal level, which alone will concern us here, the main functions of government are relatively clearly set forth in the Constitution itself. The most important concern the conduct of foreign relations, the regulation of commerce between the states, the enforcement of rights (personal freedom, opportunity, property), the ensuring of justice and internal order, and the promotion of the "general welfare." Broadly, this constitutional mandate is to implement within a certain framework the goals of the society as sketched above.

The functions of the polity, as contrasted with those of government I conceive to center in creating the conditions necessary if those assuming responsibility in government are to be able to assume and discharge this responsibility. Given the American value system these may be said to be: (1) the legitimation of the powers of government and the statuses of its various subcollectivities and offices; (2) the requisite share in the control of the basic facilities available in the society, especially control of the productivity of the economy through the establishment of "rights to intervene"; and (3) the mobilization of "support" for the assumption, by office holders in government, of leadership roles and the corresponding responsibilities for formulation of more specific goals and their implementation.[4]

The theoretical analysis of this chapter concerns the third of these conditions of responsible leadership. I shall call this the "goal-attainment" process of the polity as a system. *Its* goal, which must be distinguished from that of the society as a whole as sketched above, is to generate power in the political sense, i.e., to mobilize "resources" that can be used to implement societal goals. There are two main levels on which this goal is (more or less effectively) achieved. The more general is the provision of effective *leadership* in the goal-specification and goal-implementation processes on the requisite collective level. The more specific is arriving at *decisions* which are binding on the society as a politically organized collectivity. For present purposes the subsystem that functions as recipient of these outputs of the polity may be referred to as the "public."

We are, however, speaking of a boundary-interchange process and must be concerned not only with outputs from the polity but also with the inputs to the polity from the public—which on the one hand are essential factors in its functioning, on the other are in certain ways contingent on its performance. I should like to suggest that support (point 3 above) is the appropriate input category (from public to polity) which matches the outputs of provision of leadership and making of decisions. At the more general level, the support that is exchanged with and contingent upon leadership is *generalized*. It takes the form of broadly based confidence in those assuming responsibility for leadership in governmental affairs which is necessary to enable them to act with real power, i.e., to make necessary and far-reaching decisions responsibly in the sense that elements of the population affected will accept the consequences. Such consequences inevitably include burdens and obligations that affect some elements adversely and bear unevenly on different groups. On the lower level of generality, the relevant type of support which corresponds to decision-making may be said to be the *advocacy of policies*. By this I mean an accepting attitude on a level more general than that of specific decisions but less general than that of an "administration" in the American or a "Government" in the British sense (which is a term of generalized support).

In the above formulation I am thinking self-consciously in terms of a parallel with the corresponding boundary-interchange of the economy, the one involved vis-à-vis the household with labor as a factor of production and the production of consumers' goods. On the higher level of generalization the primary output of the economy to the household is the production of *income* in the monetary sense—in the labor case, wage income. On the lower level it is the production of specific commodities made available to consumers. The corresponding inputs to the economy from the household are, on the high level, labor in the factor sense and, on the lower level, consumers' spending.

These relations of interchange of inputs and outputs—on the one hand, between the economy and the household—may be represented diagrammatically in a simple way as follows:[5]

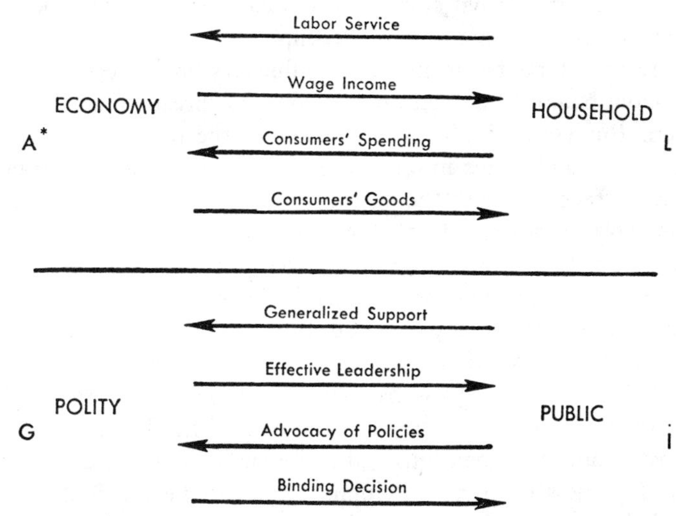

*For an explanation of the notation, A, G, I, L, see final section of this chapter entitled: Technical Note.

I shall have this parallel in mind throughout the following analysis. It should be clearly understood, however, that it is a parallel, in the strict sense an analogy, and not an identity. Power as an output is not income in the economic sense, decisions are not commodities, support is not labor, and consumers' spending is not advocacy of policies. In an analytical sense the "public," as the source of support and advocacy of policies, is altogether different from the household, as the source of labor and consumers' spending, though members of households are at the same time parts of the public. I shall delineate the relevant characteristics of the public as we go along.[6]

Let us now attempt to apply this abstract analytical scheme to some familiar facts of American political structure. I have stated that the focus of political organization on the collectivity level is government, in our case the federal government. The boundary-interchange just outlined is that set of processes by which control of the federal government is decided, its major policies are worked out, and public attitudes toward them are influenced and brought to bear. The focus of the mechanisms by which the processes work out is what we call the party system. At the support level the most important single process on the side of the public is voting because, under our constitutional system, this decides who is to assume the primary roles of responsible leadership.

There are of course many other influences on leadership: media of opinion, behind-the-scenes persuasion and threats, financial interests, etc. But voting is the central focus of the process of selection of leadership and hence in one sense all other influences must channel their effects *through* the voting process.

The most important fact about the American situation is the existence on the national level of the *two*-party system which, with some interruptions, has proved stable over a long period. This means that the presidency must at any given time be occupied by the candidate of one of the two parties, and that the majority party in each house of Congress has the opportunity to "organize" its house through the speakership (in the case of the House of Representatives) and chairmanships and majorities of committees. In spite of the looseness of party discipline there can be no doubt of the overwhelming importance of this two-party structure.

Within the complex of operation of the two-party system this analysis, in line with the empirical studies with which it is concerned, will be confined to the voting processes which determine the incumbency of the presidency. It is of course vital to realize that the process of electing the President, considered as a system, is only part of a larger one. It has been noted that a variety of influences operate to determine the decisions of voters. But even where the voting mechanism itself is concerned, voting for presidential candidates is only part of the voter's function and opportunity. The separation of powers means that he also votes for congressional candidates and for state and local offices.

A salient fact of American politics is that there is only a rough correlation between party votes for President and for these other offices. The looseness of party discipline and the plural voting opportunities provided in the American system mean that in no sense can the determination of the presidency be considered a *closed* system. For example, tensions generated by being forced to choose between only two candidates for President may be expressed in supporting for other offices candidates not in sympathy with the presidential candidate, or candidates of the opposing party. Empirical statements made in the following analysis should always be qualified with these considerations in mind.

Nevertheless I think it is legitimate to consider the voting process by which Presidents are elected as authentically a *social system.* It is a set of processes of action and interaction which may be treated in terms of specific modes of interdependence which can be analytically separated from other influences. Furthermore, in our system, the Presidency is the focus of integration of the political system as a whole. Of course the concrete data that will be reviewed are affected by factors emanating from outside this particular system—including the other voting processes in other subsystems of the political structure. But in principle this is true of any social system that is a subsystem of a larger one, i.e., less than the total society.

To return to the substantive discussion, the main function of political organization is the facilitation of effective action on collective levels. The two-party system may be regarded as a mechanism that makes possible a certain balance between effectiveness through relative centralization of power, and mobilization of support from different sources in such a way that there is genuine contingency—the supporter is offered a real alternative.[7] Dictatorships naturally are different; their concern is to avoid losing support lest the opposition become dangerous, and there is a strong tendency to use coercive measures in coping with actual or feared opposition. But the two-party system, as has often been pointed out, makes it possible for the holders of power to be changed without upsetting the system. Naturally this depends on definite institutional conditions, notably the acceptance of electoral results by the losing side without impairment of basic loyalties, and the restraint of winners from using their power to suppress opposition. It depends overwhelmingly on the firm institutionalization of such "rules of the game."

All this I take for granted. The point of present interest is that the two-party system, as distinguished from a many-party system or one of an indefinite number of shifting factions, has certain implications for the structure of support in its relation to leadership. This way of structuring the situation forces a high level of *generalization* of support on the one side, of responsibility on the other. This is particularly true in a society with a social structure as diverse as the American, in economic, class, occupational, regional, ethnic, religious, and other terms. Support, focusing on the presidency, must be given to one of two party candidates: the alternative is a "protest" vote for a minority-party candidate, or nonparticipation altogether. Many votes are motivated by more particularized considerations having to do with specific interest groups, etc. But *whatever* their motivation on lower levels of generality, all the votes have to be *counted* as support for the party candidate and his administration, and on some level for the power of the party in Congress. This point brings out in one context very sharply the difference in significance between the problem of the *motivation* of the individual voter, and of the *consequences* of his vote for the political system.

A word may now be said about the line of differentiation between the two major parties. This line is less one of ideological "principle," and more pragmatic, than is the case in European politics. A broad line can, however, be discerned. I would like to characterize this distinction as that between "right" and "left" in a sense appropriate to American conditions. The focus of the American right in this sense is the organization of the free-enterprise economy. This is by no means "conservative" in a general social sense; it is in fact the main center of dynamic development in the society. But it is *politically* conservative because the economy is institutionalized on a private-enterprise basis in such a way that positive political action can readily be defined as threatening to interfere with the conditions of operation of this type of economy.[8] Connected with the "business" interest in this sense are various other elements with a tendency to fear innovative change, notably in our recent history the rural-small town elements of a large part of the country.

The "left" on the other hand, has been the focus of those elements predisposed to favor positive action on the political level, who have been favorable to "reform" of various sorts, to control of the economy, to promotion of "welfare," and not least to "interventionism" in foreign affairs.[9] On a broad basis this distinction adequately characterizes the *main* line of distinction between Republican and Democratic tendencies. Of course the Solid South has been a special case, and at the present time major processes of realignment seem to be going on. It is my judgment, however, that the realignments will result, not in substituting a new major axis, but in reshuffling the elements involved in the support groups about the present axis. Business will continue to be the major focus of the more conservative party.

In our system the party leader, as candidate and as President, must appeal to a variety of diverse groups and interests for the support necessary to elect. He must come up with some balance involving compromises and creative syntheses. The general meaning of the aggregate of the support he receives cannot be more than the endorsement of a broad *direction* of action for the polity. More specific interests can be endorsed only as they fit the general direction; they always stand in competition with others. There can never be any "absolute" commitment to particular interest—economic, ideological, religious, or other—because this would lead to burning of bridges connecting with other elements necessary for an effective support-coalition, elements that would not "go along" with such a commitment. For example, in pre-Nazi Germany the Center party was definitely committed to represent the interests of the Catholic Church. It had considerable range for maneuver, but was prevented by this commitment from becoming a genuine national party in a religiously divided society. Similarly, an American Catholic party under our system could not conceivably become one of the two general parties.

Let us return to the parallel with the input-output boundary of the economy. What I have called the generalization of support is parallel to the "mobility of labor," the readiness to co-operate in the production of goods and services that do not themselves satisfy one's own personal needs or those of one's family. The individual worker must in an important sense relinquish control of the product of his labor. Similarly the political supporter, in our case the voter, must not claim direct control of the consequences of his vote; if he did, political support would be reduced to a "barter" basis and the political integration of a complex social system would become impossible. What then does the voter receive which is analogous to the money income of the worker? He receives the expectation that many *kinds* of measures that he approves will be implemented if his candidate wins, but without exact specification of particular policies. The directional orientation of a party candidate is a kind of political "currency" which, if he wins, will improve the probabilities that a *kind* of direct political action, over which the voter does not have direct control but which *in general* he favors, will be taken. In taking money wages for his work and relinquishing control of the product, the worker evidences "faith" that by spending the money he will be able to get something he values as much or more than the product of his work. Similarly the voter evidences faith that, if his candidate wins, the "way things will go" will be relatively in accord with his wishes, but he cannot directly control the specific decisions that will be taken.

This generalized support is, I have noted, a fundamental ingredient of power. It, along with the other ingredients, is used to help produce concrete decisions, binding on the collectivity, which are analogous to specific goods. The support is necessary because without it the decisions could not be responsible, i.e., could not be made to "stick." But if the support is to be of any "use," its consequences must eventuate in concrete decisions that deal effectively with the real problems of the collectivity. The quality and quantity of these decisions and of their consequences in turn justify the acts of faith involved in giving political support. But it is the *aggregate value* of such decisions, not their particularities, which is the basis of the community's political "income" from its commitments of support.

Perhaps it is worth while to carry the parallel between the economic and the political one step further. The keynote of economic organization has rightly been said to be the division of labor. Through it the individual "producer" makes a sacrifice and receives a gain. The sacrifice is essentially one of self-contained independence; he can no longer meet his own needs from his own efforts and resources. The gain is one of "efficiency." He gets more by pooling competence and resources with others than if each operated alone on a self-sufficient basis. In the political case the axis is the differentiation of responsibility. The giver of support makes a sacrifice—loss of immediate control of collective decisions that affect his own interest; he "delegates" this control to the holders of power. But he also receives a gain, which is his share in the benefits of the *effectiveness* with which collective action can be taken. If the responsibility of every voter, including the President, for collective action were exactly equal, in effect *no* collective action would be taken at all. But in exchange for this gain the voter has to take his chances that the *particular* decisions in which he is most directly interested will be forthcoming.[10]

A built-in element of the conflict of interest is always present in any system of the economic division of labor—for example, the terms of the contract of employment. But this is greatly accentuated in the political case because of the commitment of the collectivity as a whole which is involved. At the leadership-support level this is, in our system, dramatized by the duality of the parties and the fact that in an immediate presidential election, what is gained by one—namely electoral victory—is by definition lost by the other. Hence there are inherently divisive potentialities in political "competition" which are not present to the same degree in economic competition. The control of such divisive potentialities is, in our society, attained through the institutionalization of the two-party system referred to above.

So far we have attempted to do two things. The first was to outline a general model of the relation between the organization of leadership and the mobilization of support in a political system. The second was to apply this to the main facts of the American two-party system so far as it involved the processes of election to the presidency. It is clear that the operation of such a system is dependent on the firm institutionalization of the "rules of the game" by which certain standards of fairness are insured, by which the losing party accepts the legitimacy of electoral victory of the winner, and by which in turn the winners do not use the power of the state to make it impossible for the losers to have a real chance of winning in future elections.

In addition to this condition of general institutionalization, it follows, I think, from the above analysis that there are certain further conditions necessary to the successful operation of a democratic two-party system. These conditions may be stated in the following four propositions:

1) There must be mechanisms by which the average voter can come to a "responsible decision that is meaningful to him. He must not, in too many cases, withdraw to nonvoting, nor be too

susceptible to appeals that would be grossly disruptive of the stability of the system. Since the intellectual problems involved in a rational solution are not practicably soluble, my thesis is that the mechanisms are typically nonrational. They involve stabilization of political attitudes *in terms of association with other members of the principal solidary groups in which the voter is involved.* In terms of party affiliation this may be called "traditionalism." The traditionalistic operation of nonrational mechanisms is a condition of the stability of the system. That they root in the solidary groupings of the society follows from the fact that support is mobilized from the integration subsystem of the society.[11]

2) Pure traditionalism, however, would result in a rigidity of the system which would be incompatible both with the shift of conditions under which problems of public goal-specification and attainment must be posed and with the necessity, for a two-party system, that there be realistic opportunities for each party to win in its bid for leadership through the election of a President. A certain proportion of voters must shift from time to time in party allegiance, if a flexible balance is to be maintained. The data show that this takes place mainly through what has been called above the "indifference" reaction—the voting change of people under cross-pressures who show relatively low levels of interest in the campaign and have difficulty in making their decisions. This finding will be interpreted as in line with the importance of solidary groupings as foci of political loyalties. It is a mechanism which on the whole minimizes the dangers of instability, inherent in political shifting. But it is primarily a condition of effective attainment of *new* goals as they become salient.

3) Under two-party conditions a limited polarization of the electorate is essential—a choice between only two realistic alternatives is offered. This means that the inherently divisive potentialities of political power-struggle are increased. There must clearly be mechanisms which prevent this polarization from producing a progressively deepening rift in the electorate. In the subsequent discussion, it will be shown that there are two main foci of such mechanisms. First, there is the supraparty consensus referred to above, which institutionalizes the duality of party organization, prescribing rules of political fair play. Second, there is the involvement of voting with the solidary groups in the society in such a

way that, though there is a correlation, there is no *exact* correspondence between political polarization and other bases of differentiation. Hence, pushing the implications of political difference too far activates the solidarities between adherents of the two parties which exist on other, nonpolitical, bases so that members of the political majority come to defend those who share other of their interests but differ from them politically. These mechanisms serve the effective integration of the system.

4) American society is not static, but dynamically evolving. The political system must be adapted to this fact and must include mechanisms of adjustment to social change. Under American conditions the main autonomous processes of social change do not operate through government, but largely through the development of the economy. The business element, which is the core of this process of change, tends to be politically conservative because positive use of the powers of government has been felt, since the early thirties, to imply interference with the process. The left, on the other hand, is relatively residual, tending to gather together those elements in the society on whom the problems and difficulties arising from the dynamic process impinge, and who see in governmental action an opportunity to remedy their situations. There must be mechanisms in the political system which mediate the balance between right and left without running the risk that either set of elements will be oppressively overwhelmed by the other. They are mechanisms that are essential to adapt the system to *changes in the structure of the society*.

The reader will note that, with some differences, these four conditions bear a close relation to the balances on which the functioning of the system depends, as formulated by the authors of *Voting* in their final chapter. The authors speak of the balances between "involvement and indifference" and between "stability and flexibility." Both of these balances are related to each of my first two statements about conditions of functioning of the system. The relations between involvement and indifference are highly pertinent to the nature of the nonrational mechanisms on which the stability of the system depends and to the anchorage of the voter in the solidary groupings of the society. But the same nonrational mechanisms operate in maintaining the type of flexibility which is most important in what may be called "normal" functioning. Hence, in my more detailed review of the findings of the studies, especially *Voting*, I shall treat these two together in connection with my own first two statements of conditions.

A further balance discussed by the authors is that between "consensus and cleavage." This directly concerns my third condition, that of the integrative basis of the voting system, and will be discussed under that heading. Finally, the fourth of their balances is that between "progress and conservation," as they call it. It is clear that this is essentially the same as my fourth condition which concerns adaptation to changes in the structure of the society. The fifth of their balances, that between "individualism and collectivism," seems to me to stand on a different level from the other four. It is very close to what I have called the balance between leadership responsibility and the necessity of support. This has already been discussed and will be a continuing theme throughout the remainder of the chapter.

Under the three rubrics just indicated I would now like to attempt to spell out the implications of the above analysis and relate them to some of the more detailed findings of the studies. This will both show the degree of goodness of fit between their findings and my model, and lead to a few theoretical conclusions that are not explicitly stated by the authors.

STABILITY, FLEXIBILITY, AND THE SHIFT OF POLITICAL ALLEGIANCE. Perhaps the most striking group of findings come in the first of the three main areas: stability, flexibility, and level of interest in the campaign. These concern in a sense the status of the "independent voter"; and, from the point of view of some of the ideologies dear to intellectuals, the findings may seem rather shocking. The fact seems to be that the groups most likely to escape from the traditionalism of habitual and inherited voting patterns are those least intensely interested in the issues of the campaign. They are not particularly well informed and, indeed, often are on the margin of not voting at all. These are the groups that provide the main element of flexibility in the system, the main source of the shifters from one party to the other.[12] It is also important that these are the same kind of people who, as they report their recollection of previous votes, are most likely to have shifted allegiance between campaigns. Furthermore, intensification of the campaign tends to drive them back to their previous habits of voting.

A second very important and closely related finding is that a large proportion of the voters susceptible to shifting are people subject to "cross-pressures."[13] These are people who, in the cross-cutting status structure of our complex society, belong simultaneously to solidary groups membership in which would predispose them to vote in both of the two major directions, so that they are exposed to a role-conflict. An example would be the well-to-do businessman of Irish-Catholic origin. The evidence seems to be that a considerable proportion of the people thus exposed to cross-pressures resolve their conflict by not voting at all. In any case, those who do vote make up their minds later than those not so exposed, and shift from previous allegiances more frequently.[14]

Another primary fact, of course, is that the great majority of voters are settled in their party allegiances and will not be influenced to vote for the opposing party by either the personality of the candidate or the discussion of issues. These in general include those who feel most intensely about the outcome and take the most active part in politics at all levels.[15] This evidence, combined with other facts, seems to make clear a fundamental connection between the psychology of voting behavior and the mechanisms by which the balance of stability and flexibility are maintained which is of great interest here.

On one level we may say that the nonshifters vote "from habit" or that they are "traditionalists," but these statements do not carry us very far. Fortunately data are presented which enable us to look considerably deeper for the bases of these habits and traditions. These data show that there is a marked tendency to agree in voting preferences with certain categories of others. This is so true of the family that the authors say the family rather than the individual perhaps ought to be taken as the unit of voting behavior. The tendency to agreement then extends to friends, and somewhat less intensely to occupational associates, fellow members of ethnic and religious groups, and class associates—this last the more so in proportion to the individual's class identification.[16]

In considering the implications of these findings, let us again note that when a rational decision is not possible but at the same time there is pressure to make commitments, there has to be some stable set of reference points so that beliefs can give meaning to the commitment and people can feel "comfortable" about it. The "issues" are in general too numerous and specific to provide a focus, the individual can directly "care" about only a minority of them, and the chances are good he will disapprove of his candidate's stand on some. Furthermore, his own action can have little decisive effect on the outcome–he casts only one of millions of votes–and the direct effect of the immediate outcome on his own personal interests is usually slight.

In this situation the individual seems to vote, other things being equal, with the people whom he most directly feels to be "his own kind," who are in social status and group memberships like, and hence like-minded with, himself. It may be said that the question is not so much, on the levels of psychological determination, *for what* he is voting as it is *with whom* he is associating himself in voting. There are many questions about the specific psychological mechanisms involved in this behavior, especially because it is largely unconscious in a considerable proportion of cases. Presumably processes akin to those of natural selection have been at work. One point, however, of congruence with the social situation can be brought out. As outlined above, the relationship of political leadership and support must be in some sense one of mutual trust. The leader is dependent on the stability of his support in order to carry out the responsibilities he has assumed, and supporters have performed an implicit act of faith in the necessary relinquishment of control of their affairs to leadership.

Broadly the solidary groupings of a social structure are those on whose members political developments will have some sort of common impact. Probably the tightest solidary grouping in our society is the family and this seems to show the greatest cohesiveness in voting. Certainly the members of this grouping share to a high degree a "common fate" in the face of whatever vicissitudes may come and go. Occupational, ethnic, religious, class, local, and regional groupings have similar characteristics to lesser and varying degrees. I suggest that it is symbolically appropriate that, in performing an "act of faith" which establishes a relation of trust the consequences of which, however, cannot be directly controlled, a person should feel most secure in associating himself with persons who, by virtue of their real solidary relationship to him, are the ones he feels most naturally can be trusted.

In any case, whatever the more specific psychological mechanisms, the *effect* of the "pull" of the solidary groupings of the social structure on individuals, as a result of which they vote with their fellow members of such groups, is to contribute greatly to what I have called the generalization of support. As the authors of *Voting* state several times, the individual tends to vote as a group member. But it is precisely as a structure of groups that a society is stable and integrated. If people vote as members of the stably important groups of the society, this provides an element of stability in the structure of political alignments itself which matches and is a consequence of the stability of the social structure.

It was noted above that the primary problem of the generation of power was the requisite integration in a political action context of the social system in which it occurs. At the top, this integration is organized around the two-party alternative within the institutional framework of a constitutionally guaranteed set of alternatives and the opportunity for the losing side to try again. But at the bottom, the process is dependent on the statistical outcome of millions of individual acts. I have argued that the direct rational determination of those acts without intermediary "nonrational" mechanisms is out of the question. The attachment of the individual to his solidary associations as a voting reference builds the society up in a series of graduated steps from the more elementary units of the society to units that can be meaningfully related to the important issues of the day, the realistic alternatives facing the political system as a system. As a structure of political integration, the top of this structure is constituted by the two national parties. That there should be such a structure of integrations is directly deducible from general theory.[17] The clarity with which the studies have provided empirical evidence of its existence and concrete nature is impressive.

This line of argument does not, however, account for flexibility, which is also necessary to such a system. It is here that the findings about the changers and shifters and their relations to relative political indifference and to cross-pressures are so interesting and significant. In spite of the empirical difference, it can be said that the basic theme is the same. The phenomenon of cross-pressures means that many people are involved in solidary groupings which politically, and certainly in other ways, are not well integrated with each other. The potential voter is, by his solidary associations, being pulled two ways at once.

Of course the fact that these are the main sources of the shift in votes, both between elections and during campaigns, brings out the importance of group attachments for those whose voting orientation is more stable. But there are two other particularly important aspects. The first is the psychological reference: the "cross-pressure" people are the more indifferent (many on the margin of not voting at all) and make up their minds later than others.[18] Psychologically this is an understandable reaction to conflict, namely vacillation and the postponement of decision, and the tendency to withdraw from a difficult dilemma by avoiding decision altogether. These tendencies are of course facilitated by the fact that generally in American society there is little strong sanction brought to bear on nonvoters, and the ballot is secret.

There is also, secondly, an important social aspect of the phenomenon. It is through the mobility of individuals between groups and the formation of new groups (and correspondingly the weakening and eventual disappearance of old ones) that the social structure itself changes. It therefore seems legitimate to conclude that on the whole the people exposed to cross-pressures are, in terms of social structure, among those most directly involved in processes of social change. Thus, for example, the upward mobility of immigrant populations produces the Catholic of high socioeconomic status who is a type case of involvement in cross-pressures. Surely the result of this process will in the long run be to split the Catholic vote far more evenly between the parties than was true in the New Deal era. In the other direction, we may cite the large-scale process of migration of rural people to the industrial areas and their eventual incorporation into trade unions, a process which occurred a little earlier. The Republican predilection of many rural pople thus was crossed with the Democratic predilection of many union members. On the whole one would expect the concomitant growth of industry and of unionism to produce a relatively stable increment to Democratic strength—though particularly in the light of the 1956 results, and also of facts cited in *Voting*, there must be some qualifications of this generalization. In any case, however, the cross-pressure element in its relation to social change provides the primary element of flexibility in a system which, were the factor of group solidarity too strong, might well be unduly rigid.

These facts about solidarity and its loosening through cross-pressures provide an empirical setting for the theoretical problem I posed above about the nature and significance of the levels of generalization of support.[19] This problem is very much involved in the distinction the authors of *Voting* make between what they call "position" issues and "style" issues."[20] Position issues are close to the level of what I have called binding decisions and advocacy of policies–typical examples from the 1948 campaign being revision of the Taft-Hartley Act and price control. Style issues on the other hand are closer to the ideological level and to that of "generalized support" which requires broad bases of justification–communism in government would be such an issue, though it was not yet very prominent in 1948. My essential point is that these types of issues correspond to a distinction between levels at which people are integrated in the solidary group structure of the society. Promotion of what is ordinarily called an "interest" involves acting with people who feel they have a common interest, sometimes in opposition to others.[21] It is usually thought of at a level which can be coped with by relatively specific "policies." But at this level interests are too diverse and sometimes too conflicting to serve to integrate the electorate at the level of generalized support. Hence we would expect to find symbolizations at higher levels of generalization which can come closer to setting off the two parties against each other as a whole.[22]

CONSENSUS AND CLEAVAGE. Let us now turn to the problem of "polarization" or what Berelson *et al.* speak of as the balance between consensus and cleavage. It is important that the studies provide direct evidence of the underlying consensus that is essential if a party system is to work at all without disrupting the community, i.e., polarizing it in a radical sense. This centers on the recognition that there are common "rules of the game" binding on all participants. But consensus seems to go beyond this. Though some distortion in perception of candidates and issues can be detected, it seems fair to say the notable thing is not that distortion exists, but that it is relatively small. Thus there seems to be fair agreement across party lines on the characteristics of the candidates and the relevant criteria to judge them, on what the major issues of the campaign are, on various expectations for the future, and on expectations of the voting tendencies of various blocs of voters. There is, to a fair degree, a common framework both of institutional norms and of cognitive definition of the situation.[23]

This supraparty consensus should, I think, be regarded as the top of the more general hierarchy of politically relevant solidarities. Its existence and continual reinforcement through symbolic expression should be regarded as the essential condition of the tolerance of division at the next lower level, which is the division between the major parties as such. For sociological reason, if this division is to be considered as "tolerable," it must be based on a genuine *differentiation* of function with reference to the system as a whole. The line of division between right and left in American politics suggests a framework in which our main party structure may be interpreted. The chief problem here concerns the balance of conservation and progress, but certain problems with respect to the nature of the cleavage and the limitations on it need to be taken up. My broad thesis is that divisive tendencies are controlled by being placed in the context of the hierarchy of solidarities which I have outlined, so that the cleavages that develop tend to be toned down and muted on their own level and referred to higher orders of integration for resolution.

We have had a prominent recent example of the operation of this mechanism. One can scent a certain danger to this higher level consensus when, particularly in the heat of campaigns, spokesmen for the parties go beyond stating their differences from their opponents as differences of desirable directions and policies, and raise doubts about the "fitness to govern" of the opposite party and its candidates. Almost inevitably there is some of this in every campaign. On occasion it may go further, as it did in the 1952-54 period. The theme of the threat of communism was played up by the Republican extremists until it began to be applied, by inference if not explicitly, not just to certain limited allegedly subversive elements, but to the Democratic party as a whole. This culminated in McCarthy's slogan of "twenty years of treason." For a moment it seemed as though this would be taken up by the Republican moderates; a few speeches by such spokesmen as Attorney-General

Brownell and Governor Dewey were couched very nearly in this vein. But this provoked a strong reaction from specifically *conservative* Democrats, such as Sam Rayburn; and in general the Republican moderates, after a brief "flirtation" with the idea, drew back sharply from it. Essentially what happened is that the vicious circle of divisive cleavage began to activate the sentiments clustering around the higher-order solidarity of the national supraparty consensus. To accuse a person of disloyalty or treason is to place him outside that consensus. To extend this accusation to one of the two major parties as such is to break national solidarity at its most critical point. It gradually became clear that at most a small fanatical minority really "meant it" in this radical sense. The anxieties aroused by this really radical implication probably had a great deal to do with making the final resolution of the McCarthy episode possible. Though this was not an explicit item in the Senate indictment, it was fundamentally McCarthy's challenge to the higher-order consensus which was the underlying basis of his censure.

Only once in our national history has such a cleavage been driven to a really disastrous point. In the events that led to the Civil War, the question of loyalty to the Union could be related to a whole series of issues and ideological symbols on which the two regional sectors of the society could divide. There were in fact real and deep differences of social structure underlying the symbols and slogans, differences that divided the population into two sufficiently equal parts. McCarthyism could not split the country in this way because it did not reflect any clear-cut *structural* division but cut across the main structural divisions. The most generalized "style" issue of the Communist threat could not split the more differentiated structural solidarities. No clear-cut line could be drawn between elements that could be activated pro and con around the Communist symbol as they were around slavery and secession. Later in this chapter I will say a little more about the nature of the disturbance that made it possible for McCarthyism to get as far as it did.

The level where the problem of cleavage and consensus next arises involves bases of solidarity not in the *first instance* political. The broad picture has already been sketched and is clearly delineated in *Voting* and the other studies. The general relationships between party alignment and socioeconomic status, occupation, ethnicity, and religion are by now well established.

Almost equally important, however, is the looseness of this relation. Shifts in the alignment are continually occurring, largely reflecting processes of change in the social structure, but with an important feedback from political action.

The very looseness of the relation between structural solidarities other than political party and the party structure itself can be said to constitute an important protection against the divisive potentialities of cleavage. The essential fact here is that most structurally important groupings in the society will contain considerable proportions of adherents of *both* parties.[24] To an important degree therefore the structural ties that bind them together on nonpolitical bases cut across their political allegiances. Hence the tendency to political cleavage will tend to be checked by a set of mechanisms that operate *below* the level of party division as well as by the more general national consensus that operates above that level. The pressure of political cleavage—by activating ties of solidarity at the more differentiated structural levels that cut across the line of cleavage—tends automatically to bring countervailing forces into play. The point of view of an individual voter is likely to be, "My fellow union member (lodge member, coreligionist, office colleague, etc.) who is intending to vote Republican (Democratic) is in general a pretty decent guy. I just can't see how all people who hold his views can be as bad as they're made out to be." Awareness that this type of sentiment will be activated may put a certain restraint on extremism in the campaign.

This mechanism may be said to be the obverse of what the authors of *Voting* and of *The People's Choice* call "activation."[25] In the case just described, the activation of essentially nonpolitical sentiments of solidarity acts as a brake on processes leading to divisive cleavage. Activation in the meaning of the studies, on the other hand, works as a stabilizing mechanism with reference to party alignments. It is clear that the pluralistic nature of the general social structure is so important that if nonpolitical solidarities were too strong, the necessary generalization of support which the party system requires could not be assured. The evidence from the studies seems to show that the principal direct effect of the political campaign itself on vacillating voters is to reactivate the voting preferences that predominate in the individual's past history and predominate in the solidary groups to which he is currently attached.[26]

At the psychological level this process is related to nonrational mechanisms. The very conception of rationality implies a certain ordered responsiveness to changes and shifts in the external situation. There is hence an inherent connection between nonrationality and the relative absence of such flexible *responsiveness*. If the nonrational reaction, however, is to be *ordered* it must, inherently I think, lead to a conservative response. In its impact on the individual voter the effect of the campaign is to intensify the urgency of situational stimuli. Insofar as the response is an orderly one, it has to be in terms of established patterns of voting behavior, i.e., a "traditionalistic" response.

There are two main alternatives to this traditionalistic pattern of response. One is clearly delineated by the authors, the other not. The first has already been discussed as the response to cross-pressures—namely, low intensity of political interest, relative indifference, and readiness to shift political allegiance. The other, illustrated by McCarthyism, is openness to a certain type of "charismatic" appeal, to extremism and emotionalism.[27] The first is well integrated in the political system and may be said to be the normal mechanism that mediates shifts in the political balance. It is, I think, an example of what Durkheim called an "egoistic" response to strain. The second is perhaps the major type of "pathology" of our system and, if not controlled, may have highly disruptive consequences. In Durkheim's term, it is the "anomic" response. Let us discuss each of these briefly in turn.[28]

The "indifference" reaction results when the individual, faced with a difficult conflict situation, reacts with conservative caution. Typically, he is playing with the idea of taking a new venture, of voting contrary to the voting traditions he himself has observed and/or which are observed by many of the people with whom he has important solidary ties—his relatives, friends, or associates. He hesitates, and is slow to make up his mind. If he actually does make the shift, he is likely to have been considering it since before the campaign began. But if the pressure on him is intensified through the campaign, his tendency is to retreat from his tentative overtures to the safer haven of his own accustomed pattern or that of his older and more tried associates. Finally the steps he takes are, typically, not radical ones, but from the more conservative side of the Democratic spectrum to the liberal side of the Republican or vice versa. These findings are of the first importance to the understanding of how the system functions.

By this process the voter is moving cautiously into unknown territory. He feels his way and does not actually move until sure he "has a place to go," assured that he will be accepted into the solidary groups with whom he newly identifies himself by his vote. Furthermore there is another important finding, namely that called by the authors the "breakage" effect. When the solidary groups in the voter's immediate personal environment are badly split, he is more likely to vote with the prevailing majority in the larger local community—he shifts his solidarity identification to a higher-order grouping.[29]

It is true that these tactics of the voter do not correspond to the stereotype of the classical independent voter with his sophisticated rational choice. But this newly discovered changeable voter has one trait consistent with that stereotype: he shows a kind of (albeit negative) sense of responsibility. He does not jump or panic lightly into extreme shifts of allegiance. When he does move it is cautiously and not very far. When pressed he tends to retreat to safe ground. By and large he does not rock the boat. But he is the primary agent in shifting the balance of political forces. In favorable circumstances this shift is accomplished without any deep or lasting cleavage.

In addition to the considerations already brought forward it is perhaps relevant to note that voting is marginal and peripheral for the average citizen. He has many role-involvements in his sphere of private affairs and simply cannot be a sophisticated political expert. When the various factors playing on the "average voter" are combined, they add up to a relatively well-adapted set of mechanisms that facilitate shifts of balance without activating seriously divisive cleavages—as the authors of *Voting* clearly point out.

The mechanism *can*, however, get seriously out of order, and then the types of "secondary defense" just discussed become necessary. The most recent example is the McCarthyism episode; hence a few further remarks about it may be in order.[30]

By and large the people to whom McCarthyism appealed were people subject to cross-pressures (for example, members of ethnic groups of recently low but rising status, and members of other ethnic groups, such as people of German origin in the Midwest who in World War II felt a conflict between their patriotism and their German traditions.[31] It seems very likely that many of them were members of solidary groups that were severely split.[32]

It may not be amiss to suggest that they represented a second sort of "breakage effect," not into the safe haven of the majority position in the community, but in response to a violently emotional symbolic appeal, sharply dissociated from the realities of the domestic scene. The central symbol—"communism"—represented a magical danger. Behind the scenes a treasonous conspiracy allegedly threatened the security of everything American. In this context communism can be interpreted as a symbol to which many of the relatively free-floating anxieties of our society could be transferred. Above all it was anxiety-generated. Associated with it was regression to a romantically nostalgic fantasied "Americanism" from which many of the realities of the modern world were pleasantly absent—not only Communists in a literal sense, but bureaucrats, intellectuals, and various others, even in the wilder flights the income tax itself. This anomic response was not the "rational" alternative to the indifference response, but was wildly aggressive scapegoating and irresponsible withdrawal from disturbing reality. I suggest that too serious disturbance of the conservatism of the indifference response is likely to activate the McCarthyite type—which in content might be a "radical" rather than a "reactionary" Populism next time.[33]

In this connection it may be appropriate to make a few remarks about the phenomenon of Eisenhower popularity. This also is something of a departure from the main normal type called above the indifference pattern. Eisenhower, that is, seems to have exercised a kind of "charismatic" appeal that has shaken a certain proportion of voters out of their normal allegiances. The appeal seems to run in a "conservative" direction and may be likened to a "breakage effect," which the authors of *Voting* discussed on the level of the local community. At the present moment the country may have at the presidential level a *small* Republican majority. The mood of the country may be relatively conservative, more concerned with stability and integration than with positive action—though it is by no means certain that this is true, and even less certain that this will still be true in 1960. In any event, the Eisenhower margin of 1956 substantially exuded such a "normal" Republican majority if it existed then.[34]

One further aspect of consensus and its relation to political balance may be discussed briefly. The authors of *Voting* seem to show some uncertainties in their assessment of the effects of the campaign. It is, of course, striking how few votes it seems to change and how it tends to drive the vacillators back into their more traditional allegiances. It is further true that, in the "classical" theory, the function of the campaign is to "persuade" the voter to adopt the "reasonable" position. Though it clearly does not have this effect (as it should according to the classical formula), may it not be possible that there are certain other consequences of importance?

A few straws of evidence in the findings suggest this may be true. First, it is noted that in the course of the campaign *political* bases of solidarity are strengthened at the expense of *social* bases.[35] Secondly, it was found that opinion leaders support the party position on subsidiary issues more strongly than do voters who are not opinion leaders.[36] It is also true that opinion leaders are politically more interested than others and, though dispersed throughout the social structure, are slightly higher in status than those they lead.[37] Finally, it is noted that exposure to the mass media increases interest in the campaign and strength of feeling about it, but also that voters select media matter to confirm their presuppositions.[38]

From the point of view of bringing about the main shift of political allegiances, the campaign seems relatively "functionless"; it is a "ritual." But from another point of view, if I interpret this evidence correctly, it seems to serve a very important function. This is, essentially, *to reinforce the generalization of support*, which has been shown above to be an essential condition of the functioning of a two-party democratic system.[39] Thus, first, the "social" bases of solidarity are, from the point of view of *political* integration of the society, more particularized than the political. The greater emphases on the political solidarities may thus be interpreted as a shift in the direction of generalization.

Second, the opinion leaders seem to be agents of this process in that, through supporting the party position on subsidiary issues, they serve to integrate the levels of generalization—what appeals to the more particularistic "interests" of special solidary groups, with what appeals to the more generalized level of the party. That the sources of such influence should be of somewhat higher social status than its objects is sociologically understandable. Generally the higher the status, the higher the level of political responsibility.

Third (and it would seem to fit the same context), the influence of the mass media works in the direction of increasing interest and strength of feeling. Interest and strength of feeling in this case concern the *outcome* of the campaign, which cannot be other than victory for one of the two major party candidates. Hence the interest and feeling become less concerned with the lower level interest-issues and more with the generalized question of which *party* is to win. Essentially this is to say that the effect of the campaign is to increase motivational commitment to the generalized support of the party, and thus to inhibit tendencies to particularistic fragmentation of the political system. The importance of this set of mechanisms is the more evident when it is considered that "when the chips are down" there is a strong tendency for people to revert to the more unproblematical loyalties. In a pluralistic, i.e., highly differentiated, society like ours, this means loyalties closer to the "social" than to the "political" level of solidarity. In the major hierarchy of solidary integrations in a political reference, it means the decision of voters are shifted closer to the "top" level of general societal integration than would otherwise happen.

PROGRESS AND CONSERVATION. Finally, I would like to discuss briefly the balance between what the authors of *Voting* call "progress" and "conservation."

They emphasize the conservative tendencies activated by the campaign to reinforce established patterns of voting in different population groups. Yet, in the more "relaxed" periods between campaigns the newer trends, which almost by definition involve "deviance" from established patterns, establish a foothold. Usually the main question is whether this foothold is solid enough to withstand the stress of the campaign itself. In 1948 the Republican trend was not quite solid enough, but by 1952 it had become so. With all this I entirely agree.

There is, however, another aspect of the conservation-progress problem clearly brought out by the authors in one connection, though there are other important bits of evidence bearing on it in their findings which deserve further comment. This is its relation to the right-left balance of the two-party system discussed briefly above. One way of putting it is to say that (in one sense and on one level) the two-party system is a relatively "symmetrical" system, more or less evenly balanced between two trends on the most generalized level of support. From this point of view the political process has an oscillatory character, a swinging from relative predominance of one trend to that of the other and back again.

But looked at in the perspective of the dynamic development of the society, there is another aspect of this process, namely a structured relation to the general process of social change, which introduces a factor of *asymmetry* into the party structure. This aspect is, as noted above, structured in the form of division into a relatively "conservative" party in the political sense (the Republican, of course) and a relatively "liberal" party (the Democratic). I have stressed above that the conservatism of the Republican party is a conservatism in the field of *political* action; it is reluctant to sponsor too much *positive* use of governmental power for collective goals, particularly the *extension* of governmental power into areas where it has traditionally not been exercised. The Democratic party, on the other hand, has been more hospitable to positive political innovation, particularly in the fields of control of the economy, of welfare legislation, and of new commitments in foreign affairs. The traditional attitudes of the two parties in the field of government spending and fiscal policy reflect this difference.

The first bit of evidence that bears on this asymmetry is the authors' account of the type of appeal put forward by the two candidates in the 1948 campaign. As they say, Dewey stressed "style" issues that emphasized general consensus and tended to avoid controversial particularities. Truman, on the other hand, stressed "position" issues on which he advocated positive action. Dewey on the whole suggested that his election would have a quieting, unifying effect on the state of affairs, but did not stress positive new measures that needed to be taken; Truman did stress such measures, including repeal of the Taft-Hartley Act as a "new measure."[40]

The authors interpret this as the difference between a strategy appropriate to a candidate expecting to win, who hence does not wish to antagonize any important groups by advocating things they may oppose, and the strategy of one anticipating a struggle, who has to mobilize what support he can in order to come up from behind. This may well be an important factor in the difference, but I feel confident that there is another aspect equally important. This is that the *conservative* party, in the sense just outlined, has broadly an interest in quieting things down politically, in damping the urgency of demands for specific and positive action. The *liberal* party, on the other hand, has an interest in arousing the public to the urgencies of action and tends to stress such action issues whenever they seem to be politically opportune.

Of course there are occasions when (rightly or wrongly) a threat to stability is felt to exist. Then there may be a demand for urgent action from the right. The "communism in government" and the "corruption" issues in 1952 are cases in point.[41] But by and large the policy of emphasizing consensus certainly has been the main Republican trend in the last three elections. Stevenson's attack on the (to him) too negative conception of the presidency by Eisenhower in the last election illustrates the point directly. Of course confirmation of this generalization would require a wider basis of fact, going back into earlier campaigns, which unfortunately has not been possible in connection with this chapter.

A second finding of the study illustrates a slightly different, though related, aspect of the right-left differentiation of the system. I have emphasized the central position of our business system in defining the relations of right and left. Differential wealth, particularly benefits to a conspicuously wealthy upper economic group, constitutes one of the most publicly salient consequences of situations favorable to the business system. This raises questions of the justice of the degree of inequality of wealth thus highlighted. Throughout our national history there has been partisan controversy about the justice and relation to national welfare of the financial rewards of the highest income groups, starting with the Jefferson-Hamilton differences. It is not surprising that the position of the wealthiest should be a target of attack from the left.

Republican voters held the view that a Republican electoral victory would benefit all classes of the society without exception, but the Democratic voters felt that a Democratic victory would benefit all classes except the wealthy.[42] This element of asymmetry in the views of adherents of the two parties is directly congruent with the interpretation of the nature of the difference between the parties, which has been put forward here. It is a special case of the general tendency of Republicans to emphasize highly general consensus, of Democrats to emphasize more specific issues that demand positive action.

There is, finally, the interesting line of evidence bearing on the question of the right-left problem, which is presented directly in this light by the authors. They outline a very interesting conception of a time sequence in which issues come to and leave the center of political controversy. They speak of a "gateway" to political relevance.[43] Before the time is ripe, by approaching this gateway, an issue may be seen, particularly in hindsight, to be gaining in importance, but it is not politically resonant and somehow does not serve to create much interest or excitement in a campaign. Then there is an optimum time when taking up the issue pays handsome political dividends. Finally, the issue later fails to continue in the center of attention and gradually becomes "dead." It seems fair to say that "communism in government" could not have been made a central issue as early as 1948, that in 1952 it was moving into the "gateway," but that by 1956 it had become a dead issue. The Republicans not only did not, but could not, make important political capital of it as late as that—and not only because a Republican administration had been in office for four years.[44] It would be my prediction that though the issue of federal aid to public education was in the 1956 election just approaching the "gateway" but not yet close enough to be a big issue, by 1960 it will be in the middle of the gateway.

This pattern applies, I think, to issues pressed by both sides, indeed I have used one from each side as example. But, nonetheless, as the authors themselves suggest,[45] the basic asymmetry that has appeared in the other connections applies here. The Republican issues that come through the gateway tend to be "defensive" issues, namely they tend to concern real or alleged "dangers" to the system which must be warded off. Restriction of immigration, which came to a head in 1924, is an example, as are pressures for tariff increases. The Democratic issues, on the other hand, tend to be positive innovations that require political mobilization to be put through.

The gateway theory thus formulates a very important pattern of the history of American politics, of which the element of party asymmetry is the aspect in which I am primarily interested. The central phenomenon starts with the pressing of a policy by the party of the left, in recent times the Democrats. The policy is opposed by the right, i.e., the Republicans, sometimes bitterly. There are many alarmist views expressed that the policy will ruin the country and destroy the unique virtues of the "American system." Then the measure, or a series of them, is enacted. Relatively quickly after enactment the excitement dies down, and the new situation comes to be accepted by its former opponents, for the most part with good grace, though there often is a little company of die-hards who remain irreconcilable for a long time. As the authors point out there is a spectrum of relative enthusiasm from left to right. But when the next Republican administration comes along it does not try seriously to reverse the policy or restore the *status quo ante*. There may well be some modifications of what are felt to be "abuses," but on the whole the main phenomenon is acceptance; indeed there is probably as much modest extension as paring back. The main pattern introduced by the new policy thus becomes institutionalized and an essential part of the social structure of the country.

The more obvious examples come from the fields of control of business practices and social welfare legislation. Thus the Federal Reserve Act, the Securities Exchange Act, the Wagner Act, and the Social Security Act, were all Democratic measures—every one of which was strongly contested by the Republican party, not merely the "radical right" but the main party. Every one of them has come to be fundamentally accepted by that party with no attempt to undo the work. For example, the changes in the "charter of labor" introduced by the Taft-Hartley Act are on the whole secondary, and the present administration boasts of having extended the coverage of Social Security benefits, although their party predecessors of the 1930's widely predicted that the Act itself would destroy the moral independence of the American working population.

I am not in a position to present here a careful appraisal over a long historical period, but I think it is safe to generalize, first, that in American history the considerable majority of policies judged to have resulted in major modifications of the social structure through government action have been sponsored by the party of the left and, at the time, opposed by the party of the right.[46] Secondly, however, the majority of these policies have resulted in fully institutionalized features of the society–their consequences have come to be accepted in the society as a whole, and we have "gone on from there."

The findings of *Voting* clearly indicate that the American two-party system is a mechanism by which, at any *given* time, a relative equilibrating balance in a pluralistic society is maintained, so that conflicts and divisive tendencies are controlled and more or less fully resolved. It is also, seen over a period of time, a principal mechanism–though by no means the only one–by which the process of structural change in the society operates. The position of government in any modern society is such that it cannot be insulated from the broader process of social change. What happens at the governmental level both reflects these changes and is itself a major instrumentality in carrying them through. The main mechanism which adjusts the balance between the "reflection" aspect of the process and the "instrumentality" aspect is the raising and finally the resolution of issues through the operation of the party system. The essential point is that new things do "get done" and that the consequences do come to be accepted. In view of what sociologists now know of the intensity of the tensions and stresses generated by major processes of social change, the relative effectiveness of this set of mechanisms is impressive. Again, in view of the importance of this aspect for the whole process of political adjustment, the importance of the mechanisms involved in what has above been called the "conservative" or "indifference" pattern of the change of position of voters is again emphasized. There is a great deal of sociopolitical dynamite in the political process in a rapidly changing society. That it breaks over into charismatic "radicalism"—of right or left—so seldom and that these "fires" have usually been so relatively quickly extinguished, is testimony to the power of the mechanisms of social control which operate in this area. The authors of *Voting* have given us notable insight into the way these mechanisms operate.

CONCLUSION. It has not been possible in this chapter to review more than a sample of the rich and suggestive findings presented in *Voting*, to say nothing of the other related studies. My purpose has not, however, been to present a complete review, critical or otherwise, but to try to establish the relations between certain of these findings and a theoretical model of the operation of a two-party democratic political system. I have therefore selected for consideration the findings that seemed to be most directly relevant to the empirical problems involved in the model.

The model has been constructed essentially by extending a pattern of theoretical analysis which had been worked out in connection with the economy as a subsystem of the society, in interaction with other subsystems,[47] to the "polity" conceived as another subsystem of the society cognate with the economy. The polity in this sense is essentially the set of societal mechanisms which makes the generation of power in the political sense possible. In constructing this model I have of course leaned heavily on the literature of political theory.

It was possible to discuss here, as specifically relevant to the voting process, only part of an as yet incomplete model. This part, however, deals with a crucial aspect of the total system, the process by which the "goal-attainment" adjustments of the polity work out through interchange with another subsystem of the society, here vaguely referred to as the "public." The interchange in question is thought of as involving, at a higher level of generalization, the interchange of "leadership" responsibility for "support," at a lower level, that of "binding decisions" for "advocacy of policies."

On the gross structural level the essential facts about the American system are that it is a constitutionally regulated, "democratic" two-party system operating in a society that is primarily oriented to growth of economic productivity and involved in a dynamic process of general internal social change as well as a highly unstable international situation. Within this framework, if the political system is, in the relation between leadership and support, to be a relatively stable one that can integrate multifarious pluralistic interests and yet adapt to changing conditions, it must, within broadly specifiable limits, have certain characteristics. By applying the model to the general structure it was possible to identify four main areas in which to look for mechanisms relevant to these functional requirements.

These, the reader will remember, concerned (1) the relations between the nonrational psychological mechanisms that must be imputed to the "average voter" and the reference points of voting decisions in the structure of solidary groupings of the society which formed the main basis of stability of the system; (2) the element of flexibility necessary to allow sufficient shift of votes to permit a two-party system to function effectively without introducing unduly disruptive elements into the system; (3) mechanisms that will organize the limited polarization that a two-party system requires and yet protect the integration of the society against too deep-seated divisive forces; and (4) mechanisms that will mediate the processes of adaptation to structural change in a rapidly evolving society.

These requirements were found to correspond very closely with four of the balances formulated by the authors of *Voting* in their final chapter. The first two of my functional requirements were related to the balances of stability and flexibility and of involvement and indifference, the third to that between consensus and cleavage, and the fourth to that between progress and conservation. The fifth of the authors' balances, between individualism and collectivism, seemed to me to correspond to the more general need for balance between effective leadership and the generalization of support which has formed the main analytical thread of the whole discussion. It hence seems to me to stand on a different level from the other four. For these reasons I organized my more detailed review of the relevant findings of *Voting* about the relation between my four propositions and the first four of the authors' balances just mentioned.

Particularly in their final chapter, but also at various points throughout the volume, the authors make generalizations from their findings which come halfway or more toward the generalizations that would have been generated deductively by use of the theoretical model with which I have been working. Hence it is not any originality of empirical insight into the workings of the American political system which I wish to claim; most of what is relevant is present and clearly stated in the book.

What is important in the present connection is rather the *fit* of these findings and conclusions with a more generalized conceptual scheme. This fit strengthens the impression from the authors' own exposition that there is an important *internal consistency* in the main structure of their findings and interpretations. In the light of the above discussion it seems to me inconceivable that the facts should be just a random collection of discrete items with no essential connection with each other. But beyond the question of internal consistency, such a fit strongly suggests the feasibility of extending a coherent analysis of the American political system in its connections with other aspects of the society, economic, institutional, and otherwise. Here I have stressed only that *theoretical* congruence exists with a part of a model for the analysis of the economy. But the political and the economic analyses are both parts of a still wider theoretical scheme that I may call a general theory of social systems.

I have attempted to take only a first step in the codification of the data of empirical studies of voting with this body of theory. These results, and of course other data, as noted, need to be fitted into other aspects of the problems of the polity. Only part of the American political system has been treated here. The American case needs to be treated in wider historical perspective and, comparatively, in relations of similarity and difference, with other political systems. Finally, of course, the political aspect of society needs to be much more systematically related to other aspects of the societies in which political systems function.

In spite of the modesty of the step here taken, it seems to me that it illustrates a kind of opportunity of which social scientists should take careful cognizance. If detailed empirical studies of the type of the voting studies can produce findings and empirical generalizations that fit as closely with deductions from highly general theory as seems to be true in this instance,[48] the prospects of a *cumulative* development of codified and systematic knowledge in this field seem to be better than they have often been thought to be. In my opinion this is not an isolated instance. Intensive work on both sides, and repeated attempts at codification, should produce important results.

TECHNICAL NOTE. As has several times been noted in this chapter, the main framework of the analysis it contains was not generated *ad hoc* in an attempt to interpret the results of the studies of voting behavior, but was developed independently and applied to these results. For the reader who may be interested in the technical aspects of the scheme employed, it seemed advisable to include a brief outline of the most important elements of the scheme, and their genesis.

The main background of the analysis is a generalized conceptual scheme for the analysis of social systems, which in turn is part of a still more generalized scheme for the analysis of action.[49] The basic outline of the social system scheme which is employed here was set forth first in *Working Papers in the Theory of Action.*[50] The most essential feature of this latter formulation was the merging of a scheme of "pattern variables" put forward by Parsons and Shils with a scheme of the functional requirements of social systems originally put forward by Bales.[51]

The basis of this scheme is the idea that any social system may be analyzed in terms of four logically independent functional requirements, which we formulate as *adaptation*, *goal-attainment*, *integration*, and *latent pattern-maintenance*. For these we have, for convenience, adopted the notation A, G, I, L. These four functional requirements were interpreted as the *dimensions* along which variations in the state of a social system could be analyzed.[52]

Within the framework of this general scheme special attention has been paid to the fact that complex social systems should be conceived as differentiated into (hence made up of) a plurality of *subsystems.* Following the general lead of biological theory we have conceived that the most promising *initial* approach to the nature of the differentiation of such subsystems, and hence of their classification, lay in the concept of function as the basis of differentiation. Starting with the conception of a highly differentiated society, this conception was applied to the idea of the *economy*, as this has been used in economic theory, and it was found that the economists' conception fitted admirably with the specifications of an adaptive subsystem of a society as worked out in terms of this general theory of social systems.[53]

The whole conception of a social system which was delineated as distinct from "situation" or "environment" external to it, has implied the existence and importance of processes of interchange between system and environment which could be formulated in terms of the concepts of input and output. But further, if the system of reference is a subsystem of a larger system, these inputs and outputs would not likely, with respect to their sources and destinations, be randomly distributed over the environment as a whole, but would have relatively specific sources and destinations capable of theoretical identification.

Since we were operating with a theoretical scheme that involved four basic functional categories, and since we had been able to treat the economy as *primarily* (in an empirical sense *never* exclusively) identified with *one* of these categories (the adaptive), it seemed sensible to attempt to work out the logic of a system in which each of the four categories was the basis of a differentiated subsystem of the society. By elementary logic each such subsystem would have three boundaries internal to the system vis-à-vis each of the other three, and a fourth boundary in some sense "external" to the system. Once seen in this light, the logical requirements of this reasoning corresponded with startling exactitude to the scheme, well established in economic theory, of classification of the factors of production and the shares of income. The factors of production, that is, could be treated as categories of input into the economy from "outside" and the shares of income as categories of output from the economy to the outside.

The next analytical problem was to identify the source-destination subsystems for each input-output and to determine which was the one "external" boundary. The key to this identification turned out to be the conception of the *goal* of the economy as *production* vis-à-vis the "consumer" identified as a member of the household. The output of production was conceived to be the goal-attainment output of the economy and to go to the household, which had already[54] been identified as belonging to the "pattern-maintenance" subsystem. With two further steps, which are detailed in *Economy and Society* and hence need not be repeated here, this type of reasoning led to setting up the following paradigm[55] of boundary-interchanges between four functionally primary subsystems of a society:

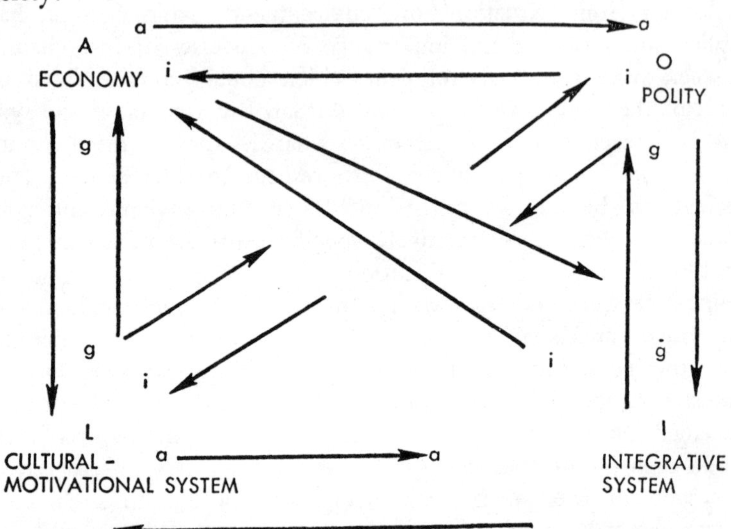

Three further implications, of special interest in the present context, followed from this. First, the category of "land" and its output cognate, "rent," clearly constituted the focus of the "external" boundary of the economy as a system. The sense in which land is a special case among the factors of production in economic theory corresponds directly with that in which the function of pattern-maintenance has been treated as a special case in general social system theory.[56]

Second, as had already been well established in economic theory, it was, in a sufficiently differentiated society, not possible to limit consideration to a *single* interchange of inputs and outputs at any one boundary, but it was necessary to consider a *double* interchange. In the economy-household case this is a direct consequence of the division of labor and means that the source of wage income (the employing organization) is typically not the same as the producer of most consumers' goods purchased. Hence money, as income and as a medium of exchange for the purchase of desired goods, is a necessary intermediary mechanism in an economic *system.*

Third, it became clear that the boundary-interchange between a postulated polity, as the goal-attaining subsystem of the society, and the integrative system should be theoretically cognate with that between economy and household. To put it in the terms used above, the main output of the polity to the integrative system is effective leadership, which is a form of power, and the main input into the polity from the integrative system is generalized support. Or, to put it a little differently, the *goal* of the polity is the production or generation of effective leadership and, on the less general level, of binding decisions.

It was within this framework of analysis of input-and-output relations between primary functional subsystems of the society that a beginning has been made in the attempt to work out a conception of the polity as cognate with the economy and of its goal-attainment boundary interchange, which has been the main subject of this chapter.

Certain features of the adaptive boundary of the polity were already given because it stood (in our scheme) vis-à-vis the economy. From the economic point of view it was the boundary concerned with the input of capital resources to the economy from the polity. But it proved to be a long and difficult task to formulate the categories relevant to the double boundary-interchange at the *goal-attaining* boundary of the polity which, according to the logic of our paradigm, stands vis-à-vis the integrative system and does not directly involve the economy at all. It was only here that the scheme used was fully worked out, though the categories of support and binding decisions had been worked with for some time. The scheme in its present form is obviously tentative.

The reader who has followed this rather involved theoretical argument (which he very likely cannot do without familiarity with the sources cited) may comprehend why it was so exciting to find that the results of the voting studies placed the primary basis of political support in the structure of solidary groups of the society: in our theoretical terms, *this is the integrative system* which, on the most general theoretical grounds, would be *predicted* to be the *primary* source. More generally, the deduced characteristics of a double level of interchange between polity and public turned out to fit the empirical findings of the studies with exciting exactitude.

One further technical point may finally be made: It should be clearly understood that, in terms of the technical paradigm I have used, this analysis does *not* deal with the polity as a system. The system of reference is the processes of input-output interchange between polity and integrative system (as "public"). In *Economy and Society* we dealt extensively with this type of system, the economically relevant prototype being a market. Thus we held that the interchange between economy and household may be treated as composed of two primary markets, the labor market and the market for consumers' goods. Similar logic was applied to the capital market and all of these were, in a strict sense, treated as social systems.[57]

Of course, empirically, the process of election of a President is most emphatically *not* a market in the economic sense. But in formal theoretical terms it was the paradigm worked out for the analysis of markets which proved most fruitful in analyzing the voting process. Seen in these terms, my first proposition about non-rational mechanisms in relation to solidary groupings concerned the "latent pattern-maintenance" basis of the system; the second about flexibility in pursuit of goals concerned its goal-attainment function; the third about control of divisive polarization concerned its integration; and the fourth dealing with its relation to the changing structure of the society concerned its adaptive function. These propositions are thus not arbitrary functional generalizations plucked "out of the air" and not dictated by the formal theoretical scheme, but are carefully formulated to meet the specifications of a specific generalized theoretical paradigm.

This demonstration that the the voting process can be considered a social system in the fullest technical sense and can be analyzed in terms of the analytical resources of social system theory, seems to me the important contribution of this chapter.

CHAPTER 5

The Problem of Irrationality and Neuroticism Underlying Political Choice

ARTHUR J. BRODBECK

Among the mass of material spread throughout the voting studies, one problem always remains more or less in focus. It is an issue which cannot fail to command the attention of psychologists and psychiatrists. *How do people learn to select and define one type of social action as a better way to satisfy their social wants than some other type?* A motive can be satisfied in many alternative and sometimes numberless ways, even so basic a motive as the sexual or economic motive. What determines the variation within and between personalities in the choice of means toward the satisfaction of the same kind of motive?

The voting studies deal with this general problem *only in the political sphere* of social action within a democracy and then *only in the very limited sense of choices at the ballot box*. The general problem, however, turns up in many other theoretical systems than those used by the authors of the various voting studies, and in many different areas of social action than those of political behavior and ballot-box choices. Psychoanalysts have dealt with it under the rubric of "choice of symptom," and the voting studies may be looked upon as providing interesting information about the "choice of symptom" problem *within a conventional range of political choices*. The same problem is potentially present in studying the choice of a mate in marriage, the choice of profession, and the choice of one type of house and neighborhood rather than another.[1] It is by no means "special" to a study of voting behavior.

Everybody knows that science *responds to* as well as *acts upon* the cultural life in which it is embedded. The problem of social action has come so strongly to the fore in social sciences in the last decade probably because it has become so critical an issue everywhere in our contemporary life. The way in which psychological wants can be "rationally" satisfied in social action is no longer as clear as it once seemed during the eighteenth and nineteenth centuries. There have been discovered irrational, unforeseen, and unintended consequences of such seemingly "rational" action in the recent past which often dismays and repels us. We fear the unintended consequences of action and we have something more to fear than fear itself. We fear ignorance. Psychoanalysts have, by way of explaining such dilemmas, made us aware of irrational and unconscious forces in the individual, and sociologists have made us aware of the tremendous gaps there are bound to be between theory and practice when these become institutionalized.[2] An intelligent way to read the voting studies is with the problem of "rational" action in mind. This chapter is an attempt to concentrate on some of the psychological aspects of the problem of "rational action," especially exploring the way in which contemporary motivational and learning theories may be related to it.

Professor Lazarsfeld has provided, in a still unpublished manuscript, a very explicit revelation about the psychological assumptions and problems underlying the two studies on voting behavior with which he has been associated. He makes clear, if I may briefly sketch from his very stimulating unpublished paper, that he is concerned with the way in which *motives* give rise to *intentions.* By "motive," he includes sexual or aggressive drives and, speaking less within the "behavioristic" tradition, such wants as a need to maintain self-esteem. By "intention," he refers to predispositions to choose one way of acting rather than another way, or one object rather than another object, so as to satisfy such motives. Speaking behavioristically, all "position habits" are "intentions" as, for instance, when a hungry rat tends always to go to the *left* side of a maze in order to look for food rather than the *right* side. An "intention," within psychoanalytic theory, would be a tendency to choose older "motherly" women rather than younger ones for coitus. Within a self and communication theory frame of reference, an intention would be a tendency to be overly modest about one's achievements rather than brag openly about them, using "modesty" as an alternative technique to call attention to the self and satisfy a need for reassurance of one's worth.

Starting with this distinction, Professor Lazarsfeld then concerns himself with the problem of how such "intentions" are *crystallized* out of "motives." Furthermore, he is interested in the process by which, once they are "crystallized," they are *maintained or modified over time* within the environmental conditions among which they must operate. Lastly, he is interested in factors which *block* such "intentions" *from coming to actual or full expression.*

To give an example, let us suppose that a man has grown up with a strong "motive" to be dependent on others. He is now an executive in a large corporation and he is looking for a secretary. Let us say, to simplify matters, that he acknowledges his "dependent drive" to himself (which is very seldom likely to be true of the type of business executive who develops an ulcer). His rational problem is now to choose a secretary who will gratify his dependent needs. He may have at least the following types of choices: A secretary who appears to encourage dependency but is actually frightened of gratifying a boss's dependency needs (Type 1) or a secretary who not only encourages dependency but delights in it to the point where she practically does the boss's job for him (Type 2). Let us say we watch this man over ten years' time and discover he has had six secretaries who have left the position for various reasons. We might discover that he consistently chooses one type of secretary rather than another. The theoretical questions then arise. What made him predisposed to satisfy his dependent drives with a Type 1 secretary rather than a Type 2? What made it impossible for him to move from a Type 1 to a Type 2 choice? Or, indeed, is it possible that his successive choices of secretaries moved away from *extreme examples* of Type 1 choices—i.e., he chooses secretaries with less fear of a boss's dependency although still basically "fearful." This is the type of analysis Professor Lazarsfeld has in mind. (The choice of a successor to fill one's shoes and the choice of people for employment and/or for membership in an organization are especially important areas for such an analysis.)

It is an "accident" that Professor Lazarsfeld chose to study these questions in terms of voting decisions. They could have been answered in many other areas of applied social science. However, voting behavior is in some ways *simpler* than the choice of a mate in marriage or the choice of a brand of coffee. The choices open to people in America (not in France!) in the political arena are not quite as wide as in marital mates or brands of coffee. This is an *asset* in terms of the simplicity with which measurements and relationships can be stated; it is a *debit*, however, in terms of translating whatever findings about these problems turn up in the voting studies into other areas of social action in which the choices involved become more numerous and complex. It is wise to remember both the limitations of and generalizations from any concrete investigation bent on discovering abstract laws. For instance, there is perhaps needed a certain distinction that helps to clarify the notion of "intention." The term is used by Professor Lazarsfeld to refer primarily to the *preferred object choice* of an individual in attempting to satisfy "a motive." However, when a man chooses a profession, he is not choosing an object, but *a set of preferred activities* by which he earns his bread and butter. Thus, Professor Lazarsfeld wants the term "intention" also to refer to *preferred ways of behaving* in attempting to satisfy "a motive." A man may satisfy an "oral drive" by smoking rather than overeating, but he may still be a real connoisseur of good pipe tobaccos or he may smoke some cheap brand of cigarettes which give him little real smoking pleasure. There is no harm in fitting both kinds of preference under one rubric, as long as the distinction is kept in mind.[3] It could very well be, however, that abstract laws governing preferred object choice are different than those governing preferred ways of behaving. If so, a single term like "intention" to cover both will eventually confuse the clear statement of laws.

There is no doubt, no matter how much we may want to re-examine some of Professor Lazarsfeld's reasoning, that a stimulating set of problems for psychiatrists and psychologists is raised which require us to integrate psychological and psychiatric research more seriously with that of the sociologists than has been done up till now. This chapter is an attempt at such an integration.

We can begin with some historical considerations. The psychology of motivation, an area which at present is in a state of great flux and adventurous experimentation,[4] grew out of theology and philosophy. When psychology attempted to emancipate itself from these two disciplines, it was concerned with appearing "respectable" to its older scientific siblings, the physical sciences. Thus, it attempted to rid itself of all damaging theological and philosophical trappings, which might look "meta-empirical." The area of motivation was an especially difficult one in which to maintain such a type of reputation for the maturing science of psychology. Motives were "unseen"—John B. Watson forcefully placed them among the "ghosts" in psychology—and to talk about them, so psychologists bent on being "naturalistic" were led to believe, in any terms that suggested a revival of theological or metaphysical interests had to be studiously avoided. Hence, motivation had to be given a naturalistic flavor, and biology offered a way of resolving the dilemma of maintaining scientific self-esteem while getting ahead with the job to be done. The concern with motivational theory became urgent at the turn of the twentieth century, at which time there were published a rash of lists of "instincts" over which tiresome "internal" professional wars were waged. Motivation was spoken about in biological metaphors and conceived of in terms of biophysical models.

Psychoanalysis shared in this general trend and manifested much of the same "symptoms" that appeared in the more academic writings of psychologists. The difference was that Freud was more economical and tried to get along with only two instincts (for a while only *one* until Adler, as he put it, "bequeathed" Freud the "aggressive instincts"), whereas psychologists like McDougall wanted a plethora of them. The "libido" notion was based on a physicalistic model, partaking of the Helmholtzian materialism of the time. Reputable physiologists, like Ralph W. Gerard, tell us that there is little physiological evidence to support the "energy" assumptions within the psychoanalytic theory of "libido."[5] Nevertheless, it did succeed in discussing "the unseen movers"—and *really* "unseen" since they were *unconscious!*—in a way that demonstrated scientific "intentions" to the chaste eye of physical and biological scientists alike.[6] Much happened during this period of the growth of motivational theory which is quite fascinating and important, but it is not of immediate concern here.

Since these early stages in the development of a motivational theory, psychologists and psychiatrists have begun to deal with social wants rather than purely biological wants, and to concern themselves with relating the two. Ego psychology and the social behaviorism of the followers of Clark Hull represent these new directions. By and large, the application of these advances in motivation theory to problems of the group sciences—i.e., sociological, historical, economic, and political problems, for the most part—have been few and not overly successful.[7] Yet, the group sciences are developing rapidly and psychologists should perhaps see in this fact some encouragement for a psychology of motivation that is not based too narrowly and thinly on biological concerns.

Our current categories of motivation like "aggressive drives," "dependency drives," and "conformity drives" are probably only partial attempts to accomplish the required job. They sometimes *confuse skill with motive,* probably because of an historical genesis in Darwinian and Watsonian models. A person may be aggressive or conforming or dependent for quite different reasons. It is what the behavior is *being used for,* what social changes it attempts to bring about, that matters to the group social scientist, not the mere fact that it occurs. Aggression in one context may be used as a way of increasing one's wealth (getting a raise of salary) and, in quite another, may be used to extract affection or respect which has been justifiably or unjustifiably denied one. In still others, it may be a way of decreasing the amount of "sin" in the social environment, where "sin" is defined either by cultural standards or by the aggressive actor. Furthermore, some aggressive acts may or may not work in bringing about desired social changes for the aggressive actor, and some aggressive acts may be prosocial rather than antisocial as O. H. Mowrer has contended.[8] In short, *what has happened in motivational theory is that we can lump together a series of social techniques under one rubric like "aggression" without taking into account whether all instances included under the rubric are being used to maintain or modify the social environment of actor in the same way, and with the same degree of intelligence.* Although the tendency is to define social "behavior" in increasingly abstract terms, getting away from the delineation of simple reflexes bound up with instincts, nevertheless the descriptions and categories are still made in terms of the abstract biological (rather than social) features of the actor's movements, and not in terms of the social *outcomes* which such movements, consciously or unconsciously, *are designed to bring into existence,* nor the intelligence in the skills utilized.

We are nonetheless moving in this direction. Goal specifications always play some part in contemporary motivational theories. Thus, an "aggressive drive" may be defined by followers of Hull as "an attempt to 'injure another'." Yet, confusion often arises when such logical definitions are applied to the varieties of human action and experience. Striking another is without doubt (for most people) a sign of "an aggressive drive." But a parent often strikes a child for going too near a radiator in order to prevent the child from burning his body. Is that response to be considered the same sort of "sign" as another in which an adult tyrannizes over a child just to see the child suffer, as in *Oliver Twist*? If so, some of the most important personality distinctions of social life are being blurred by so "positivistic" an approach in using both acts of striking as the same kind of signs of "aggression" and conceiving of both as arising from a similar motivational system. Social context is neglected.

Any motivational theory must account for the complex development of civilization. This development has come about through the subordination of biological impulses and the refinement of biological skills to and by *social values*,[9] and each complex contemporary culture has accomplished this in slightly different ways. The term "socialization study" is used when there is concern with such problems of subordination and refinement of biological processes. The concept of values has, unfortunately, a way of reminding us of philosophical ethics and theology, but there is no particular reason why such value categories cannot be constructed in as naturalistic a way as biological categories or as categories which deal with social behavior in terms of the "biological features" of social behavior. Such categories of social values will have to be comprehensive enough to include all the social outcomes that people of all cultures strive for empirically, but they must also be economical and subsume these social outcomes under the most abstract terms possible.[10]

An "intention," the predisposition to choose one object or one way of behaving to achieve a certain end rather than another alternative way, bears some resemblance to what Hullian social psychologists call "secondary drives." There is, at best, probably only a matter of the level of abstraction involved. The category of "an aggressive drive" could be used, for instance, only for responses which involve (*a*) hitting another or (*b*) calling him "names" instead. Such an analysis of alternative ways of acting would be analogous to a choice between voting for a Democratic or Republican candidate. The interest would be in the factors leading up to the choice of alternatives. Psychologists realize, however, that there are all sorts of subtle, alternative ways in which "injury to another" may occur. The term has often been expanded to include, under the impact of psychoanalytic and clinical observation, such acts as a child's failure at school when success means much to his parents and when they have turned the full focus of their affection away from him toward a newborn sibling. So, too with a child's constipation or wetting of his bed. Adults often "kill with kindness" by making others totally dependent on them for the maintenance of their self-esteem. Professor Lazarsfeld might begin to speak of "a political drive"—with great justification, since there seems to be so much "apathy" among the citizens to whom the vote is available—and use voting as one index of the strength of such a drive just as hitting or calling names would be an index of "aggressive drive" and constipation, enuresis, and school failure more subtle indicators of aggressive motivation. I am reminded of a friend who refused to interest himself in voting at all, or in discussing voting issues with his friends and associates, but who loved to tell political jokes. His mother and father were deadlocked between Republican and Democratic loyalties and he was unable to take the side of one against the other! It could be suspected that his "political drive" was as strong as "the aggressive drive" of the "good" constipated child.

Some increasingly abstract and subtle definitions, however, probably would not do as much as might first appear in helping sociologists to analyze group behavior in terms of a more adequate motivational theory, and it is to Professor Lazarsfeld's credit that he has not chosen this way to move. Yet, he has *not* moved toward a systematic analysis of the values of the individual voter, nor of certain categories of voters, to see how they line up their vote with their value system. It is here probably where the greatest contribution toward building upon the voting studies might be made in the future. If education is a strong value for a certain group, and if one party has acquired a "reputation" for advancing that value, then we would expect that group to line up solidly behind that party. Yet, politics has its mysteries and sometimes we find just the opposite process occurring. It is at such points that future voting studies would contribute much toward the problem of rational action, if they operated with some value theory of motivation in mind.[11] We will return to this idea later.

Professor Lazarsfeld and his associates have provided still another area of concern, that of interest in the *maintenance and modification of "intentions."* It is at this point that the voting studies touch upon learning issues, especially issues involved in social learning and socialization study. In *Personal Influence*,[12] Professor Lazarsfeld has done much toward providing interesting information about such social learning taking place through the influence of "opinion leaders," mass-media exposure, and personal conversation. For him, learning issues would arise in at least three connections: (1) How are intentions "crystallized" out of motives? (2) Under what social conditions can such "crystallizations" be intensified or weakened or modified in any way? (3) How can such "crystallizations" be inhibited from full overt expression, even when not basically influenced in any fundamental way?

Psychologists working in the area of learning theory[13] will take heart that their academic, experimental studies provide laws and produce phenomena which are not too different from what appears in such applied field studies as the voting books represent. We learn that "intentions" are acquired in primary groups and are influenced by ethnic, religious, and social class identifications and reinforcements. We learn that "intentions" are kept from modification to some degree by the individual's unwillingness to expose himself to the influence of persons and groups with whom he is not identified or what Professor Lazarsfeld calls a refusal to be "cross-pressured." Inability to keep himself from being exposed to contrary opinions of other groups and people, makes him more likely to change his intention and/or be blocked in going to the polls. Voting behavior emphasizes the importance of social reinforcement as an explanation for the potency of certain forms of voting patterns. It suggests, too, that learning theorists who have attempted to integrate psychoanalytic thinking into their studies via the concept of "identification" have been moving in the right direction toward integrating laboratory experiments with complex human situations involving learning.

Yet, learning theorists have traditionally avoided the problem of rational action since they avoid formulating a theory of intelligence and deal purely with reinforcement, and perhaps psychoanalytic theory sometimes shares to some degree in the avoidance of this problem through a tendency to convert the study of rationality into a study of "rationalization." And it is here that the voting studies are hazy about why the "crystallizations," or processes of learning to vote as one does, have arisen in just the "mechanical" way they have on the individual and group level. Antecedent and consequent factors in voting behavior are not examined for their "rationality." Actually, voting behavior, as portrayed in the Elmira and Michigan studies, as well as the British study of the Bristol elections, looks very irrational, governed wholly by group identifications and family loyalties rather than by independent and thoughtful reasoning, and swayed by certain historical-sociological regroupings of allegiances.

When values are obliquely touched upon, the voting studies show that the political party and group one belongs to or identifies with *is perceived as sharing one's values*, sometimes mistakenly. The individual refrains from identification with political parties who do not seem to share his value system. He tends to attribute ego-alien values to nonreference groups. Personality factors seem uninvolved except when the individual does not line up with his reference group and votes contrary to his ethnic, religious, and social class affiliations. An ambiguity arises here. Is the "neurotic" the person who lines up his political choices on the basis of emotional ties to his primary and secondary group affiliations? Or is the "neurotic" the person who breaks such emotional bonds and votes in either "independent" terms or in terms of "outgroup" affiliations?[14]

To put it another way, is "neuroticism" to be equated with "irrational" political behavior? And if so, does "irrational" mean something else than a simple inability to satisfy one's value system through political action or an inability to learn how to do so in better and better ways (to continue to learn)? May not both the type of person who lines up his political vote with the groups toward which he is emotionally involved and the type of person who refuses to do so *both* have neurotic people within them? And may not both these types of "neurotic" people *sometimes* be considered as acting "rationally" to satisfy their value systems through political action? It is here where I find the voting studies skirting answers and working with an underdeveloped and perhaps misguided model about the relationship between personality and political choice in the interests of simple demographic descriptions of a normative sociological nature.[15] Slick empiricism begins to mask social complexities.

One would suspect that where no identification with primary groups takes place, the socialization procedures in the family have been faulty. Evidence for such an hypothesis comes from a "scouting" study provided by Eleanor E. Maccoby and her associates.[16] Yet, nothing follows from this about "neuroticism" or "irrationality." If parents with Democratic affiliations cannot socialize their children as successfully as those with Republican affiliations (or vice versa), in any community, there is some reason to believe that those parents are "disturbed." They may, however, produce sons and daughters who line up with the opposite political party in a "nonneurotic" way (as "independents," perhaps) in which their primary identifications are not completely overthrown. Much will depend on community factors other than child-training procedures. If the opposite political party, for instance, does not demand "true believer" political attitudes from its supporters, then a person moving away from his parent's political preferences may do so in a more "rational" way, without violent emotion and with a high amount of attention to issues. Furthermore, if the importance of political affiliations is not strong in the eyes of parents who unsuccessfully socialize their children, the movement away from parental political affiliations may not be attended with as much heat and emotion and, hence, perhaps with less neuroticism and irrationality.

If the opposite political party is in a minority position within that community, it may be that the person who breaks with a parental political tie will do so with more heat and emotion and less calm rationality than where the opposite political party is in a majority, since the movement is not only away from parental choice, but also from majority choice of the entire community. And the individual who is successfully socialized by his parents may, if the political party of their choice is in a minority position, still approach his political choices with little rationality and with much neurotic involvement of the sort that has been emphasized in the studies of "the authoritarian personality."[17] It thus seems that loyalty or disloyalty to primary groups in terms of lining up or moving away from their traditional political choices can do little toward resolving the problems of personality and neuroticism involved in voting behavior, or resolving problems of rationality and the ability to continue to learn how to satisfy one's values through political action, unless they are supplemented by both depth study of the socialization of political attitudes within any community and of the way in which political parties function within that community itself.[18]

A hunch would be that the social learning issues involved in the crystallization of "intentions" on a demographical level are rather trivial and minor. But the social learning issues involved in the acquisition and implementation of value systems within the family and community may be quite decisive and important in settling questions about the role of neuroticism and irrationality in political choice. *Change of "intention" takes place primarily, in this view, when the individual voter sees an opposing "intention" as an equal or better way to satisfy his value system, whether his value system is different from or similar to that of his primary group.*

Conversation and contact with people having a different political choice produces no magical modification of "intention." Undoubtedly, some contact and conversation with those having opposite intentions does have a "magical" effect upon *some* voters. For instance, among the socially mobile, conversation with those in superior status positions may produce a change of political choice. The vote may be seen as a symbolic way of proving to oneself that one is "moving upward" on the social ladder, whereas in actuality nothing of the sort is occurring at all.[19] The somewhat masochistic voter who cannot argue for himself or his position may become inhibited after conversation with those with differing intentions. The conversation may result in his feeling "unworthy" to vote since he cannot defend his position with as much intellectual perfection as he would like, when actually he may be better informed about issues and have worked out his political interests with greater thoroughness than the majority of voters. Discussion with a voter with opposing intentions may evoke unconscious emotions which are frightening and lead to magical rituals. (I am told by a person who worked at polling places that one individual explained that he voted by the number of letters in the names of candidates which he has a "theory" about, and another asked if he might use the magical system of voting for those with first initials which contained "lucky letters"!) We do not yet recognize the forms of "magical thinking" a political campaign may call forth from the various sections of the public and the specific way in which conversation with others about politics may inhibit or accentuate magical thinking about politics. Yet, one can judge the rational or irrational and magical quality of the change in political intentions primarily by examining the values of the voter and the reasoning by which he sees his political choice implementing the attainment of those values in sociopolitical reality.[20]

Social learning theory is, along with contemporary motivational theory, in a state of flux. Those psychologists working within a neo-behavioristic framework, and psychoanalysts moving toward a more highly developed theory of ego functioning, have begun to emphasize the need for the "self" concept as a way of understanding social learning issues and problems associated with social maturation.[21]

The "self" concept has been under attack by empiricists since David Hume examined it and found it without empirical substantiation. It suggests the type of theological and philosophical trappings which appear inimical to a naturalistic approach. Yet, like the concept of "motivation," it may be one of those "ghosts" which manage to materalize again and again in surprisingly naturalistic ways. The concept seems to me to emphasize the importance of studying individual differences, even group individual differences, and to stress that one must move away from simple biological categories which tend to minimize individual differences. Each group and each individual maintains "self-esteem" in different ways and with different values. A study of "the self" is a crude reminder that we must list the full array of values in terms of which people maintain their self-esteem and seek to perpetuate it, no matter what part or aspect of their biological security is at issue. It emphasizes less an attention upon "part functions" of the personality and a greater attention to the organization of the "total" personality in differing social contexts in which the person behaves and in which one kind of social value is involved more than another.

Theories of learning which emphasize the "self" concept tend to be central rather than peripheral theories. Yet, they attempt to tie together in a more "molar" way the part functions with which peripheral theories of learning deal, so that principles of "social learning" coming out of simple situations can be applied to more complex ones. The use of the "self" concept involves "composition rules" of which the logical positivist speaks.[22] Personality disorganization and organization is more and more seen to be explainable in terms of the threats or hopes people are made to entertain about the central values by which they maintain their self-esteem whether in sexual, political, economic, or other kinds of social contexts.[23]

Recent experiments in social psychology tend to bear out this line of reasoning. We find that a result is obtained in one laboratory which cannot be reduplicated in another. Part of this lack of verification may be due to *not standardizing the value systems* of the subjects that participate in such experiments, a matter which can become quite crucial the farther away geographically the subjects of one experiment are from those of another, since value systems are notoriously different in different parts of the United States. Some of what looks like wonderfully "controlled" experiments may actually leave a crucial determinant of social responses —the value system of the subjects, in terms of which self-esteem is maintained—relatively uncontrolled and unmeasured. So, too, the "social rewards" administered by an experimenter who values those rewards greatly may be administered in much different ways and with different social cues than those who do not value them. The highly revered experiments of Kurt Lewin and his associates on "democratic atmospheres" could easily have been influenced by the values of the experimenter about "authoritarian" methods. Some of the results of these "classical" experiments are being severely challenged by new experiments in which the values involved in self-esteem are being more elaborately controlled, both in terms of the persons administering "social rewards" and the persons exposed to them.[24]

It may very well be that the voting studies partake of the same errors. The *same* political loyalties of *one* group in the *same* community may have a *different* value base (increase of employment and wealth for the members of that group) than the value base of *another* group (increased respect and deference, since an important member of that group is a candidate). So, too, the *same* group may have a *different* value base for supporting the same political party when operating in one community (the South) than when operating in another community (the West). Even more interesting, however, is where the same group forms quite different political choices in different sections of the country *even though their value base remains quite similar*. Here it becomes a matter of how the two groups perceive each party as furthering or curtailing the realization of the same value system. One of the two groups, when the issue is part of a national election, is behaving more "irrationally" than the other; a comparison of the two groups would provide a masterful little field study in community, personality, and family factors producing rational and irrational political behavior at the ballot boxes. The findings from the voting studies suggest many similar types of further, more compact studies designed to lay bare the influence of neuroticism and irrationality in voting behavior.

Summarizing, the voting studies can be looked upon as *encouraging innovations* in the psychology of motivation and social learning. In some ways, they partake of some of the "cultural lag" in psychological and psychiatric theories with respect to the study of values and the "self" concept. In other ways, they help psychologists and psychiatrists to see that laws coming out of the experimental laboratory and clinical settings can be transferred, with some modification, to complex social conditions. In still other ways, they go beyond the simple studies in laboratory settings or clinical interviews and provide a host of new problems for the psychologist and psychiatrist interested in social motivation and social learning within the field of social action. Further interaction between sociologists undertaking field studies of the sort that Professor Lazarsfeld has promoted (plus the equally interesting Michigan studies), and the theories and findings coming from the studies of social-learning theorists and psychoanalysts, cannot help but enrich the depth and breadth of laws and generalizations about human behavior. This chapter has attempted: (*a*) to provide a number of suggestions for further research in voting behavior in which psychologists and psychiatrists might both make decisive contributions to the general problem of irrationality in social action, and (*b*) to provide suggestions as to how to develop theories to deal with irrational behavior both in more complex and less traditional areas and under less extreme conditions of choice than those customarily provided by the study of extreme clinical disorders of personality.

CHAPTER 6

Political Theory and the Voting Studies

EUGENE BURDICK

In the last chapter of *Voting* the authors grapple with the problem of reconciling political theory and the data of their study. They conclude the book with an admirable statement from Cobban. "For a century and a half the Western democracies have been living on the stock of basic political ideas that were last restated toward the end of the eighteenth century. That is a long time. . . . The gap thus formed between political facts and political ideas has steadily widened. It has taken a long time for the results to become evident; but now that we have seen what politics devoid of a contemporary moral and political theory means, it is possible that something may be done about it."[1]

One would lack both humility and common sense to attempt to "do something about it" in a fragment of a single volume. However, the Elmira study, the Michigan study, and the Bristol study all raise questions of high relevance for political theory. By a process of radical condensation I shall attempt to lay some of their findings parallel to some facets of democratic political theory and indicate the implications that flow from such a comparison. Necessarily the attempt will be more heuristic than exhaustive. The effort, however brief, is justified not only by Cobban's advice, but also by the widespread feeling among students of politics that when political theory becomes too divergent from political practice the polity is in some sort of danger.

In this chapter data from the voting studies will be used to re-examine four ideas of democratic theory. First, the "citizen" of classical democratic theory will be compared with the "voter" of the voting studies. Second, the question of how adequately the voting data support a theory of political pluralism will be examined. Third, political concord and the voting studies will be considered. Fourth, a contemporary theory, Lippmann's notion of "civility," will be examined in light of the voting studies.

For reasons that are not completely clear to me the voting scholars have not brought their findings face to face with general problems of political theory. They have in fact recoiled sharply from such a confrontation.[2] There are at least two strong reasons for this. First, the positivistic suspicion that ethical values had little or nothing to do with the empirical world and that proof in one of these worlds has no relevance for the other has made empiricists shy away from ultimate problems of political value.[3] Secondly, the voting scholars have been beset by substantial problems of internal meaning and consistency or what are usually known as "problems of methodology." These problems of method are so substantial and persistent that little energy is left over for consideration of more speculative problems. As a result the generalization from voting data to political theory has been slight indeed.[4]

In one sense the caution of the empiricist is well founded. It is doubtful, for example, that any amount of data can conceivably validate or invalidate either a theory of intention or an ethical theory.[5] For this reason no attempt will be made here to consider problems of pure ethical theory. Rather the effort will be to discuss elements which both empiricists and theorists would agree are real, e.g., political nature, psychological motivation for political acts, and, perhaps less certainly, political concord.

At this point one must face a very central problem: To what extent are the findings of the voting studies "real"? Without raising the philosophical technicalities it is clear that between voting studies there is not only considerable ambiguity in definition, but that even when they ostensibly search for the same thing they do not find it.[6] Or they find it in different quantities and valences. Voting scholars are well aware of this difficulty and are attempting in a number of ways to meet the problem. In this chapter it will be assumed that a phenomenon that appears frequently in various studies has something of the nature of "reality" about it. Time or data are unlikely to solve this problem and for a simple reason: in a field so dynamic and changing the results will never be final.

It will be seen, furthermore, that even the qualified "realities" which emerge from the voting studies raise serious problems for political theorists.

THE "CITIZEN" OF DEMOCRATIC THEORY AND THE "VOTER." *Rationality*. Central to almost every democratic theory has been the idea of the essential rationality of the citizen. Locke conceived this rationality to be so durable that in his famous "state of nature," autonomous rational men were reasonably happy. Indeed each, being possessed of rationality, was able to exercise a form of "executive power"[7] and the over-all effect was one of harmony—blemished only by occasional miscalculations. Locke further conceived that man lost none of his rationality when the civil society was formed.[8] He wrote that men entered civil society "only with an intention in every one the better to preserve himself, his liberty and property for no rational creature can be supposed to change his condition with an intention to be worse."

Very little in classical democratic theory refuted Locke. Rousseau, despite the recent uncertainty about his work, was firmly in the tradition which viewed political man as rational.[9] If the eighteenth century was optimistic in this regard the nineteenth was even more so. The Utilitarians saw man not only as rational, but they thought that his moral life could be made scientific and orderly. For Bentham the state was nothing more than a means by which the pains and pleasures of each perceiving and rational individual could be remorselessly added and subtracted and the "felicific calculus" of the entire society computed. Adam Smith might sound an eccentric warning about the nonrationality of humans,[10] but as late as 1890 Sidgwick had to "demonstrate" that "unreasonable action" was possible.[11] The American tradition was essentially the same. Although a number of the Founding Fathers had reservations, both public and private, about the limits of reason, the necessity to argue a theory of rights also drove them to embrace, at least, a modified theory of rational political man. When Paine remarked immodestly that he was "unconnected with any party, and under no sort of Influence, public or private, but the influence of reason and principle," he expressed a dominant mood.[12]

The "voter" who emerges from the studies discussed in this

book has little of the rationality of the "citizen" of democratic theory. Even when rationality is given a minimum definition the American voter does not meet the test. If rationality is defined merely as the possession of the information necessary to make a decision, ratiocination on that information, and the *self-conscious* evolution of a decision, the voter is, by and large, not rational. In Elmira over a third of the respondents knew correctly only one stand taken by Dewey and Truman on issues of the utmost gravity.[13] In the Michigan study only a third of the respondents were "greatly interested in the election" and only a fifth thought it made a "good deal" of difference who won.[14] There is also ample evidence that the perception of the political world was highly selective and often inaccurate, e.g., the respondent "saw" what he wanted to see, even if this defied common sense and the stated position of a candidate.[15]

This is not to argue that the voter is irrational. It will be indicated below that his interest in politics is so slight that his behavior in this field is no true test of his rationality. But he most surely acts unrationally in his political choices; the voter of the Elmira and Michigan studies quite obviously is incapable of the kind of rationality which Locke expected of him, to say nothing of his ability to make the kind of intricate "felicific calculus" which Bentham required of his citizen.

Political Nature of Man. The citizen of classical democratic theory was conceived to be both interested and active in the political discourse. Knowing that the question of *who* is to be sovereign and *how* this power was exercised were the most fundamental questions of social life, classical theorists, quite logically, could not conceive that any citizen would ignore the discussion by which the decision was made.

But it is abundantly clear that the voter of today does lack both high political interest and an urge to participate in the political discourse. The voting studies indicate that political discourse is limited, sparse, and desultory. Indeed, most voters make up their minds, and act ultimately on that decision, even before the campaigns begin. Family background, cultural milieu, all of the inchoate pressures of "socioeconomic status" seem subtly to work on the voter in a process which is neither rational nor accompanied by high interest. The conveyors of political information are massively ignored, except by small nuclei of partisans.[16]

Political Principles. The citizen of classical theory was supposed to vote in terms of a set of values or principles. The ultimate referent might range from a luminous hagiolatry, to an enthusiasm for revolutionary slogans, to a cold calculation of interest; but that the citizen might make his political decisions in an unprincipled manner, classical theory could not concede. More recently there has evolved a more realistic theory based on the assumption that the plurality of principles in a complex modern society was amalgamated into the principles of a political party.

The voting studies, however, do not allow even this last slight image of the principled citizen to remain. The voting studies seem agreed that "if this requirement [of principled voters] is pushed at all strongly it becomes an impossible demand on the democratic electorate."[17] The political party is not regarded as a variegated repository where the conflicting principles of the electorate are merged and made compatible. Much more it is viewed as a traditional allegiance of one very low affect or another in a series of acts aimed at coming to adjustment with one's environment.[18]

In summary, the voting studies etch a portrait of the contemporary voter as a person who votes with relatively high frequency, but on very low information, with very little interest, and with very low emotional involvement in the entire process. The act of voting seems divorced from any coherent set of principles. The original cause of the voter's attitude, the steps by which it is modified before coming to formal decision (what voting scholars call intervening variables), and the whole subtle process of change in political attitudes and institutions are, of course, not so clearly known.

But although the etiology of individual voter motivation and the over-all process of collective political change are not clear, the image of the contemporary voter is clear enough to give serious pause to political theory. For it is evident that the "citizen" of the theorists is really an ideal construction; more paradigm than reality.

Now as has been indicated above this changed version of the citizen does not necessarily destroy previous ethical theory nor does it damage theories of intention. But it does substantially alter some parts of political theory by supplying relatively firm answers for what were previously conjectures or mere statements of preference. The relevance for much of classical theory is so obvious that it need not be remarked. Theories of consent, majoritarianism, the role of elites, the nature of individual and collective will, and theories of social contract are areas which would need radical revision if the findings of the voting studies on the nature of political man and political participation are accurate.

The relevance for contemporary political problems is even more striking. One wonders, for example, if in recent attempts to involve "the public" more directly in international relations, the involvement is either possible or desirable. Given the demonstrated low interest in domestic politics and the even lower interest in foreign affairs one wonders how this is to be accomplished. If the only manner in which their heightened interest and affect could be achieved is through the adoption of a form of "total politics," the fact would have to be faced that a corollary of high political interest might be a sharp rise in ideology with a parallel rise in tensions and rigidity. Can popular participation mean anything less than "intrusion of the masses" into politics? And if it can, what are the educational and motivational means which must be developed? And how will these means be controlled and to what end?

PLURALISM AND THE VOTING STUDIES. The authors of *Voting*, in their concluding chapter, strongly suggest that their findings are compatible with a pluralistic theory of sovereignty. They argue that in the same way that economic complexity has resulted in economic specialization the "same kind of division of labor—as repugnant as it may be in some respects to our individualistic tradition—is serving us well today in mass politics."[19] They go on to suggest that the very indifference to politics which they found in Elmira results in a sort of resilience and malleability which is necessary to survival and progress in an increasingly complex situation. They imply that the extreme ideologies of left and right will find little following in a society which gives slight importance to politics and has a very dim opinion of the efficacy of political action. There is, on page 323 of that volume, a nicely modulated bell-curve which pictures the balance between "sociable man" and "ideological man" in the middle; the suggestion is that the bulk of citizens fall into the swelling of the curve labeled "political man." The pleasing symmetry of the curve—its utter lack of jaggedness—seems to imply a compatibility between the data in their book and the democratic society which is vastly reassuring.[20]

The theory is, however, peculiarly unconvincing. In the same way that one might find in the midst of one of Hieronymous Bosch's terrifying pictures a pleasing cherubin and take that as the standard of Bosch's intention, one has the sensation that the compatibility between the data of the voting studies and pluralism is somehow misleading.

Upon close examination it is clear that the voting data are not really supportive of the theory of political pluralism. What the voting studies do illustrate is that American and British societies are extremely "pluralistic." That is, they are heterogeneous in character, complex in structure, and the individuals within such societies differ widely in motivation. This is undoubtedly true; the voting studies have spelled out this type of "pluralism" with skill and ingenuity and added greatly to the dimensions of our knowledge of social and political complexity.

The plain fact is, however, that such heterogeneity is not the equivalent of political pluralism. Political pluralism recognized heterogeneity and complexity as *fact* and then proceeded to invest this fact with the cloak of sovereignty.[21] To do this, two things are necessary which are quite lacking in *Voting*. First, however arcane the language now sounds, it was necessary to give the subordinate associations a genuine legal personality. Secondly, these subordinate associations were actually to have a portion of the sovereignty formerly assigned exclusively to government.

In none of the voting studies and in none of the commentaries on them is there a proposal to fracture the existing sovereignty into parts and then reassign it to the subordinate associations. Much more there is the suggestion that the heterogeneity, which the voting studies have discovered and described in valuable detail, is itself "pluralism." It is indeed plural, but it is not "political pluralism" as the theory is known to political theorists and for a simple reason: no way is known to assign legal personality to the associations described.

This would be logic-picking or trivial were it not that this fact points to a very major problem for the political theorist when dealing with the voting studies. The problem is this: How real and concrete are the groupings described in these studies and how durable are they? Are they durable enough to be treated as legitimate associations?

Take, for example, the phenomenon known as "socioeconomic status," the famous SES, of the Elmira study. For anyone interested in political behavior it is a valuable term. It suggests that each voter is the center of a world of external pressures. These pressures come crowding in on him from all directions and in all intensities. Family background, social aspiration, religion, occupation, place of work, ethnic background, income, neurotic propensities, and endless other factors are involved. Most of these pressures are subliminal to the voter, at least as far as his voting intention is concerned. On some obscure level they are measured, ignored, valued, but in the end reconciled—and he votes in a certain way. All three of the studies being discussed give much attention to what the different elements in this complex environment are. Future work, presumably, will give even sharper care to this.

The immediate question on which the theorist needs guidance is this: Is the sociologist of voting suggesting that an SES category, say such as "upper-middle-Catholic-urban," not only exists, but is durable? At times one has the impression that what at first were defined as abstract categories are hypostatized into concrete collectivities. What was first viewed as a category for lumping "variables" becomes something more viable and substantial. One emerges from the studies with the distinct impression that "status," "occupational level," and similiar terms are as tangible as the phenomenon which the theorist calls "political institutions." I am not here questioning this suggestion as much as remarking the problems it raises for students of politics. For example, it is clear that the voting studies do violent damage to the conventional notion of the political party.[22] The conventional view of the political party is that it not only represents a shared principle of political policy, but that it has high efficacy in elections. The voting studies give a much different view of political parties.

What much of the material of the voting studies suggests is an existing situation in which the two major parties really are only administrative cores around which a vast congeries of smaller associations and webs of motivation cluster. All that is shared is the name and, occasionally, a limited administrative apparatus. Now *if* the suggestion were made that SES categories really described self-conscious groupings, a theory of political pluralism could be formulated which would give legal personality to the groups and thus assign them a fraction of sovereignty.[23] Such a theory could be made pluralistic in the classical sense as well as in the technical sense.

It has been indicated above that the "pluralism" of the voting sociologist is not the equivalent of the "pluralism" of the political theorist. The data of the voting studies are unquestionably of high interest and value, but there are great difficulties in moving to the level of political formulation of the significance of the studies. Political theory must, necessarily, deal with relatively durable and stable institutions. At the present time the political theorist has great difficulty in knowing if the "variables" of the voting studies are durable and stable enough to be considered as some variety of association.[24] When Durkheim argues that mere similarities suggest a basis of solidarity he may be speaking a simple sociological fact: for political theorists he raises problems of the most striking magnitude without suggesting limits to the answers.

CONCORD AND THE VOTING STUDIES. The authors of *Voting* cite an excellent quotation from Judge Learned Hand that, without using the word, focuses upon the problem of concord in a diverse modern society.[25] Hand, after commenting that the act of voting "is one of the most unimportant acts of my life," remarks that if he were to acquaint himself with the facts on which his vote ought really to depend he could only bring a "fatuous conclusion to a fatuous undertaking." He then goes on to say, however, that the system, for all its difficulties and uncertainties, "abuse it as you will, it gives a bloodless measure of social forces—bloodless, have you thought of that?—a means of continuity, a principle of stability, a relief from the paralyzing terror of revolution."

Hand states, however puckishly, a paradox. It seems *not* to be true that the chaos of democratic government, the irresponsibility of political parties, the blatant appeal to interest, and the confused political warfare could actually result in public concord. But this *is* what happens. Whatever the qualities of the individual voter, whatever the defects of political parties, whatever the shortcomings of the democratic process, it has, at least in the United States and Britain, resulted in a remarkable degree of concord.

The problem of concord is, of course, most central for political theory. Theories of cyclical development, notions of social contract, problems of individual and social will, the basis for tyrannicide—indeed, almost every problem of political theory comes to bear upon one problem: How *is* concord achieved and what can *make* it legitimate?

The voting studies under consideration, I shall argue, supply a partial answer to the problem of concord, but leave very basic problems of etiology unanswered. Before turning to this matter, however, it is necessary to dispose of a theory of concord which it has frequently been alleged that the pollsters, survey experts, and voting scholars advocate. This is the notion that concord is achieved by allowing public opinion to be expressed in public policy. Or, more crudely and explicitly, the argument that simple majority opinion should find a quick and ready response in political policy.[26]

Whatever may be said by other polling, survey, and voting experts, the authors of the three volumes discussed advance no such theory. Only by committing some form of the fallacy of *petitio principii* could they be conceived as supporting a crude form of majoritarianism. In all three cases they seem fully aware that the mood or opinion of the whole society is far from being the equivalent of desirable political policy.

However, the three studies do seem in agreement in suggesting that concord, at least in two modern democratic states, flows from simple disinterest in politics. *Voting* states directly that the very low affect of most voters, their lack of ideological commitment, and the low faith in the efficacy of politics make political concord relatively easy to achieve. One is instantly reminded of Bagehot's statement that the true strength of the government of England is the stupidity of the population and his thesis that the very boredom of the citizens and the mediocrity of the statesmen makes for a "rut of freedom."[27] This hard conclusion, needless to say, none of the voting studies are prepared to make.

The reluctance of the voting studies to pursue the more pessimistic aspects of their data is, I think, altogether regrettable. For some time there has been a recognition by political theorists that the irrational impulses of individuals were a substantial element in politics. The findings of psychoanalysis and psychiatry, because they emphasize so strongly the individual, have answered few of the questions which would be helpful to students of politics. At the same time they have made a consideration of irrationality in politics incumbent upon political theorists. By explicating the more pessimistic and melancholy of their findings, the voting scholars might do much to reconstruct both political theory and politics.

There is, for example, no reason why a theory of concord could not be based on the assumption of passivity and low information on the part of most of the voters. Acceptance of such a state of affairs might, for example, allow us to explore more energetically the nature of elites in modern society. Samuel Stouffer has suggested that among elites there is a remarkable unanimity of view: leaders tend to be more alike in viewpoint than do their followers.[28] It is conceivable that a liberal theory of concord might be quite consistent with a theory of political elites. A necessary prerequisite, however, would be the willingness of behavioral scientists to explore, and present, all of the possible evidence on the matter. At the present time, however, the voting studies seem directed at supporting existing theories, even when the strain of fitting data into conventional and optimistic theory is very great.

I have suggested that the voting studies, as they stand, might be incorporated in a theory of concord based on the notion of low citizen interest and information. One hesitates, however, because of an implicit warning within the studies and because of explicit statements by their critics. The voting studies make it quite clear that in terms of the etiology—the true causation of political partisanship and of political attitudes—they are at a loss. The authors of the studies still find the basis of concord as "deep, silent and obscure" as did Calhoun.[29] *The Voter Decides*, for example, suggests that membership in large regional, ethnic, and social groups "determines" one's voting preferences. The authors are as aware as their critics that this is a descriptive statement having little to do with causation. *Why* Catholics vote more heavily Democratic or farmers more heavily Republican is still unknown. *Voting* draws the focus more sharply and states that, in Elmira at least, "it is the socioeconomic classes, on the one hand, and the religious and ethnic groups, on the other, that serve as the social carrier of political traditions."[30] Apparently the voter is caught in an intricate and invisible web of religion, desire for security within status, social aspiration, economic class, and family background. But *how* these elements work on him, *why* one argument is persuasive at one time and ineffective at another, the *way* these attitudes are transmitted is still unknown. Until these elements are isolated and explicated it is impossible to conscientiously draw up a theory of concord based on contemporary empirical data from the voting studies. That the voting studies raise doubts about classical theories of concord is beyond question. That they supply the material for a sure new theory of concord is in great doubt.

CIVILITY AND THE VOTING STUDIES. I have indicated above that the voting studies do not technically lend support to a theory of political pluralism. I have also indicated that the studies are either moot on the question of concord or give only partial answers. There are, however, a number of contemporary theories of politics to which the studies, in part or whole, give considerable support. I have selected one of these to indicate how reconstruction of theory might take place and also how this process might be instructive to the voting scholar in terms of his future research.

One such theory is the notion of "civility" advanced by Walter Lippmann.[31] Lippmann's theory of civility is complex and ultimately is based on a theory of natural law which is not relevant to our discussion here. However, Lippmann's effort is directed at isolating the proper qualities of citizenship and leadership and the relations between the two. His exploration is classical in the most literal sense of the word. However, when Lippmann advances empirical evidence for his theory of civility there is a remarkable parallel between his evidence and that of the voting studies.

Lippmann in response to the question "What are the true boundaries of the people's power?" answers: "The answer cannot be simple. But for a rough beginning let us say that the people are able to give and to withhold their consent to being governed—

their consent to what the government asks of them, proposes to them, and has done in the conduct of their affairs. They can elect the government. They can remove it. They can approve or disapprove its performance. But they cannot administer the government. They cannot themselves perform. They cannot normally initiate and propose the necessary legislation. A mass cannot govern."[32]

Lippmann goes on to argue that a proper balance between skills and interests and capabilities, in short, civility, has been disturbed by the gradual domination of Jacobin ideas. By this he means the notion that any person is competent in government, that everyone possesses equal talents, and that politics is the means by which the sentiment working up from the masses comes to political expression.[33] The result has been that the masses have either intruded into public policy or been invited to. In either case the result was catastrophic. By arguing the *individual* was possessed of political competence (as differentiated from general political judgment) and by emphasizing the individual above the needs of the collectivity, the Jacobin revolution has resulted in a theory of politics which is wholly incompatible with reality.

This, admittedly, is a conservative and pessimistic point of view. But when we turn to the voting studies we find considerable empirical justification for the argument. All three of the studies under consideration indicate a remarkably low degree of political information. The Jacksonian notion of sound political judgment "trickling up" from the citizenry is, in our time and situation, obviously feckless.

The authors of *Voting* are, in the end, very close to Lippmann when they suggest that classical democratic theory by concentrating upon individual qualities of citizenship lost sight of the over-all demands of the political system. "That is the paradox," they say. "*Individual voters* today seem unable to satisfy the requirements for a democratic system of government outlined by political theorists. But the *system of government* does meet certain requirements for a going political organization. The individual members may not meet all the standards, but the whole nevertheless survives and grows."[34]

Presumably the authors of *Voting* and of *The Voter Decides* and *Straight Fight* would not be sympathetic to the theory of natural law outlined by Lippmann. At the same time they find themselves addressing the same secret: How in a popular democracy are individual imperfections able to add up to a rather superior political order? The equation is more difficult than it looks. It supplies not only a challenge for those studying concrete political behavior, but it calls, I believe, for a radical reorientation by political theorists. Neither has yet supplied adequate answers. Each is aware that firm answers will be difficult to obtain. Given this mutual disquietude there is, however, a reasonable chance of success.

CHAPTER 7

The Voting Studies and Consumer Decisions

IRVING ROSHWALB

The distinguishing feature of panel research, as it is employed in the voting studies, is that the actions and attitudes of each individual at some point can be compared with his actions and attitudes at other points in time. This kind of check makes possible the analysis of changers and nonchangers to determine—to some degree, at least—those factors that play a role in the constancy or variability of attitudes. The voting studies all deal with the sort of direct observation of the decision process which should shed a great deal of light on consumer behavior. This contribution stems from the analysis of change which panel research makes possible.

An initial interview of a sample of consumers, plus a series of reinterviews of the same people, using questionnaires designed specifically to identify and investigate those who change attitudes and those who make decisions contrary to earlier statements of intention —as well as those who carry out their intentions—should reveal a wealth of information on such matters as:

—Which consumers are predisposed to a particular product, and to a particular brand of that product?

—How soon does a predisposition eventuate in a purchase? What factors bring about the closing of this gap? Are there factors over which the advertiser has any immediate or long-term control?

—What factors enter into a decision to buy? What part does advertising play? What part is played by the dealer, by friends, and by family? Who are "the Joneses" that are to be kept up with, and what is their role? What is the role of past experiences with both the product and the brand?

–How does the decision process vary with the type and price of product?

–What is the background of an *impulse* purchase?

The value of the panel in obtaining answers to these questions—and many others—rests in the longitudinal study of individuals it permits. The macrocosmic approach of the opinion survey—involving the observation of gross changes—is replaced by the microcosmic approach of the panel, which has as its basis the study of a single individual through a number of interviews. The continuity from study to study, provided by this direct comparison of the testimony of a single individual from study to study, is the methodological basis of the voting studies. Applied to the problems of consumer-buying decisions, the panel adds the dimension of analysis of change which is needed to obtain the answers to some of the questions listed above and to many others.

Before proceeding to a discussion of specific areas in which panel studies might contribute to a better understanding of consumer-buying decisions, it might be well to consider the conceptual differences between the voting- and buying-decision processes and the problems which may stand in the way of the wider use of panel studies in consumer research.

In attempting to apply the lessons of the voting studies to marketing problems, it becomes clear immediately that there is no one-to-one correspondence between the steps in any one voting study and the steps that should be taken in a study of consumer decision-making. The reason is evident: the voting decision is not the buying decision. There is basis, for example, for the contention that voting decision is less *rational* than some buying decisions. "The usual analogy between voting decisions and the more or less carefully calculated decisions of consumers or businessmen or courts . . . may be quite incorrect. For many voters political preferences may better be considered analogous to cultural tastes—in music, literature, recreational activities, dress, ethics, speech, social behavior. . . . While both are responsive to changed conditions and unusual stimuli, they are relatively invulnerable to direct argumentation and vulnerable to indirect social influences. Both are characterized more by faith than by conviction and by wishful expectation than careful prediction of consequences."[1] Thus, in the buying decision the buyer has a pretty good idea of the benefits he will derive from his decision: the ownership and use of a given item if he decides to buy; the savings he incurs by refraining from buying. The voter, on the other hand, cannot foresee the benefits of his decision so clearly.

What other differences between the two decision processes may we observe? First, there is the mechanical difference involving the deadline for a decision. There is a legally set deadline for voting decisions. No matter how devious the route taken, by the end of election day the voter must have made a decision. His decision may be not to vote; or his decision may be to vote and to vote for a given candidate. In the consumer's decision process, however, there may be some general—but different—deadline in the mind of each consumer. However, as the deadline approaches and finally arrives, the consumer may choose from yet another pair of alternatives which is not available to the elector—shall he make his decision at this point or put it off awhile longer?

Then there is an important difference in terms of the alternatives available to the decision-maker. As a voter, the decision-maker votes or he does not vote. If he votes, he chooses one of the candidates presented to him. As a consumer, the decision-maker is faced with a high-order multiple-choice situation. The consumer possesses limited resources but many desires of varying degrees of urgency. He is faced with the classical problem of economics: How shall he distribute his limited resources among the various ends so as to maximize his sense of well-being? For the consumer, the buying decision involves, first, the selection of a certain class of product in which to make his expenditure; and, second, the selection of a particular brand in that class. For the producer of a particular brand of product this implies two objectives: first, to increase the likelihood that every consumer will choose to spend in the producer's product area; and, second, to get the consumer to buy his brand of that product. It seems that the panel study could offer clearer insights into both of these aspects of the decision process.

A third difference between the two decision processes, which is closely related to the last, deals with the competing forces in each type of campaign. In the election campaign, directly competing parties and candidates try to influence voters to take certain action. In the advertising campaign, one advertiser must overcome not only directly competing advertising for similar products but also the less direct competition of advertising for other lines of goods which too are struggling for a share of the consumer's dollar.

A final difference between the two types of decisions is the nature of the campaigns involved. The election campaign is one of mounting intensity over a short period of time, covering perhaps four months of an election year. Most large-scale advertising programs never reach the peak intensity of election campaigns but are maintained at lower levels for longer periods of time.

Some of the problems that may stand in the way of the use of panels in consumer research are panel errors, panel analysis, and the ever-present problem of cost.

Panel errors are errors peculiar to panels—*panel mortality* and *panel bias.*

Co-operation of *all* persons contacted for interview is an unattainable goal in public opinion research. The longer the panel is in operation, the more people refuse to co-operate and the more serious the question of the panel's representativeness becomes. The refusal rate drops quickly after the first or second reinterview. The implication of any rate of refusal is a function of the homogeneity of the entire population from which the panel is drawn. A high refusal rate may have no effect on the measurement of a variable whose value is the same for respondents and nonrespondents.

Panel bias, or panel effect, refers to the tendency of some respondents to become *experts* on the subjects on which they are being interviewed. This, too, may destroy the representativeness of the sample making up the panel.

The magnitude of the problem created by these two sources of error, however, can be kept under constant watch and control. One method of control is suggested in *The People's Choice.*[2] In this study three control groups were set up, each reinterviewed only once during the course of the study. Each reinterview coincided with a reinterview of the main panel, in order to obtain some measure of the panel bias among members of the main panel.

In analyzing the effects of mortality and the repeated interviewing of panel members in this study, the authors report that both were small.[3]

A second form of control is one which calls for periodic replacement of a fixed portion of the panel. At any given interview period, the panel consists of several groups—those who are being interviewed for the first time, those who are being interviewed for the second time, and so on up to the group being interviewed for the last time. Each of these groups, in effect, constitutes an independent subsample of the population of the study. At each interview period, one subsample—that being interviewed for the first time—serves as the control group against which the combined effects of panel mortality and panel bias may be measured. The scheduled replacement of the complete panel places an upper limit on the length of time a panel member may be observed. Thus, if one-fourth of the panel is scheduled for replacement every six months, a single panel member will be observed over a period of two years. The optimum scheduling of interviews and replacement appears to be a function of the kind of decision being observed. A study of the decision process involved in the choice of a brand of beer, for example, may call for more frequent interviewing and replacement than a study of the automobile-buying decision.

The second class of problems deals with the analysis of panel data. The analysis of change, in terms of past attitudes, characteristics, and influences must contend with complex collections of data. Conceptually, the forms of analysis which come to mind immediately are applications of regression or difference-equation analysis. Thus if x_i is the measure of an individual's attitude at time i, the relationship of this attitude measure to a similar measure at the time of the previous interview might be written as

$$x_i = ax_{i-1} + b + e_i$$

where e_i is some independent random effect. This expression, known as a first-order linear stochastic difference equation[4] is an example of one form of analysis which may describe shifts in attitudes as observed through the panel.

Anderson[5] has discussed the construction and application of probability models to the analysis of attitude change. In his paper, Anderson considers in some detail several simple models—simple in the sense that of the many factors influencing an attitude they deal only with attitudes that have been held previously.[6] He also indicates how his approach may be generalized to the problem of considering more than one attitude.[7] Anderson treats opinion change as a stochastic process which "is a sequence of events (a set of events ordered in time) together with the probabilities of these sequences."[8]

Another area, which has as yet not been studied intensively in this connection but which may be fruitful, is the application of the concepts of Communication and Information Theory to the measurement of advertising and communication effectiveness.[9]

The implications of the mathematical theory of communication for research on the factors affecting the buying decision are present in the following analysis of the communication problem by Weaver.[10]

"Relative to the broad subject of communication, there seem to be problems at three levels. Thus it seems reasonable to ask, serially:

Level A: How accurately can the symbols of communications be transmitted? (The technical problem)

Level B: How precisely do the transmitted symbols convey the desired meaning? (The semantic problem)

Level C: How effectively does the received meaning affect conduct in the desired way? (The effectiveness problem."

Although Shannon's mathematical theory of communication deals directly with the problems at Level A, it deals with Levels B and C to the extent that they can use only that which is transmitted at Level A.

In order to extend Shannon's engineering model of communication to the study of the communication of ideas among people with the purpose of influencing behavior, one must consider not only the problem of random interferences with the communication process but also the problem of semantic interferences with this process and, ultimately, the effect of this communication on certain aspects of the target audience's behavior. Thus, an advertising program designed to bring about greater consumption of a product must deal first with the mechanical problems of transmission, such as the format of the message and selection of a medium for transmitting the message. It must deal also with overcoming the more or less random disturbances—called "random noise"—set up by other campaigns aimed at the same audience and by other activities of the audience which may cause a breakdown in the mechanics of carrying the message from the transmitter to the receiver. Then, the campaign must deal with the problem of "semantic noise," which involves the receiver's assignment of a meaning to the message different from that intended by the sender.[11] Finally, the question must be faced as to how much, and what kind of, effect does the message have on the activity it was intended to influence.

The value of Weaver's analysis of the communication process is that it breaks down the problem of influencing consumer decisions into three critical parts, each of which must be clearly understood before a successful program of persuasion can be designed and used. Most commercial advertising-rating devices, for example, deal with Levels A and B as one problem. These services rate an advertisement in terms of how many people see it, how many remember the name of its sponsor, or how many readers remember what parts of its message. The "effectiveness problem" has not received the same amount of attention and study. The panel, it would seem, can provide information on this level as well as on the others. If a panel respondent purchases a certain product, his purchase can be related to his contact with advertisements and other sources of information regarding that product. The repeated interviews which make up panel data should also produce information on the relationship between the frequency of exposure to an advertisement and its effectiveness.

This discussion of the effectiveness of influences on behavior implies the ability to measure—or at least assign ranks to—the various factors which influence consumer behavior. Some very interesting work on evaluating influences has been published recently by Katz and Lazarsfeld.[12] The method of measuring impact of influences consists of two parts. The first deals with *specific influence questions*, which ". . . are designed to bring out through the retrospection of the respondents, all the cases in which a personal contact or an advertisement or a story played however minor a role in the whole process which ended with the specific decision under consideration."[13] The second deals with a number of *assessment questions*, which ask each respondent to name the most important single factor influencing a specific decision he has made. An index of the impact of an influence may then be computed by singling out those persons who were exposed to that influence, and computing the proportion of persons who thought this influence most important.

In addition to the technical problems mentioned above, there is the problem of cost. The research that may be carried on with the panel approach is more complex and costly than the standard research approaches. In spite of this, on the basis of the results that panel research has produced in the election studies, the marketer would do well to apply the panel device to the study of consumer decision-making. The justification for research expenditure should not be solely the number of dollars involved but how this research expenditure may increase the effectiveness of advertising and marketing procedures. For the marketer, the problem is in the realm of decision functions—what are the likely consequences of each of the several research approaches (including no research) available to him; what are the costs of each of these procedures? He must make his choice in the light of these two sets of data.

Panels have been used in market research for years. Although some of these panels have been concerned with problems of analysis of change, most have not.[14] The rationale for most market research panels set up and used in the past has been the greater economy and/or greater reliability of the panel as compared with independently selected samples of respondents.

If several waves of interviewing are needed to complete a study, it may be less expensive to select one sample (and interview it on each wave) than to select a new sample for each wave.

As for the greater reliability of panel results: if the aim of the study is to measure differences between the successive waves of the interviews, an observed difference between two panel visits is, under certain conditions, more likely to be real than the same difference observed between two independent samples. This can be seen if we compare the variances of a difference between two panel interviews and the difference between two independent samples.

In the case of two panel interviews, the expression for the variance of an observed difference is $\sigma_p{}^2 = \sigma_1{}^2 + \sigma_2{}^2 - \rho_{1,2}\sigma_1\sigma_2$ where
$\sigma_1{}^2 =$ variance among observations taken at time 1
$\sigma_2{}^2 =$ variance among observations taken at time 2, and
$\rho_{1,2} =$ the correlation between observations taken at times 1 and 2.

In the case of two independent interviews, the variance of an observed difference is $\sigma_i^2 = \sigma_1^2 + \sigma_2^2$. Thus, when $\rho_{1,2}>0$, as is often the case, $\sigma_p^2<\sigma_i^2$.

Although these reasons for using a panel are real enough and deserving of the consideration received, the real contribution of the panel lies in the keener insights into consumer decision-making that it must lead to.

Only in the last two decades have social scientists attempted to study directly and in detail the processes by which individual citizens decide to vote and choose their candidates. The most fruitful device used in these elections has been the panel—at least two interviews with the same people in order to study how earlier voting intentions are carried out. In *Voting*, the authors compare the panel device to *process analysis*, an analytical concept developed by econometricians for studying the interrelationship of events occurring at different points in time.[15] A major problem in applying this kind of analysis to any problem such as decision-making, is the selection of key variables, knowledge of which would help to understand and predict these decisions. The contribution of process analysis to the identification of the key variables is that it is a *feedback* mechanism for research when feedback may be defined as "a method of controlling a system by reinserting into it the results of its past performance."[16] In this sense, hypothesized key variables may be tested by observations among panel members. The rejection of certain hypotheses leads to the rejection of the corresponding variables as controlling factors. At the same time, these same observations may suggest other hypotheses concerning key variables.

The richness of panel data, presented clearly in the voting studies, indicates the tremendous payoff that might be expected from a large-scale undertaking designed to trace the paths consumers take toward buying decisions and to describe the influences that guide them along these paths. For widest circulation of the results, such a study might well be sponsored by a group of companies or trade associations interested in learning more about consumer behavior.[17]

The meaningfulness of panel data on voting is amply illustrated in the voting studies in many areas, as, for example, the reported relationships between attitude changes and ethnic backgrounds and exposure to various media. Although the most important implications of the voting studies for market research are methodological, some of the substantive findings must be taken into account. For example, the conclusion that attitude changes tend to bring members of subgroups of the population into closer harmony with fellow members and to sharpen the differences among subgroups leads to very obvious questions about the consumer decision process: Are there similar group standards for buying patterns?[18] How strong are they? How likely is a member of a subgroup to violate these standards? Is the existence of a group standard a function of the type and price of product? If there are group standards, how are they set, how are they enforced? What roles are played by the various media, by dealers, and by friends?

The panel can locate such standards, if they exist, and then, through the several interviews, determine which respondents veer from these standards and under what pressures such deviations take place.

How else may panels contribute to market research? One of the more elusive problems of consumer research is obtaining validation of data collected in a consumer survey. The usual check on the validity of respondent testimony is a gross one: Survey A predicts that consumers will buy M million models of Brand X refrigerators in a given period. The actual number of models purchased is then compared to the estimate. Actually, this comparison confounds the concepts of *reliability* and *validity*, where "reliability" deals with reproducibility of the research results and "validity" concerns the value of the specific questionnaire as a predictor.

This entire area of choosing the correct or best predicting instrument has achieved prominence in recent years in the discuscussions of the applications of projective techniques to market research. The problem in selecting the correct predicting instrument is essentially the problem of questionnaire design. What questions will most accurately report what the respondent "really" feels or plans to do? Does the question "Do you plan to buy an automobile this year?" evoke a response in terms of well-laid plans or in terms of wishful thinking? Or will a more accurate prediction of automobile purchases this year be made on the basis of those respondents who can give evidence of having made plans to purchase a car?

The contribution of the panel toward assessing various predictors is that the difference between the actual and the predicted outcomes can be compared for each individual.

Another area in which panels could prove useful is in the evaluation of *test city* programs. It is common practice in marketing and advertising research to pretest new products or new campaigns in a "typical" city before their nationwide introduction. The measure of acceptance of the new product or the success of a campaign is the change in sales following the introduction of the product or campaign.

These tests could be made more effective by the use of panels that throw light on the decision process as influenced by the promotion campaign.

Still another area of the usefulness of panel research is its value as a control or checking device. As an integral part of an advertising and merchandising program, the panel would serve to indicate the changes—or lack of changes—the program may be effecting. These indications, in turn, would lead to recommendations to make those revisions in the promotional campaign which would either counteract or reinforce the observed changes among panel members.

In product advertising, the sales of a product are often a rough, albeit debatable, guide to the effectiveness of an advertising campaign. There is one area of advertising, however, which does not have even this gauge. This is the area of public relations or institutional advertising.[19] Large sums are spent annually on trying to establish good will on the part of the public toward some company, industry, or trade group. The attitudes of the public toward such bodies is a very nebulous thing—more subject to the level of economic activity, perhaps, than to advertising.

Although there may be no direct evidence to bring to bear on this point, the following relationship is suggestive. Correlation of the respondent's politico-economic position with his estimate of how well off he was at the time of the survey, produced the following percentage response in answer to the question: "Considering your income and the cost of living, would you say you are doing well today, just fair, or having a hard time getting by?"[20]

Politico-economic group	*Doing well*	*Just fair*	*Having a hard time*	*No opinion*
Strongly free market	41	48	10	1
Middle group	22	57	19	2
Strongly socialistic	11	54	34	1

That one's sense of well-being and one's position on free-market principles are related at least suggests the hypothesis that attitudes toward business groups may be related to one's well-being as influenced by the level of business activity.

Because institutional advertising involves such large sums annually, and because there are few indirect measures of its effectiveness, the lack of an adequate control program—such as the panel might provide—must mean a less than optimally effective advertising campaign.

Finally, the panel serves as an apt vehicle for testing hypotheses suggested by other areas of research. For example, learning experiments conducted by Hull suggest that, although the promise of reward for the performance of an action leads to better performances, the many repetitions of the sequence *stimulus-reaction-reward* tend to contribute to resistance to the desired performance which could in time result in deterioration of that performance.[21] The *inhibitory potential*, as Hull labels it, exists beyond any fatigue factor.

The finding suggests that the panel could be used to investigate the value of repetitive advertising in terms of negative as well as positive effects.

Other hypotheses are worth exploring in experiments on the effectiveness of communication—the audience's view of the sponsor and the effect this has on any communications from him; the effectiveness of a message which gives "both sides" of the story; etc.

In summary, the discussion presented above has dealt with the apparent value to market research of the panel as it has been employed in the studies on voting. In the analysis of change it permits, the panel yields insights into the "dynamics of . . . behavior" which are absolutely necessary for a more complete understanding of the consumer's actions.[22]

CHAPTER 8

Primary Groups and Political Party Choice

HENRY W. RIECKEN

One of the consistent findings of recent voting studies is that an individual's political preference is likely to be the same as that of his closest associates. There is ample evidence in the Elmira study that the individual voter tends to choose the same party his father customarily prefers; that husbands and wives tend to vote for the same candidate; that the same sort of agreement characterizes the friends, and, to a lesser extent, the co-workers of most of the Elmirans interviewed; and, finally, that people tend to vote like others of the same socioeconomic status and religious affiliation. In short, the Elmira study says that, for a given individual, the social environment tends to be politically homogeneous. Furthermore, most individuals are not exposed to opposite political views, for they discuss politics mainly with those with whom they agree.

In the light of this evidence, it is reasonable to believe that an individual's political party preference is stable. Most individuals are born into Democratic or Republican families, the evidence implies, choose as their spouses and friends people whose views are congenial to their own political heritage, and do not associate or communicate much with people of opposite persuasion. The picture emerging from this evidence is one of considerable political stability and homogeneity within primary groups. Before we accept such a depiction, let us inquire whether there is any support for it outside the Elmira study. For it might be argued that political stability of this sort would occur only in a town like Elmira, only in a predominantly Republican climate, or only in an election like that of 1948.

Fortunately, we can answer such objections without even asking that they be rationalized, for there is excellent supportive evidence for the findings of the Elmira research in several other studies.[1] Four of these (covering three different U. S. presidential elections and one British election) obtained the same finding regarding political homogeneity within the immediate family of the voter. Two of the studies substantiate the relationship found in Elmira between the vote of the present generation and that of their parents. Two surveys bear out the conclusions of the Elmira study with regard to relationship between one's own vote and that of friends and co-workers. In addition, there is a single study of young voters (aged 21-24) conducted in Cambridge, Massachusetts, in 1952 that offers corroborative evidence on all of the above-mentioned points.[2] These corroborative instances—drawn from a wide variety of places, times, and political climates—justify considerable confidence in the generalization that people who are closely associated tend to vote alike.[3]

GROUP MEMBERSHIP AND CONFORMITY. Several theoretical explanations have been put forward to account for the uniformities of behavior and belief observed among members of face-to-face groups. George Homans, for example, has developed a set of propositions using the variables of sentiment, interaction, activity, and norm. Assuming that norms (ideas about how one ought to behave or believe) exist or arise in primary groups, Homans has asserted that an individual will be the recipient of positive sentiment (i.e., liking) from others to the extent that his behavior and/or beliefs "live up to" their norms.[4] The generalization about voting behavior with which we are presently concerned can be derived from Homans' proposition by simply inverting it and assuming that individuals want to be liked by other members of the primary group, or groups, to which they belong. Therefore, they will endeavor to bring their opinions into line with the norms of each group.

An equivalent set of propositions (at the present level of generality) has been put forward by Festinger, Schachter, and their associates in the group dynamics school of social psychology.[5] Asserting that groups are characterized by varying degrees of cohesiveness (defined as the attractiveness of the group for a member), and that uniformity of opinion within the group on a relevant issue is, for various reasons, desired by group members, these researchers have demonstrated that group members will bring pressure to bear on those who deviate from a group standard (a belief or behavior, virtually equivalent to a "norm" in Homans' usage). Such pressure will take the form of communications to the deviate to bring his belief or behavior into line with the group standard. If the members of the group are unsuccessful in their attempts to persuade, they will tend to reject the deviate (i.e., express dislike for him). Finally, the power of a group to exercise this sort of influence successfully over its members will be a positive function of the cohesiveness of the group.

Although the focus of interest is slightly different in these two theoretical schemes, it should be clear that the observed generalization about voting behavior can be derived from either of them: that conformity in political opinions and voting behavior will bring rewards to the individual in the form of acceptance and liking from other members of his primary group(s); and that deviation will be followed by attempts to bring the deviate into line, or, if these do not succeed, by rejection. In short, to the extent that an individual likes his associates and wants to be liked by them, he will conform to their views on relevant issues. There seems to be no reason why this statement does not apply with as much force to political views as it does to other views, as long as political views are "relevant" to the particular primary group under scrutiny. This last phrase will turn out to be an important qualifier of the primary generalization and merits some discussion. Before embarking on that topic, however, some other points deserve emphasis.

The generalization being considered and the theoretical formulations about it are concerned with explaining stability and homogeneity of opinion among associated individuals. The actual findings of the Elmira study are that there is less than perfect homogeneity of political views and voting within primary groups, and that some people do depart from the voting habits they "inherit." If the explanation offered by the theoretical formulations cited above is sufficient for the moment to account for existing stability and homogeneity,[6] the next task is to investigate the conditions under which there will be instability and heterogeneity of political views.

It will be the object of this chapter to suggest some of the ways in which change may come about in political opinions.

More specifically an attempt will be made to account for both stability and change in only one aspect of political behavior; namely, adherence to or defection from one of the two major parties in the United States as reflected in the popular vote for presidential candidates. Restricting the aim of this chapter in such a fashion does not imply that other aspects of political behavior are unimportant; rather it is motivated both by limitations of space and by the intention to stay within the primary frame of reference of *Voting*. Furthermore, the attempted explanation will be deliberately biased in centering on sociopsychological variables concerned with interpersonal relations, and it will try to account for as much of the data on party preference as possible in these terms. Again, the restriction of purpose does not imply that variables other than changes in interpersonal relations are of no consequence. It is imposed mainly to see how much work a simple set of variables can perform.

SOURCES OF POLITICAL CHANGE IN PERSONAL RELATIONSHIPS. The foregoing account of stability and homogeneity in political attitudes and behavior has attempted to explain these phenomena in terms of the individual's relationship to primary groups—their attractiveness to him and his desire to live up to their norms in order to be accepted in the groups. A consistent formulation therefore demands that we seek the sources of instability and heterogeneity in the same terms, that is, in terms of relationships to primary groups. We can begin by suggesting the general hypothesis that when an individual becomes detached or alienated from the primary groups in which his political views were acquired or maintained, then these views will be open to change. Furthermore, we might reasonably expect that whether his views do in fact change or not will depend on the norms of the new groups in which he acquires membership. Let us now examine what evidence there is for such an hypothesis.

Alienation from Parental Opinions. In a recent study, McClosky and Dahlgren found that the voter's family of origin has a very important influence on both the formation and maintenance of political preferences. Furthermore, these investigators found that the stability of political preferences acquired from parents was directly related to the frequency of contact between the voter and his family of origin and to the attractiveness of its members for him. "The more often one sees and the more one likes his family, the greater is the probability that he will agree with parental views on politics."[7]

On the other side, in her study of the young voter in Cambridge, Massachusetts, Eleanor Maccoby reports that "it is the children of the parents who attempt to exercise strictest control over children in their teens who most often change away from the political preference of their parents."[8] She infers from this finding that the young voters subjected to strict control by their parents were rebelling against such treatment and taking political opinions as an avenue to demonstrate their resentment. Parenthetically, Dr. Maccoby notes that there is some evidence, though not definite data, that "the effects of parental training methods on political conformity seem greatest when the parents have a high level of interest in politics."[9] In short, when politics is a relevant issue for the family group, attempts at overstrict control are more likely to produce rebellion manifested as political difference from parents than when politics is of little importance or relevance. As Dr. Maccoby remarks, in the latter case, presumably children "will choose *some other area* of values in which to . . . register their protest."[10]

While Dr. Maccoby's data are concerned with one specific source of feelings that may lead to alienation from parental opinions, a recent paper by A. J. Brodbeck and H. V. Perlmutter suggests a more general proposition.[11] These authors assert that unsuccessful socialization may, through generating self-dislike in a child, lead to exaggerated rejection of parental values and strong preferences for out-groups. Brodbeck and Perlmutter provide evidence that self-dislike in an individual is correlated with xenophilic tendencies. They found that college students who expressed strong and consistent "agreement with . . . statements favoring the European 'way' over the American" had significantly stronger feelings of self-dislike than those who held European culture in lower esteem. The researchers provide no data on parental attitudes, but if one makes the plausible assumption that the parents of their high self-dislike subjects were not themselves xenophilic, the finding can be interpreted as indicating another source of tendency to rebel against parents' values.

Although this evidence is not directly relevant to the topic of intergenerational changes in voting preferences, the generalization of Brodbeck and Perlmutter's findings to our present concern does not seem exaggerated. Perhaps children who had dissatisfying experiences in the socialization process and thus came to have low self-esteem may tend to vote for the party opposite to that chosen by their parents. Such an hypothesis needs to be tested, but even in its present, tentative state, it suggests some highly interesting explanations of the process of change in political party preference. Furthermore, it is important to note, this hypothesis is consistent with the theoretical position of research workers in group dynamics outlined above.

Vertical Social Mobility. Strong self-dislike or rebellion against overstrict control are not the only, nor even the most common kinds of alienation from one's family of orientation. A much more likely—and perhaps more subtle—shift in values may take place when young adults move up the ladder of social mobility to positions higher than those occupied by their parents. To the extent that primary groups at the higher socioeconomic levels have different values from those at lower levels, it is reasonable to expect upwardly mobile individuals to experience a shift in values toward those of the higher level groups as they begin to associate with members of the latter and seek social acceptance from them. It is a well-demonstrated fact that, in the United States, the higher the socioeconomic status of members of a group, the more likely they are to have Republican political preferences. Upward mobility, therefore, signals not only alienation from parental values in general but the likelihood that political preference will shift from Democratic to Republican since the upwardly mobile person will be moving into predominantly Republican affiliations in primary groups.

That such a shift in political preference does take place is well substantiated by the data in *Voting*. Young voters whose occupation is higher in status than that of their Democratic fathers show stronger Republican tendencies than do those voters who have occupations that are the same or lower than father's. The tendency is particularly marked when father's occupation is in the lower half of the occupational status range. Dr. Maccoby's data illustrate the same phenomenon even more clearly; upwardly mobile young voters are more likely to be Republican and less likely to be Democratic than the nonmobile individuals in the class where the upward mobiles originated. Except for the fact that they are much less likely to declare themselves "Independent," the upwardly mobile show a pattern of political choice quite similar to that of the nonmobile individuals in the class to which the upward mobile are moving. The data of McClosky and Dahlgren also give support to this relationship between mobility and deviation from parental opinions.[12]

The Instrumental Function of Political Opinions. Implicit in the view taken here of these data is the notion that political preference is often used in an "instrumental" fashion to forward one's acceptance in a group—peers, neighbors, co-workers, and the like—or to express rebellion against one's parents. In the vast majority of cases, changing one's party preferences is an unconscious process that takes place gradually as one becomes persuaded of the correctness of the views held by members of the groups he is joining. Sometimes, of course, changing one's opinions may be more self-conscious, especially if the new opinions are regarded as prestigeful or as characteristic of a group by which one explicitly wants to be accepted. Such self-conscious adoption of new values is a kind of "anticipatory socialization," which both aids people in being accepted in a new group and also eases their adjustment to its characteristic activities and attitudes.

This kind of anticipatory socialization has been found in other contexts. Merton and Kitt point to the instrumental role in acceptance that certain attitudes (especially toward entering combat) may have for the replacement in a veteran division, but not for the inexperienced soldier in an untried division.[13] To draw the parallel closer to our present interest, we can hypothesize the same sort of anticipatory adoption of prestigeful political views among those with aspirations toward upward social mobility. In short, the more ambitious members of lower socioeconomic status groups are more likely to be Republican in their political preference, even though their actual status has not yet changed. None of the studies considered here provide the data needed to test this hypothesis, but, if it is correct, it may well help to account for some of the apparent contradictions between political choice and rational economic self-interest, especially among lower-paid white-collar groups.

The "instrumental" use of opinion change, in the sense used here, does not mean simply that individuals will change their opinions to accord with the norms of groups into which they are moving, but that such change will occur only if the individual wants to be accepted by and identified with the particular group. Opinion change will not occur if the individual's membership in a category or a group is involuntary and unsought—perhaps even rejected—by him. Thus, in Eleanor Maccoby's study of young voters, *downwardly mobile* individuals are more likely to be Republican than the class into which they descended and slightly more Republican than even the nonmobile individuals in the class from which the downwardly mobile came. In Dr. Maccoby's own words: "It appears, then, that those who move up the social scale seek to identify themselves with the political values of the higher group, but those who move down cling to the symbols of their former status."[14]

The foregoing discussion of social mobility and opinion change has tended to slur a distinction that is important—the distinction between sociological categories, such as socioeconomic status, and actual membership in particular primary groups. It is important to make clear here that the process of opinion change being hypothesized does not rest on the fact of sociological classification, but on the assumed corollary of actual membership in primary groups, such as families, neighborhoods, clubs, or working or recreational groups. When an individual's socioeconomic status changes there is a parallel change in his associates—his neighbors, co-workers, and his friends off the job. The new job or the new neighborhood supplies social pressures that act on the newly arrived person to bring him into line with the norms of the group. Some individuals may be able to resist such pressures and continue to find affiliative satisfactions in the company of their former associates, but they are probably the exception rather than the rule.

Horizontal Social Mobility. While vertical social mobility is perhaps the most common, it is by no means the only occasion for change in political opinions. Indeed, any sequence of events that separates an individual from the primary groups in which he has had membership and presents him with others in which he *wants* membership offers an opportunity for change in his values, opinions, and behavior. Moving from the city to the suburb or from the South to the North may alter one's political stand. The only requisite for a particular change (e.g., from Republican to Democratic preference) is that the groups into which the individual moves have different norms about the opinion, value, or behavior area in question, and that the area is relevant to the interests of each group. Thus, for example, being drafted or going to college may offer the young voter an opportunity to switch political allegiance. The latter case is perhaps best documented by Newcomb's well-known study of a college community during the late thirties when the political climate there was fairly "liberal."[15] He showed that those students from "conservative" homes who achieved acceptance in the college community (and who, presumably sought it), rejected the political opinions of their parents and switched to the prevailing liberal norms. Furthermore, those students who retained the conservative opinions they had acquired at home failed to be accepted by their college mates. In this connection, it is important to notice that politics were an important, a relevant, a salient issue at the college during the period of study. At another time or another college, the sort of opinion upheaval that Newcomb observed might well fail to happen.[16] It is not simply the fact of going to college that produces political (or any other kind of opinion) change—it is going to a college where politics are a relevant issue for the academic community (or for the subgroups of that community in which a particular student moves) that makes change likely.

ASPECTS OF RELEVANCE. Although relevance, or importance, is a familiar psychological variable, its dimensions and properties have not been very clearly spelled out, and the multiplicity of terms that have been applied to essentially the same phenomenon attest to the difficulty of conceptualizing it. Intuitively most people would agree that some issues or some areas of behavior and belief are more prominent, salient, relevant, important, significant, crucial, central, essential, critical, or serious for a group than others are. Somehow, all of these terms point to the attention, time, energy, and other scarce resources that are devoted to such issues; or to the weight attached to them; or the interest taken in them. Some things matter more than others. Some things are appropriate for a group to act upon and it is worth taking effort to try to influence members on such things. A teacher tries to influence a child's conception of arithmetic but not his taste in clothing; the opposite may be true for his parents. A scientific society has norms about the papers a member reads at a convention but cares little about his behavior in the hotel bar; often his wife and children reverse the priority. Such examples can be indefinitely multiplied at this obvious level, and the same phenomenon is only a little less obvious when one looks at families or groups of friends or co-workers in connection with politics. Although there may be quadrennial cycles of interest in political affairs. it is clear that some primary groups are much more interested, active, and concerned about political matters than others are. No attempt will be made here to deal with the question of what forces or events make a particular issue relevant in a particular group. Obviously, however, an issue connected with the success, survival, or major purpose of a group will be considered relevant. In the absence of such an issue, importance may be attached to a topic, a problem, or an area of behavior or belief for reasons of tradition or because the idiosyncratic interests of prestigeful members of the group lead them to concern themselves with it.

Correspondingly, there are differences among individuals in the degree to which political matters concern or interest them, entirely apart from whatever level of interest there may be in the various primary groups to which they belong. Again, only some of the reasons for individual differences in level of interest can be suggested here: personal involvement in political activities, the demands of a particular occupation, or perhaps the continuance of an interest fostered by having read about or having known a political figure. Whatever the origin, the fact of differential relevance of politics is as well established for individuals as it is for groups.

The Effects of Relevance on Homogeneity of Opinion. At several points in this chapter the relation between relevance and the operation of group pressures toward uniformity of opinions has been noted. It has also been said that we should expect to observe change in political opinion or voting as a result of joining new groups of people, only if political behavior was "relevant" or "important" to the members of the group—especially, relevant or important enough for the group to have a standard or norm about how one should vote or opine on political issues. What is true of change is also true of stability; that is, we should expect to find stability of political opinion only in those primary groups whose members attached sufficient importance to politics to support a group norm about political behavior. Such an expectation is confirmed by the observations of McClosky and Dahlgren who say: "The greater the initial intensity of political belief and affiliation of parents, the more likely are their children to hold the same party preferences and to hold them stably."[17] To extend this line of reasoning further, we could say that the greater the importance (or "relevance," etc.) of political behavior in a group, the more strictly will the standard of appropriate political behavior in a group be defined, and/or the stronger will be the pressure applied to group members to conform to that standard. Consequently, we should expect to find homogeneity of opinion increasing as the relevance or importance of an issue becomes greater in a group.

Furthermore, the salience of politics for an individual can be expected to exert a parallel effect on his relationship to his social environment. It has been asserted frequently that there is a general tendency for friendships to develop among people of similar values, tastes, and opinions and also a tendency for individuals who have formed a friendship to adjust differences in values by changing or modifying their original positions in the direction of greater agreement. The existence of these general tendencies toward "value homophily" would lead us to expect homogeneity between the values and opinions of an individual and the norms of those primary groups to which he belonged.[18] Therefore, if politics are a salient matter for an individual, then we ought to find that the political norms in his primary groups supported the same party and candidate as he did or vice versa.

Such an expectation is partly borne out by the findings of the Elmira study, for it was observed that most respondents tended to agree politically with most of their associates in primary groups. But a sizable proportion (at least one-fourth) of the voters studied did have some co-workers, some friends, or perhaps even a family member with whom they disagreed on political matters. To say that such heterogeneity would inevitably arise, out of chance, in a population that was divided about 60-40 between the two major parties, is not a sufficient explanation. (If chance alone were responsible for assorting the political preferences of voters and their friends, co-workers, spouses, and relatives, the individual's social environment would have been observed to be much less consistent and supportive of his views than it actually was.) Rather, we should inquire why there was not a perfect homogeneity of political opinion among primary associates. Certain obvious answers suggest themselves: a man may choose a job because it pays well, or offers attractive work or good conditions—or for a dozen reasons—even though he opposes the political beliefs of those with whom he works; a man enters marriage in the expectation that it will be an emotional, psychological, and material improvement over his bachelorhood—not that it will be a political debating society; and a man chooses his friends because they are amusing, convivial, or enthusiastic about the same baseball team as he although they support the presidential candidate whom he disfavors. But all of these reasons can be reduced to the same general one: politics are less salient, important, or relevant for the relationship than is some other consideration.

Heterogeneity of Opinion and Relevance. Assuming the correctness of the analysis thus far, it would appear that a sizable number of voters in Elmira (and everywhere else, of course) find themselves in somewhat of a conflict. They are, on the one hand, attracted to certain friends, co-workers, and family members; on the other, they disagree politically with these associates. Unless politics are completely unimportant, the desire for affiliation with a particular person conflicts with the individual's desire for consistency in values and opinions between himself and his social environment. There are a limited number of ways in which this conflict may be handled. Breaking off the association means depriving oneself of gratifying friendships; but tolerating the inconsistency at an overt, conscious level may be painful. Perhaps the best technique for many people is to reduce, in essence, the salience or importance of political opinion to the disagreeing other. There is, of course, always the possible course of attempting to convert the other to one's own view, but the evidence from the Elmira study suggests strongly that such a resolution of the conflict is a minority activity. About 72 per cent of the voters interviewed in October in Elmira said that their latest political discussion had been with a person whose political preference was the same as their own. Furthermore, although about 25 per cent of the respondents had associates from the *other* party, only about 6 per cent of the discussions involved "some degree of argument between the discussants."[19]

A further piece of evidence from the Elmira study appears to support the notion that heterogeneity of political preference in one's primary associations is accompanied by a lowering of the importance of politics. Voters who belong to politically mixed friendship groups (i.e., where two or fewer of three friends agree with the respondent's political choice) are less likely to feel strongly about their voting intentions than are voters who belong to politically homogeneous friendship groups (i.e., where all three friends agree politically with the respondent). We should like a more precise measure of "importance" than we have here, but strength of feeling may be an approximate indicator.

It is possible to raise the question of direction in regard to the relationship we are examining: Do individuals to whom politics are of lesser importance exercise less political discrimination in selecting their friends? Or do those who find themselves in politically mixed company tend to play down the importance of political activity? There is no evident reason to believe a priori that one or the other of these sequences is the primary or the predominant one. The actual distribution of the sequences is a matter for empirical investigation, for whatever use there may be in knowing whether the chicken usually precedes the egg or vice versa. Certainly, some people do weigh political position in choosing their friends and yet there is some evidence that finding oneself involuntarily in a politically heterogeneous environment leads to diminution of the importance of politics.

The Elmira study confirms the earlier finding of the Erie County research that individuals subject to cross-pressures have a low degree of interest in the election. The authors of *Voting* use the term "cross-pressures" to refer to a variety of inconsistent and conflictful factors in the individual voter's situation—to the fact that he takes stands on issues that are inconsisent with his party preference; that he belongs to a socioeconomic class that is predominantly Republican, but to a religious group whose members are predominantly Democratic; and so forth. It does not seem unreasonable to believe that cross-pressures that are identified by sociological categories (e.g., "religious affiliation" and "socioeconomic status") are represented concretely in the individual's life-space by personal associates. In short, the cross-pressured voter is one who has two Republicans and one Democrat for friends. If this line of reasoning is correct, then surely the foregoing finding is evidence for the reduction of importance of politics when the social environment is politically heterogeneous. We may also note, in passing, that such cross-pressured individuals show other signs of conflict, such as delaying their voting decision and switching or alternating party choice. Perhaps these manifestations are also symptoms of attempts to reduce the salience of political behavior, or of having done so.

Finally, we note in the Elmira study that people for whom politics are not a salient issue often comment on the futility, unpleasantness, and danger of political discussion. From the more detailed study by Baxter,[20] the authors of *Voting* list several reasons Elmira respondents gave for not discussing politics. Some of the accompanying illustrative quotations sound very much as if the respondents were making a conscious effort to avoid political discussion because of the conflicts and cross-pressures in which they find themselves: "I don't talk politics at the store because it's bad for business"; "All my neighbors are Democrats, so there's no use talking to them about it"; and, gloomiest of all, "Through the years I've seen different arguments and it is just not worth it."

Homogeneity of Opinion and Political Discussion. The picture of political activity in primary groups that emerges from the Elmira study then is quite different from the traditional notion of free and open controversy of ideas at all levels of society, which leads the individual voter after an examination of all sides of a political question to arrive at a considered choice of "the best man" or the better party. Rather, it seems, as the authors of *Voting* note, that political discussion is concentrated among people of the same political preference and "consists more of the exchange of mutually agreeable remarks than of controversial ones. . . . there is relatively little political exchange among the electorate in the sense of open differences of view.[21] This finding accords with what is known about the self-selectivity of voluntary audiences; namely, that the hearers or readers of the material presented by a particular side of a controversial issue are mostly those who are already convinced of the correctness of that side's position.

What, then, is the function of such discussion? What roles does the "exchange of mutually agreeable ideas" have? It seems most likely that it serves to reinforce the decision already made, to reduce any doubts the individual may have about the correctness of his choice, and to bolster sagging confidence. This interpretation is supported by the findings of an ingenious experiment by May Brodbeck.[22] She found that individuals whose confidence in their opinion on a controversial issue had been weakened by exposure to a strong speech for the opposite point of view preferred to listen to arguments in favor of their original position following the speech, and that, when they were given the opportunity to do so, they tended to regain their confidence in that opinion.[23] The parallel between Dr. Brodbeck's experiment and the situation of the average voter is almost exact. No doubt the voter is exposed, during an election campaign, to mass-media presentations of the views of the "other side" from his own. Perhaps, as he hears or reads speeches by the leaders of the other party, his confidence in his choice is weakened, temporarily. But it can be, and evidently is, restored in primary group discussions, by the "exchange of mutually agreeable ideas" favoring the original choice he made.

The role of primary groups in political behavior, then, is to reinforce the opinions the individual originally acquired in such groups. When an individual's group memberships are stable and all of the groups he belongs to are politically homogeneous, there is every reason to believe that his political preferences will also remain stable, perhaps even throughout his life. Each assault on his convictions through the mass media or through interpersonal communication can be countered by supportive arguments for his original position from within the primary groups. It is only when some break in these attachments appears that the opportunity for change enters.

FACTORS AFFECTING CHANGE IN POLITICAL OPINIONS. When the opportunity arises for the individual to join another primary group with opposite political norms, the likelihood of a break from old attachments depends partly on the relative importance, or salience, of politics as an issue for the individual and for the groups concerned. To the extent that some other kind of behavior is more important to an individual than politics are—say, for example, getting a college education, holding a better job, marrying a particular person, or moving to a better neighborhood —the opportunity for political change is opened. If the alternative primary group attachments accompanying these new kinds of behavior also imply group norms (about politics) that are contrary to the individual's initial political position, then he may change his position. Whether he does so or not will depend on several factors: (1) the relative attractiveness of the new primary groups compared to the old ones; (2) the relevance, or importance, of politics in the new groups and in the old ones, which will determine the amount of group pressure that will be brought to bear on the individual in any attempt to influence his political opinions; and (3) the importance, or salience, of politics to the individual himself. Factors (2) and (3) will strongly influence the individual's ability to tolerate inconsistency between his own views and those of his associates.

These three factors probably interact in complex ways, and it is difficult to make a general statement as to which are "independent" and which "dependent" variables; or to say, a priori, what the most common empirical relationship among them is. We can, however, make a few guesses that may suggest hypotheses for research. Obviously, the individual who is born into a family where politics are highly salient, and who finds few issues more interesting and few groups more attractive than those in which he grew up, is not likely to show either political change or appreciable conflict. Although there may be many such people in the world, they are of little interest for research. They contribute to the stable core of the contending political parties, and help to account for political stability in this country.

Somewhat more interesting is the individual who grew up in a primary group environment where politics were of relatively low relevance or importance. In the first place, he would probably select his associates and group memberships on a nonpolitical basis. If his other interests should lead him to form attachments to new primary groups with contrary political norms, we might expect to find him switching his political preference, and doing so with relatively little conflict, while retaining his attachments (perhaps in dilute form) to the "old" primary groups, provided that politics were not a salient issue in the new groups he joined. If politics were important in the new groups, we should expect to find the individual experiencing moderate conflict. He would probably cut off contact with the "old" groups, and he might well find politics becoming a much more important part of his life. Alternatively, he might try to retain both sets of attachments and to make politics a relatively unimportant issue personally.

If politics were fairly important in both the old and new groups, we would expect to find the individual in high conflict and to exhibit the characteristic symptoms of the cross-pressured individual—low interest in an election, changes in voting choice during the campaign, and delay in voting decision. Depending on how successful these evasive maneuvers were, and how much power the individual had to alter his primary groups relations,[24] we might expect him to remain in the conflictful situation for varying lengths of time. Ultimately, we would predict, the pressure of the conflict might become strong enough to cause him either to break off with the "old" groups or to cease trying for membership in the "new" ones. Which of these alternatives he would choose would depend presumably on how he valued the rewards or gratifications that each group could hand out. In part, then, cross-pressured voters may be people who are in social transition—from one social class to another, or from one set of primary group attachments to another. There may be others who are somehow caught between primary groups in political disagreement, and who have no alternative but to minimize the role of politics—e.g., a Republican storekeeper whose customers are mostly Democrats.

There is one further strategy open to the cross-pressured individual when politics are a salient issue among his associates. He may follow a course of overt agreement with the views of his associates while covertly he remains attached to the opposite party. The privacy of the voting booth and the utter anonymity of a single vote in a sizable electorate favor this sort of "public compliance without private acceptance."[25] Such an adaptation to the conflict may be fairly common, although there appears to be no information on it and it would be understandably difficult to secure accurate data on this kind of behavior. But, no matter what the empirical frequency, it seems likely that publicly agreeing with one party while privately supporting its opponents is in itself painful, because of its inconsistency, and the more painful if politics are important. We would predict, therefore, that such behavior is at best a temporary adaptation which tends to break down either through an effort on the individual's part to rearrange his primary group attachments toward greater consistency, to change his own (private) opinions, or to reduce the importance of politics.

Finally, we are able to construct from this model, a tentative picture of the typical "independent" voter, a picture that is in striking contrast to the stereotype of the politically rational, alert man who has not sold his loyalty to either party but who judges candidates and issues on their merits. He is probably an individual who, if he has strong primary group affiliations at all, is likely to be linked to politically heterogeneous groups where politics are of low relevance, and he himself probably considers politics fairly unimportant. He is likely to associate with people who do not talk much about politics, and probably avoids attachments to groups where politics are of major concern. As the authors of *Voting* remark: "The classic 'independent voter' of high interest but low partisanship is a deviant case."[26] Independence of vote, as inferred from our model, is equivalent to political indifference.

A MODEL OF POLITICAL CHANGE. What will be proposed below is a scheme for explaining political change that depends fundamentally on changes in the primary group affiliations of the individual. It is suggested that: (1) homogeneity of political preference in primary group affiliations will lead to stability of an individual's political opinions; (2) the relative attractiveness of primary groups that are politically opposed will determine the individual's decision for or against joining a new group or giving up an old one [note that the "attractiveness" of a group may depend in part, or for some individuals, on the political complexion of the group]; (3) joining a new group or leaving an old one may change the amount of pressure on an individual toward conformity to a norm of political preference; (4) when political heterogeneity is introduced into the individual's primary group affiliations, and politics is moderately or highly important in these groups, he will be put into conflict, and may well try to reduce the unpleasantness of the conflict by minimizing the importance or relevance of politics to himself or by avoiding any kind of political activism or expression of opinion; and (5) if the unpleasantness of the conflict is stronger than the positive consequences of maintaining a particular association or set of affiliations, the individual will cut off his attachment to the group(s) on one side of the conflict. When there is some orderly sequence of change in the political complexion of one's associates, such as seems to occur typically for the upwardly mobile person of lower-class origin who moves from a uniformly Democratic through a politically mixed set of affiliations to a uniformly Republican society, then we should expect to observe the sequence: convinced Democrat; Independent (or indifferent); convinced Republican. Depending on the speed with which the social transition is accomplished, the middle stage of conflict and indifference may be brief and difficult to detect because evidence of it may not appear in readily observable behavior. But it seems doubtful that this stage is ever entirely absent.

This model is only a plausible one. There is comparatively little evidence for the sequence of movement hypothesized above, and, indeed, most of the evidence available from studies of voting is either tangential or else ambiguous enough to permit other interpretations than the one suggested here. A more rigorous test, employing data more closely fitted to the needs of the model, is desirable.

The Utility of the Model. It should be obvious that the power of the model to explain stability of political adherence is greater than its power to explain change. It suggests plausible reasons why individuals continue to vote consistently for the same party in election after election, and it helps to account for the enormous stability of the proportion of popular vote that each of the major parties has received in presidential contests over the last thirteen decades. In the thirty-one presidential elections (1832-1952), there have been thirteen in which the Democratic party's share of the two-party popular vote has changed by more than 5 percentage points from the preceding election and in only six of these did the change exceed 10 percentage points. On the thirteen occasions since 1828 when control of the presidency has changed hands, the shift in popular vote has usually been small: in only five elections (1840, 1860, 1912, 1920, and 1932) has the Democratic party lost or gained more than 10 percentage points compared with its share of the two-party popular vote in the preceding presidential election.

It is in explaining these major shifts of party allegiance that the proposed model shows its weakness most clearly. Yet, even here, it is not without value. Consider the five elections named above: three of them (1840, 1920, and 1932) occurred shortly after a major depression or a major war—in short, in times when there was unusual social mobility, both horizontal and vertical. Just how much contribution the factor of social mobility made to the variation in popular vote on these occasions is not at all clear, nor would it be contended here that the model can account for all of the change that occurred. But the connection between the events and the prediction from the model is plausible.

In the two remaining elections (1860 and 1912), where the proportion of two-party popular vote changed radically, there was no immediately preceding war or depression. Both years were, in fact, peaceful and relatively prosperous. The striking feature of these two elections is the effect of major third parties in draining off votes from the Democrats in 1860 and the Republicans in 1912. Analysis of these two elections in terms of our model is greatly complicated by the third-party vote. In point of fact, in both of these years the proportion of total popular vote received by the party that was *not* split did not change greatly from the immediately preceding election. (In 1856, the Republicans received 42.0 per cent of the popular vote, and in 1860, 45.7 per cent; in 1908 the Democrats received 45.5 per cent of the popular vote, and in 1912, 45.0 per cent.)

Such competitions for votes from third parties are not to be considered "extraneous factors," however, or *ad hoc* explanations to take care of defects in the model. Rather, they point to a feature of primary groups that we have heretofore ignored and that we can touch on only very briefly here, that is, changes in group norms. In other words, although primary group affiliation may remain stable, the norm or standard of behavior to which group members adhere may itself undergo a change. The circumstances under which norms change are manifold and their exposition is outside the scope of our discussion. To some extent, norms change because opinion leaders in a particular group may be influenced toward change by their attachments to other groups or to prestigeful people outside the groups in which they are leaders. To some extent changes in the social or economic environment of a group, uninitiated by its members, nonetheless may affect the welfare or purpose of the group and thus become a matter for concern and for the appearance of a new or a changed norm. For example, by 1860 the question of slavery had become so important an issue in both economic and humanitarian terms that most primary groups in the nation had defined group standards about it; and correspondence between these norms and the perceived stands of the presidential candidates seem to have been of overriding significance in the outcome of the election.

In 1912 there does not seem to have been any single issue of the sweep and significance of slavery. Rather, it seems that the personal attractiveness of Theodore Roosevelt was in great measure responsible for the 27 per cent of the popular vote he received, for his party ran far behind him—all but 4 per cent of the House of Representatives elected in 1912 were either Democrats or Republicans. Perhaps presidential candidates of great personal appeal are able to swing some voters away from adherence to group norms, or perhaps, like great issues, great men can be the source of new norms in primary groups.

CONCLUSION. Obviously, there has been space to give only the most superficial consideration to the many conditions that may have influenced the outcome of elections in which there have been spectacular swings in the division of the two-party vote. It would be absurd to imply that our model has explained such changes, for at most we can claim that the evidence can be interpreted in a fashion consistent with the terms of the model. It should be quite clear that the reach of the model is presently greater than its grasp. Potentially, it can contribute to the understanding of a wide variety of political behavior. In its present stage of development it is too abstract to yield specific predictions about concrete events in the natural world, and, if it is ever to make such predictions, several things must be done.

In the first place, further theoretical and logical development of the concepts of "relevance" is required. The psychological dimensions and conceptual properties of relevance need to be brought out, and some ingenuity and exploration put into ways of measuring the relevance of issues to individuals and groups. Secondly, there ought to be better ways than are now available to researchers for detecting and measuring pressures toward uniformity or conformity to norms in natural groups observed in the field. Similarly, more information is needed on how norms arise and change in groups, and some way of relating the *content* of norms to other properties of groups. Finally, the predictions of the model cannot be unequivocally tested with the kind of data presently available in most studies of voting. Specifically, it is necessary to demonstrate that group pressures toward uniformity do operate under the natural conditions of everyday political life; that political issues vary in relevance, and that pressures toward uniformity vary with the degree of relevance; and, finally, that individuals who change membership to groups with opposite political norms do experience pressure toward conformity and, under the specified conditions, conflict. If these requirements seem enormous in comparison to the present accomplishments of the model, let us notice that they are, at least, specific requirements that suggest programs of research.

CHAPTER 9
Voting and Voting Studies

LESLIE A. FIEDLER

It is a terrible thing to be a lion in a Daniel's den; but a humanist fallen among social scientists can scarcely help seeing himself in that absurd role. I have been interested for a long time in voting: in the meaning of the act itself and of the choices which that act involves. My interest has been especially poignant because so Platonic; I have, that is to say, actually voted only once in my life —and regretted it immediately afterward. There are, I tell myself, good superficial reasons for my failure to go to the polls: changes of residence and a consequent lack of knowledge of local candidates and issues, an early Marxist indoctrination against the whole notion of parliamentarianism. But I am not really sure why I have so strong a reluctance to vote; and I have sought to answer my questions about myself by speculating on my neighbors. Do they really believe that they are acting meaningfully when they put a cross before one of two names on a printed ballot? Do they vote to make a choice or make a choice in order to be able to vote; that is, is voting an act of social conformity. a symbolic gesture of belonging rather than a way of influencing government? Why do societies succeed in getting more and more people to vote as they become more and more totalitarian? Has the act of voting in its modern mechanical form (I see the voting machine as the visible and outward form of an invisible and inward process of dehumanizing choice) anything to do with traditional democracy at all?

I was disconcerted in turning to the three recent studies of voting I have been looking through (*Straight Fight*, *Voting*, and *The Voter Decides*) not so much by their failure to ask some of the questions that strike me as fundamental, as by their method. Different men must ask different questions, I know; for a study, whatever its pretenses at objectivity, is an attempt to define oneself as well as a social problem. But the dispassionate, scientific air of these approaches left me feeling inadequate, overwhelmed by their modesty and impersonality, and dazzled by the charts and diagrams, the clinical vocabulary (no one "thinks" or "guesses," but "conceptualizes"), the sophistication in the matter of statistics, and the precision of the sampling methods. I am almost ashamed to admit that the very notion of the "panel" interview was unknown to me; and that I had vaguely assumed all my life that a "random sample" was one made at random.

In the face of such professionalism and abstract concern, my own interest seems not merely amateur but almost animal, that is, passionate and instinctive; and so I have been indulging in the sentimental image of myself as a member of a lower species trapped in the lair of the prophets of science. Yet when I have turned to their prophecies, that is, to the results of their investigations, I have been disconcerted once more in quite an opposite direction. *Straight Fight*, for instance, informs us that, in one English urban constituency at least, a greater portion of the old, of women, and of the upper classes vote for the Conservative party, though, indeed, all three factors may be reducible to the single one of social class. To which the only adequate response is, "Uh-huh," or in more literary terms: we need no prophet come back from the grave (or panel interview) to tell us this! And when the same study goes gravely on to observe that "the behaviour of electors may perhaps be classified in terms of long-term trends and short-term fluctuations," the modest "perhaps" with which this platitude is proffered seems the final insult to one trained to wince at belaboring the obvious. I am similarly offended when it is ponderously established in *Voting* that Catholics tend to vote Democratic, or noted, with the air of having discovered some arcane truth, that "opinions are really formed through the day-to-day exchange of observations and comments which goes on among people." This even the naïvest of poets has observed, as he has also observed, merely by living, what *The Voter Decides* includes in its summary: "the results of both studies may be said to conform to the basic psychological principle that when strong and opposing forces act on an individual the resultant behavior will demonstrate the characteristics of conflict." This assertion, stripped of its technical vocabulary, does not even make the grade of a platitude but remains a simple redundancy: where there is conflict, there is conflict! And such a pleonasm is scarcely redeemed by applying it to the political situation and producing the further conclusion that a voter with contradictory convictions is less likely to vote and more likely to vacillate in his choice than one without them.

I do not wish to appear Philistine on this score; and I want to go on record as believing that sociology will yet survive such self-evident "discoveries," as it will survive parallel ones in other subfields, i.e., that rumors are less accurate as they spread out from a center, that people who talk about moving move more often than those who don't, and the like. I feel, however, that such banalities are the price American social science is paying for its current anti-intellectualism, its flight from theory; and I cannot help making some observations on the sociology of such sociology from the point of view of a not wholly unsympathetic outsider. I feel obliged to preface those observations with a note on the sociology of my own sociology of sociology; this is a process which opens up possibilities of endless regression, but here I promise I shall stop!

The humanist's image (or as we prefer to say, "myth") of the contemporary sociologist is that of a heavily subsidized, much-touted and honored scholar, torn at each moment between offers from industry and government—scarcely knowing, indeed, whether to take the rewards offered by the Coca Cola Company or the Air Force—for his latest documentation of some wearly cliché about man, long since a commonplace of literature. The humanist, made especially aware of the spiritual dullness and lack of intellectual curiosity in contemporary society by its indifference to great art, cannot help thinking of the sociologist's statistical wisdom as an ersatz for real insight into the social being of man; and he is likely to be caught muttering bitterly: "Sufficient unto the day is the social science thereof." Perhaps the wittiest expression of this rather unfair, but thoroughly understandable, reaction is found in two lines of Auden, a new commandment for modern life:

Thou shalt not sit with statisticians
Or commit a social science.

The humanist's case must, then, be discounted a little for the professional pique of the excluded which lies behind it; yet it is not without merit. The sort of statistical sociology (or political science) represented by these texts seems to him the result of two phenomena, both peculiar, in their strongest forms at least, to contemporary America: an almost neurotic impulse to self-examination and an almost religious regard for "scientific method." The spiritual hypochondria, the eternal feeling of his own pulse by the contemporary American is a standing joke among Europeans; and this eternal self-examination (rivaled only, if we can believe Dostoevski and Chekov, by nineteenth-century Russians) is not merely a matter of maudlin self-exposure at cocktail parties, but of endless polls, interviews, exposures, and candid statements to the press, ranging from the crassest journalism to the most cautious and methodical research.

These, the average American is not only delighted to participate in, but is pleased to spend his leisure time reading. From Kinsey's improbable best seller to the latest Gallup or Roper report in the daily newspaper, the American is at once creating and consuming a never-ending "Song of Myself": a monument to obsessive self-concern beside which Whitman's poem seems a masterpiece of selflessness. His voting habits are of especial concern to him, since the act of balloting tends to become his only even remotely political activity; and he wants to be told first how he is going to vote, then how he is voting (at two in the morning, he is still up beside his radio; and the great electronic gadgets of which he is so proud are adding him to all the other nameless units awake beside their sets), at last how he has voted. And he is not even averse to being told why, though the simple, gigantic figures are what interest him most. Like the sociologist on his more sophisticated level, the man by the TV believes that only quantitative truth is real.

Once given official sanction (and large budgets), such organized curiosity is insatiable; from the polls, to the altar, to the sickbed, to the grave—the experts we have hired to tell us all pursue us doggedly, notebooks in hand. I presume that the only reason we did not drop sociologists and psychologists into Hiroshima with the Bomb was a technical one; and I sometimes have a nightmare of our world after its final war, in which the sole man and woman left alive turn out to be a pair of sociologists, who after questioning each other scientifically, instead of getting down to reproduction, separate to write rival studies of "The Single Survivor." Yet the interest in self which lies behind such phenomena is not, however untrammeled, in itself really reprehensible. As a nation, we come by it honestly enough, out of the tradition of soul-searching so unexpectedly handed down by the Puritans to the emancipated, contemporary American of whatever origin. There is something really satisfactory and amusing in the notion of the social scientists as our Last Puritans.

It is only what the "self" becomes in the electronic calculating machines that gives me pause; for what the IBM cards can record or newspapers report is a statistical datum, abstract and unreal. I cannot finally convince myself that in our desire to know first especially and then exclusively the existence we share with others, experience that is *statistically* meaningful, there is a retreat from inwardness and the person as defined in literature and art. There is a kind of comfort, I am aware, a delightful sense of actuarial helplessness in learning that we are Democrats because of certain probabilities inherent in our generation and ethnic group—or adulterous because of our level of education. The panel method, for all its avowed desire to come to grips with individuals rather than with rows of figures, cannot handle those individuals except as instances of, say, the male sex, the forty-year-age group, the Protestant religion. The sort of peace with himself that man used to seek in the conviction that we are all sons of God, he seems now to find in the conviction that we are all specks on a bar graph between the covers of a scholarly book.

I do not believe, of course, that the studies I have been reading are the work of conscious or deliberate enemies of inwardness. They are written by men doing a job as conscientiously as they can in a society organized on the lines of a rigid division of labor. They are, in short, "specialists" rather than men at the moment that they write, and in that sense, the victims of a general panic in our culture, a flight from the person. A first symptom of this is their resolve to attest to their objectivity by drawing their metaphors for the individual from science rather than the humanities. The "sciences of man" (as they are sometimes called in the phrase that already gives away the game) hesitate between the natural sciences and literature and philosophy; but the poles do not stand still. And how can one blame the sociologist for abandoning traditional notions of man, when critics and philosophers, too, are abandoning insight to statistics, poetry to methodology—and even the professor of literature likes to boast that he is producing "research."

The embarrassment of the scientizing political philosopher and literary man alike is that he deals with a field in which there is (in a sense analogous to that of the physical sciences) nothing new to discover; though, indeed, certain older wisdom has to be taught again and again in new languages. I think at this point of Freud's plaint about having to tell men as if it were a revelation what every nursemaid knows. Both poet and social scientist are, therefore, necessarily engaged in redeeming platitudes; but the method of the poet is to specify and complicate the cliché, while the method of the sociologist is to quantify and simplify. A poet's pondering on the problems of filial ingratitude produces *King Lear*. A sociologist might by a series of panel interviews decide that ("perhaps" and "at least in one rather typical small court of pre-Christian England, selected because of etc., etc.") there is more of a tendency among grown daughters of kings showing signs of senility to evidence open hostility, if such kings give over their property completely to such daughters. A really canny investigator might even be able to show, within the normal statistical margin of error, of course, the percentage of such cases in which the father would finally be shoved out into a storm. To put it mildly, such information is irrelevant to any central human concern; though, to be sure, more than one Department of Welfare might be persuaded to put up funds for a continuing study along the same lines.

Yet the notion that knowledge about the relations of men to each other is not useful—not even really *true*—until it can be quantitatively expressed has taken over not only in the social sciences. The accidental (from any philosophical point of view) predominance of physical science in our culture and the confusion of that science in the popular mind with technology have lent prestige to all graphs, mathematical formulations, and equations, however, meaningless. The social sciences, precisely because they have come late into the field to which they aspire, and because they are suspected of continuing fraternization with such outmoded elite disciplines as religion, philosophy, and literature, feel obliged to ape especially sedulously the outward appearance of the more prestigeful methods of investigation. In the way a schoolgirl imitates the hair style of the reigning movie actress, so the social scientist imitates the mathematical statement and laboratory attitudes of the physicist. His world, too, can be reduced to numbers! *Wie m' goyisht sich, azoi m' yiddisht sich* (As the gentile is a gentile, so the Jew is a Jew)—the folk saying puts it.

Of course, there are rationalizations. "True," the sociologist retorts, "everyone always knew that things fell when one dropped them; but until such knowledge was quantitatively expressed as $S = \frac{1}{2}gt^2$, that knowledge was not practically of any consequence, and in the same way. . . ." But it is, alas, never the same way; at least, I have never seen any "sociological law" of the order of the law of gravity emerge from the most statistical analysis of a platitude. Indeed, one could scarcely look for such an event until the vagaries of the individual man become as indifferent to us as the wanderings of individual atoms. At this happily scientific stage, I trust we shall never arrive; and, indeed, it is because I feel an impulse in such a direction in statistical sociology and political science that I am a little wary of those disciplines.

One does not have to move to such large objections, however, because of the lack of smaller ones. The "quantitative method" as exemplified in these three studies leads to an insidious sort of half-conscious falsification, disturbing, I am sure, even to advocates of the method. For instance, in *The Voter Decides*, there is a striking instance of the tendency to hypostatize imaginary psychological categories, which can then be statistically manipulated in their interrelationships. In this case, the "manageable number of variables" turns out to add up to the fairy-tale number of three: issue orientation, party orientation, and candidate orientation; and though the writers begin by speaking of these as names, convenient labels, they end by the logic of their method in treating them as *things*.

More disturbing to me and more inevitable, I fear, is the way in which all three books are driven, for the sake of merely getting on with the problem, to treat all Republican or Democratic votes as equivalent to each other. I suppose that if one is to make any generalizations at all on this level about voting behavior, one must assume that all voters are making a choice between two relatively constant and distinguishable alternatives. Yet such are the complications of our party system to begin with, and of human motivation in the second place, that two people who are "black radicals," opposed passionately and ignorantly to the educated and rich, may vote one Democratic ("for the party of the people") and the other Republican ("for the party of the investigators who showed up those Harvard boys in the State Department"). Each of these may be paired off with a quite genuine conservative, one of whom takes the Whiggery of Eisenhower to represent his ideal, the other of whom finds the same ideal better personified in the genteel New Deal nostalgia of Stevenson. In such cases, is it not more bewildering than informative to treat arbitrary labels as indications of a real choice? The same impulse to make quantitative lists rather than qualitative discriminations leads to a lumping together of all non-voters, though certain refusals to vote may be real political acts, just as certain resolves to go to the polls may be abject surrenders to conformism, the rejection of politics. Such distinctions are perhaps impossible to make inside such an approach as we are examining; and I suspect that many of the investigators would find them as pointless and finicky as a qualitative distinction between orgasm and orgasm would seem to a Kinsey.

My final and chief objection to the statistical method in the social sciences in general is that it represents the triumph of an anti-theoretical drift, which seems to me one of the most regressive aspects of American scholarship. It strikes me, to put it as bluntly as possible, as yet another facet of a widespread, academic anti-intellectualism—part of the (real American!) quest to find a democratic substitute for something so aristocratic as ideas, some bureaucratic ersatz for the insight of the individual thinker. Sociological investigation becomes not merely quantitative in method but bureaucratic in its organization, not the child of pure science it would like to claim itself but a hybrid offshoot of mass production and industrial engineering, with techniques as impersonal and ultimately mindless as the production methods of a movie or a newsmagazine. One imagines the director of research with three phones on his desk, dreaming of the day of complete automation.

"Specialization" first and now "bureaucratization," these have been in the American university, in the schools of a country notorious for its resistance to general ideas, the respectable methods of substituting technology for theory. Such a retreat from speculation to "fact" begins with a healthy desire to escape the "ivory tower," to bring political science, say, down to the level of practical politics—to be immediately useful to ordinary men in their everyday concerns. This is not on the face of it an ignoble ideal; but it turns out to be merely the noblest disguise of the heresy of practicality which has turned our colleges into trade schools. To be sure, the investigation of opinion formation is *useful*, and it is no accident that it blurs into big business on the one side and journalism on the other; but such a usefulness is not the usefulness of science or of pure mathematics. It is the hallmark of the technological: and technology is the slave of the system it serves; it cannot challenge or teach, only blindly implement.

I suppose that below such theoretical levels, the development of mass faculties in mass universities has created an economic pressure for the invention of co-operative disciplines to replace individual talent. Only in an academy of the elite, can one expect Platos and Aristotles; we must find, and are finding, ways in which the mediocre can at once maintain their self-respect and be useful to their society. This is a necessity in a day in which the university is becoming more and more overwhelmingly a refuge for men of indifferent talent in search of status and security. In the beginning, the fact-compilers and the statistics-gatherers were humble and spoke as temple servants. They were mere collectors bringing in a fresh harvest of data against the day when some great, synthesizing mind would make of their harvest a new theory. But let anyone now dare to try to synthesize with the proper rashness and brilliance, and hear the vituperation heaped on him as a popularizer and robber of other men's ideas. The fact-snufflers, the truffle-hounds of science, have come to think of themselves as their own masters; the temple servants have set themselves up in the inner sanctum as priests. And who is there to challenge them in a society that more and more thinks of "facts" as more honorable than theories, of impersonality as more acceptable than personality, of graphs as more worthy than poems?

Of the three books I am discussing, *Straight Fight* is by all odds the worst offender in this regard: no idea contaminates the purity of its research. *Voting* is, in many respects, an honorable exception. Certainly, in its last two chapters, especially in the latter on "Democratic Practice and Democratic Theory," it moves out freely and interestingly into the realm of speculation; but, truly, I must confess that I find it hard to see how the detailed documentation that precedes those chapters is necessary to the posing of a question of which most of us are surely aware: How is it possible to maintain a belief in classic democracy now that we are conscious (and weren't the formulators of that doctrine conscious of the same thing, after all?) that the individual voter does not come up to the ideal qualifications they dreamed for him? The book does, however, resist the temptation to stay safely ensconced behind its figures and easy clichés, asking finally some of the questions at least which properly follow such an investigation.

It seems to me, however (speaking with all the irresponsibility of one whose primary commitments are elsewhere), that some theoretical speculations must be engaged in before *an investigation.* No one can begin, of course, without prior ideas and expectations; if he is not conscious of those ideas and expectations, he is likely to begin with ill-perceived general assumptions that will betray the finest sampling methods and questioning techniques. There are two areas especially where the lack of insight and theory seems to me evident in the studies with which I am concerned. First, the matter of class. In England, conventional notions of class status, resting on the traditional socioeconomic basis, seem to yield viable results; at least, there appears to be a real correlation between "class" in this sense and the way a voter makes his limited party choice. But in America, ordinary (which is to say, European-oriented) conceptions of class are confusing rather than helpful when applied to voting habits.

Let me deal here quite briefly only with the criterion of "education" which is used in *Voting* as one of the three main measures of SES. To ask only the quantitative question, "How many years of education?" is to establish a standard so gross that all really interesting distinctions escape it. I have a hunch that in America at the present moment a university education is in the process of becoming so general a cultural possession that it can scarcely be considered a cutting line between classes. The important questions now tend to be: night-school or day-time classes? city college or college away from home? agricultural school or arts college? general curriculum or school of education? Ivy League or Big Ten? A real distinction in status now could be established not so much from where a person happens to get his education as from where he is able to imagine getting it. If one insists on turning these things into questionnaires anyone can administer, perhaps the key question should be: Where do you look forward to sending your children to college? It seems to me, at least, that the limitation of ambition, even of imagination in such regards, is the clue to actual class status in the United States, not so much the matter of legally or even economically limited possibilities as of the limitation of aspiration and desire.

It is not, for instance, how much money a man has that fixes him in a certain class (for our classes, as they most effectively function, seem to me clearly "cultural" rather than economic), but what kind of ties, say, he would buy if he had money enough to make a free choice. What kind of clothing, what sort of house, which magazines, what books (if any) would he own? Would he drink beer or Martinis? Would he go to wrestling matches or polo matches? These are the matters that count. Indeed, a distinction closer to that we make in ordinary conversation between "highbrow" and "lowbrow" (in which years of education and income are secondary considerations) would be more to the point than inherited notions of socioeconomic class, or even the self-ranking of people who do not really share in this regard the assumptions of the questioner.

At least, if one began with such a standard, he would not produce the really useless and confusing conclusion arrived at by most of this research, namely, that the more educated group votes more Republican. This baffles my own firsthand knowledge, for instance, that university faculties (who are, after all, more educated than anyone) tend to be Democratic—or the special fact that in three English departments with which I have had intimate connections less than 5 per cent of the members voted Republican. What are the operative factors here? I certainly find no hint of them in any of the studies. In what groups does one lose caste by voting Republican? In what groups does he gain status by such a vote? What makes a vote either way *what one does?* The authors of *Voting* make the point quite clearly in one place that the voting decision is parallel in its formation to the formation of taste. I should guess that it is, often at least, precisely like other manifestations of taste, a way of asserting one's belongingness to a particular group, and that it should be studied in respect to the whole syndrome of taste. How many readers of comic books vote for Stevenson? How many people who do not know what an artichoke is prefer the Republicans? What is the connection between wearing hand-painted ties and party choice?

Finally, it seems to me (and here I return to where I began) that there is not in any of these studies sufficient prior speculation on the social meaning of the act of voting as such, opposed to the act of choosing one or another candidate; yet I do not see how one can begin to study the latter until he has distinguished from it and clearly understood the former. In recent years and in direct proportion, I would venture to guess, to the decrease in a really passionate concern with the outcome of elections, there has grown up an increasing public concern with having people *just vote*, no matter whom they vote for. Institutional propaganda in the press and over the radio insists more and more (even at the cost of time for publicity for the competing parties) on everyone's getting out to the polls; so that in the consciousness of the American citizen there is slowly established (of all people, he has been in his freedom of movement and choice relatively immune to this) the notion that not the considered act of deciding on candidates and issues but the mere mechanical act of voting is in itself his essential patriotic duty. To "go to church" (but what church?), to vote (but for whom?), to send his children to college (but what *sort* of college?)—these are the demands on anyone who asks respect from the community.

The whole mythology of voting has been transformed; the vote comes to be regarded as a public act of allegiance to an abstract "democracy" rather than a private decision as to what is good and what bad for the state. The "secrecy of the ballot" becomes an outmoded slogan; what matters is that the act of entering the polling place be *not* secret, known to everyone. That this is merely one symptom of a general drive for *participation* as a good in itself—regardless of its end—should be obvious. It links up closely with the parallel propaganda that nags at us from radio and television: Go to church this Sunday. Not to one church or other, just any church—not to assert your difference but your sameness: everyone the same in different places. It is notorious that we are in the midst of the strangest of all religious revivals, a renewed commitment to the abstract idea of religion rather than to any particular manifestation—in a nation where "man" is any man, "the church" is any church.

On every level of cultural life, this hunger for total participation replaces the older ideal of personal preference and threatens especially the freedom simply to withdraw or hang back. Even school children become subject to such pressures; the coming of Valentine's Day, for instance, no longer means that a boy brings, shyly or boldly, to some girl he has mooned over all year a lacy heart and a declaration of love; but that every kid under pressure brings for every other kid in his entire class some machine-produced greeting remembered the day before at the Five-and-Ten. One does not choose a special Valentine, but celebrates Valentine's Day. I have a hunch that our situation is already far gone in this respect when it comes to voting; but I should be interested in having the problem investigated (as long as the machinery is in motion) by someone with the means and techniques for such research. We seem to be at a critical point; for the abandonment of choice is one of the essential symptoms of a drift toward a totalitarianism of spirit and attitude which can presumably grow even inside a technically open society.

It is well known that in the full-fledged, total state, voting (once sentimentally regarded as the sufficient guarantee of democracy) far from being discouraged reaches new heights of enthusiasm and participation. It is pointless merely to speak of a perversion of the practice; something in the act of voting itself has apparently all along contained the seeds of its present uses. To be sure, in a totalitarian culture, the element of choice, already narrowed for us unredeemably, it seems, to two parties, is further minimized or eliminated altogether; and the whole process becomes purely what it was before only in part, a mass ritual of acceptance and conformity. In what sense and to what degree voting has already become for some of our people such a symbolic gesture of the surrender of personality is a question whose significance cannot be exaggerated. This question, so vital to us at the present moment, I would hope that some future researcher would have the intellectual temerity to ask.

CHAPTER 10

Suggestions for the Study of Mass-Media Effects

HERBERT BLUMER

A goodly number of social scientists and psychologists have studied the effects of mass media of communication. Their problems have ranged from narrow ones like comparing retention between oral and visual presentations to broad ones like determining the influence of mass media on voting behavior. Similarly their plans of inquiry range from broad exploration to exacting, if simulated, experiment. In spite of the variety of the studies, a basic similarity underlies the way in which the problem is approached. The student identifies the influence in the medium which he wishes to study, he identifies the people who are subject to this influence, and he seeks to ascertain the effects that result from the play of the given influence on the given universe of people.

Nothing would seem more natural or proper than to approach the problem for study in this manner. One pins down the influence, the people being influenced, and the results of the influence. This "pinning down" of the three objects of concern is customarily made by following the logic of "variable analysis." The aim is to make each of the three objects as precise and detached as possible. The medium-influence, as an independent variable, is isolated in a clean-cut fashion so that it stands forth as a discrete and qualitatively independent item. The people on whom the influence operates are given a fixed qualitative composition in such terms as age, sex, nationality, and socioeconomic status. The behavior presumed to result from the medium-influence is treated as a specific and qualitatively homogeneous item or series of items. The purpose of the study is to isolate a definitive and stable relation between these three objects, so that one may say that a specific medium-influence playing on a specific type of population will have such and such a specific result. To increase the likelihood of such a definitive finding, efforts are made to draw an accurate sample of the population, to eliminate or stabilize other influences that may be playing on the population, to use control groups, and to cast the independent and dependent variables into the form of quantitative units. It is believed that, if the study meets these methodological desiderata, the changes noted in the dependent variable represent the effect of the independent variable under the conditions specified. From such findings a set of generalizations is constructed on the influence of mass media.

This simple framework of inquiry, so characteristic of research into the effects of mass media, seems to be open to question. I wish to present reasons for suspecting that it does not faithfully reflect the operation of mass media in the real world, that it gives rise to the setting of fictitious problems, and that it favors false generalization.

The explanation of these suspicions must begin with a commonplace characterization of mass media and of the world of their operation. There are three simple features that need to be noted and discussed: (1) the variability in the presentations, or so-called "content" of the media; (2) the variability in the responsiveness of people due chiefly to an intervening process of definition; and (3) the interdependent connection of all forms of communication.

What is presented through mass media—the so-called "content"—varies enormously and continually. This variation becomes obvious not only by comparing the media but also by examining the content of any one of them. I am not referring merely to different kinds of material in a given medium as in a newspaper with front-page news, editorials, financial page, and sport section. Instead, the reference is more to the varying character of what is presented from day to day in any one of the component parts. This changing character of the presentations is true obviously of all mass media—motion pictures, newspapers, radio programs, and television programs. Mass media are geared to a moving world; all of them seek, so to speak, new presentations and indeed are forced to give such new presentations. The professionals who man the media and are responsible for what is presented are under pressure to offer something new and different; satisfying such a demand is part of their job. These commonplace observations show clearly that what is presented by mass media is highly diverse and undergoing continual alteration. What their "audiences" see, hear, and read is essentially always changing.

Next, a similar variation exists in the sensitivity or responsiveness of the people touched by mass media. By now students of mass communication realize that effects cannot be safely gauged from the "manifest" content of what is presented through a medium. It is necessary to consider how people in the audience are sensitized to the presentation and prepared to interpret it. Such sensitivity and responsiveness differ not only between people in the given audience but more importantly in given people through time. People are caught up in a world of moving events, which foster new objects of preoccupation, new lines of judgment, and new orientation of feeling. As issues arise or subside, as new interests emerge or recede, as sophistication replaces naïveté, or in many other ways, people shift in their sensitivity to presentations and in their interpretation of them.

Finally, the different media of communication are interdependent. They deal to a considerable extent with the same series of happenings; the producers in each medium are familiar with what is presented in the other media and are guided in measure by such presentations; further, people usually attend to a number of media and thus merge in experience different presentations of the same things. The consequence is that the media cannot be regarded as operating in separate and clearly demarcated areas, but rather as flowing into a vast common arena. For instance, much of what is handled in the press is treated over radio and through television, and is considered, further, in conversation and local speech. What emerges as striking in local discourse may gain expression or reflection in mass media. All major channels and forms of communication are intertwined in a vast communicative process.

The variation in presentations, the variation in responsiveness, and the interdependency of media challenge seriously the methodological scheme which, as explained above, is followed in practically all research into the effects of mass media. As suggested above, this prevailing scheme presupposes the following: (1) the isolation of an independent variable, consisting of the given form of communication under study; (2) the identification of the given universe of people and of the given type of their behavior subject to the play of the form of communication; and (3) the identification of the resulting influence, or so-called "dependent" variable. Under the scheme the independent variable is necessarily qualitatively homogeneous, constant, and disparate; also, the universe of people, their given type of behavior, and the surrounding conditions are treated as set and as having a logical constancy.

This scheme is brought into question by the shifting nature of presentation, sensitivity, and interconnection. It is highly doubtful if the type of communication chosen for study can be taken as qualitatively homogeneous, constant, and disparate; and it is doubtful if the people constituting the universe of study can be regarded as constant in their sensitivity and responsiveness. Let me spell this out further.

The varying and changing nature of what is presented by mass media does not favor the setting up of an independent variable with the true characteristics of homogeneity and constancy. Further, the intertwined and interacting nature of diverse forms of communication robs any of them of disparateness. Because of these conditions the setting of problems in the study of the effects of mass media has all too frequently a spurious character. Let me illustrate by referring to the current interest in studying the effects of mass media on voting. In such study some students seriously entertain the intention of treating mass media, collectively, as an independent variable, so that one could say that the effects exercised by mass media on voting behavior are such and such. This is as ridiculous as asking what the effects of conversation on voting behavior are. Like the content of conversation, the presentations made through mass media differ greatly in substance and manner and, further, are likely to evolve and change to meet newly developing conditions. Thus, to treat mass media as a single, homogeneous, and constant factor is to ignore their real character. Obviously, the same difficulty exists in selecting any single medium as an independent variable, as in recent studies designed to determine the effects of television on voting. Here again, the variable and changing character of the presentations whose influence one seeks to ascertain clearly robs the medium of the homogeneity and constancy that would warrant its treatment as a variable. This same difficulty holds for practically any influence that one selects for study. In every instance one is not handling the same presentation, the same condition of responsiveness, and the same setting.

These variations place under suspicion the frequent tendency to assert a given influence of mass media on the basis of the findings of a study of some instance of their presumed play. This can be illustrated in a current view that the Erie County and Elmira studies by Lazarsfeld and Berelson show that the influence of mass media is restricted and minimal. Considering the wide range possible to media presentations, the wide range of the varying sensitivities of people, and the different possibilities in the moving developments in political settings, such a view is indeed pretentious. There is no established ground for taking the two studies as a representative sample of the universe of voting situations.

The form of setting problems here under criticism is further exemplified by efforts to compare the presumed effects on voting of different kinds of communication. The authors of one recent study, for example, venture a comparison between the presumed influence of mass media with the presumed influence of face-to-face discourse. Other students entertain an interest in contrasting the effects of radio with television, or television with newspapers. To set problems of these kinds seems to ignore what occurs in the real world. In a political campaign the various media are participating in a total evolving process, treating to a large extent the same events and responding to one another's presentations. What they present is filtered and organized in diverse ways in the experience of people, with much of it picked up and used in the arena of local communication. This intertwined, interacting, and transforming make-up of the communicative process stands in noticeable contrast to a scheme wherein each form or channel of communication is regarded as exercising a distinct influence that can be kept separate and measured in some parallelogram of forces.

Further difficulty arises because whatever influence is exerted by the presentations of mass media depends on the way in which people meet and handle such presentations. Their interests, their forms of receptiveness, indifference, or opposition, their sophistication or naïveté, and their established schemes of definition set the way in which they initially receive the presentations. Usually there is a further intervening stage before the residual effects of the presentations are set in experience and behavior. This additional stage is an interpretative process which through analysis and critical judgment reworks the presentations into different forms before assimilation into experience. This process of interpretation in the individual is markedly guided by the stimulations, cues, suggestions, and definitions he secures from other people, particularly those constituting his so-called "reference groups." Account must be taken of a collective process of definition which in different ways shapes the manner in which individuals composing the "audience" interpret and respond to the presentations given through the mass media. Although this collective process of definition may settle into a stable set of views, images, and positions, it is always subject to movement in new directions as people, collectively, face new situations, meet new problems and crises, and find it necessary to take account of new happenings.

Studies seeking to ascertain the effects of mass media are easily led to overlook the state of sensitivity of the "audience," and particularly the process of collective definition that is so powerful in shaping and sustaining this state of sensitivity. Generally, the student is inclined to take the audience as it is—to characterize it in terms of conventional categories of age, sex, religion, education, class position, and the like—and to assume that the responsiveness of the people in the audience is naturally tied to such categories. Even when the state of sensitivity is measured through a questionnaire or an attitude test, there is little realization that a process of collective definition forms the state of sensitivity and holds it in place. The failure to recognize and consider this process of collective definition leads easily to a deceptive generalization of the findings of one's study. A given group subject to an unusual and critical run of experience may shift significantly its state of sensitivity without any change in the formal categories by which it is identified. A set of findings yielded by a study of the group in its earlier state of sensitivity could not be safely projected to the group after developing a different state of sensitivity. For example, it is readily conceivable, although admittedly unlikely, that the Elmira subjects in the Berelson study who steadfastly favored the Republican candidate could have been dislodged from this preference by some happening or series of happenings which brought disgrace to the candidate or to his party. If the presentation of such happenings had occurred through media like the press, television, and the radio, an influence on voting behavior would have been attributed to such media quite different from that actually suggested by the Elmira study. This is not a point of sheer conjecture. There are indeed plenty of historical instances of profound shifts in the political preferences of people resulting from critical collective experience. The possibility of such shifts, whether gradual or abrupt, should be respected by studies seeking generalized knowledge of the effects wielded by mass media. This recognition is rarely made in current studies. Indeed, it is largely precluded by the way in which the problem is put—one cannot allow open-ended variability in the setting in which the independent variable operates and hope to pin to this variable a set of specific effects.

Many readers will reject the foregoing discussion as having no merit. They will argue that its criticisms could apply only to sloppy studies. They will declare that studies rigorously designed on the model of the experiment and carried out with exacting care would not lead to the risky and faulty generalizations that have been hinted at. Such an exacting and careful study would eschew the choice of a broad and heterogeneous variable such as a given mass medium and select, instead, something indubitably precise and constant like, let us say, the major campaign addresses of a presidential candidate. One would present these through a clearly defined and fixed medium like that of recordings. The composition of the audience would be carefully determined in all relevant respects, including their "state of sensitivity" before hearing the recordings. Use would be made of carefully matched control groups. A clear identification would be made in advance of the precise area of behavior or make-up in which effects are to be observed. The effects of responding to the recordings would then be carefully spotted in this area. Any proposition resulting from the study would be cast in terms of precisely defined items—the presentation, the make-up of the population, the area of response, the given responses, and the degrees or difference between the responses and the original behavior.

Such a study would indeed avoid some of the sources of error and the faulty generalizations commented on in the previous discussion. But these virtues are achieved, unfortunately, only by sacrificing the possibility of generalizations that can be applied meaningly to real-life situations. The exacting study establishes a situation necessarily unique, because of the rigorous restriction of the factors being dealt with and the resolute elimination of the conditions found in the real world. Whatever generalization it allows is restricted to the particular composition of factors embodied in the experiment. Because of the uniqueness of this composition, which is a necessary consequence of the design of the study, the results do not fit real-life situations.

Paradoxically, the more exacting the study and the more faithfully it adheres to the schematic framework of a precise relation between variables the less it allows generalizations that can be applied to the crude but real world. What appears as a paradox will be found, I suspect, to be a genuine dilemma. Students may be expected to continue their efforts to isolate an exact relation between a given form of mass-medium influence and its effects. In doing so they will strive to reduce their variables to items that are homogeneous, qualitatively constant, and clearly disparate from each other, for without these features the items are not true variables. They will endeavor, further, to stabilize the setting of the relation they are seeking to delineate, for without this stabilization they are checked in their efforts to establish a clean-cut relationship. Yet the very pursuit of study along these lines forces them to structure a setting whose parallel is not to be found in the real world. To generalize the results of the study to the real world is perilous, from a scholarly point of view, because the structured setting does not match a class of instances in the real world. Most contemporary students ignore or gloss over the question of difference between the structured setting of their study and the make-up of the real-life instances to which they project their findings and interpretations. More cautious students will face this question of difference and note that in the real world the designated items lack the character essential to variables and that such items are lodged in shifting and unstable settings.

The dilemma to which these remarks point is not inherent in studying and analyzing the world of mass communication. I suspect that it arises instead from the scheme used to make such study and analysis. This scheme, as suggested above, forces into being a study at odds with the character of the real world it proposes to study. Let me summarize some of the chief points of variation. First, the medium-influence has to be treated necessarily as a discrete and qualitatively constant item; whereas, in real life it is interwoven with other communicative factors and is subject to a flow of change in its content. Second, the audience or population exposed to the medium-influence has to be treated as having a fixed and constant composition; whereas, in the actual world it has a shifting composition. Third, and more important, the effect of the medium-influence on the "audience" has to be taken as direct and necessary under the specified conditions; whereas, in actual experience the medium-influence is subject to variable interpretation by the people before its effect is set. And, fourth, the scheme presupposes logically a world composed of set factors arranged in set relations; whereas, the real world of media communication is caught up in dynamic transformation of experience, of factors, and of relationship.

What seems to be needed is a different scheme of analysis—one that will respect the central features of the mass communicative process as it exists in the world of real happening. This process is not an addition or combination of single lines of influence coming from discrete and fixed items acting on a fixed and neutral audience and leading necessarily to specific changes. Instead, as mentioned earlier in this chapter, the features of this process seem to be: the variant and changing character of the presentations of the media, the variant and changing character of the sensitivities of people touched by the media, the process of interpretation that intervenes between the presentation and its effect, the interdependent relationship between forms of communication, and the incorporation of media, presentations, and people in a world of moving events that imparts an evolving character to each of them. To study such a world implies the following: (1) the items used for study and analysis should not be treated as discrete but should be caught in their interlaced position—the aim should not be to isolate cleanly such an item but to handle it with its lines of attachment; (2) the items must be construed not as qualitatively constant but recognized as undergoing formation; (3) the "audience" or people must be viewed not as responding to stimuli but as forging definitions inside their experience; and (4) the network of relations must be seen and taken as involved in a developing process and thus moving out along new directions.

It is not easy to devise a convenient research model to accommodate these features. It calls for a perspective, a way of setting problems, a type of sampling, and a manner of selecting data that are alien to those found in current procedure. The construction of an appropriate model is a hope of the future. I wish merely to enumerate and comment on some of the principal considerations that should guide the task.

1) A study of the effects of media-influence should seek to reflect accurately the empirical world in which the influence is operating. This interest should be paramount in place of an adherence to conventional procedure.

2) An effort should be made to determine the state of sensitivity of people toward the media-influence. This means a need of catching the dispositions of such people in the form of their developing experiences. The roots of their sensitivity will extend back into a body of previous experience that has given some structure to their interests, their views, and their feelings. This previous experience has been involved in a process of interaction and interpretation between people as they develop orientations inside a moving world. In the flow of such previous collective experience, so-called "eddies and currents" operate to incline the people to certain kinds of responsiveness. To determine the sensitivity or responsiveness of the people in any meaningful way it is necessary to catch it in terms of the moving line of its development instead of in the present moment. It is also necessary to note the sensitivity of the people as a collectively formed complex and not as a congeries of separate and detached lines of individual experience. The introduction of this temporal dimension and this contextual dimension seems essential as a background to the study of the effects of media-influence. Life in a mass society is a moving complex. Any faithful study of it must respect this character.

3) Any given media-influence should be studied *in relation to* other influences which may be operating in the area of concern. In the legitimate effort to isolate the given media-influence it would be erroneous to block out of consideration other operating influences. The real experience of people comprises a combination of the influences at work; to understand any one of them in operation it is necessary to trace its play *inside of the combination.*

4) It is necessary to consider how the media-influence *enters* the experience of people rather than to turn immediately to its

presumed effects. What is presented in the media-influence becomes subject to interpretation by those on whom it plays. A process of interpretation which involves the play of the suggestions and definitions coming from many other sources, particularly from one's associates, intervenes as a crucial stage before the establishment of the effects. This process selects features of the presentation, shapes them into objects, determines the kind of significance with which they are endowed, and guides the way in which they come to be set in thought, feeling, and action. This process of interacting definition should be traced in the fuller context of the moving complex of developing life of the group.

5) In line with the foregoing considerations the effects of a given media-influence should be sought in breadth. To single out only one line of effects, even though this be the avowed intention of the study, may weaken seriously an analysis of the findings. For example, in a study of the effects of television presentations on voting intentions it would be highly desirable to include inquiry into how people are influenced on related matters by the presentations. Thus, findings on how the presentations shape views of the political parties aside from the candidates, definitions of issues as against parties and candidates, beliefs about politicians and ideas of political life—such findings put the voting intentions in better perspective and yield an account more in line with the context of relevant group life.

The study of the effects of media-influences with proper regard to temporal and spatial contexts, the joint participation of such influences in the experience of people, the moving process of collective interpretation made of them, and the wider order of orientation that results from them sets new questions of sampling, selection of data, and lines of analysis. It is hoped that these questions will come to engage the serious attention of scholars in this field.

To accommodate these five features, it is clear, requires a different type of approach, a different way of setting problems, a different scheme of sampling, a different selection of data, and a different form of relating data. The approach calls for a historical dimension in order to trace the line along which people become prepared or sensitized to respond to media-influence. It calls for an extended spatial dimension in the need of catching the way in which people are defining to one another the content of the given media-influence under study. It calls for handling the media-influence not in isolation but in relation to other sources of communication which challenge, oppose, merge with, or reinforce its play. The scheme of sampling should represent the "population" as a developing organization and not as an array of differentiated individuals. The data would have to be selected to reproduce a moving process and not to isolate disparate and simple relations.

It is hoped that such radical changes in the scheme of study, needed to remain faithful to the empirical world, will come to engage the serious attention of scholars in this field.

CHAPTER 11

Second Thoughts on "Straight Fight"

R. S. MILNE

The second thoughts[1] are of three sorts. They are concerned with comparisons between survey findings in Great Britain and the United States, with shortcomings and criticisms of *Straight Fight*, and with present and future developments in this field in Britain.

By judicious selection, a case could be made out for regarding the survey findings in the United States and Britain as remarkably similar. By equally judicious selection they could be conclusively demonstrated to be radically different. There are obvious broad similarities in the behavior of women voters as opposed to men, of different social classes, and in the demographic data of Republican/Conservative voters and Democratic/Labour voters. The findings in *Straight Fight* on party images[2] resemble less closely the conclusions of *The People's Choice*.[3] Even sampling difficulties sometimes run parallel in the two countries. The familiar problem in the United States of obtaining samples with a high enough proportion of Democrats is matched by the tendency of Labour voters to be underrepresented in British samples. This difficulty persistently afflicted the British Institute of Public Opinion, and it was rectified only some months before the 1955 election. Both the 1951 (*Straight Fight*) and 1955[4] Bristol surveys contained too small a proportion of Labour voters in the sample.[5] Further points of resemblance may be found in Appendix A of *Voting*.

The dissimilarities, however, are not less striking. The association between religion and voting does not seem to be nearly as pronounced as in the United States.[6] Also, for reasons of expense, no British survey has yet been made of voting in a rural area. It has therefore been impossible to set up the equivalent of an index of political predisposition. There remains only the single yardstick (or rather multiple yardstick, because the term can be defined in many ways) of social class. Until 1955, also, it seems that estimation of turnout was not an important problem in Britain. At the 1950 and 1951 elections, an average of about 83 per cent of the electors voted. Allowing for deaths, errors in the electoral register, and for electors completely incapable of voting, even by postal votes, the electors who abstained amounted to only about 10 per cent of the total. There is little room, compared with the United States, for election predictions being upset by large shifts of electors from voting to nonvoting, or the reverse. But at the 1955 election, turnout dropped to just under 77 per cent. To be sure, turnout fluctuations are a headache mainly for pollsters interested in *predicting the results* of elections. But the low 1955 turnout is also perplexing for those who conducted surveys at that election. To what extent did the swing to the Conservatives result from Labour abstentions being greater than Conservative abstentions?[7] And, supposing that they *were* greater, which was mainly to blame, the Labour party's inadequate organization or its unsatisfactory policy?[8] If, however, British elections revert to the 1950/1951 pattern, changes between voting and nonvoting will be decidedly less important than in the United States. On the other hand, the activities of the Liberal party, which contests some seats at one election but not at the next, are a fertile source of complexity to students of British elections.

To take one further example, the concept of "candidate orientation," used in the 1952 Michigan survey,[9] would be quite inapplicable in Britain. Only about 1 per cent of the voters mention a candidate as a factor in their voting decision. The orientation is, if anything, toward the *party leaders,* the men who will constitute "the Government" if the party wins. This is in accord with the view that British general elections are in reality plebiscites on the next Government rather than elections of individuals. But such orientation was confined almost entirely to *Conservative* voters, who saw their party leaders as possessing brains, education, managing ability, and like qualities. To some extent this is a modern version of the "deference" to superiors in Britain, described long ago by Bagehot. It is also consistent with the role of the leaders, and particularly of *the* leader, in the Conservative party, compared with the Labour party. Admittedly, as has been pointed out recently,[10] Conservative party leaders may not be so effectively insulated from shocks from extraparliamentary sources as they appear to be. But this is precisely the point. Mr. McKenzie's demonstration was necessary and useful *just because* the role of the leader was *reputedly* so pre-eminent. It was this reputation that produced the Conservative voters' images of leadership. Labour voters were not oriented in this direction; in 1955 they were actually *repelled* by the divisions in the party leadership.

These dissimilarities should warn the reader, if any further warning were necessary, of the dangers of too facile comparisons between elections in the two countries. An acute criticism of Maurice Duverger's brilliant book on political parties[11] was that it might lead less brilliant readers to imagine that in a number of countries there were similar entities, "political parties," which could be directly compared. This criticism applies with equal force to election surveys in different countries. However, fruitful speculation has sometimes been stimulated by the consideration of similar topics in wildly contrasting surroundings. The British educational administrator, Sir Robert Morant, is said to have owed some of his most penetrating insights into British education to his experience of quarreling religious sects in Siam. Consideration of *Straight Fight* in this book may, on a lower level, be of benefit to American readers.

Accepting that *Straight Fight* merits brief notice in an American volume, what are the second thoughts of one of its authors several years after writing it? It is difficult to avoid appearing pretentious in answering this question about an unpretentious book. Perhaps the chief regret about the survey is that the sample was not larger. The two samples contained only between four and five hundred voters each; just one sample was interviewed twice, the other was interviewed only once. This is "small stuff" by American standards. The basic problem in Bristol was lack of money. For this reason the interviewers—students—were unpaid, the sample was small, and there was delay in publication. The design of the sample, the instruction and supervision of interviewers, the coding of the questionnaires, the perforation and sorting of the cards, the tabulation of results, and the actual writing of the book were done almost entirely by the two authors.[12]

The problem was a little more complicated than this, however. Presidential elections occur at regular intervals; general elections in Britain do not. Normally the maximum life of the House of Commons is five years, but, as in 1950-51 and 1951-55, it may be substantially less. Consequently it is hard to plan an election survey when the notice given may be as short as six weeks. Only if Parliament has already lasted about four years, is it possible to draw up a fairly definite plan for repeated panel interviews. This could be done in Greenwich by the directors of the 1950 survey in that constituency;[13] it was not possible at the 1951 and 1955 elections.

A really large sample survey (of, say, 3,000 electors), interviewed at intervals before the election and also after it, would require a large corps of professional interviewers. And to be *completely* sure of obtaining interviews over a period of six months before an election, interviewing would have to start quite soon after one election in case the next followed quickly on its heels, as in 1951. If interviewing were left until just after the announcement of an election—for example, five weeks before polling day—then no data could be secured on the important question of the electors' attitudes *before* the announcement. There would also be the practical difficulty of obtaining a large number of professional interviewers at short notice.

The 1951 samples, then, were too small. Consequently when the figures in the samples were broken down into small groups, say of two-party changers or of party members, the sampling error was large and the results suggestive rather than significant. In the absence of a sufficiently large sample the interpreter is driven to consideration of findings in a number of roughly comparable small samples, for example, Bristol North-East in 1951 with Bristol North-East, with altered boundaries, in 1955, or Bristol North-East in 1951 with Droylsden in 1951. This involves a good deal of guesswork about what is "roughly comparable" and what is not.

Apart from the smallness of the sample—a glaring defect and a source of many separate imperfections—it is hard for the writer, who has not seen the rest of this book, to divine the exact lines of criticism which may be leveled at *Straight Fight.* One stricture, made in a newspaper but unlikely to be repeated in this book, was the familiar one directed against many sample surveys—that *Straight Fight* documented the obvious. The tables and statistical appendices were treated with respect by the reviewer, but he claimed to have known previously that women were more Conservative than men, that former Liberal votes largely went to the Conservatives in 1951, etc., etc. There was no evidence that the reviewer, so patronizing on the "easy" questions, had even attempted to grapple with the more difficult ones, such as age, voting and differential death rates (Chapter 5), or party images (Chapters 11 and 12).

Nevertheless, it is perhaps worthwhile to consider briefly two other criticisms, already made of the book, from slightly better-informed sources.

One criticism was expressed in the discussions on political parties and public opinion polls held at the International Political Science Association Conference at Stockholm in August, 1955. It was not directed specifically at *Straight Fight*, but the book was clearly *one* of its targets. While conceding that polls and surveys performed dazzling technical tricks, it was alleged that they were of little use for providing information about the structure of party organizations. Party structure was much more effectively studied directly than via polls or surveys. This statement is indisputable. It is also, as it happens, irrelevant. It could be made only by political scientists, so absorbed in questions of party *structure* that they had become oblivious of the *content* of party policy and party propaganda. Polls and surveys do not claim to answer questions about party structure. They do, however, as was pointed out in material prepared for the Stockholm conference, among other things tell us something useful about the impact of party symbols on the voter.[14]

Another criticism, in a review of *Straight Fight* in a learned journal, maintained that Bristol North-East was too "mixed" an area and not "sufficiently socially homogeneous" for an election survey. The authors, it was alleged, had been too impressed by the need to study a "typical" constituency. Perhaps the authors were indeed to blame for this inference. In *Straight Fight* they went to considerable pains to point out that, save in one interesting respect,[15] the constituency was fairly typical of provincial borough constituencies. But the reason for their pains was apparently misunderstood. They had not sought after typicality when choosing Bristol North-

East for the survey; it had been selected because it was conveniently near the university and because a close fight was expected which would make the local party organizations work at full pressure. But, once it had been selected, it was evident that readers would like to know how it compared with other constituencies where surveys had already been carried out, e.g., Greenwich and Droylsden, or would be conducted in the future. If a "socially homogeneous" area is preferred, there are few British universities that have such a constituency within close enough reach to make use of student interviewers. Alternatively, an area smaller than a constituency, such as a housing estate, might be chosen. But there would be two serious objections. Figures for voting obtained from a sample survey could not be checked against actual voting figures, because in Britain these figures are not available for any unit smaller than a constituency. Because one of the objects of a survey is to study party organization at an election and since the parties are organized on a constituency basis, the constituency is the obvious unit to choose.

In any case, it is doubtful if the time has yet arrived to search out "socially homogeneous" areas for sample surveys. So few surveys have been made that the work is still at the exploratory stage. Larger samples of electors are a much more important priority than socially homogeneous areas.[16]

In the light of the defects in *Straight Fight* and the most recent developments in United States research, what lessons for British sample surveys can be learned? The most obvious one, which has already been mentioned, is that larger samples should be used. One possible variant of this, if the interviewing were done professionally and not by students, would be to choose half a dozen constituencies of varying types and put the same question to a random sample of about 500 in each. Sampling on a nationwide scale, after the fashion of the British Institute of Public Opinion, would be difficult, unless the operation were conducted through an existing market research organization with interviewers all over the country.

Another improvement on the 1951 survey would concentrate on gaps by asking questions on religion, education, interest in the election, and the like. Questions of this sort were asked in the 1955 survey. In 1951 there was no deliberate search for opinion leaders. In 1955 an attempt was made to discover the opinion leaders in the sample, but not opinion leaders *outside* it. To find the "outside" opinion leaders, long preparation is necessary. Unless ample time has been allowed (as in a current survey in the Netherlands) for making the aims of the project known locally, there is bound to be suspicion and resentment if the electors in the sample are asked for the names and addresses of "outside" opinion leaders with whom they have held conversations.

In the 1955 survey rather more attention was given to the question of issues and party images. The concept of the "gateway" for issues, used in *Voting*,[17] proved useful for a more detailed analysis of British issues. A study was made of the electors' images of the opposition party as well as of their own.

In 1951 no great effort was made to look back over the voting history of individual electors. In 1955 two main elaborations were attempted. Questions were included on how an elector voted the first time he was entitled to vote, whether he had ever voted for a party different from his 1955 party, and, if so, for which. Some electors were also asked additional questions; these electors' answers were used in the preparation of about twenty-five case histories, which attempt to give a précis of the elector's previous voting behavior and to show him "in the round" during the 1955 campaign.

However, by far the most promising developments seem to lie in the possibility of relating sample survey findings to political theory. A masterly outline of the possibilities in this regard are given in the last chapter of *Voting*.[18] A very brief treatment of one or two of the headings for investigation in Britain was sketched in *Straight Fight*.[19] One of the applications referred to there concerns the doctrine of the "mandate." What is meant by saying that the victorious party at a British election has been given a mandate to do X? Political theorists are suspicious of the doctrine and have pointed out some of its difficulties and pitfalls. But only a sample survey, by revealing the voter's customary disregard of election issues in arriving at his voting decision, can put the problem in a fresh perspective by describing what the voter himself says in his mind when he actually votes.

Moreover, the extent of the electors' ability, intelligence, knowledge, and civic consciousness goes to the very root of the theory of representative government. The problem was, of course, widely canvassed when the extension of the franchise was debated in Britain. John Stuart Mill was willing to accept universal suffrage only along with provisions designed to give greater weight to the votes of educated persons. The qualities of the electors are still relevant today. The general level of education, although not necessarily of *political* education, may be higher now in Britain than ever before. But the proportion of electors who voted in the 1950 or 1951 elections was also higher than ever before. Apathetic and ill-informed electors, who might formerly have "cushioned" the advent of universal suffrage by abstaining, now turn up at the polls, impelled by social pressures or the efforts of the party organizations. The findings of *The People's Choice* on electors who change their parties, largely confirmed since both in the United States and in Britain, stimulated Mr. Max Beloff to voice his fears in a celebrated article: "It is far more likely that the marginal voter is someone who is so inadequately identified with one major set of interests or another and so remote, therefore, from the group-thinking out of which political attitudes arise, that his voting record is an illustration, not of superior wisdom, but of greater frivolity."[20]

It is necessary, therefore, to push analysis further along the lines traced in *Voting*, and to consider the implications for theories of representative government of findings such as those on the qualities of changers and on personal contacts, both inside and outside the family. Paradoxically, polls and surveys, which in their routine aspects seem far removed from political theory, at the same time in their description of voting decisions, illuminate one of its central problems.

CHAPTER 12

The Mass Media and Voting

KURT AND GLADYS ENGEL LANG

After each national election students of political behavior comment on how little effect the mass media appear to have had on the outcome. Franklin D. Roosevelt and Harry S. Truman won *in spite of* the press. The personal nature of the Eisenhower victory in 1952 showed that the campaign was so much shouting and tumult; the election was won before the campaign had even begun. Still, all of us—politicians, candidates, public servants, symbol manipulators, members of the Great Audience, and even students of political behavior in our private capacities as interested and partisan citizens —much as we may publicly belittle what the mass media do, act most of the time *as if* we believed in their potency. Republican members of the faculty pay for a newspaper ad supporting their candidate; the Democrats must counter with their own publicity. The vagaries of research lead us away from a principal concern with the impact of press, radio, television, and magazines, but nothing would seem to have banished our not yet empirically demonstrated beliefs that the mass media are more influential than we would sometimes wish. Outcries against certain political television shows during and between campaigns, as well as the enduring and enthusiastic acceptance accorded to George Orwell's *1984*, indicate vividly that our research may not tell us what our common sense reveals is there to be told.

At first glance recent research on voting behavior appears to go along with this emphasis on *how little* the mass media determine the vote. The reader's attention is called to influences that intervene between the content itself and the individual's voting decision.

Emphasis also moves away from a concern with the power once attributed to mass communications to the personal dispositions and group influences that circumscribe it.

None of the three voting studies—Elmira, 1948; Bristol North-East, 1951; the U. S. national survey in 1952[1]—draw any explicit conclusions to the effect that mass communications are *not* an important influence in voting behavior. They all point to their own methodological inadequacies, and in the most recent of the three studies the problem of mass-media impact has actually been avoided.[2] At many points, the importance of the mass media is stressed; nowhere is their role in connection with the vote actually belittled. Yet there may be a difference between the author's own interpretations and more or less popular understandings of what their findings mean.

MASS COMMUNICATIONS DURING THE CAMPAIGN. Exactly what do we learn about the influence of mass communication on voting behavior by studying its effect within the scope of a single campaign?

Both the Elmira and the Bristol studies reiterate findings of earlier research. In Elmira the group who changed their voting intentions during the campaign, compared with those who followed through, included fewer people who were interested in the election. They were less "exposed" to the mass media, and they arrived at their decision later. Likewise in Bristol, "floaters [those inconsistent either in their intentions or in their vote], no matter what their final party, listened to fewer broadcasts and read fewer national newspapers than the regular voters."[3] These observations are consistent with the most widely accepted finding on mass-media impact: "Media exposure gets out the vote at the same time that it solidifies preferences. It crystallizes and reinforces more than it converts."[4]

Accordingly, then, the election period serves less as a force for change than as a period for reclarification. There are several concrete circumstances in a campaign which severely circumscribe opportunities for observing the influence of mass-media propaganda.

Most obvious in this connection is the observation, confirmed in different contexts and by different methods, that the minds of most voters are closed even before the campaign officially opens. At various places and at different times, this figure has been set at anywhere from 50 to 84 per cent of the voters.[5] But even if a voter arrives at his decision late in the campaign, he is not necessarily in a constant quandary, endlessly pulled in opposite directions by conflicting propaganda. Evidence from panel studies indicates that in most cases where the final decision comes late in the campaign, prior leanings are crystallized into a firm intent. The impregnability of voting intentions as a whole limits drastically the number of people who are, so to speak, potential converts.

Moreover, during a campaign, people cannot help but be aware, however unhappily, that they are the targets of deliberate propaganda. Neither side enjoys a monopoly of available space or time, and so propaganda is almost always exposed as such. Expecting attempts at persuasion, voters come prepared with stereotyped meanings. It is not altogether unusual to hear speeches discounted as so much campaign talk. People, being aware of the intent of the messages, tend to avoid views contrary to their own. They tend to believe their own side and to question the arguments of the other. As long as old loyalties are activated, selective perception will serve as an effective screen.

Campaigners themselves limit the conversion potential of their propaganda. While their aim is to activate partisan loyalties and to persuade the small undecided group, their speeches and political shows must not alienate anyone disposed to be on their side. The lore of politics is replete with the terrible specter of candidates who lost elections because of a few ill-chosen words.[6]

The campaign period, then, would seem inherently to be less a period of potential change than a period of political entrenchment, a period in which prior attitudes are reaffirmed. This may well be a real paradox of political life: We are accustomed to think of campaign periods as the dynamic times when political passions are aroused and wholesale changeover results, and of periods between as the quiescent years, when people tend to forget about politics and are less attentive to the larger political environment. Yet changes in political opinion and in the general political climate may be less characteristic of the days of arousal than of the "quiescent" times between campaigns.

At any rate, the number of people who have already "made up their minds" before the campaign begins, the overwhelming importance of "filtering" effects resulting from self-selection and selective perception of media content, and the awareness of the intent with which all campaign statements are phrased all work together to make "conversion" through any medium particularly difficult during an election. But, in addition, there is something in the way the problem is approached which may obscure certain ways in which the mass media are effective.

Let us briefly review how the impact of the mass media is detected in the panel studies.[7] The authors of these studies investigate the initial voting intention and how it crystallizes and changes during the course of the campaign. They record individual "exposure" to the campaign—mostly in terms of attention paid to campaign materials, sources relied on, and the operation of self-selection. Then, by relating the voting intention to "exposure" within a framework of contextual factors, they infer the impact of that exposure. But among all the relevant "exposures," specifically what influences a vote cannot be easily inferred. More direct evidence about the content of that "exposure" and what it signifies to the consumer is necessary. To this end the researchers did ask at least one open-ended question that might (and did) elicit reports of particular speeches, news events, and broadcasts that helped voters "make up their minds." Yet the authors attribute no high validity to these retrospective answers. Consequently, the over-all amount of attention paid to the campaign remains the main index from which to infer mass-media impact.

This approach allows the authors of these studies to relate generally "high" exposure to a rising interest in the campaign and to a strengthening of partisan conviction.[8] Milne and Mackenzie point to a "hardening of opinion" after the campaign, which they find it "not unreasonable" to attribute to "persistent and concentrated propaganda."[9]

But to relate "exposure" to interest and partisanship is not to explain why people vote as they do. For such explanation the authors of the panel studies revert to an examination of people's prior political predispositions, their group identifications, and other variables which, by comparison with mass-media exposure, can be deemed relatively impermeable. These group measures, used in *Voting* and *Straight Fight* to "explain" voting decisions, are analogous to, though less explicit than, the set of "motivational" variables[10] which the more recent Survey Research Center study focuses upon.

To be sure these generalized motivational variables—issue orientation, party identification, and candidate orientation—allow for the comparison of elections but still unexamined are the processes by which "weights" come to be assigned to various elements involved in the voting decision.

As long as the loyalties and imagery of the electorate are treated as "givens," as they have been, rather than as themselves in need of explanation, the probability of understanding the nature of mass-media impact is duly minimized. The very emphasis on change *within* the span of a campaign makes it almost inevitable that whatever realignments occur are limited by the more permanent identifications and loyalties existing at the time the study is started. In the same way, both the amount of attention paid to campaign materials and the sources on which people rely follow motivational and social dispositions as they follow prior political opinions. All of these habits and orientations have their roots outside the campaign.

To sum up, whether the "strain toward consistency" which characterizes the campaign period is observed on the *individual* level as bringing attitudes into line with motivations or as the adjustment of a voting decision to the local pressures emanating from the *social* environment immediately relevant to the voter does not much matter. In either case, examination of change within this short span fails altogether to account for the cumulative impact of media exposure which may, over a period of time, lead to such changes in the motivational patterns as differentiate one election from another or to a breaking away of many "primary" groups from older allegiances.

POLITICAL CHANGE. The study of long-range effects leads us to a comparison of elections and especially to a second look at the occasional election in which long-standing habits seem to be upset.

What, we have to ask, do the results of any election mean? What is a "vote of confidence" for a party in power returned to govern, and what marks a political turnover? The vote recorded at the polling place, though a climactic and discrete act, is after all but a summary measure. "Whatever we may not know about the act of voting itself, we do know that it is highly complex, the net result of influences from many other activities in which voters are engaged and of other experiences than those directly associated with political campaigns."[11] We cannot explain the vote unless we know the influences that are at work during the so-called "quiescent" times. What do the mass media contribute to political stability and to political turnover?

Underlying the "strain toward consistency" observed in election periods is the basic stability of the vote. This stability also extends over longer periods. There is a high correlation between a person's first vote and his subsequent choices. Moreover, geographic, demographic, and social groups often display surprisingly consistent (over time) voting rates and patterns. Such consistent loyalties are fostered, above all, through the linkage of party images which class (and other status) symbols and the reinforcement of these loyalties through the relatively homogeneous political environment in which a majority of voters appear to move.

The study of the Bristol constituency highlights this basic stability. It indicates the importance of party images and the relative insignificance in British politics of "candidate appeal." Only 19 per cent of the respondents admitted that, in any of three elections since 1945, they had voted for a party other than the one they were supporting in 1951.[12] Indeed, in 1951 not a single candidate in all of Britain was able to win for Labour a previously Conservative seat and reverse what was a slight (though politically decisive) shift toward the Conservatives. This may be attributed, in part, to the fact that candidates considered valuable to a party may be run in "safe" constituencies. Yet it principally reflects the decisive role of the national party struggle and the importance that must be attached to the efficacy of party images as such. "However unthinking many electors may be," a British scholar writes, "their votes do seem on balance to represent a general judgement between the merits of the national parties."[13]

What seems to matter in British politics is the party image—what the party stands for. As economic and social conditions change, so do the self-images of voters. Inasmuch as party loyalties reflect class loyalties, the successful party must manage to alter its image even if ever so slightly to take account of these shifts. The role of the mass media in disseminating the "appropriate" party image is apparent in *Straight Fight*. It is the national news sources that largely serve to channel to the electorate the party image with the pertinent symbols and clichés. Although the processes by which and the conditions under which these images are successfully communicated remain to be explained, Milne and Mackenzie conclude that national propaganda sources (as contrasted with local sources) have more "powerful direct effects."[14]

Such party images are obviously not the product of a single campaign; they are in existence, ready-made, long before the official contest begins. Their reinforcement through local pressures helps to give the vote its fundamental stability and to make much of voting a highly institutionalized and conventionalized activity, especially when, as in Great Britain, the party ties are closely linked with class organizations, trade unions, and the like. But it is not only stability that we have to understand. Also to be explained is how long-standing habits are upset, and upset among many divergent local groups. The mass media would seem to play an indispensable role in producing the cumulative changes that are given expression in a turnover at the polls.

A possible turnover in the United States was forestalled in 1948. A rally back to the Fair Deal "decided" the outcome of the presidential vote in Elmira that year. In particular, the "waverers," strays from the Democratic fold, returned largely because of the salience of class issues, exactly those issues stressed by Truman during his campaign. National surveys confirm this Fair Deal rally as a nationwide phenomenon. Truman's benefits from those who in the early part of the campaign had been "undecided" or did not follow through on their original voting intention were twice as great as Dewey's.[15] These late changers were 1944 Democrats switching back to the administration.

The importance of the mass media for the Fair Deal rally is flatly stated in the Elmira study. (The "salience of class issues was brought home through the mass media.")[16] Though the image of Truman did *not* change, the image of what was important in the campaign did change. As the campaign progressed, socioeconomic issues became dominant. The change was most noticeable among persons high in mass-media exposure. The Fair Deal rally, based on renewed attentiveness to class issues which was helped along by the mass media, enabled the Democrats to chalk up still another victory. Not very much attention has been paid to this finding on the mass media.

Legend already has it that Truman, as he whistle-stopped across the nation, took his own case to the people and won despite a hostile press. What Truman actually did, it would seem, was to make "news." The press—or magazines or radio—could editorialize against the administration; their presentation of the news that Truman was making could be more or less subtly biased through headlines, spacing, choice of words, and the like. But since what Mr. Truman said was news, his appeal to class interests commanded attention and helped bring the strays back into the fold.

Nevertheless, the Truman victory in 1948 called attention primarily to what the mass media could *not* do. The results in 1952 surely have led us to reconsider the assumption that people will not, on the whole, cross party lines. The proportion of voters who did cross was undoubtedly small. But there were enough of these, together with previous nonvoters, to produce the Republican landslide. Primary group pressures, local influences, latent dispositions of voters throughout the country failed to reinforce wavering allegiances to the Democratic party. The motivational pattern of the vote was different. If 1948 was largely a party year, in 1952 the "more variable factors of issues and candidates" assumed unusual importance.[17] Some analysts have pointed to the long-term trends underlying these cyclical changes, such as the general prosperity prevailing, the upward mobility of minority groups, the trek to the suburbs, the industrialization of the South, and the general change from "interest" to "status" politics.[18]

That the mass media were a significant force in defining and structuring the decisive issues of the 1952 campaign and in "projecting" the candidates" personalities should be beyond dispute. The extent of this influence can unfortunately only be inferred. The campaign may have reactivated old loyalties, but, if it did, they were not the same old loyalties as in 1948. The issues were drawn differently. Where socioeconomic issues had invoked Democratic loyalties, the issue of national security, especially the Korean war, exercised a new attraction which worked in favor of the GOP. And, along with this, the public personality of General Eisenhower appealed to Democrats and Republicans alike, though not always for the same reasons.

Plausible as it may seem to impute a great impact to advertising techniques employed during the political war, to the novel role played by TV, and especially to the saturation of TV with filmed "spots," there is no evidence that the official campaign propaganda, as such, changed many votes.[19] The "turnover" away from the Democrats had taken place before the official campaign opened. The campaign found the Republicans with a number of issues ready-made. From a postelection perspective, it appears evident that, in order to win, the Republicans had but to bring these vividly before the public. The real influence of the mass media, then, is to be sought in the play given communism and corruption in government and the controversies over Korea. These had been spelled out on front pages and in radio bulletins for some time. How, during the weeks of the campaign, the stalemated Korean war was restored from the back to the front pages of newspapers has been duly noted, though not yet systematically treated.[20]

The campaign talk on Korea may not actually have "converted." It nonetheless kept open the psychological wound inflicted by a peacetime war. Straight news and campaign oratory were joined to keep attention on what could, it seemed, only redound to the benefit of Republicans. Only in this sense may the campaign talk have "converted" by preventing the return of Democrats to their party.

We can inquire similarly about media influence on the Eisenhower image. He was, in 1952, not simply the "man of the year." Already in 1945, Eisenhower enjoyed an immense popularity, though for a war hero not a popularity without precedent. The political appeal of the General seems to have resided less in what he stood for than in what he did not stand for. Few Democrats or Republicans, who, as early as 1948, were advocating an Eisenhower candidacy, seem to have been familiar with his views on important issues. His political ("partisan") leanings were not on public record, and what was on the record had not been publicized.

Neither, for that matter, do early Eisenhower enthusiasts seem to have placed any emphasis on his political views. It was the "personal character" that counted. Eisenhower seemed to appeal most to those voters who "placed less emphasis on ideology and more emphasis on personal qualities in their choice of a candidate."[21] Yet, at that time very few people had met Eisenhower "intimately" via TV and there is no evidence that the personal image of Eisenhower originated with or was most prevalent among veterans of the European theater. But the image was there, ready for political exploitation, and it must be understood as a mass-media-built image.

PERSONAL INFLUENCE AND MASS INFLUENCE. The mass media, then, exert some of the influence they do because they are more than a channel through which national party policy is brought before the local electorate. In filtering, structuring, and spotlighting certain public activities, the media content is not confined to conveying what party spokesmen proclaim and what the candidates say. All news that bears on political activity and beliefs—and not only campaign speeches and campaign propaganda—is somehow relevant to the vote. Not only during the campaign but also in the periods between, the mass media provide perspectives, shape images of candidates and parties, help highlight issues around which a campaign will develop, and define the unique atmosphere and areas of sensitivity which mark any particular campaign. Any long-run view, therefore, reveals certain differences among elections which make clear that in each case voters, much as they may respond to traditional allegiances, also respond to a unique historical situation.

The scheme of analysis outlined in *Voting* barely touches upon the role of the mass media in creating a secondhand reality, through which public policy is elaborated and the effects of that policy on the voter clarified and made tangible. The "main concern," we are told, "is with the electorate itself. How many individuals pay *direct* attention to the campaign via the mass media?"[22] In this scheme the mass media act primarily as transmitters of content supplied by the national parties and by their candidates and subsequently consumed, in one way or another, by the electorate. The personal network of communications within the community hooks onto and makes use of the mass media. Opinion leaders usually pay more attention to the mass media than their peers, and they relay relevant information to those less firm in their partisan convictions.

In this transmission system which passes along arguments and information required in voting decisions, personal influence often seems more crucial and persuasive than mass-media content. The reasoning seems to go as follows: The opinion leader can induce compliance not only through *what* he says; he can exert his influence in a flexible fashion and also provide gratifications that go with compliance.[23] The prestige of opinion leaders is often interposed between the mass-media content and those who, on their own, pay no direct attention (or only very little attention) to the content itself. It is in aligning voters with their peers that personal contacts reactivate latent dispositions.

Opinion leaders thus seem often to counter the possible impact of counterpropaganda and to make effective the propaganda favoring their own side. This signal discovery of the ubiquity of opinion leaders has led many to pit the measure of personal influence against that of the mass media. Nothing could obscure the real character of mass-media impact more than to pose the problem in this way. Personal and mass-media influence do not act in the same way. Personal influence may govern a larger segment of any individual's behavior than do the mass media—and it may be easier to demonstrate how a husband influences his wife's voting decision than to demonstrate what the mass media have to do with her voting behavior—but from the viewpoint of the larger society, it is the influence of the mass media which is the most potent.

The persons generally designated by social scientists as "opinion leaders" prepare the ground for mass-media impact. They translate the mass-media reality into the experience of local groups. Some persons may enjoy informal status as opinion leaders precisely because they attend to the relevant mass-media content. Or it may be that in order to wield influence a man may have to be especially knowledgeable about what the mass media do and say. In either case, the opinion leaders exhibit greater responsiveness to the mass media, channeling for their peers—to whose dispositions they are particularly sensitive—that which the mass media have already made significant.

Theirs is essentially a transmission function and through them the views and interests of persons not directly exposed to the content of the mass media are involved. Yet these leaders select what they will transmit, and hence such influentials need not act only as a stabilizing influence. An emergent local leadership at odds with the official party may make use of whatever prestige or credibility the mass-media content has per se to subvert older loyalties.

The short-run frame of reference, with its primary concern with the electorate and how it lines up within the course of a single campaign, has perhaps exaggerated the dominant role of personal influences and the effectiveness of "normal" social pressures. For it puts the accent on the type of changer who is most susceptible —perhaps by a sort of default—to such influences, that is, it draws attention almost exclusively to changers who are converted or whose decision crystallizes only *during the campaign.* In the first place, such persons are, quite logically, those with a relatively low interest in politics and for whom political loyalties are not ordinarily salient; second, they are further characterized by low mass-media exposure.

Moreover, people who do *not* vote with their peers as well as people who do *not* vote in accord with their predispositions appear only as deviant cases among the over-all consistencies found in the panel studies. Deviants somehow get lost in the concern with how A influences B and how both A and B vote in line with their basic predispositions. Yet in order to understand the nature and extent of mass-media influence—and especially their impact on the larger political trends that often mark off one election from another—it is precisely these deviants upon whom we may be forced to concentrate.

By way of brief explication, take the situation described in the Elmira study: Women as a group are less interested in the campaign than men. In their voting decisions, they tend to follow their husbands. Yet at the same time, the "women's vote" is less clearly linked to social class than the male vote. To put it more succinctly, women from the higher socioeconomic levels are less Republican than the men from those classes, whereas women among the working and lower classes are less strongly Democratic.[24] Somehow or other women follow their husbands' leads and yet, by comparison with their husbands, vote less in accord with their class interests. Many plausible explanations commend themselves, but clearly the pattern of the "women's vote" cannot be explained as the simple outcome of personal influence, however helpful this approach is in explaining individual vote changes.

The Bristol study does distinguish the "waverer" from the "changer." And a follow-up of this distinction may serve to sharpen our knowledge of influences upon voting behavior. The "waverer," although consistent in his vote over time, may move into the "undecided" column during any particular campaign or his "intentions" may (judged by what he tells us) appear inconsistent. The "changer" is one whose vote "at present" differs from that of the past, whether or not such a change is recorded within the span of a single campaign. We would contend that there is nothing in the Bristol or other data to indicate that the short-run regularities that mark campaigns reflect accurately the patterns associated with party turnover between elections and over longer periods of time. "Waverers," for instance, may mostly be political indifferents who give way under the pressure of the campaign. But is this true of "changers"? Especially if their conversion occurs during the "quiescent" times between campaigns, when personal pressures are least likely to be deliberately exerted in a politically partisan way, it raises the possibility that such change, or the disposition to change, follows from their private communions with the mass media and the trickle of news reports. During a campaign, women will in all likelihood move toward greater agreement with their husbands. But when the political battle is less obviously joined, the influences weaning women as a group away from the class loyalties of their husbands may well be of a different sort.[25]

The significant question at issue is, then, the pressures that cause people to vote out of accord with their local surroundings and out of accord with their group-anchored attitudes. No speculative answer can be accepted as adequate. Nonetheless, the response of individuals in the mass audience to certain nonlocal influences, however vaguely or indirectly they are perceived, is a problem with which research must contend. Voters, much as they interpret their secondary and symbolic environment in terms of their local milieu, do as individuals acquire certain general political perspectives that shape their responses during campaigns. Notions of politics, of parties, of issues, of candidates, and of their own roles as participating citizens cannot be satisfactorily explained by study of local communication networks. Along these lines, more than along others, ideas are affected by what the mass media present.

SECONDHAND REALITY AND THE MASS AUDIENCE. Persons in the mass society are, as we all know, members of many more or less formally organized groups. Some of these memberships are, of course, more politically relevant than others. Trade unionists in the United States tend to vote Democratic; in England they most often side with Labour. Some minority groups "stick together" politically, and some organizations formed to defend "majority" interests have their own characteristic voting patterns. We know a considerable amount about the political perspectives that derive from such memberships and about the cross-pressures exerted by multiple allegiances.

We are also aware that most of what people know about political life comes to them secondhand—or even thirdhand—through the mass media. The media do structure a very real political environment but one which, even in these days of TV, we can only know "at a distance." Because of the way people select from the political content of the mass media and interpret what they select, the political communication system serves to transmit materials peculiarly relevant to persons in various milieus. Beyond this, however, the mass media also structure a larger, nonlocal reality from which it is hard to escape. The content filters through, even though people are not directly exposed to it or do not claim to be paying a great deal of attention.[26] There is something obtrusive about what the mass media present, something that makes their influence cumulative.

The mass media have, then, another function. They not only transmit materials that feed into the political perspectives of relevant groups; they leave an impress of their own. There are political perspectives that rise out of an individual's position as a member of a mass, as the object of direct and indirect stimuli coming from the mass media. The relationships between voting behavior and the perspectives developed by virtue of one's position in the mass have as yet been inadequately investigated, perhaps because of the very real methodological difficulties involved, perhaps because we overestimate the difficulties or fear to risk criticism of our results.

The subsections that follow outline briefly *some* ways in which the media shape the perspectives of voters, so to say, en masse. Whether individuals accept the media content as "authentic" or discount it as "propaganda," they nonetheless respond to it. The relationship of the following three areas of mass-media impact to voting, however apparent their relevance to politics, has so far not been systematically investigated.

The Dissemination of Distrust. The mass media, by the way in which they structure and present political reality, may contribute to a widespread and chronic distrust of political life. Such distrust is not primarily a mark of sophistication, indicating that critical "discount" is at work. It is of a projective character and constitutes a defensive reaction against the periodic political crises known to affect a person's destiny as well as against what are defined as deliberate efforts to mobilize political sentiment.

How, we may ask, do the media encourage such distrust? Who is most prone to it? And how is it counteracted? The answers must be sought in the way in which the mass media tend to emphasize crisis and stress it in lieu of the normal processes of decision-making. Such distrust also has its roots in the complexity of events and of problems in which the mass audience is involved. For instance, since viewers bring little specialized knowledge to politics, even full TV coverage of major political events does not allay this distrust. In fact, it may abet it. The efforts of telecasters, in 1952, to let the viewer in on everything happening at the conventions sometimes boomeranged.[27] Viewers, being overwhelmed, often felt less that they were being "let in on the inside" than that they were being kept out. People low in political competence and those who tended to take a sinister view of politics were especially prone to such hostile stereotypy.[28]

The Channeling of Trust. How does this distrust express itself in voting or nonvoting? After all, people, in order to act politically, must form some credible picture about political questions. If we knew more about who trusts what mass-media sources and how this trust is channeled, this knowledge would be a springboard for assessing how persons who withdraw from political mass-media materials may periodically be stirred out of their apathy.

To study this, we might start with the characteristics of the consumers rather than those of the media. Certainly not all consumers of mass-media materials approach the political content with the same orientations. Persons with above-average political sophistication (and therefore less subject to a "chronic distrust" of politics) are in the habit of checking one source of information against another. While, like all others, dependent on the mass media for information, they have a sort of natural immunity to the news slant of any particular medium. They are a "high" interest group and usually firm in their voting decisions.

But what about those others who feel disbarred from channels of political influence and who would also seem most suspicious of politics in general? Will they distrust all mass-media sources and believe only what their friends tell them? Paradoxically, the withdrawal of "interest" from political mass-media materials may go hand in hand with high reliance on some particular trusted "medium" somehow exempted from the contamination imputed to the mass media as a whole. This would seem to put a high premium on "sincerity" and "honesty" and on a public personality radiating confidence. And, thus, under certain conditions, it would make those most distrustful of politicians most susceptible to mobilization.

The relation between chronic distrust and reliance on TV as a source of political information seems a particularly rewarding avenue for investigation. Pilot research suggests that television has an especially strong appeal for the chronically distrustful. Members of the audience feel themselves taken "to the scene of the crime," free to explore and follow their own clues. Inherently, TV is therefore the most authentic of the media. The viewer is ready to believe that he "sees for himself," though what he imputes to the picture often originates in other news sources. The immediate and apparently "firsthand" experience of television makes seem as direct experience what may be the end product of a careful build-up. If politicians employing TV can find a successful formula for channeling the trust of persons usually apathetic to and distrustful of politics, the newly mobilized might become a dynamic force in politics, highly volatile and acting with great conviction at election time, but not necessarily out of sustained interest in public policy.

The Dictation of Public Imagination. The mass media force attention to certain issues. They build up public images of political figures. They are constantly presenting objects suggesting what individuals in the mass should think about, know about, have feelings about. There is implied in the way they address their audience, moreover, an appropriate way of looking at politics. By the materials they choose, the media may give us the semblance of an "acquaintance with" the political world, though most of us have but a most indirect knowledge of what it is all about.

The media can also stifle debate and criticism by defining certain elements in a situation as not *actually* subject to controversy. This is most easily done in relation to public personalities and "moral" issues. For example, during the Truman-MacArthur controversy in 1951, the press reported a striking unanimity of public sentiment. In addition to the official hero's welcome for the ousted General, they reported many minor public demonstrations aimed against the Truman administration and indicating sympathy for MacArthur. In retrospect, the unanimity of this sentiment appears to have been misstated.[29] For some months, however, public discussion took its cues from this assumed sentiment, and only the brave politician dared to raise his voice publicly against MacArthur. Most waited until the storm "blew over" and MacArthur was no longer headline news. In much the same way, Democratic criticism of the Eisenhower administration appears to have foundered on the rocks of the unimpeachable hold of his personality on public imagination. How much, we may inquire, has the assumption of reporters about this unshakable popularity prevented them from featuring less popular images of the Eisenhower personality and thus helped to maintain the popular public image as such? This is one type of impact study which we need.

Such definitions of overwhelming public sentiment—"landslide perceptions"—tend to be cumulative. They influence political strategy; they inject a tone into news reporting; they seem to produce a certain reserve in personal discussion, since much conversation revolves around what is assumed to be held in common (like views on the weather). Politicians themselves believe in the importance of band-wagon effects in victory or defeat, and there have been attempts to assess the impact of election forecasts on election results. But this is not merely a matter of confidence or wanting to be on the winning side. For the communicator, assumptions about the public temper "legitimate" what is communicated to the mass. These assumptions likewise "legitimate" omissions. If the assumption about the unanimity of a public mood is erroneous, omissions of news about dissenting views or dissenting imagery make the unanimity much more marked than it is. For it tends to withdraw from personal discussion the very stuff that can be assumed as common political experience and, conversely, leaves uncriticized what everyone else is believed to approve. By influencing both public and private discussion, the saliency of what is at stake is affected, and where this influence enters campaigns, the election itself may be determined.

Individuals in the mass are likely to imagine what others in the mass are believed to be imagining.[30] Thus not only local influences but the beliefs imputed to nameless others exercise their pressure in the mass. Surely, one of the more interesting approaches to mass-media impact on political participation must be the study of private and public imaginations in relation to each other, and their joint relation to what we consider group-relevant reasons for casting a vote.

CONCLUSION. In this chapter we have set ourselves the task of exorcising the currently prevalent emphasis on *how little* mass media determine votes. We all are constantly exposed and sometimes concerned about mass-media influence, and yet this influence escapes our research endeavor.

Studies in voting behavior have dealt with both long-run trends and short-run changes. In either case, since voting rates and voting decisions can be determined with a high degree of validity, we seek inferences about antecedent conditions influencing these end products of political activity. Such influences as age differences, regional locations, and traditional political affiliations which may affect voting habits can with relative ease be isolated for examination. When we come to deal with mass-media influences, however, these are much more difficult to single out. They operate among a multitude of other factors and their effects do not always take tangible shape. Consequently, the measures of mass-media exposure are usually crude and the effects looked for are relatively specific and short run.

Quite naturally, campaign studies such as we have been considering, have focused on the short-range influences operating during the period of active electioneering and on how these culminate in a final voting decision. It so happens, as we have tried to point out, that this approach to the problem, with its emphasis on individual conversion during the "official" campaign, minimizes the important cumulative influences of the mass media and emphasizes instead how political communications are transmitted through personal networks and how latent tendencies are activated. In this way, attention has been focused on the limits to mass-media influence.

Where the question for study is "What makes the electorate tick?" research is naturally shaped to fit the problem; the mass media become just one among many concerns. On the other hand, experts in mass communications have not in recent years distinguished themselves by probing the long-range influence of mass media on political life—and more particularly on voting behavior. The cumulative and society-wide effects about which we often talk vaguely as shifts in public moods or drifts in political opinion are hard to demonstrate; yet, if we would further our knowledge of political behavior, such effects are much in need of clarification. And they can only be clarified through research specifically designed to get at them.

In turning attention to the continuous, and not only the intermittent, aspects of mass-media influence, we must deal, first, with the role of *mass* communications as such, focusing not only on the communicator's job as a transmitting agent for party propagandists but on the direct impress the communications have on what individuals in the mass society know of the larger political world. We have to get at the political perspectives that rise out of the individual's remote participation in politics as a member of the mass and at the relationships between voting behavior and these perspectives.

Moreover, we must develop a more apt definition of relevant changes and "changers." In place of turnover during a campaign, changes in party allegiances between one election and the next, together with discrepancies between "fundamental dispositions" and voting decisions, ticket splitting, and the like, are suggested.

A few specific problems for study have been directly outlined or indicated. The imagery made especially relevant by the mass media—the imagery of the "public imagination," of public personalities, of what politics is really like—and the relationship of such imagery to party alignments seem noteworthy. Among other subjects, the specific role of television, its authenticity and the exploitation of that authenticity by public officials and publicity directors, and the impact of such exploitation on voting participation constitute important areas for inquiry.

CHAPTER 13

TV: A New Dimension in Politics

ITHIEL DE SOLA POOL

VOTING STUDIES AND THE IMPACT OF THE MEDIA CONTENTS. We know little about the political effects of TV—or of any of the mass media, for that matter.[1] Politicians want to know what TV will do, and social scientists cannot begin to answer. Politicians have their own lore about the effectiveness of public speaking, press releases, and other conventional media; they do not ask too many embarrassing questions about them. TV, however, invites questions that political research should have been asking all along. What effects do different campaign methods and messages have?

Topics studied are often functions of the research methods available. Before the seminal Erie County study of 1940,[2] the traditional methods of political science and history had almost a monopoly on voting studies. These methods were often biographic and produced studies of political leadership and of the strategies and programs with which leaders concerned themselves. There were many fine studies, for example, of how Boss X built and worked his machine. The early methods were often documentary and covered platforms, speeches, and editorial comment, treating them as the realities of public opinion and of political battle. Finally, there were studies based on voting statistics. Since the data were geographically distributed, they could be matched with census data. Such studies examined correlations of votes cast in a given election with results at other elections, and the age, sex, income, and ethnic distribution of the voters.[3] That was the status of voting studies before the public opinion polls introduced the survey method to voting research. With it came a fresh and fascinating set of topics.

Surveys tend to focus on the feelings and behavior of ordinary voters. At the same time they tend to refrain from observing the politicians, the campaign organizers, and the reporters. The authors of *The People's Choice* admit candidly that it was only "toward the end of the interviewing we learned from our respondents how important the local Republican machine was in influencing the formation of opinion. By that time, however, it was no longer feasible to study the political situation adequately."[4] But surely they are too self-critical. Men such as the authors of that book and of the chapter in *Voting* on "Democratic Practice and Democratic Theory" were not unaware of the ABC's of politics. More to the point is that their study was an experiment in panel surveying, a valuable method of research but not suited to examining internal machine politics. In the 1948 follow-up reported in *Voting*, the authors made a valiant effort to redress the balance by including in the interview material on the voters' perception of the machine and by supplementing the survey with a separate study of the parties in Elmira.[5] The results add greatly to the book, but are hardly used in interpreting the survey of the voters' behavior. The two analyses do not meet.

That, too, is the limitation of the recent voting studies with respect to mass media, but the later studies show no progress over the earlier ones.

The data collected in the surveys cover what the voter reports having read, seen, and heard. Questions asked carefully and in detail, as they were in Elmira, elicited reasonably objective information on the respondent's exposure to campaign materials vivid and salient enough for him to recall. But without some objective way, independent of the respondent's own consciousness, of determining his response to that material, little can be said about the effects of the varied contents of these campaign messages. Politicians believe that voters are affected by what campaigners say about farm prices, or war and peace; whether they smile or scowl; whether they are seen in person or not; in short, by the character of the messages they put forth. But how far and in what ways this is true we do not know. The recent voting studies have not come to grips with that question.

The People's Choice attempted to come to grips with the relationship of campaign messages and the response to them. An elaborate content analysis was made of campaign materials in the hope that differences in stress at different times or in different media could be related to differences in behavior of respondents exposed to the materials. The results were essentially negative. The crude and vague responses of the voters did not reflect the subtleties of the propaganda contents. Content analysis was reported in only its broadest categories (i.e., general direction of bias), in a short chapter on "What the Voters Were Told."[6] *The People's Choice* contains much fascinating material on the role of the mass media, but not on their effects. It tells who used them; that their use was cumulative; that people attended to material that agreed with their established bias; that in the cases when they did not they were more likely to change. (How far each variable was cause or effect we do not know.) "The campaign activated the indifferent, reinforced the partisan, and converted the doubtful."[7]

Voting, with its greater attention to interpersonal influence, adds little to the earlier volume in its treatment of the mass media. It merely confirms the earlier results. It reports in a few pages the main themes of the campaigns and deals at length with the voters' perceptions of the issues and how these perceptions affected behavior.[8] What it does not deal with is the relationship, if any, between the themes and their presentational methods and the themes as perceived by the voter.

The Voter Decides is much more sketchy in its treatment of the impact of the campaign messages. The interview asked two almost projective types of questions (in contrast to the detailed factual questions in the Elmira survey). The Michigan interview asked: "Did you read about the campaign in any newspaper? (If yes) Would you say you read quite a lot or not very much?"

Similar questions were asked for radio, TV, and magazines.

Then the question was asked: "Of all these ways of following the campaign, which one would you say you got the most information from?"

The results, simply in terms of the number of media used (not which ones), are reported in two pages of the book.[9] The same authors, however, did publish a more detailed analysis of the responses to the above questions in an article in *Scientific American*.[10] Their data suggest that television, though it was in only 40 per cent of homes in 1952, was the most influential medium in the campaign. The authors say, however, quite candidly, "We cannot tell from our studies whether television had a distinctive impact on voters." They also say, "No one really knows, because no specific studies were made to measure the impact of TV on the thinking of the electorate." That is not quite correct, but the authors could not have known when the article appeared of the few isolated studies that were then being made. The drift of what they say is true. Voting studies by 1952 had virtually ceased attempting to ascertain the effect of either the contents or the form of campaign messages on the thinking of the electorate.

Why this abdication? The main reason is that previous attempts had met with failure. In the laboratory it was easy to establish experimental situations in which attitudes could be measurably affected by controlled stimuli. Thus in the work of Hovland, Janis, Kelley, Asch, Festinger, and others, the effects of one-sided or two-sided presentations, the effects of the social environment, the effects of visual and oral presentation, the effects of repetition were all established with reasonable conclusiveness for the limited circumstances of the experiment. In the real-life situation, however, attempts to observe or measure the impact of such variables failed repeatedly. In an election campaign, it seemed impossible by existing research methods to relate the voters' behavior to what was said or how it was said. The candidates might as well have been saying "blah blah" as far as our studies indicate voter reaction.

In retrospect, it is possible to speculate on the reasons for the failure of research to shed much light on what had always seemed by common sense to be among the most significant aspects of the campaign. Several reasons come to mind:

1) The interview method, relying as it does on the voter's own perceptions of the influences on him, is not well suited to measuring the relationship between the actual stimuli and his response to them. How often, in successful laboratory experiments where subjects in different test groups responded differently to different stimuli, could the subjects have described explicitly how they were reacting? Learning better on a second repetition, for example, does not depend on knowing that the repetition is a repetition. Responding to a smile on TV does not depend on recalling the fact of the smile. Asking a voter in a survey which medium he relied on most may sometimes tell us which medium influenced him, but some-

times it may tell us which medium he used most often, or thought most appropriate to the question, or found most reassuring and least disturbing, or likes best for pleasure. These variables may, but need not, determine actual influence, the sources of which may often be forgotten. More use of direct and carefully controlled observation may prove useful in future voting studies.

2) In the real-life situation of voting studies, weak stimuli are working on highly structured and strong attitudes. In the typical psychological experiment, on the contrary, a captive student is devoting his primary attention to doing the odd things the experimenter requires; those of his attitudes, changes in which are being measured, concern some abstract and secondary issue that will not affect him directly. In the electoral situation, on the contrary, attempts are being made to move a man from his lifelong party and social identifications by means, for example, of words that drift into the living room while members of the family wash the dishes, diaper the baby, do homework. There are, of course, political rallies and similar exceptional stimuli, but on the average the salience of the stimulus is lower, the structure of the attitudes on which it works firmer, than in ideal experimental situations.

3) More important, the voter is a free, not a captive subject and chooses the stimuli he will allow to hit him. As *The People's Choice* showed, he is highly selective and prevents strongly alien or provocative stimuli from coming to his attention.

4) To the extent that he does not control the stimuli that touch him, neither does the researcher. The campaign serves, as *Voting* pointed out, to bring him a mass of messages despite himself. The very mass tends to blanket any one message, and among the mass are almost always some that partly contradict and neutralize any given message. This means that the respondent's reactions are reduced. It also means that the observer's clarity in identifying the relevant stimulus is reduced.

5) Perhaps, then, the *direct* impact of the mass media is in fact small. This seems to be the implication of the recent stress by Paul Lazarsfeld and his associates on the opinion leader and personal influence. The opinion leader, well described in *The People's Choice*, moves people face to face. He derives the information and arguments that he uses in part from the mass media. He acts as a relay point in the communication net. Conceivably, the direct

impact of the mass media on the total public may be small, and the media important only as armories for the opinion leaders.

Perhaps that is true in elections and perhaps not. We do not know.[11] The phenomenon of opinion leadership has been demonstrated to exist and is important. Yet it would be surprising if it were important enough to obliterate the direct effects of the mass media. Most political scientists believe, to the contrary, that with the use of radio and TV, and the decline of party machines and political fervor, the direct impact of the media is increasing and that of opinion leaders declining.

This is not to deny the importance of the opinion-leader concept. It marks a major step forward in communications research. We here merely affirm the probable importance of some direct media impacts, although we do not know what they are. After all, the opinion leader selects material from the mass media. This is an impact of the media, and certainly he is not alone in being susceptible to such influence.

6) The opinion leader's *using* the mass media suggests the last and most important point. The voter is not a passive target of the messages of the mass media. Rather, he is a repository of countless bits of previous information. He retains within him a lifetime of earlier messages that have been structured into a series of predispositions. The new message adds one more, but its net effect in changing the balance is infinitesimal compared to its effect as a trigger to responses already determined by predispositions. At any one moment the voter's predisposition is likely to be a far better predictor of his response to a stimulus than the character of the stimulus. A strong enthusiast for candidate X will say that his TV speech was good, regardless of its specific content (within wide ranges). The candidate's mere presence will elicit positive responses. But, of course, a series of disappointments, which individually may not be admitted, may over time change the predispositions. Observation of real-life situations is, however, usually too brief to allow us to note more than the trigger effect of a new stimulus. This has been a major barrier to successful study of the impact of messages.[12] Yet the specific character of the messages received does have its effect. The predispositions are, after all, simply a structural collection of previous messages.

The question becomes how to study the effects of campaign arguments, of the personalities of the candidates, of dramatic staging, of the use of propaganda devices, of the use of one medium rather than another—all the questions, in short, with which campaign managers primarily concern themselves. We know very little about what difference the contents of the campaign make. What can this medium do that the other media cannot do? How will it change American politics? These are among the questions facing students of American elections, and yet little research has been done on them. There is little doubt that the effect of TV will be profound. To say something about the specific quality of its impact is a challenge to students of communication.

The remainder of this chapter reviews one exploratory but only partly successful study which was designed to sort out the specific effects of TV in 1952. Better studies can be built on its lessons. But it, and a few others which will be mentioned, are all we have now.

THE IMPACT OF TV ON CANDIATE'S IMAGES IN 1952. Four main conclusions can be drawn from a set of questionnaires about TV and politics distributed in November 1952.

1) Since the campaign saturated all media it made astonishingly little difference whether a person got his information about the candidates through radio, TV, or some other medium. The voter was likely to gain almost the same image of the candidate. But it was not completely the same. There were small but important differences.

2) TV humanized Eisenhower by revealing him to be somewhat more sensitive and withdrawn than the iron soldier the public had previously imagined. TV did not improve the image of Stevenson though it certainly helped him to become known. Radio was the medium that conveyed an overwhelmingly favorable image of Stevenson.

3) Both candidates were liked and respected by both supporters and opponents. Stevenson was held in somewhat higher esteeem on a couple of skill traits, Eisenhower on personal amiability traits.

4) Except for the powerful impact of Stevenson on radio, the pattern seems to be that TV conveys a more vivid message and makes people more firmly partisan in their own views, whichever candidate they favor. It sharpens the issue.

TV and the older media. Some persons believe that TV will change the character of the heroes of American politics. Many believe that it favors the relaxed, easygoing, friendly campaigner over the demagogue.[13] Perhaps McCarthy wrote himself out of history when his smirking snarl came into America's living room. Nobody has been able to prove these hunches, but they may be true. Many TV artists, producers, and writers believe them, but if TV works that way its impact is so slow, gentle, and subtle that until the present study no one has been able to isolate an effect on a political image, and this study shows at best a mild one. Some small differences appear in the impact Stevenson and Eisenhower made in 1952 on persons who saw them on TV and those who heard them on radio.

The effects of TV appearances on the image the public forms of a candidate do not register alone. Each medium makes its contribution to every other and to the total effect. Whatever image of Ike or Adlai came over the airwaves in turn colored the man later described in gossip or writing. Thus discrepancies among the various media are held to a minimum. As soon as they become sufficiently great to be noticeable, they become newsworthy in other media. This process, which can be technically described as negative feedback, prevents wide differentiation between the contents and effects of different media. It makes it hard to measure the effect of a new medium, for the new medium works not only directly but sends ripples through all the other media. Something useful may be learned from the small differences in the way the two candidates registered on TV and elsewhere.

The research opportunity of 1952. The campaign of 1952 was unique in the way in which it reached the voters. Twenty years before, radio had taken over from the mass meeting and parade. Now TV takes precedence over radio. In 1952, the airwaves were divided. Some people saw TV and some still did not. The 1952 presidential campaign was the only one in which it was feasible to sort out the viewers from the listeners and to compare their reactions. For the researcher it was a unique opportunity.

A few individuals seized the opportunity. Herbert Simon did a study in Iowa where some counties had TV and others did not.[14] Oxford Research Associates did a study in Ohio.[15] Kurt and Gladys Lang did a study in Chicago.[16] The present study was done in California.[17] To seize the moment, with limited resources which precluded any polls, the author collected 1,833 questionnaires from students at Stanford University (very much of an Ivy League school) and San Francisco State College and San Jose State College (schools that partly redressed the social balance). On these questionnaires the students told in detail when and how often each had read, witnessed, or heard a speech by either candidate—in the movies, in the press, in person, on TV, or on radio. Thus we could sort the watchers from the listeners.

The student also listed his voting preference and other vital statistics, and (most important of all) rated each candidate on thirty-eight personal traits. The following are the traits, not in the scrambled order in which they were presented, but sorted out for understanding:

Aggressive
Extroverted
Open
Sturdy
Rousing
Coarse
Cheerful
Good-natured
Likeable
Modest

Withdrawn
Shy
Sensitive
Weak
Uninspiring
Refined
Angry
Spiteful
Disagreeable
Conceited

Folksy
Unreliable
Indecisive
Honest
Sincere
Clear-headed
Brilliant
Practical
Fatherly
Eloquent

Snobbish
Reassuring
Domineering
Crooked
Hypocritical
Dreamer
Unintelligent
Emotional

Clearly, most of these traits can be grouped as "good" or "bad," or they can be grouped in clusters relating to the manifold aspects of the image of man. The problem was to learn whether seeing the candidate smiling and gesturing, walking into the living room through the screen of TV would endow him with traits different from those of a disembodied voice.

To test this we sorted out from the 1,833 students those few whose impressions of a candidate were most purely the product of a single medium. In the case of radio we call these people *the listeners;* in the case of TV, *the viewers.* Listeners were persons who had heard at least two campaign speeches by a candidate but had not seen any—whether in person, on film, or on TV. Viewers were persons who had seen at least two speeches on TV (but none in person or on film), and if they had heard a candidate on radio, it was less often than on TV.

There were, of course, small and distinctive groups. There were:

115 Stevenson listeners	97 Eisenhower listeners
147 Stevenson viewers	124 Eisenhower viewers

It would be risky to draw conclusions from 200 to 250 persons, or less than one fifth of the people who answered our questionnaire. For that reason, we drew as a check a somewhat less restricted second set of comparison groups: persons whose reliance on a single medium was not quite as pure. The movies seemed the most reasonable adulteration to permit in our sample. Rightly or wrongly, we reasoned that people do not go to the movies for politics. Furthermore, the newsreel occupies only a few minutes in the midst of other excitement. From such reasoning we surmised that the impact of the movie image might not too far distort the image received through two or more radio or TV speeches. Therefore we took as our second group of listeners those who otherwise met the requirements but who had also seen the candidate on film. The second group of viewers deviated in the same way from the pure viewers. To our satisfaction it turned out that these larger comparison groups showed much the same contrasting patterns as the pure groups, though less clearly and strongly. In view of this fact, we have felt reassured as to the significance of the results and have done our entire analysis below with the small pure groups. We report herein only results the general trend of which also holds up in the larger less pure comparison groups. The larger groups plus the pure groups encompass a reasonably substantial portion—about 40 per cent—of the total sample, though it still omits the politically apathetic (who had not heard or seen two speeches), the politically avid who went out of their way to *both* hear and see (and maybe even see the candidate in person), and those individuals who through circumstances happened to come on some TV along with radio exposure. Our usable groups numbered as follows:

VIEWERS			*LISTENERS*	
Movies too	*Pure*		*Pure*	*Movies too*
378	147	Stevenson	115	187
377	124	Eisenhower	97	216

The Groups Differed Little in Their Images. What do we learn when we compare these groups? The first and most manifest discovery is how little the groups differed. It would be easy, though not entirely correct, to conclude that the same image came through regardless of the medium to which a person was exposed. On trait after trait that seems to be the case. Take, for example, the percentage rating of Stevenson for cheerfulness.

VIEWERS			*LISTENERS*	
Movies too	*Pure*		*Pure*	*Movies too*
54	54	Fits very well	53	57
36	35	Fits somewhat	35	33
2	6	Does not fit	1	2
9	6	Don't know	11	8

There are no differences there. The audience saw Stevenson as cheerful, and it did not matter through which medium they met him. His reputation for humor and his jokes set a pattern, somewhat modified by his seriousness, which came through to all. The viewer or hearer experienced no new individual reaction as a result of his TV or radio contact. Stevenson had a fixed stereotype in regard to humor which exposure did not contradict. We shall find in this study that the TV image is sometimes used by the viewer as a check upon his stereotypes. If it contradicts them he may change them, but as long as it is somewhat in line, he will see in the picture what he expected to see.[18] If the newspapers have said that Eisenhower is a great leader and he is seen waving to a crowd, that will show Eisenhower to be a great leader. But if the newspapers have said Eisenhower is a great speaker, the same picture of a cheering crowd would prove him rather a great speaker. Thus on traits regarding which established stereotypes and visual experience were not in gross discrepancy, viewers and listeners did not differ.

That psychological propensity (as noted above) helps account for the lack of measurably separate effect of TV and other media. In addition, no medium in a national campaign works by itself. We may now list three reasons why there is consistency between the image that comes out of TV and the image in the rest of the media.

1) Partly it is because the image in each medium is a true reflection of the same man.

2) Partly it is because the same writers put out the same view in each medium.

3) Partly it is because the image that comes through any one medium is then repeated by writers and speakers in other media.

These are the reasons for similarity of the media and are aside from the fact, more closely examined above, that the viewer reads into the picture what he has heard elsewhere and therefore sees the image as even more uniform than it really is. For all these reasons it is not surprising that on so many of the thirty-eight traits there is no discernible TV effect, that is, no difference between viewers and others.

The rating of Stevenson is clearly unaffected by TV on all these traits:

Extroverted	Shy	Weak
Open	Sensitive	
Coarse	Refined	
Cheerful		
Likeable		
Unreliable	Reassuring	
Sincere	Crooked	
Practical	Unintelligent	
Fatherly		

That of Eisenhower is clearly unaffected on:

Open		
Likeable	Spiteful	Snobbish
Indecisive	Domineering	
Sincere	Crooked	
Clear-headed	Unintelligent	
Practical		
Fatherly		
Eloquent		

On the above traits there is *no* TV effect. It should not be assumed that there is a TV effect on *all* the other traits. Some of the other results are merely ambiguous or confused. The above are the traits concerning which our first conclusion, the uniformity of image regardless of channel used, can be asserted affirmatively and with some confidence.

Both Candidates Came Across Well. The second conclusion that stands out is that *both* candidates were regarded as fine and great men by people on *both* sides of the political fence. Eisenhower supporters liked Stevenson and Stevenson voters liked Ike. It was not a struggle of good versus evil but of good versus good.

The following profiles are derived from all 1,833 respondents, not merely from those who used a particular source of information. The profiles held by students who favored Eisenhower are presented separately from those held by students who favored Stevenson, for of course they are different.

Table 13-1—Eisenhower Supporters' Rating of Eisenhower

Percentage saying	*he is:*	*he is not:*
Over 80	Good-natured	Unintelligent
	Sincere	Disagreeable
		Uninspiring
		Unreliable
		Weak
		Snobbish
		Crooked
70-79	Honest	Conceited
	Cheerful	Coarse
	Clear-headed	Withdrawn
		Spiteful
50-69	Sturdy	Indecisive
	Practical	Shy
	Reassuring	Dreamer
	Aggressive	Hypocritical
	Open	

The traits on which there was most consensus in the rating of Eisenhower by Eisenhower supporters are presented in Table 13-1. Besides these:

48 per cent said not *angry*. A little over half divided over the other three choices: Don't know, fits very well, fits somewhat.

41 per cent said not *domineering*. The rest divided showing doubts and uncertainty.

On: Brilliant
Refined
Rousing
Folksy
Modest

they divided between saying it fits very well and it fits somewhat.

On: Eloquent
Extroverted
Emotional

they divided between saying it fits somewhat and it does not fit. On "sensitive" they divided between saying it fits somewhat and saying they did not know, and on "fatherly" they divided between saying fits very well, fits somewhat, and don't know.

The pattern is clear. These Eisenhower supporters saw their man as a strong but happy warrior. The positive traits on which they agreed were: likeable, good-natured, sincere, honest, cheerful, clear-headed, practical, reassuring, and aggressive. Negative traits were mostly rejected out of hand.[19] Doubts entered in two areas: political skill (is he brilliant and eloquent?) and overbearingness (which is the negative side of the image of a great leader). Is he as modest as he should be? Or is he angry and domineering? (These were the bad traits which were least firmly rejected by Ike's supporters.)

Stevenson supporters saw Eisenhower in much the same way. We have already noted that they also liked him, though of course not quite so much. It follows that their percentages of agreement

Table 13-2—Stevenson Supporters' Rating of Eisenhower

Percentage saying	*he is:*	*he is not:*
Over 50	Likeable Good-natured	Unintelligent Withdrawn Snobbish Crooked Shy Weak Unreliable Disagreeable Conceited Coarse
40-49	Cheerful Aggressive Honest Sincere Sturdy	Uninspiring Spiteful Dreamer

on Eisenhower's traits were lower. Thus, for example, 91 per cent of Eisenhower supporters said he was not unintelligent. Stevenson supporters agreed on the whole, but a few more of them pleaded ignorance or even said that he was somewhat unintelligent; so the percentage saying he was not unintelligent was only 79. Similarly, while both Eisenhower and Stevenson supporters felt that the trait "likeable" fitted him very well, the percentages saying this were 89 among Ike supporters, but 60 among Stevenson supporters. Whereas the same pattern holds, the percentages are all down.

The realm of substantial agreement is portrayed in Table 13-2. Once more we note a consensus that Eisenhower has the good traits and does not have the bad. But let us turn to the traits about which there is more doubt. There are traits on which the questionnaires divided between "fits very well" and "fits somewhat." These traits were:

Folksy	Extroverted
Rousing	Emotional

In some instances the doubts were resolved by most respondents by saying the trait fitted somewhat. Over 40 per cent said "fits somewhat" of:

Refined	Clear-headed
Brilliant	Practical

It is worth noting that these traits evaluate not so much Eisenhower the man as his ability.

Then there are the traits on which the division was between "fits somewhat" and "does not fit." These traits are:

Modest	Hypocritical
Angry	Domineering
Indecisive	Eloquent
Reassuring	

Again we find high in the area of doubts the possibility of the General's being "a man on a white horse," immodest, angry, and domineering.

Finally, there were a few traits on which the Stevenson supporters' reaction to Eisenhower was to plead ignorance; notably is he "fatherly" and "sensitive." There was no pattern of agreement on whether he was "open."

So much for the image of Eisenhower. Now what of the image of Stevenson? Here again the image is overwhelmingly favorable both among his supporters and among those who were going to vote against him. He was not as well known as Eisenhower. As a result, the "don't know" replies are more frequent and the other percentages thus somewhat lower, but the image of him is no less favorable.

Table 13-3—Stevenson Supporters' Rating of Stevenson

Percentage saying	*he is:*	*he is not:*
Over 80	Clear-headed	Unintelligent
		Weak
		Unreliable
70-79	Sincere	Uninspiring
	Brilliant	Crooked
	Likeable	Coarse
	Honest	Disagreeable
	Refined	Indecisive
50-69	Good-natured	Spiteful
	Cheerful	Snobbish
	Practical	Conceited
	Eloquent	Hypocritical
	Reassuring	Angry
	Open	Withdrawn
		Dreamer
		Shy
46	Sturdy	
41		Domineering

The items on which his supporters rated Stevenson with much agreement are presented in Table 13-3. They divided, however, on whether he was very or only somewhat: aggressive, rousing, modest. They also divided on whether he was "somewhat" or "was not": folksy, extroverted, emotional.

The parallelism between the images of Eisenhower and Stevenson is striking, but there are some differences. One notable difference between the image of their own candidate held by Eisenhower and Stevenson voters is that Stevenson is held to be brilliant and refined by his supporters while Eisenhower supporters are not sure on these points. The only notable difference besides that is Stevenson's higher rating on eloquence. Otherwise the general ranking of the traits is much the same. In Stevenson's case, as in Eisenhower's, an area of reservation about his character concerned whether he was modest, angry, domineering. Both men were viewed as strong leaders; both as honest and sincere. Many of our respondents did explicitly comment on how much alike the two men were. While the resemblance between the two 1952 candidates may have been greater than is usual, the uniformity of trait rating is also partly a reflection of the strain for consistency which makes it hard to assign other than good traits to good men.

Having said that, let us turn to the last image: the image of Stevenson among Eisenhower voters. We will not be surprised this time to find once more substantially the same pattern. It is portrayed in Table 13-4.

Table 13-4—Eisenhower Supporters' Rating of Stevenson

Percentage saying	he is:	he is not:
Over 50	Clear-headed	Unintelligent
		Coarse
		Shy
		Weak
		Unreliable
		Disagreeable
		Withdrawn
		Crooked
		Uninspiring
40-49	Brilliant	Indecisive
	Good-natured	Spiteful
	Aggressive	Snobbish
	Cheerful	Conceited
		Angry

The Stevenson traits on which the Eisenhower supporters divided between "fits very well" and "fits somewhat" were: rousing, honest, sincere. Those on which the general answer was "fits somewhat" were: likeable, sturdy, practical, reassuring, open. Those on which there was division between "fits somewhat" and "does not fit" were: folksy, hypocritical, modest, domineering. "Don't know" was the predominant answer about: extroverted, emotional, fatherly. And in the case of dreamer, the division was between "does not fit" and "don't know."

One important difference between the Eisenhower image and the Stevenson image emerges in the last set of data. With the Eisenhower voters Stevenson does not do as well on such traits as: likeable, conceited, snobbish, as Eisenhower did with Stevenson voters. This confirms a pattern barely noticeable in evaluating each man's own candidate too. Eisenhower did better on these amiable personality traits, whereas Stevenson did somewhat better on ability traits.

TV and the Candidates' Images. The images we have just detailed were part of the context in which TV operated. What details of the stable favorable image of each candidate were affected by his appearance on TV? We have already noted that they were few. We may now examine which they were.

First let us look for traits where TV had a similar effect on Republicans and Democrats alike. In the entire list of thirty-eight traits Eisenhower is seen consistently differently by TV viewers on only two. People who saw him on TV found him more "sensitive" and "withdrawn." More accurately, a larger majority thought the word "sensitive" fit him either "well" or "somewhat," and a larger, though still small minority, thought him "withdrawn." The pattern is shown on Figure 13-1. The proportions for the whole sample

FIG. 13-1.—Aspects of the Eisenhower image affected by TV. ("Don't know" responses omitted.)

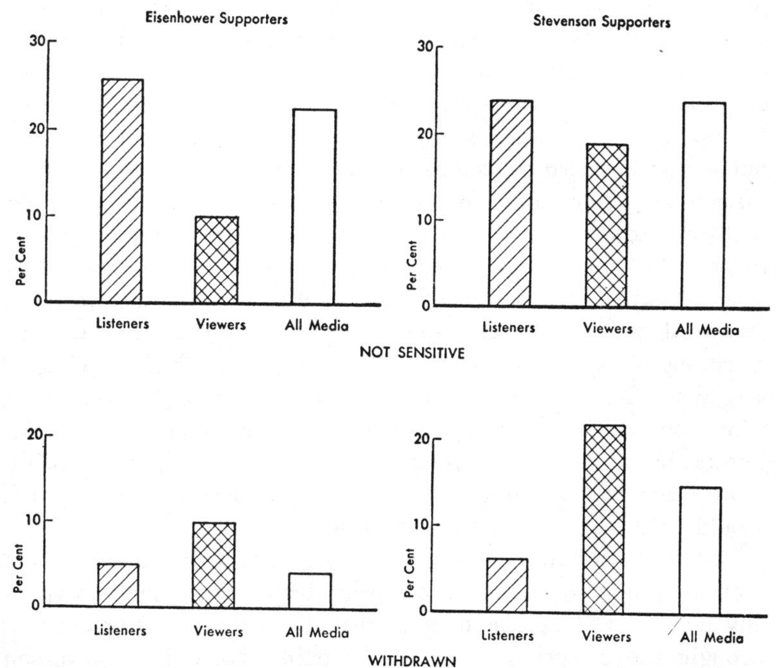

are shown as well as the proportions for the small groups of pure radio listeners and pure TV viewers. Results with the larger comparison groups who also saw him on film follow the same pattern. So do separate results for men and women, high authoritarians and low authoritarians, as well as for Eisenhower supporters and Stevenson supporters. These separate tabulations were made to guard against some adventitious variable accounting for the finding. Only these two related traits, sensitive and withdrawn, met this rigorous test of TV effect. Thus the evidence suggests that TV exposure accounted for the difference in Eisenhower's rating on these two traits.

If so, that tells us something about the Eisenhower campaign and also about the effect of TV in it. It is a curious pair of traits to show up as affected by TV, for they are not part of the normal image of Eisenhower. They are in fact traits more often assigned to Stevenson. The normal image of Eisenhower, at least in 1952, was that of the conquering hero home from the wars—the great General. He was far from unknown to the public, but what the public knew was for the most part a rather abstract figure of a savior and conqueror, gracious to his men as a hero should be, but hardly a simple human being with foibles. What TV did was to chip the graven stereotype. The man who showed up from overseas to appear on the screen was a less overawing character than the public had been led to expect. The discrepancy was not excessive. Eisenhower made no fool of himself. On the whole his image fitted the great expectations that had been built up. But he did turn out to be more of a likeable, good-natured man (the traits most often assigned him) than a powerful, decisive warrior. He was sometimes awkward and sometimes hesitant. His viewers saw him react to situations as a man not cast of iron. The traits on which his viewers saw him differently from those who had only heard his voice were a pair on which he did *not* fit his stereotype. This probably did him no harm, for while "sensitive" and "withdrawn" are probably more negative than positive, they are negative in a mild way that would only add to a hero's humanity.

Unlike Eisenhower, who had a national, even if somewhat abstract, reputation when the campaign began, Stevenson was virtually unknown. This would mean that TV or any instrument that brought the campaign closer to the public could help Stevenson more than it helped Eisenhower. That that actually was what happened has been well documented in the study by Oxford Research Associates, who used a panel survey. Stevenson's problem was to get a public image fast and in that he succeeded. In any case, by the time our questionnaires were answered, in the last week of the campaign, the population we tapped had almost, though not quite, as clear and uniform an image of him as they did of Eisenhower. "Don't know" responses were somewhat more common regarding Stevenson (and, it might parenthetically be added, overwhelming on Sparkman. But already the Stevenson image was sufficiently all-pervasive in the mass media so that his special TV image was no more distinct or identifiable than it was for Eisenhower.

The traits on which, across the board, Stevenson viewers saw him differently from listeners and from the general public of respondents were again only two: snobbish and domineering. These again were not part of the general image of Stevenson. Many more respondents of each party denied that he was snobbish than held him to be even somewhat so, and a plurality of Republicans and most Democrats held him to be not domineering. But in these ratings, the TV viewers were less favorable than the rest. The data are shown in Figure 13-2. The Stevenson who came over on TV was a bit less appealing in these respects than the Stevenson who came through to the rest of the population, however helpful TV may have been in making himself known.

It is hard to pin down the roots of this particular and rather narrowly defined negative effect of TV for Stevenson. We would have been less surprised if the negative image were that of the "egghead," a dreamer, weak, indecisive, for these are the accusations often made by critics. But that was not at all the effect on our respondents of visual or oral contact with Stevenson. He came over as a strong and decisive man. Indeed, as with Eisenhower, immodesty and domineeringness among the negative traits were the ones of which he was suspected. For some reason his TV appearances, instead of putting those fears to rest, added fuel to them. Perhaps the obviously educated and literary character of Stevenson's presentation (which made him seem more brilliant, decisive, and eloquent than Eisenhower, whereas Eisenhower carried off the laurels for being likeable and good-natured) did contribute to the fears of his superiority. Perhaps, however, another

FIG. 13-2.—Aspects of the Stevenson image affected by TV. ("Don't know" responses omitted.)

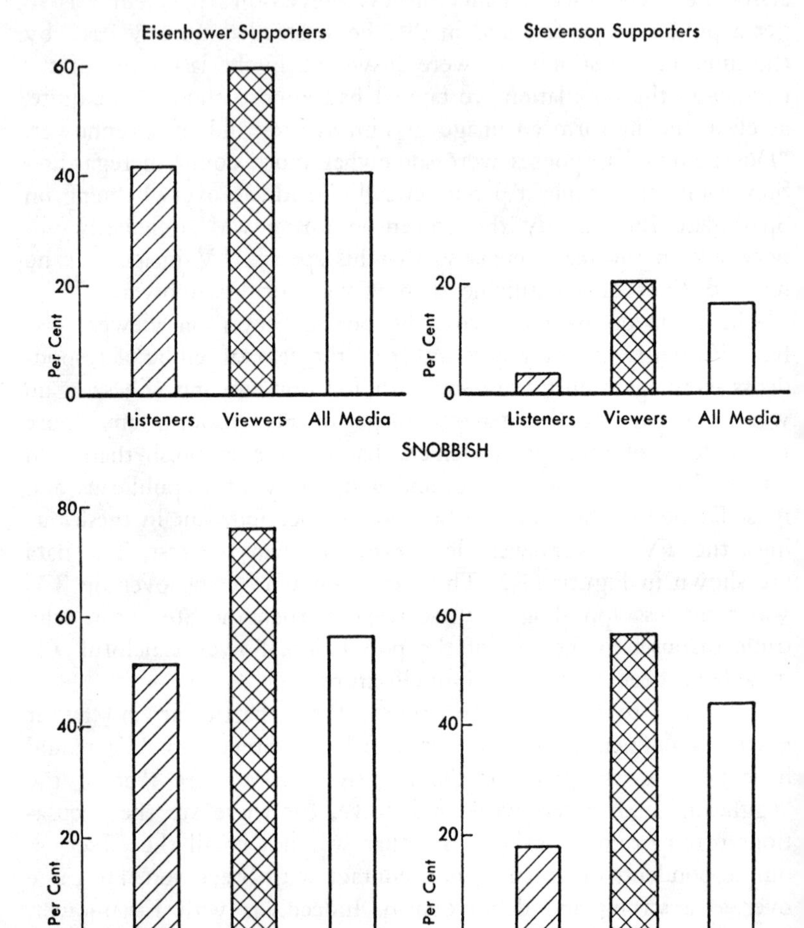

factor specific to TV was even more important. The Eisenhower campaign was a Madison Avenue campaign. The TV programs were produced with all the wisdom and folklore of the public relations and advertising professions. The TV programs had action because that is what TV producers believe in. The shots showed Eisenhower walking, conversing, interacting with other people. Relatively less often was he a lecturing face. The Stevenson campaign, on the other hand, stressed the speech. It lacked the interpersonal touch which the experts fed into the Eisenhower "crusade." It nevertheless had a very favorable impact, but perhaps a Stevenson who had said the same things during shots of conversation or walking and talking and meeting other people (particularly unimpressive "regular" people) would not have affected the TV audience less positively than the radio audience—or might even have affected them more favorably still.

Did TV Intensify the Campaign? If the reader has been examining our figures closely, he may have noted that most often the radio listeners did not deviate appreciably from the total audience in their reactions, though once in a while they did. That is a clue which leads us to our last major conclusion: the way in which the different media heightened attention to the different candidates.

It would be well to note again a few of the things we know from previous voting studies about the relationship of interest and partisanship in political campaigns. Studies such as *The People's Choice* and *Voting* have shown that as a campaign heightens interest, it heightens partisanship; that the people who are most interested are most partisan, that the less partisan people are not as interested in the campaign and do not follow it as closely, and finally that people listen to and read a lot more of their own side than the other side. It is clear that our viewers and listeners are not a cross section of the populace or even of our student sample. They have paid enough attention to the campaign to stamp them as being in the more interested, and therefore more partisan, segment of the population. The Stevenson listeners and viewers are more likely to be for Stevenson, whereas the Eisenhower listeners and viewers are more likely to be for Eisenhower. (This does not affect our previous analysis because we examined the Stevenson voters and the Eisenhower voters separately.)

Now the question arises whether TV is not sufficiently more vivid and exciting than radio so that it would serve to:

1) Make the TV viewers more interested in the campaign.
2) Make them as a result more partisan.

3) Make them as a result more different from the general populace of respondents than the radio listeners.[20]

As a matter of fact, there is some evidence that on the whole this is true, but the picture is a bit more complicated. Let us start by examining once more the image of Eisenhower among TV viewers and radio listeners, for regarding him the above propositions seem largely to hold. It will be recalled that earlier we listed thirteen traits on which there seemed to be no difference between the listeners and viewers. Then we noted two traits on which there was a very significant difference. What of the rest?

In regard to these other traits we found a pattern which we designate as partisan polarization among the TV viewers. What that means may be illustrated by the trait "cheerful." Among the radio listeners 67 per cent of the Stevenson voters and 68 per cent of the Eisenhower voters thought him cheerful; i.e., substantially the same image. The TV viewers, however, were more partisan. Among them, 87 per cent of the Eisenhower voters thought him cheerful, whereas only 43 per cent of the Stevenson voters thought so. If results went consistently this way we would be justified in speculating that TV heightened the impact of the campaign, roused more interest in the viewers, and led them thus to a strengthening and reinforcing of their partisan predispositions. Another example of this is the trait good-natured. Among the Eisenhower listeners, 76 per cent of his supporters and 60 per cent of Stevenson's thought that term fitted him very well. Among the viewers the split is sharper: 87 per cent to 40 per cent. Democrats seeing the same TV performance by Eisenhower came to see him as less good-natured; Republicans as more so. Ten Eisenhower traits show this partisan polarization among the TV viewers. To Eisenhower the reaction of listeners is indeed less extreme and more typically that of the whole population than is the reaction of viewers. It was viewers who gave sharp expression to their political feelings. Perhaps Eisenhower on TV did have more impact in mobilizing those feelings (on both sides) than he did on radio. Perhaps his TV presence was more vivid.

When we turn to the Stevenson data, however, the simple hypothesis of TV vividness is no longer adequate. Often the radio listeners differ most from the average. The point seems to be that Stevenson came over on radio better than on TV. People from *both* sides of the political fence who heard him more than once on radio seem to have been favorably affected. The way in which the pattern of party polarization emerges reflects this fact.

FIG. 13-3.—Two Stevenson trait-ratings showing a frequent pattern of media effect.

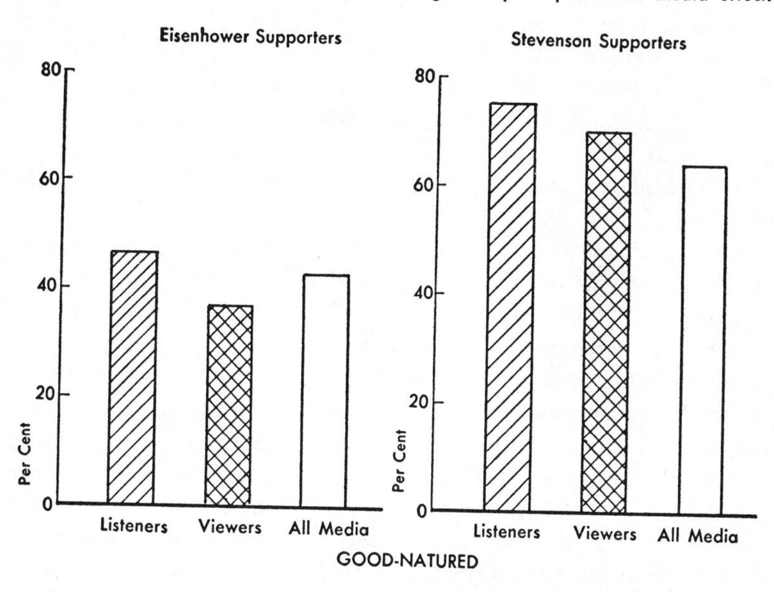

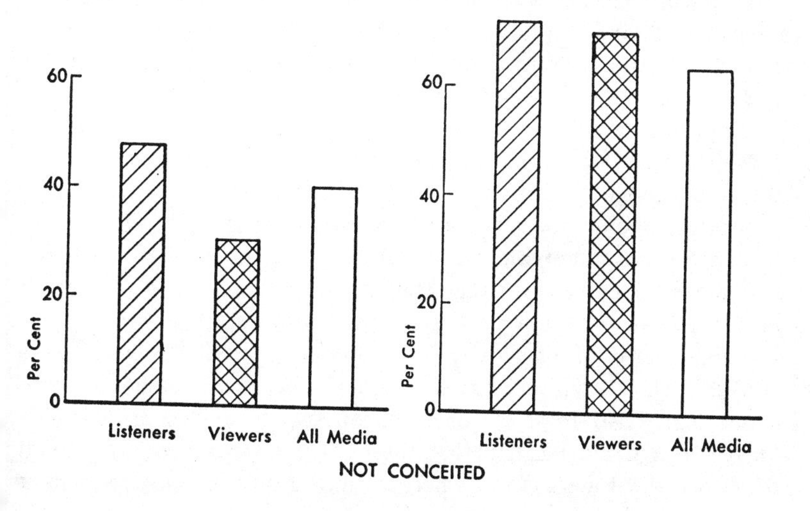

Let us illustrate by reference to two sample traits: good-natured and conceited. A glance at Figure 13-3 will reveal several things. First of all, those Stevenson supporters who exposed themselves to him *either* on radio or TV had a more favorable image of him than the general run of Stevenson supporters (who on the whole were persons less interested and thus less apt to follow the campaign, and less partisan). Yet among these strong Stevenson supporters falling within our listener and viewer groups, the listeners were still more favorable than the viewers. Democratic TV watchers, in short, liked Stevenson *better* than those Democrats who had not seen him but *not as well* as those Democrats who had heard him on radio.

Second, among Eisenhower supporters those who watched Stevenson at least twice on TV had, as we would expect from the above hypotheses, a less favorable image of Stevenson than the general run of respondents. TV may have intensified their reactions as politically interested and therefore partisan Republicans. The listeners to Stevenson among the Eisenhower supporters, however, were also interested and partisan Republicans. Since their communication medium is less vivid, we might expect them to be more like the general public than are the viewers (as we found when examining the Eisenhower stereotype) but also less favorable to Stevenson than the general run of respondents. Actually, they are more favorable! In summary, those Eisenhower supporters who exposed themselves to Stevenson on the radio, despite the fact that they were among the more political and therefore normally more partisan ones, actually came to admire Stevenson more. Radio did a remarkable job for Stevenson, and Stevenson did a remarkable job on radio.

Viewing the same data in another way, we can say that polarization was indeed occurring among the viewers. The Stevenson supporters among them were more favorable and the Eisenhower supporters less favorable to Stevenson than the general populace of such respondents. Among the listeners, however, there was a uniform trend in favor of Stevenson.

This pattern of partisan polarization among Stevenson viewers and uniformly favorable reactions among his listeners shows up to some degree for most of the traits on which any media effect is visible. It will be recalled that there were sixteen traits on which no effect was found. Two others showed a uniform negative effect of TV on the Stevenson image. (A glance at Figure 13-2, which deals with these two traits, will show that, even regarding them, the presently discussed more common pattern was partially operating. Radio listening in most cases produced a favorable revision of the Stevenson image.) Five other traits showed the pattern in all details and nine more in substantial part.

How Generalizable are These Findings? The behavior we have observed occurred while Stevenson was transforming himself from an unknown into a national figure in 1952. We have already noted that the specific and peculiar effect of TV in the 1952 Eisenhower campaign was to highlight certain of his human qualities, which the public had not anticipated in the military man. The specific radio and TV impact of Stevenson in 1952 was a function of the conditions of the time. There was a wave of public feeling against a supposed mess in Washington and an almost hysterical reaction to "dirty" politics in any form. Eisenhower certainly benefited by that mood, but so did Stevenson. His extraordinary speeches coming over the airwaves set a tone to which the public responded. His TV performance worked in part in the same way to bring to the public the revelation of a previously unknown great man, but at the same time his TV behavior lacked the interpersonal warmth that the medium can sometimes convey. In the particular context of 1952, the radio impact of Stevenson was therefore exceptional, his TV impact was just ordinary.[21]

CHAPTER 14

The Relation Between Primary and Secondary Identifications: Psychiatry and the Group Sciences

C. W. WAHL, M. D.

If a brick building is to be sound, the builder must know not only how the bricks are put together, but also something of the nature and structure of the individual bricks. On these two factors—the structure and composition of the individual unit, and the fashion in which they are combined—does the integrity of the building depend. Similarly, we cannot study the complex social organizations and institutions of mankind with real insight if we do not base our suppositions on an intimate and detailed knowledge of the men who make up these institutions—their secret hopes, fears, desires, and strivings, both known and unknown to them—for these significantly operate to motivate and influence their social selves. In the mass, their shared individual imperfections and blind spots, their collective misapperceptions and irrationalities form "social neuroses," distortions in the social fabric which unfortunately we are often too prone to explain in retrospect on purely sociological and economic grounds. However, it is becoming increasingly evident that the great unconscious depths of man's personality play a significant, if not crucial, role in initiating his social behavior and group formations. If we are truly interested in his group functions, we cannot afford to ignore these depths.

Voting and political behavior are prime examples of social acts and beliefs which superficially appear to have been formed preeminently by processes of conscious and rational forethought. On closer examination, however, they show evidence of influence by more subtle factors and motivations which, covertly and unknown to the thinking self, have determined their appearance and form. In political convictions, as in other areas of opinion value and belief, are concealed irrational motives of which we are largely unaware. But perhaps in no other area, save possibly that of religion, is the average person more convinced of the logical, defensible, and wholly rational nature of his decisions. We note that he can support his voting choice with animation and vigor. He can and does discuss the pros and cons of his choices with his friends, family, and associates; he can ponder the avenues of action open to him in his mind and yet remain comfortably purblind to what would appear to an external observer as the biased nature of his eventual choice. He can remain equally blind to the role of his political choice in achieving a fulfillment of extraneous wishes and desires of which he has, if any, but slight conscious awareness. The average person here manifests in a very clear fashion what has been called in psychiatry by Dr. Harry Stack Sullivan (**9**), the "mechanism of selective attention"; i.e., he perceives and notes only those observations and arguments which tend to support his point of view, largely ignoring unconsciously those which refute them. Hence, he is not often dissuaded from this stand even when the opposing arguments are cogent, insistent, and compelling.

The collectivity of psychotherapeutic experience suggests that the areas of politics and religion are for most of us more deeply immune to the rational processes than are any other portions of our conscious beliefs and value systems. Though rationality may largely govern the remainder of our lives, these two areas often are largely exempt from its purview. This supports the frequently made observation that our convictions and views thereupon are accepted by most of us as "*donnée*" and we largely exempt them from the motivational scrutiny which the average mature person is accustomed to train on his other and more personal activities. The hypothesis offered here is that the secondary identifications, such as our choice of political party, are not so much a result of family traditions of habit, class, or response to the issues involved (though these are certainly relevant factors). Instead these identifications are primarily expressions of individual needs to secure gratification of repressed wishes for a certain type of parental image; a type that will vary depending on the nature and circumstance of the past parental relationship. Hence, much of our political behavior and candidate choice are, in my view, largely unconscious, subrogative attempts to recapitulate the primary and parental identifications or to form new secondary identifications antithetical to the parental ones.

However, the view that societal and other collective forms of mass behavior are extensively influenced or modified by individual psychical forces of which the person may have very limited awareness, is not a concept which has been widely accepted by social scientists. Their position has been described by von Hayek who says in *The Counter-Revolution of Science* **(10)**, "The social sciences deal not with the relations between men and things or the relations between man and man. They are concerned with man's actions, and their aim is to explain the intended or undesigned results of the action of many men. Social sciences, in the narrower sense, are concerned with man's conscious or reflective actions, actions where a person can be said to choose between various courses open to him. *This claim presupposes that we are able to arrive at a substantive explanation of why we hold the particular views we hold*, and how additional knowledge is determined by specific conditions." [Italics mine.] Most psychiatrists, on the other hand, would probably be of the opinion that this presupposition is too sweeping and inclusive. For while no one will deny that man is, in the main, a rational animal, it is apparent that we are not always able to give substantive explanations of why we hold our particular views or why we adhere to one set of beliefs rather than to another. The many flaws and imperfections in man and in civilization, his collective product, attest to many residual irrationalities. Yet, von Hayek appears to arrogate to conscious reflection and ratiocination not the dominant, but the exclusive role in the formation of action and belief.

The widespread disinterest in the relationships adumbrated above is not an unmotivated phenomenon. Society has come to accept the desirability of an extensive and thorough inquiry into the antecedents of such activities as criminal behavior and psychiatric illness. The multitude of foundations and research groups investigating these problems attest to this acceptance, but the more recondite motivation of political activity has been almost totally ignored. Most of us do indeed derive a sense of comfort in excepting certain domains of our value systems and behavior from psychological and motivational scrutiny. Yet for our own collective safety this is an area of research which cannot long be deferred.

We are often inclined to forget that the vote is more than an individual or legislative act; it is a powerful form of affirmation or of protest. Moreover, it can be a collective coercive device whereby one can play a part in compelling others to his way of thinking and thus attempt to insure their adherence and belief. In its essence such coercion stems from unconscious forces and drives, which in other times and in other ways may take the form of criminal behavior, of revolutionary activity, of psychosomatic or psychoneurotic disorders. The power to vote, like the power to tax, is the power to destroy. And we can no more permit ourselves to survey the voting act complacently than we can ignore the power and the immediacy of the atom bomb.

What then are the unconscious factors and antecedents which may significantly motivate or modify voting and other political behavior? Lest one promise too much, it is necessary to say that it is not usually possible for the psychiatrist to be able to delineate exactly the relationship between complex social behavior, such as voting choice, and unconscious psychological factors. First of all, the patient can never be a designed experiment begun, pursued, and concluded for a specific research end. Both medical ethics and the nature of psychotherapeutic work itself largely preclude the use of historical and therapeutic materials for other than the patient's own end. Secondly, the number of patients seen in psychotherapy, even over a long period of time, are too few in number to be statistically significant for the investigation of any such modality.

Despite these disadvantages, intensive psychotherapy constitutes the most searching and the most thorough of all methods of individual human study yet devised and it offers an insight into human character and motivation which no other method can equal. For this reason psychiatrists can often be of help to social scientists in their study of such phenomena as voting behavior, since the information obtained from patients in psychotherapy often has a decided relevance to the study of the motivations of political life and mechanisms of voting choice. The practicing psychiatrist has frequent opportunity to learn of the political persuasion and voting behavior of his patients, and he obtains this information in a context of an understanding of them deeper than that possible in less searching methods of inquiry. Therefore, while the psychiatrist can not give *definitive* answers to complex social problems and issues, he can give *indicative* ones. He is obliged thereafter to relinquish to his colleagues in the behavioral sciences the task of isolating and verifying any hypotheses he has advanced.

When psychotherapy has progressed to a point where an intimate and sequentially arranged knowledge of the patient has been acquired, a remarkable correspondence is often found between his political views and voting behavior and certain factors and antecedents in his past history. Bearing in mind that the following are impressions gleaned from a relatively small number of patients, it may be said that there often appears to be a striking correspondence between the nature, quality, and intensity of the primary parental identifications, or their lack, and subsequent political choice. Among other things, it appears that if a strong identification has been made with the significant same-sex socializer (usually the parent), there is subsequently evinced a tendency to maintain and reinforce the political views held by this parent. This seems, for obscure reasons, to be more often true for men than for women. Conversely, when this process of identification has been impaired or has not ensued, there seems to be often a wide divergence in political opinion and belief between the individual and his parent. This identification can be impaired in many ways: antecedent loss of the parent by death, divorce, or separation; conflict between the two parents; intense and persistent rejection; punitive behavior; or apathy, indifference, or vacillation on the part of the parent. All these may produce conflicts. These conflicts frustrate basic needs which later appear to find vicarious and veiled expression in other secondary, nonparental activities and identifications.

It is necessary, however, to mention at this point that the concept of identification is used here in the somewhat specialized sense in which it is used in psychiatry; namely, an internalization, largely unconscious and alogical, of the attitudes held toward one by the significant persons in one's early life, usually the parents.

We know that the processes of rational appraisal, of abstraction, of conceptualization, of self-estimation, are not naturally inherent in the psyche. They are the product of learning and experience, slow and uneven in development. Unlike an adult, the child has little capacity to comfort himself by hope, reason, language, or by making a decisive change in his environment. He is largely unable rationally or objectively to appraise himself, the world, or his place in it, without the help of others. He is dependent on others not only for his bread and butter, but for any sustained conception of his worth and adequacy. This conception of his worth and merit is invariably obtained by an uncritical absorption of the prevailing attitudes held toward him by others. The child has much the same attitude toward his parents as a religious adult has toward the Divinity; i.e., he regards them as omnipotent and omniscient and tends uncritically to accept their attitudes toward him as judgments which are not to be questioned. If the parents are consistent, loving, and nurturant and if they themselves possess an approving self-regard, the child takes within himself their habits, values, and methods along with their good esteem for him. He *identifies* with them and these initial paralogical identifications are referred to throughout this chapter as the "primary identifications." These identifications change markedly, of course, as maturation proceeds. In the average person, the basic unconscious sense of personal worth is retained but there develops an increasing freedom to subject the values and opinions of the parent to logical and social scrutiny and thus to modify one's old adherence to them without experiencing excessive guilt.

Conspicuous and far-reaching results occur, however, if this development does not take place. For the growing child is ubiquitously exposed to many situations which induce rage, fear, and guilt. If, for example, the parents are essentially rejecting, vacillating, inconsistent, or highly anxious persons, then the child is faced with the dawning realization that to these persons upon whom he looks as all-powerful and all-knowing, he is considered worthless, wicked, and unacceptable. His natural needs for succor, security, and for stable and gratifying parental relationships are not met. As he grows to maturity these needs still unconsciously persist but are secondarily and irrationally displaced. His choice of friends, employers, social groups, and spouse and his attitude toward government will reflect these unconscious needs and may thus often be vicarious fulfillments of the previously frustrated infantile longings. Furthermore, the child's natural feelings of ambivalence toward the parents are immensely reinforced by these pathological parental attitudes. The result is that the feelings of hatred, as well as the strong feelings of guilt, which the wish to destroy and usurp the unloving, derogative parents induce, are usually internalized, repressed, and subsequently displaced elsewhere. Extreme oversolicitousness on the part of the parent has an effect similar to rejection because it implies to the child that he is essentially weak and unable to cope with the frightening external world, thus reinforcing his conception of himself as damaged and worthless.

We are all aware, of course, that the usual person does not come from a home which has been fragmented nor has he had parents who manifested the extremes of rejection or overprotection described here. These are pathological states which have been described, not the normal ones. But it must be remembered that the pathological states differ from normal ones in quantity rather than quality. They are bold, magnified canvases on which can be seen more clearly the processes less evidently operative in other individuals and, as such, they merit our closest attention and study. *All* early relationships, and all the needs expressed therein, whether they be gratified or frustrated, do significantly influence our subsequent interpersonal and social relationships. It must also be remembered that the experiencing of these pathological parental attitudes or of parental loss does not necessarily result in subsequent neurotic pathology. Later maturational experiences may largely bind up these early wounds to the psyche, and no subsequent neurosis need eventuate. Maturation however, is a course which by its very nature is complex, fraught with impediments, and never traversed with complete success. The result is that in all persons there is a latent core of irrationality which impels us to pursue and attempt to gratify latent frustrated needs.

This digression has been necessary to point out that an infantile need to usurp, alienate, overthrow, or defeat a parental figure, or a converse need to adhere strongly and consistently to the parents' values and teaching, or a need to achieve and gratify infantile longings vicariously all unconsciously persist into adult life. These needs can significantly motivate the decisions and extrafamilial group relationships of which political behavior is a salient example. "Homo

Politicus" does not spring like Athena from Zeus's forehead fully caparisoned and accoutered. He burgeons slowly and unevenly within the family circle and both his penchant for action, reflection, and rational thought and his emotional expectations and needs are profoundly influenced at a very early age by factors of which he may later have little conscious recollection. His subsequent political decisions and loyalties are thus laden with, and subject to, the same unconscious and irrational drives which may covertly influence his interpersonal behavior and decisions.

The same factors, therefore, which produce personal neuroses also produce social neuroses. Hence, the main sources of political behavior and the secondary identifications of which it is an example must be sought within the individual mind which was so extensively influenced by the first group of which he was a member, namely, the family.

The use of political identifications to gratify longings of which we are largely unaware appear not to have been noted, much less considered or studied, by political and social scientists. Perhaps this is true because such relationships are much less evident in America than in such countries as France. There, owing to the broad spectrum of political parties from far left to far right, the individual can choose a party which most closely represents and gratifies his unconscious interpersonal needs. In this country vastly dissimilar persons, both in political persuasion and antecedent family background, can be found dwelling, if not in comfort at least in moderate amity, together under the umbrella of our two major political parties. And it is significant that even the differences between these parties are by no means antipodal. The Russians see the Democrats and the Republicans as being no more different than tweedledum and tweedledee and express surprise at what we take for granted; i.e., that persons who are vastly dissimilar in belief and aim can find a common haven in any one party. Because of the common appellation Democrat or Republican we are often apt to assume that all persons within either party think and act alike. A vote, after all, can only be for or against a given candidate, though the processes of ratiocination or their lack may differ vastly from one voter to another. The internal satisfactions or frustrations which the vote gives the voter may differ just as widely.

Hence, the familial prototypes which the individuals may wish to resurrect in government and the vast differences among these prototypes are largely overlooked by us.

Psychiatrists, for their part, have often neither the interest nor the training to pursue the relationship between primary and secondary groups. Social scientists, whose interest and purview is normally the organization and interaction of secondary groups, for similar reasons very rarely concern themselves with the psychological ontogenesis of the persons who compose the larger group they study. The result is that between these two specialties is a no-man's land which is investigated by neither.

The extent to which these relationships have been ignored in studies of political motivation is illustrated in the very interesting book, *The Voter Decides*, by Campbell *et al* **(2)**. The authors have listed six major psychological variables which they believe to be relevant to an individual's decision to vote and to his choice of candidates. They are: (1) personal identification with one of the political parties, (2) concern with issues of national and governmental policy, (3) personal attraction to the presidential candidates, (4) conformity to group standards of one's associates, (5) a sense of personal efficacy in the area of politics, and (6) a sense of civic obligation to vote. Although personal and familial antecedents were not within the interest or scope of this study, it is significant to note that the authors apparently did not consider antecedent familial experience and presumably felt that it had little relevance to the problem of voting choice. This, if so, is in marked contravention to the totality of psychotherapeutic experience which suggests that in many instances the primary familial identifications are the vital factors which most strongly, if covertly, influence political choice.

The hypothesized relationship between primary familial identifications and secondary group identifications may also cast light on some interesting data compiled by Lazarsfeld *et al.*, in *The People's Choice* **(7)**. This group of social scientists remained in Erie County, Ohio, from May until November, 1940, in order to observe the progress and effect of the presidential campaign in that community. They noted that 77 per cent of their panel members said their parents and grandparents had voted consistently for one or the other of the major political parties and that they themselves had maintained these family traditions in the 1940 election. After the election, only 4 per cent of the 413 panel members who voted claimed that someone in their families had voted differently than themselves. Similarly, Berelson *et al.* in *Voting* **(1)** find that there is a high degree of agreement (about 90 per cent) in political preference within the family. They note, too, that voting change appeared to be related to the political preference of the family members. These data appear to substantiate the hypothesis that the primary familial identifications have a power and cogency in the role of political choice which enables the individual to be largely resistant to the group and social pressures and the propaganda efforts which Campbell *et al.* consider of primary importance in motivating political choice.

In addition, Berelson *et al.* found that people under cross-pressures (between social class and religion, between friends and co-workers, between friends and family) come to their final decision later than people of homogenous circumstances and moreover, the more intimate the conflict (as between family and friends), the later the decision.

If this is true, we should expect to find that the conflict within the most *intimate* group, the primary family, would be the most intense of all. This is to be inferred from the above statement and also from psychotherapeutic experiences. None of these three studies appear to consider the possibility that this primary group has any significant or vital role to play in later political and voting decision. A consideration of such relationship would perhaps enable us to answer questions like the following: What is the resultant political behavior if there is broad disagreement between mother and father or between one of the parents of the voter and his siblings? What effect does widespread sibling rivalry have upon voting behavior? What mutations in political views might eventuate if one or both parents have been lost by antecedent death, divorce, or separation? How does perversion of the paternal or maternal image, caused by the evincement of manifestly pathological attitudes such as rejection or overprotection, act to influence subsequent political views and behavior? How does this influence differ if such attitudes are evinced more by one parent than the other? Does severe and persistent vacillation in the display of regard to the child by the parents act to render his subsequent decision in political life indecisive, inconsistent, and belated? Social scientists have themselves never seriously considered these questions nor have they included as members of their investigating teams persons who might help to formulate and elucidate problems such as these.

These and many other similar questions must remain unanswered until investigated by definitive research, for as yet we know almost nothing about how our secondary identifications, such as political party, are related to the primary ones. It is quite apparent that our political party affiliations are highly emotionally surcharged loyalties and that we often tend to perceive one party as hero and the other as villain; one as succorant and giving, the other retentive and refusing; one interested in "the common man," the other the instrumentality of "special interests." If the primary identifications are prototypic of the secondary ones, the needs and wishes which were unfilled in childhood are irrationally transferred to the political party of our choice. We would then expect that a conflict between the maternal and paternal images in childhood would result in the conflict of voting choice. This would be an approach-avoidance conflict so that no voting action could be taken or a vacillation and postponement of voting decision. Lazarsfeld *et al.* found that of their panel 29 per cent intended to vote and knew for whom they would vote, 7 per cent intended to vote but did not yet know for whom, and an astounding 64 per cent did not intend to vote at all. These authors also noted that the panel members fell into two main groups, those who did not change their political opinion during the period of study and those who changed in a variety of ways. This they called "turnover" and 13 per cent represented the turnover which took place a few weeks prior to the election. It would be interesting to know if the persons manifesting this instability of voting behavior or failure to vote had prior experience of the kind of parental ambivalence alluded to above.

Lazarsfeld *et al.* also made the interesting observation that of the many cross-pressures, social and otherwise, which resulted in voting indecision, the most effective appeared to be lack of complete agreement within the family. These data suggest that to the congruence of social factors which influence political behavior must be added the antecedent intrafamilial ones as well.

Berelson *et al.* also make the interesting observation that among their panel voting indecision was highly correlated with neuroticism. This is not altogether surprising. Voting indecision represents conflict as does neurotic behavior. Presumably, the extensive self-preoccupation which is generally characteristic of the neurotic largely precludes his taking a firm interest in national affairs. The authors conclude that a relative freedom from personal maladjustment is required if an individual is to focus his attention on public rather than on exclusively private concerns. They measured neuroticism by the degree of affirmative response to this four-statement index: (1) I have to struggle for everything I get in life, (2) Prison is too good for sex criminals; they should be publicly whipped, (3) A lot of people around here ought to be put in their place, and (4) I often find myself worrying about the future.

In discussing this index they say, "Even the so-called 'neuroticism' index is, among other things, a measure of social rapport, confidence, and trust." Or stated in another fashion, the neurotic has impaired secondary identifications. Most psychiatrists would agree that other than superficially the neurotic is not warmly identified with mankind and with social groups. He does often lack social rapport and social interest and yet though this is a point on which the authors and most psychiatrists would be in fundamental agreement, none of the statements listed in the index appear to test the lack of social rapport which the authors themselves consider to be primary to neurosis. Even considering the limited scope of the inquiry, the panel statements above, in my opinion, are not those best calculated to delineate neurotic character formation or symptomatology. An affirmation to the first statement that one is struggling for everything in life and worrying about the future is an indication of a dilemma to be sure, but not necessarily a neurotic dilemma. An agreement with statements two and three might indicate bias and social resentment but again not necessarily neurosis. If the authors felt that a high degree of neuroticism does have a relationship to certain aspects of political behavior, then is it unreasonable to hope that social scientists would not attempt to be all things to all men but would instead avail themselves of the help which psychiatrists and psychologists might be expected to supply in such a situation?

It is not appropriate here to enter upon a detailed discussion of what constitutes neurosis. But it also may very well be that it is not possible to delineate the degree of neurosis in response to so exiguous a questionnaire. Such a determination may require a more subtly contrived and more extensive instrument but if I were forced to construct one in its place I would be inclined to favor this group of statements: (1) I find it hard to think of anything but myself and my problems, (2) I feel more anxious, worried, and troubled than I think I should, (3) I often have fearful and distressing dreams, and (4) I am somewhat inclined to be superstitious. These impinge, however slightly, on the primary symptoms and manifestations of neurotic disorders, namely, (*a*) a tendency for an excessive and ruminative self-preoccupation, (*b*) an inability to master internal conflict as evidenced by frequent painful states of emotion, (*c*) an increased frequency of attempts at mastery of these conflicts by employment of nocturnal and diurnal dreams, and (*d*) a penchant for heavy reliance upon unconscious and magical methods of problem solution.

It is interesting to note that the authors found so remarkable a correlation between neuroticism and voting indecision even though they used an instrument to measure neuroticism which is inadequate in many respects. It would be extremely interesting to repeat the experiment employing a more adequate measure. Such a study would greatly clarify many aspects of political behavior about which at present we know very little. If the neurotic who is prone to voting indecision has impaired secondary identifications with social groups, then it is even more true that he has impaired primary identifications, since it is from the latter that the former develop. Hence, I consider the evidence of Bereison *et al.* to manifest the theme I have been adumbrating, namely, that a decided though variable relationship exists between early pathology with the primary identificants—the parents—and the subsequent political persuasions, or lack of them, which develop.

Sociological, technological, and cultural factors have resulted in marked changes in intrafamilial patterns from the days of our sires and grandsires, and this may operate in many subtle ways to affect political life in this country. One change of great significance for psychological and political development is the growing tendency for the *paternal* influence in the home to be greatly minimized. We note that the complexities and patterns of modern life increasingly require the father to be absent from the home. He is usually off to work before the children arise. He returns home at the end of the day to have dinner with the family and may or may not be beguiled from the evening newspaper or television to have a brief contact with his children before they are packed off to bed. Other contacts with his children are progressively becoming fewer and farther between. The result is a high incidence of family groups in which paternal presence and authority are more theoretical than actual.

Moreover, there seems to be a progressively lessened paternal stature within the home. Frequently European obserevrs chide us by saying that American families are becoming wife-ridden. They note critically that men are willing to surrender prerogatives and status to their wives to a degree inconceivable in a European household. The British anthropologist, Geoffrey Gorer (**5**), states that most Americans seem to be intensively concerned with the problem of masculine identification and he attributes this to the predominantly feminine influence in our early lives. Perhaps it is also significant that such mass media as "Blondie," "Li'l Abner," and "I Love Lucy," to name but a few, have as themes the trials and difficulties of the stupid, bumbling, passive boy-husband who is repeatedly saved by the sagacity, forthrightness, and horse sense of the mother-wife. If the function of laughter is, as has been said, to preserve us from pain and depression—that we tend to laugh that we may not cry—then perhaps it is indeed better that such a state of affairs amuses us rather than reduces us to depression, self-hatred, or mayhem. It is noteworthy that these themes are so widespread and that they so titillate the vast majority of men and women today.

It is interesting to speculate whether this authority vacuum in the home and the transfer of the directive parental role from the father to the mother are reflected in the increasing interest in many levels of our culture for a more authoritarian and paternalistic government, one featuring a maximum of security and a minimum of hazard. May this result in a tendency on the part of many people to secure such a state by the vote?

Many political commentators are alarmed by the increasing tendency during the last quarter century for voters to seek the establishment of an ever stronger chief executive and to personify him as the whole of government. Governmental function is then perceived largely as a reflection of the person of the president and of his character, beliefs, and personal attributes. More and more he is cast willingly or unwillingly in the role of an all-powerful, all-seeing "great white father" who bears the entire personal responsibility for any governmental shortcomings and to whom all praise is due if things go well.

A most revealing illustration of the nature and extent of these displaced parental identifications was shown by the public reaction to the death of Franklin D. Roosevelt in 1945. It was striking to note that the majority of persons reacted to his death with a stunned incredulity and a deep sense of personal loss and bereavement. Orlansky (**8**) and de Grazia (**3**) have written two excellent studies of the ramifications of this event. They were both impressed by the frequency with which individuals who were most strongly affected by the President's death had projected to the President intense expectations of omnipotence and immortality in a manner comparable only to the attitudes of prelogical children toward the early father and mother imagoes. Thus the death of the President was not only a shattering event in its own right but portentous of the disillusion of the parental imagoes and through them the self and the world. Orlansky quotes many persons who described the world as stopping or appearing changed and damaged subsequent to the event. Fairbairn (**4**) describes very similar reactions among the British to the death of the late George VI. These descriptions suggest to us the extent of the object overestimation which is so characteristic of infantile identification states. One might wonder if this common propensity to identify so strongly with the Chief of State reflects an increasing need to obtain a surrogate for the pristine omnipotent father and mother of whom our changing cultural mores are steadily depriving us.

On the other hand, is the state perceived by persons who have originated from a deprived paternal environment as a matriarchal government, one functioning as a matriarchal substitute for the absent father and promising a maternal-like succor in the form of a womb-to-tomb security? Or does it motivate conversely the wish to destroy or alter the status quo and to usurp or overthrow a government which so closely resembles the ambivalently regarded wife and mother? In psychotherapeutic practice one can see convincing examples of these several dynamisms. My point, if somewhat belabored, is that psychological and socio-cultural research has not enabled us even to formulate, much less answer, these questions. Unless there is a growing awareness among behavioral scientists that archaic and unconscious intrafamilial factors such as these do subtly modify the men and women who compose the social fabric and that these modifications do have a salient effect on the secondary groups and their interactions, we shall not materially progress to any deep understanding of the complexities of political life.

Lastly, I wish to consider an almost totally neglected area and one which literally cries out for joint research by political scientists and psychiatrists. This is the phenomenon of those political movements of our time characterized by a manifest exaltation of the concept and functions of the state, and by a concomitant wish to modify the political, governmental, social, and cultural status quo by force and violence.

Perhaps also there is no area about which there is more muddled thinking in high places. In regard to one of these movements, the Communist party, the State Department proceeds on the naïve assumption that economic privation is the "*fons et origo*" and we have only to disburse enough millions of dollars for it to vanish from the face of the earth. Mr. Whittaker Chambers and a phalanx of theologists assure us that the Christian religion is the only needed remedy and they recommend, as it were, that we exchange one absolutism for another. Still another proffered remedy is the dispersal of a sufficient number of hydrogen bombs.

I submit that before we proceed to vanquish such a movement, if indeed, this is the solution, we must first study it. A search of the literature shows an appalling lack of well-designed and thoughtfully pursued studies of the antecedents of persons who compose such movements. This paucity of study is all the more remarkable since there is such widespread agreement that they do constitute a problem and since we are living in an age which uses the scientific method widely in the solution of other problems.

More specifically, we need to investigate the phenomenon of what might be called the antecedents and etiology of the "revolutionary personality." Not because such persons constitute a sizable proportion of the voting population in this country, but because they show, in magnified form, the manifestation of drives and needs which, in attenuated or altered forms, are just as apt to find expression in the Democratic and Republican parties. And we must also learn to distinguish the dissenter and the individualist from the revolutionary. The former are often execrated today as though they were the latter. The dissenter, however annoying he may be to some, manifests a quality which is of great good to mankind; our political and social life must be organized in such a way as always to give him a forum. The revolutionary wishes to force his dissenting views on the social fabric and the lives of others. This is hardly to be condoned even though it is ostensibly all for the eventual good of mankind.

What then is known about the characteristics of revolutionary groups and the persons who compose them? It has been repeatedly noticed that such groups closely emulate, and are often subrogative for, religious groups. They are characterized by the same intense group life, the same need to promulgate and adhere to dogma, and by a similar insistence upon unquestioning belief on the part of the participating members. In addition, their political beliefs are propounded with a religious-like fervor and zeal. The arguments adduced in their support show the same biased nature and inability to endure logical scrutiny as does the dereistic thinking of the schizophrenic or the zealot. The function of selective attention is very obviously manifest and all controverting arguments are studiously ignored or nullified. In other words, they show all the characteristics of "True Believers," as Eric Hoffer (**6**) has so ably described them.

Interestingly enough, the persons who compose these groups are not usually, as one might expect, members of society who have endured economic privation or social inequity, although "the class struggle" is a significant and frequent feature of their dogmatic belief. These persons are usually intellectuals and technicians who have a frequent history of rising from one social class to another in a short space of time. They tend as a group rather to be characterized by a deep, intense, and irrationally hyperextended hatred of constituted authority: governmental, religious, and familial.

Psychiatric studies of such persons (for many reasons scarce and limited in scope) suggest that individuals who might be called "revolutionary personalities," have significant, ubiquitous, and predictable pathology in their personal and familial antecedents. In my experience they tend to have experienced with remarkable regularity a relationship to the parents characterized by extreme hostility and guilt. The parents tend to be of two types, either extremely hostile, punitive, unjust persons who unfairly wore the trappings of authority, or weak, vacillating, capricious, and ineffective persons who gave little help or direction to their children. Subsequent affiliation with or membership in a revolutionary party not only supplies the strong group identification which recapitulates and is compensatory for the lost security of the authoritarian familial dictatorship, but also allows the individual to expend massively, through displacement, the hostility he was unable to express toward his familial figures without experiencing feelings of guilt and self-devaluation. The revolutionary personality achieves compromise in isolating this familial and interpersonal conflict from its painful context and allowing, through its irrational displacement to other forms of authority, a means of expression which preserves and even augments his individual sense of purpose and self-esteem.

We know that unpleasant affects, such as anxiety and guilt, can be reduced or "bound" by neurotic symptoms, e.g., an obsessional or a physical disorder. Neurotic symptomatology, irrational and unwelcome to the individual as it may appear to be, is in part a solution of conflict. It is an inefficient and often self-destructive mechanism which enables one to survive. We often overlook the fact that social activities and pursuits, as well as personal ones, may also be neurotic symptoms acting to bind anxiety. The individual "acts out" against the general good of society his neurotic symptoms in an attempt to achieve the power drives, the vengeance, and the hatred that would rationally be expended elsewhere. Such a person can, and usually does, preserve a lack of insight as to his true purposes. He conceals these from himself and often from others by a series of creditable rationalizations. One can be an "idealist" or a "liberal" who consciously wishes to modify the world and its organization for the most altruistic of reasons and yet act out in very destructive ways one's neurotic needs. This mechanism is often very clearly expressed in the case of the active revolutionary and zealot. In its milder form, however, it is not so apparent.

We often fail to recognize these drives in such persons as the ward leader, the union representative, the company official, or the man of the cloth. These factors are just as important to understand in relationship to everyday political life as they are in comprehending the *Sturm und Drang* of revolutionary activity but as yet, this entire subject is almost wholly neglected by all the behavioral sciences.

In summary, I have endeavored to adumbrate the view that early parental or primary identifications profoundly and ubiquitously affect the subsequently developed secondary ones, of which political group identifications are an example. Hence, the vote is more than a political act. It is an expression of affirmation or protest and is therefore an emotive as well as instrumental act. The act of voting or of nonvoting fulfills covert and unconscious as well as overt and conscious needs and wishes. Consequently no one discipline such as political science or psychiatry can wholly arrogate to itself the exploration of this field. It is an area in which both have a co-operative place. I have tried to outline some of the penumbral areas for needed future research. But it is only by immense further efforts on the part of all behavioral scientists, working together, that we shall have any reasonably complete answers to the questions framed here.

CHAPTER 15

Social Determinism and Electoral Decision: the Case of Indiana

V. O. KEY, JR. AND FRANK MUNGER

The style set in the Erie County study of voting, *The People's Choice*,[1] threatens to take the politics out of the study of electoral behavior. The theoretical heart of *The People's Choice* rests in the contention that "social characteristics determine political preference." Professor Lazarsfeld and his associates, prudent as they are, do not let so bald a statement stand without qualification or exception. Yet almost inevitably from this basic view, which is usually not put so explicitly, there develops a school of analysis that tends to divert attention from critical elements of electoral decision. The focus of analysis under the doctrine of social determinism comes to rest broadly on the capacity of the "nonpolitical group" to induce conformity to its political standards by the individual voter.

At bottom the tendency of the theory of group or social determinism is to equate the people's choice with individual choice. Perhaps the collective electoral decision, the people's choice, is merely the sum of individual choices. If enough were understood about individual decisions, by addition the collective political decision of the electorate would be comprehended. Yet when attention centers on the individual elector as he is led to decision by the compulsion of his nonpolitical group, the tendency is to lose sight of significant elements that both affect and relate individual decisions to the political aggregate. The study of electoral behavior then becomes only a special case of the more general problem of group inducement of individual behavior in accord with group norms. As such it does not invariably throw much light on the broad nature of electoral decision in the sense of decisions by the electorate as a whole.

The purpose here is not to dissent from *The People's Choice.* It is rather to raise the question whether its fundamental propositions do not provide a base on which, if enough effort were devoted to the matter, a supplementary theoretical structure might be erected that would bring politics into the study of electoral behavior. A few of the possible directions of development are here indicated through questions suggested by an examination of the voting record of Indiana. The simplest of techniques permits the analysis of a variety of types of electoral situations and suggests interpretations not so likely to emerge from the close observation of a single campaign. Parenthetically, it ought to be made explicit that such crude manipulation of aggregate electoral data is not urged as a substitute for the refined techniques of observation and analysis employed in *The People's Choice.*

TRADITIONAL PARTISAN ATTACHMENTS: A BENCH MARK FOR ANALYSIS. Almost any pioneer inquiry is inevitably beset by the peril of generalization that requires modification after a series of analyses has been made. What seemed a plausible general finding turns out to have been only a characteristic of the peculiar case cast in general terms. Similarly, the inspection of a cross section at a particular moment of a society existing through time may divert attention from characteristics that would be revealed by deliberate attention to the time dimension. Voting decisions made prior to the campaign itself may differ radically from those occurring during the campaign, both in the kinds of voters involved and in the factors associated with decision. Moreover, the factors relevant to decision may differ from time to time.[2]

Explicit attention to the time dimension of electoral decision would probably bring to light a variety of characteristics not readily perceptible by the observation of a single case. Illustrative is the difficulty of obtaining a satisfactory estimate of the nature and significance of traditional or habitual partisan attachments by interviewing a sample at a particular point in time. Often electoral decision is not an action whose outcome is in doubt but a reaffirmation of past decisions, at least for the community as a whole. For generations the Democrats may carry this country and the Republicans may predominate in an adjacent county.

The potency of these traditional attachments may be inferred from the maps in Figure 15-1 which show the distribution of Indiana presidential vote by counties in 1868 and 1900. Although the pattern of 1868 did not move unchanged from election to election to 1900, an astonishing parallelism appears in the county-by-county division of party strength at the two widely separated points in time. Thirty-six of the state's ninety-two counties were over 50 per cent Democratic at both elections; forty-five were under 50 per cent Democratic at both elections.[3]

Apparently the persistent pattern of party division represented a crystallization of attitudes at the time of the Civil War mainly along lines separating areas with different sources of settlement. The southern half of the state, peopled chiefly from the southern states, contained in 1868 and 1900 most of the Democratic strongholds. Other Democratic areas find a partial explanation in the greater attractiveness of that party to newcomers from abroad. Dearborn, Franklin, Adams, Allen, and Pulaski counties all had large German populations as did Dubois in the south. The Republicanism of certain blocks of counties was related also to the sectional origins of settlers. The block of 1868-1900 Republican counties in east central Indiana was settled by Quakers, whose cultural center was Richmond in Wayne County. Their antislavery sentiments and perhaps other reasons as well made them early converts to Republicanism. Other strongly Republican areas in the northern part of the state had drawn heavily from Federalist and Whig areas of the Northeast. Many of the oddities in detail of the territorial distribution of party strength find explanation in like terms.[4]

From 1868 to 1900 the potency of traditional party attachments may have been much greater than now, yet such community traits persist as is demonstrated by the scatter-diagram in Figure 15-2. The diagram relates the Republican percentage of the total presidential vote by county in 1920 to the corresponding percentage in 1948. Although most counties were more Democratic in 1948 than in 1920, a substantial correlation, +0.689, existed between the Republican percentages for the two elections. Generally where the Republicans were strong in 1920, they were relatively strong in 1948;

FIG. 15-1.—The traditional vote: Democratic percentage of the two-party presidential vote in Indiana, 1868 and 1900.

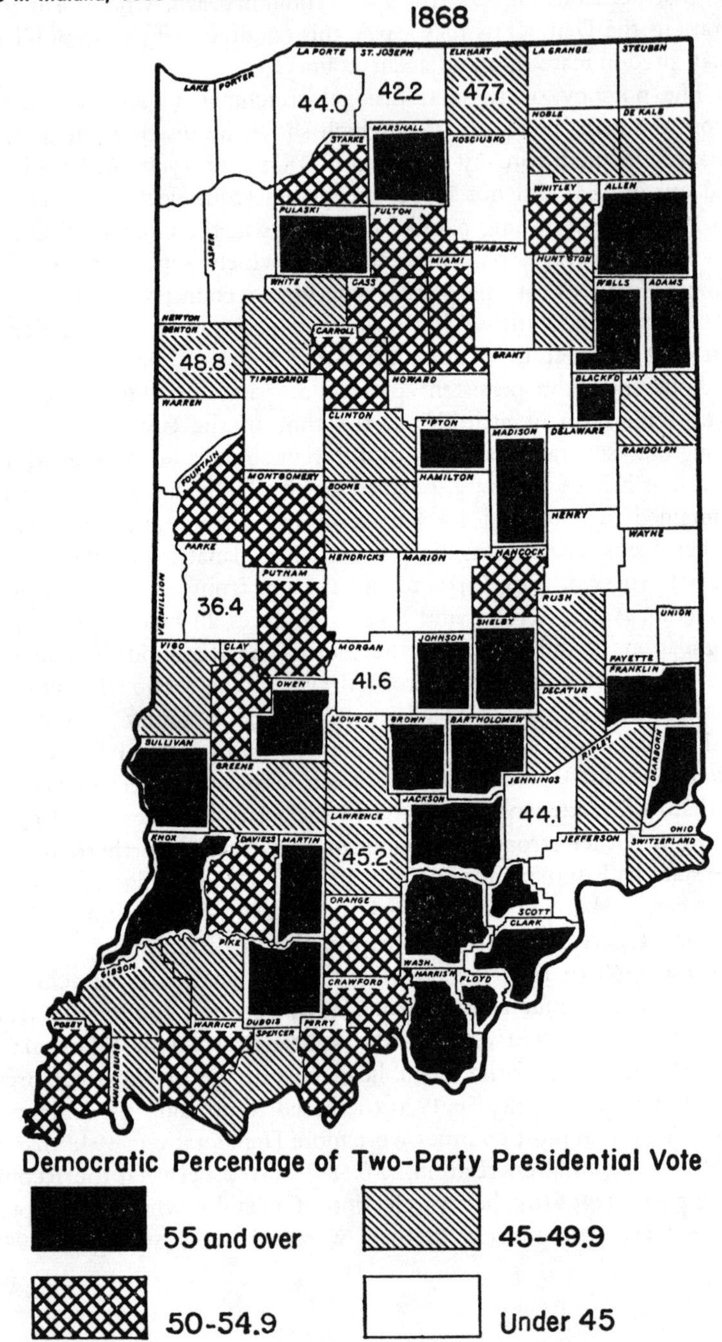

FIG. 15-1.—The traditional vote: Democratic percentage of the two-party presidential vote in Indiana, 1868 and 1900.

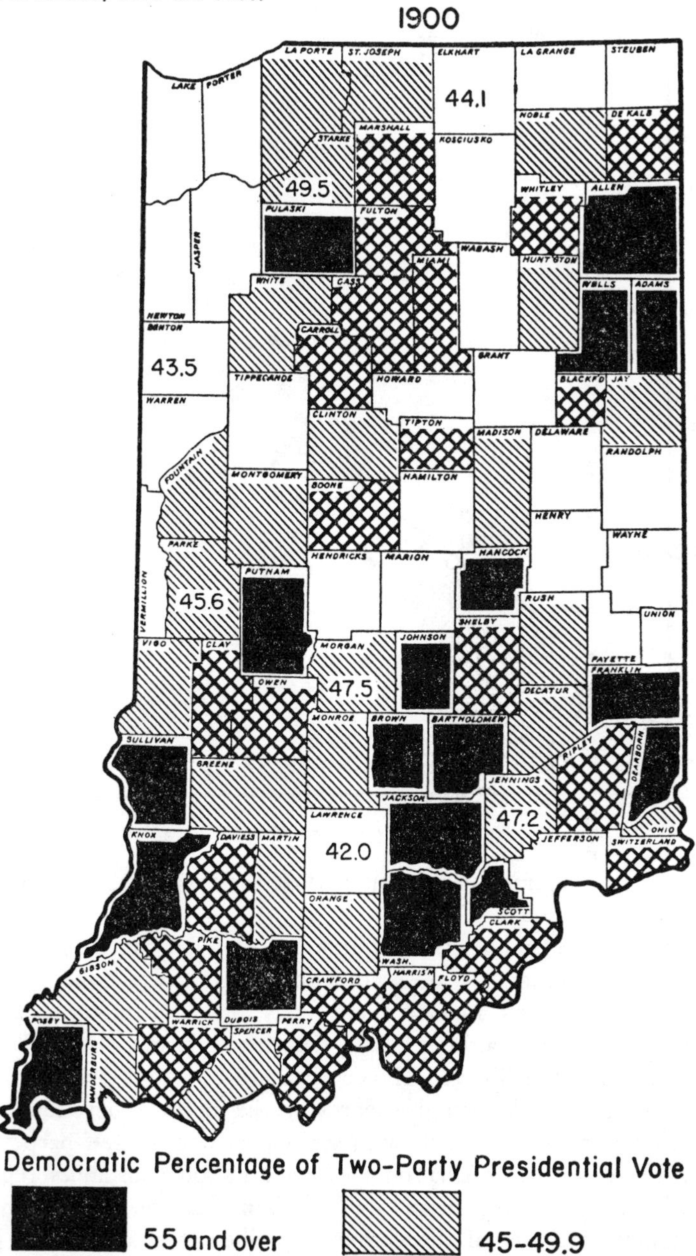

FIG. 15-2.—The traditional vote: Relation between Republican percentage of total presidential vote in 1920 and 1948 by counties in Indiana.

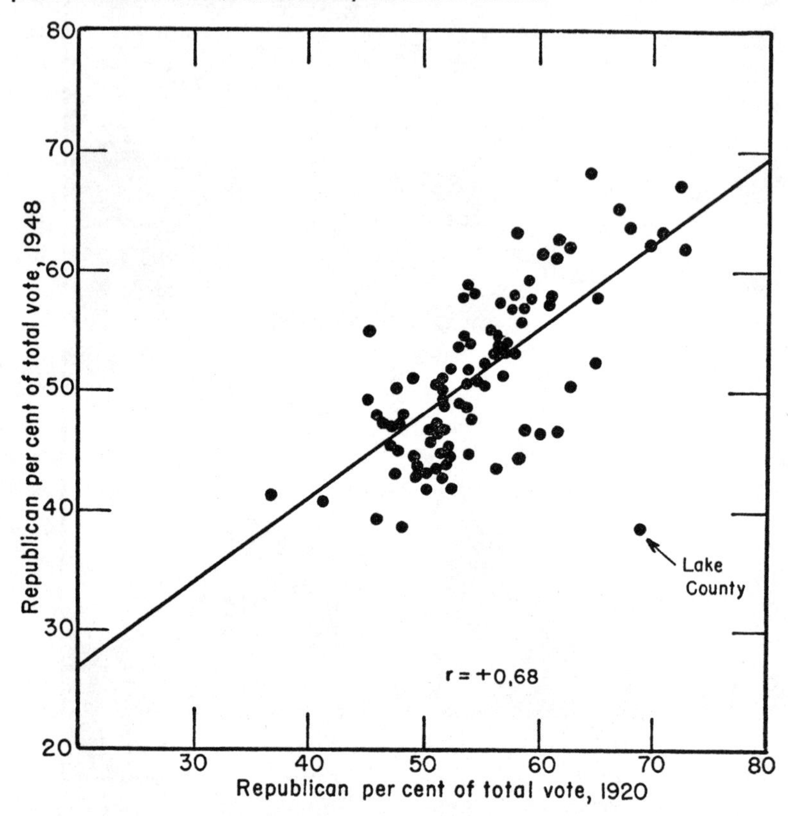

where the Democrats were weak in 1920, they were relatively weak in 1948.[5]

The analytical model that centers attention on the campaign as a period of decision obviously obscures a significant dimension of the electoral process. In fact, there tends to be a standing decision by the community, although as a descriptive term "decision" has connotations of deliberate choice that are apt to be misleading. The "decision" may simply represent the balance between two opposing party groups each with striking powers of self-perpetuation. Their original formation may have in some instances represented a simple transplantation of partisan attachments. In others the dominant classes of the community allied themselves with the party whose policies of the moment were most akin to their inclinations. Doubtless great contests and stirring events intensified and renewed partisan loyalties.[6] The clustering of interests, career lines, and community sentiments about the dominant party gives it a powerful capacity for survival.

The relevance of all this to the theoretical problem is that it raises the question whether one needs to supplement the doctrine that "social characteristics determine political preference." May there not also be a political group with to some extent an independence of exterior determinants of membership and attachment? Obviously a simple reconciliation of the persistence of party groupings and the notion of social determinism would be to assert that the stability of "interests" and people associated with geography produces a parallel continuity of partisan attachment. Yet the long persistence of county patterns of party affiliation despite changes in "interest" and the disappearance of issues that created the pattern, and the existence of contrasting partisan patterns in essentially similar counties, point toward a "political" grouping at least to some extent independent of other social groupings.[7] It may be also that the continuity of the life of the party group is not a smooth and uninterrupted flow, as might be inferred from electoral analysis alone. Each election may be accompanied by considerable churning about and crossing of party lines in both directions. From election to election varying proportions of the electorate may be affected by indecision and inner conflict. Yet the net effect over long periods is the maintenance of similar party divisions. Aggregate figures do not, of course, tell us whether this net result is accomplished by stability of individual party attachments or by the power of party groups to maintain their being through a combination of the retention of individual loyalties and the recruitment of new adherents.[8]

Recognition of the time dimension of "decision" suggests the plausibility of an analytical model built on the assumption that political groupings manage to exist, as majorities or minorities, over long periods of time.[9] Their persistence suggests that they may represent, not mere derivatives from other social groupings, but political groups with a life of their own.[10] To be properly understood these groupings would probably have to be analyzed in their behavior vis-à-vis the institutions of local government as well as in relation to national issues.

Focus on the time dimension of voting behavior compels recognition of the more or less standing nature of electoral decision, at least for a substantial part of the electorate. Yet the traditional vote does not by any means decide all elections nor govern the decisions of all individual voters. The traditional party divisions apparently fix a line of siege which moves to and fro with the fortunes of individual political battles. The balance of electoral strength varies from community to community and is disturbed in varying degrees by the impact of events and of campaigns. In any case the traditional pattern of voting provides a bench mark for the identification and analysis of particular electoral shifts. Electoral decision may be fundamentally a question of whether to depart from pre-existing decision. Under what circumstances does the electorate, or parts of it, choose to deviate from old habits of action? Does the nature of these "decisions" differ from election to election, situation to situation?

DURABLE ALTERATIONS IN PARTISAN DIVISION. Even the most cursory analysis of shifts in party strength from the more or less viscous pattern of traditional behavior suggests that an understanding of the process of electoral decision (and of popular government) must rest on a differentiation of types of electoral decision in the sense of elections as collective decision. It also suggests lines for the supplementation of the theory that "social characteristics determine political preference" to make it a more useful tool for political analysis.

Evidently one type of electoral decision consists in a more or less durable shift in the traditional partisan division within a community. The manner in which such realignments occur should be instructive to advocates of party reconstruction as well as suggestive for speculation about the nature of the party system. This type of alteration is not the work of a moment but may take place in a series of steps spread over a considerable period of time. Or at least such would be the conclusion if the Indiana data mean anything beyond the particular situation.

To identify areas undergoing a secular change in party division one must separate the electoral movements that occur from election to election from those that seem to represent a long-term trend. The long-term tendency of the areas undergoing durable realignment presumably will be retarded or accelerated by those factors peculiar to each election which affect them as well as those areas not touched by the secular trend. A crude separation of short-term movements and long-term trends is accomplished by the arrange-

FIG. 15-3.—Secular shift in partisan attachment: Mean Democratic percentage of two-party presidential vote for all Indiana counties and for fifteen counties with the most marked Democratic growth, 1920-52.

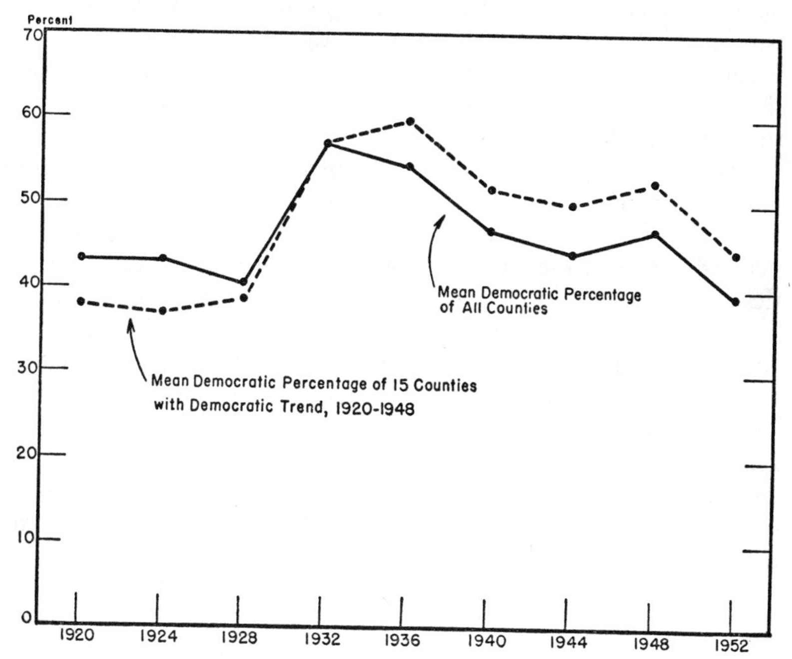

ment of the data in Figure 15-3. From 1920 to 1948 in fifteen Indiana counties the Democratic proportion of the two-party presidential vote increased by 10 percentage points or more.[11] In the chart the average Democratic percentage of these counties is plotted alongside the average Democratic percentage of all counties of the state. Although the fifteen counties evidently felt the election-to-election influences common to all counties, their long-term divergence as a group from the mean of all counties moved them in a sequence of steps over sixteen years from a Republican position to a new and relatively stable pattern of division above the Democratic average for all counties. The shifting counties were more affected by the LaFollette candidacy in 1924 than were the rest of the state's counties.[12] As a group, they withstood the general trend toward Hoover in 1928. In 1932 they moved Democratic as did all other counties but at a slightly higher rate. In 1936 their divergent trend continued and apparently that election fixed a new equilibrium in partisan division. In effect, the analysis segregates out areas undergoing a secular trend that creates a "new traditional" pattern. If the cyclical component of the fifteen-county series in Figure 15-3 were to be removed, the residual secular trend would show a gradual upward movement from 1924 to 1936 after which the series would flatten out.

The phenomenon recorded in the chart has interest purely for its isolation of a secular movement from one party toward the other. Only a panel study over a long period could determine the detailed nature of the secular change, yet from the aggregate statistics some surmises are possible. To the extent that the shift reflected a net change in partisan attachment rather than differentials in accretions to the two parties,[13] it probably occurred by the cumulation of individual shifts. Some persons became disenchanted with the major parties in 1924 and voted for LaFollette. Others were recruited by the Democrats on liquor and religious issues in 1928. The depression made permanent as well as temporary Democratic converts in 1932. The impact of the New Deal program completed the process in 1936. Party realignment may be accomplished under some circumstances by a series of steps.[14]

If this aggregate analysis identifies a type of electoral shift, can it be brought under the doctrine that "social characteristics determine political preference" or do we need a supplementary theory? If social characteristics determine political preference, it would be supposed that a set of secular social changes occurred in our fifteen counties and guided their political reorientation. Most of the fifteen counties either included within their limits considerable cities or were within the zone of influence of such cities.[15] Yet not all counties containing such cities underwent enough partisan change to be included in the group.[16] Most of the counties enjoyed a continuing growth of urban population and of industry, and in some instances notable addition to the electorate occurred with the coming of age of sons and daughters of immigrants.

It seems most improbable that changes in social characteristics occurred as rapidly as did political change during the period 1924-36. To fill in one theoretical gap one could posit the existence of a lag in the adjustment of political preference to social characteristics, i.e., that it took some time for political attitude to catch up with urbanization and industrialization. Under some circumstances the process of social determinism may encounter formidable friction in remolding political orientation.

The perspective of time also suggests the utility of taking into account other elements of the field within which the voter acts. Over the period 1920-48 the political parties and the voter's perceptions of political parties probably changed more than did his social characteristics. The pronouncements of political leadership and alternatives in program tendencies of the parties played upon the voter. Moreover, the group affiliations of the people of our fifteen counties and of the state changed but little in the period 1924-36, but through the differential effects of depression and party appeals those memberships and characteristics, if they were determinative of political preference, took on a new meaning. Social characteristics do not operate in a political vacuum. It is quite as meaningful, perhaps more, to assert that changes in the structure of political alternatives govern electoral choice as it is to say that social characteristics determine political preference.

All this discussion points, of course, to the proximate relation of group discipline to individual electoral decision. To explain the more or less durable secular shift in partisan loyalty identified here one must go beyond group theory to an analysis of factors that bring particular social characteristics to the level of political consciousness, to changes that alter radically the distribution of the electorate among categories of persons differentiated by politically significant characteristics. Collective electoral decision, at least at times, may be a product of such changes in the aggregate with group determinism functioning more or less as an accessory after the fact.

SHORT-TERM DISTURBANCES OF PARTISAN PATTERNS: THE RELATIVITY OF SOCIAL DETERMINISM. Another elaboration of the doctrine of social determinism is suggested by observation of the short-term shifts in partisan strength. Evidently at some moments in time these shifts are associated with a particular social characteristic; at other times that characteristic will be unimportant as a determinant. At one time one social characteristic may seem to fix election results; at another time another will predominate.

FIG. 15-4.—Impact of the 1928 campaign: Shift from 1924 to 1928 in the Republican percentage of total presidential vote in four types of Indiana counties.

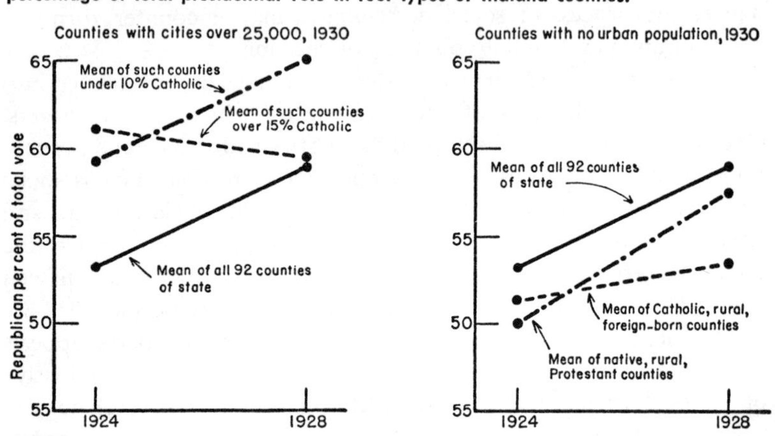

Again rough analyses of the Indiana data may illustrate the argument. The charts in Figure 15-4 indicate the movement of the mean of the Republican percentage of the total presidential vote from 1924 to 1928 in four types of counties. In the urban counties with relatively small proportions of their population Roman Catholic, the Republicans gained sharply while their proportion of the vote declined in urban counties with the highest proportions of Roman Catholic population.[17] In the rural counties with the highest proportions of native-born Protestant population, a much sharper Republican gain occurred than in rural counties with relatively high proportions of Catholic and foreign-born.[18]

Obviously these aggregate figures do not establish that Protestants moved from Democratic to Republican ranks from 1924 to 1928. Nevertheless, it is most probable that a shift associated with religion and related factors occurred. To the extent that the data indicate electoral decisions associated with such social attributes, they point toward an additional elaboration of the theory of social determinism. The social characteristics of our contrasting counties changed very little over the period 1924-28. If these characteristics determined political preference, they acquired a political significance, at least for some people, in 1928 that they lacked in 1924.

The same sorts of propositions find further illustration in the voting behavior of German and non-German counties. Although most Indiana counties from 1936 to 1940 shifted to some degree away from the Democrats, the supposition is that voters of German origin were especially antagonized by Roosevelt's policy toward the Reich.[19] In 1940 Henry Schricker ran as the Democratic candidate for governor. Of German origin, he was reputed to have a potent appeal to voters of that nationality. If the social characteristic of national origin moved in higher degree into the zone of political relevance in 1940, it would be supposed that German voters would support Schricker in higher degree than Roosevelt while the non-German groups would probably give about the same proportion of their vote to both gubernatorial and presidential candidates.

FIG. 15-5.—National origin and the vote: Democratic percentage of the two-party vote for President and Governor in Dubois and Clark counties, Indiana, 1936-48.

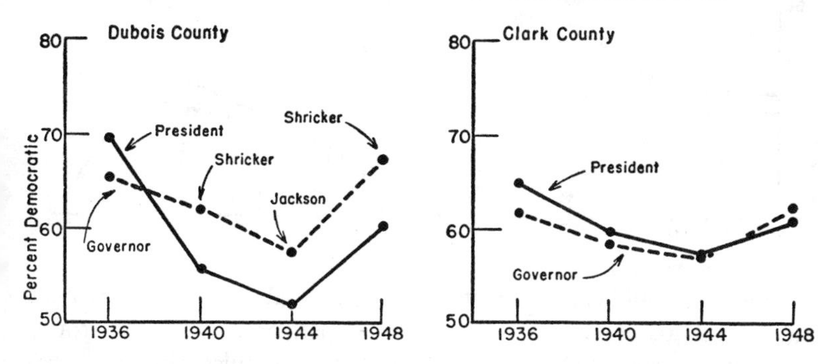

Insofar as election returns give a clue to group voting behavior the graphs in Figure 15-5 support the proposition. The chart compares Dubois County, in high degree Germanic in origin, with Clark County, an area with relatively fewer citizens of German origin. Dissatisfaction with foreign policy presumably accounted for the especially sharp drop in Dubois in the vote for the Democratic presidential candidate in 1940. The higher vote in that county for Democratic candidates for governor probably reflected primarily a loyalty to the state Democratic ticket unaffected by national policy and perhaps to some extent the special appeal of Henry Schricker, who ran in both 1940 and 1948. On the other hand, in Clark County the Democratic presidential and gubernatorial candidates polled more nearly the same percentages of the vote.

The relativity of social determinism is further illustrated by a type of fluctuation in party strength in which voters are apparently drawn away from their usual party preference by the issue or events of a particular campaign only to return to the fold when the repelling peculiarities of the election disappear.[20] It might be supposed, for example, that in 1928 some persons who usually voted Democratic supported Hoover in preference to Smith yet returned to their party when the commotion subsided. A rough test of the proposition is provided by the data in Figure 15-6, which shows

FIG. 15-6.—Mean Republican percentage of the total vote for President and Lieutenant-Governor in selected Protestant and Catholic counties in Indiana, 1920-32.

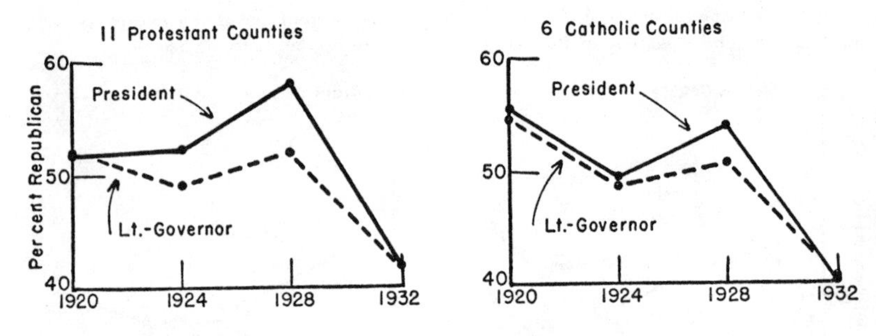

the mean Republican percentage of the total vote for President and for Lieutenant-Governor of another pair of contrasting groups of counties from 1920 to 1932. Note in particular that the predominantly Protestant rural counties reported about twice as wide a net splitting of tickets to the advantage of Hoover as did otherwise comparable counties with relatively large Catholic populations.[21] In both types of counties the gaps between the state and national votes disappeared in 1932. Such aggregate figures, of course, do not tell us who crossed party lines, whether gross ticket splitting was greater in one set of counties than in the other, or whether ticket splitting was higher at one election than another.[22] Yet the differentials strongly suggest that Protestant Democrats and perhaps

Catholic Republicans responded to the situation in 1928 by splitting their tickets. After the religious issue subsided, national and local party appeals were more nearly congruent and ticket splitting declined.

The data have an incidental utility in sharper definition of the "independent" voter. Insofar as ticket splitting is regarded as a manifestation of "independence," one type of independence apparently is not a generalized objectivity of judgment but a response of particular classes of voters to the particular issues of the day. The quantity and incidence of this type of voting would be expected to differ from time to time with the issues and personalities of the moment.[23]

All these illustrative analyses in a sense support the doctrine of social determinism of political preference yet they also point to the need for correlative theory. Social characteristics gain a political significance when political alternatives tend to parallel differentials in social attribute. One attribute may be of political significance at one time and another at another. That significance may well be the product of events and actions entirely outside the group concerned. Politicians may, in effect, invest group attributes with political significance. Appeals to group interest, prejudice, and pride are part of the stock-in-trade of the politician who often labors mightily to make the voter conscious of his social characteristics in order that they may determine his political preference.

To gain a broader understanding of electoral choice, it is necessary to account for the circumstances associated with variations in the relevance of social characteristics for electoral decision. That inquiry must lead beyond the nexus of group and individual voter to those factors associated with the political activation of groups or to those factors that bring social characteristics into the zone of political relevance. The data examined suggest such factors as the differentials in impact of market forces on different groups, the changing structure of political alternatives, the interaction of group memories of past and contemporary events. Undoubtedly many types of factors contribute to group tensions and frictions. Their identification permits one to go a step beyond the proximate relations involved in the focus on relationship of group and individual toward a more complete identification of the nature of electoral decision. Unless we can make some such step, we are left more or less with the proposition that those social characteristics that happen to be relevant at a particular time and place determine, or are associated with, political preference.[24]

UNEXPLAINED ELEMENTS OF DECISION: THE GENERAL DRIFT OF SENTIMENT. While the interaction of the structure of political alternatives and cleavages in social characteristics undoubtedly bears significantly on electoral decision, the preceding analyses implicitly suggest that social determinism may account for only part of the movement of the electorate from party to party over each four-year period. Social groups that move into the zone of political relevance in a particular campaign may transfer their loyalties in a relatively high degree, but it seems not unlikely that in many elections most groups move in the same direction. If this could be demonstrated, it would suggest the existence of some political X factor or factors which may, in most elections, play the determinative role in political decision.

The evidence on the proposition is extremely thin. Obviously the facts differ from election to election, yet it seems fairly plain that in many four-year periods a general drift of sentiment occurs that is shared to some degree by people of all sorts of social characteristics. Some of the charts point in that direction. Some broader possibilities are suggested by the data in Table 15-1, which shows

Table 15-1—Number of Indiana Counties with Increasing or Declining Democratic Percentage of Two-Party Presidential Vote, 1928-52

Period	Increasing Democratic Percentage	Declining Democratic Percentage	No Percentage Change	Total
1928-32	92	0	0	92
1932-36	23	68	1	92
1936-40	0	92	0	92
1940-44	3	89	0	92
1944-48	87	5	0	92
1948-52	0	92	0	92

the direction of movement from presidential election to presidential election from 1928 to 1952 of all the counties of Indiana. It will be observed that the more common pattern was for most of the counties to move in the same direction. A sharp deviation from this uniformity occurred in 1936 which was a crucial election in reshaping the traditional composition of the Democratic following, as was indicated by Figure 15-1.

The figures of Table 15-1 only show, of course, that the people of geographical units as a whole moved in the same direction in most elections. Only insofar as social differentiation is associated with geography do the figures give ground for supposing that various sorts of social groups moved in the same direction. A series of sample surveys covering the same period as the table would be necessary to determine the answer to that question. Yet scattered evidence suggests that it is not uncommon for people of the most diverse social groups to shift their political sentiments in the same direction. Decisions, i.e., to change, may well be conditioned, at least in some elections, by factors more or less independent of social characteristics. It could be that persons of different characteristics shift in the same direction for different reasons, yet that seems inadequate to account for the drastic shifts affecting all types of persons in some elections. Whatever the explanations may be, it seems clear that the search has to extend beyond the tendency of nonpolitical groups to enforce their norms on their members.

COMMENT. A major burden of the argument has been that the isolation of the electorate from the total governing process and its subjection to microscopic analysis tends to make electoral study a nonpolitical endeavor. That isolation tends, perhaps not of necessity but because of the blinders on perception associated with the method, to divorce the subjects of microscopic examination from their place in the larger political situation. Hence, all the studies of so-called "political behavior" do not add impressively to our comprehension of the awesome process by which the community or nation makes decisions at the ballot box.

It has been suggested that a fruitful avenue of development might be to seek to bridge the gap between microanalysis and macroanalysis, to the improvement of both. Much further refinement of our knowledge of the place of social characteristics in electoral decision, for example, would probably quickly follow once the setting of political alternatives and the matrix of objective conditions within which these determinants operate were brought more specifically into the field of observation. It seems apparent that social characteristics move into and out of the zone of political relevance, that they "explain" the actions of some people and not those of others, and that insofar as social characteristics determine political preference they encounter considerable friction.

Some of the difficulties of theory and analysis will be solved in due course, doubtless in a serendipitous manner, as the number of studies multiplies. New types of election situations will be analyzed; provisional generalizations will be modified to account for new situations; and the process will be repeated. By the observation of a greater variety of types of situations it may be possible to tie the study of electoral behavior more directly to the workings of the state. Such a linkage might enable us to talk with a bit more information about the conditions under which an electorate can most effectively perform its decision-making role in the governing process. What are the consequences, for example, of the subjection of differing proportions of the vote to determination by specified social characteristics? Of the existence of a greater or lesser proportion of the electorate loyal to party? Of the intensification of particular types of group loyalties? Of the decay of others? Of the introduction of particular types of issues into the electoral arena? Of integration or atomization of the structure of leadership? Of variations in the range of electoral indifference and in the intensity of electoral involvement?[25]

Another point that recurs is a note of doubt about the doctrine that social characteristics determine political preference. There can be no doubt that there is at times a high degree of association between readily identifiable social characteristics and political preference. At the extreme position it might be argued that political preference is a hitchhiker on social characteristics. Yet there seems to be always a very considerable part of the electorate for which no readily isolable social characteristic "explains" political preference. The query may be raised whether a rather serious void does not exist in the theory. Is there some sort of political order or system of loyalties more or less independent of the identifications of citizens and electors with these nonpolitical groups to which we have an index in their social characteristics? The identification and analysis of the political role of the voter may present considerable difficulty in research design, yet if there is no political community, if citizens, or many of them, have no political role more or less autonomous from their other roles, a good many centuries of political speculation, both hortatory and otherwise, has been beside the point. Some of the considerable variance unaccounted for by social determination might be removed by attempts to analyze the nature of the individual's identification with the community and the nation, the character of his identification with political party, his perception of the political world, his general orientation toward complexes of policy questions, his conception of his role as a voter and as a citizen. There may well be, for a part of the electorate at least, roles, identifications, and preferences of a purely political nature with quite as much reality as his "social characteristics." Perhaps some common denominator ties together the archetype Republican and the Republican unskilled laborer who always turns up in the survey.

In research the answers one gets depend in part on the kinds of questions he asks. If one inquires about social characteristics and political preference, he finds out about social characteristics and political preference. If one puts other sorts of questions into the research mill, he might well bring out other and more complex characteristics of the process of electoral decision. It might well turn out that the emerging picture would be one of an electorate, or at least of a great many electors, now struggling with great questions, now whipped into a frenzy or into fear by the demagogue, now voting against its own imputed short-term interest, now acting without check or restraint, now weighing as best it may the welfare of the community, all more or less in accord with classical democratic theory.[26]

CHAPTER 16

Emotional Factors in Voting Behavior

FRANZ ALEXANDER, M. D.

When the editors of this book invited me to discuss the psychology of voting behavior, in particular its unconscious and preconscious motivations, I accepted only after considerable hesitation. One reason for my hesitation was that as a psychoanalyst, my firsthand observations are limited; patients' voting intentions rarely are a central issue in their analyses. This itself, of course, may be of considerable interest. Obviously in the human material which the clinician observes, a patient's individual problems—we may call it his private life—are far more important to him than his political decisions. Whether this relatively low interest in politics is due to the nature of the sample which we clinicians observe or is generally true for our present era cannot be decided without a control study of relatively nonneurotic individuals. It should be noted, however, that the human material on which these observations are made comprises not only patients but also candidates of psychoanalytic institutes who are undertaking treatments primarily for learning purposes and are selected as a comparatively nonneurotic group. The relative insignificance of political issues in their material is equally valid for this group.

Another reason for my hesitation to submit my observations and conclusions is that a microscopic study of the complex fabric of motivations in a two-party system is of little practical value. There are only four decisions possible: (1) straight Democratic vote; (2) straight Republican vote; (3) split voting; and (4) refraining from voting. These four choices are disproportionate to the extreme wealth of different and often conflicting motivations which careful study of individuals reveals. While voting intentions might be determined by a large number of motivations representing intricate psychological patterns, the actual vote of necessity cannot reflect the wealth of motivations but only the end result of a complex parallelogram of forces. These patterns may be of considerable interest for those who are interested in the sociological aspects of voting. The following observations and conclusions, therefore, are submitted with full cognizance of their restricted sociological value which is due to the scantiness of the observations, to the insufficiently representative nature of the sample, and finally to the fact that these observations are focused on understanding the voting intentions of individual persons and not those of groups.

The psychoanalyst who tries to establish in the psychoanalytic situation why a person casts his vote on the Democratic or Republican ticket or why he is an independent or deviant voter is not in a much better position than an ordinary opinion taker. For a person whose vote is decided primarily on the basis of conscious and rational factors–such as that his family always voted for the same party or that he is convinced his social and economic interests are best served by this vote–voting is not a problem; his voting behavior will not enter in his psychoanalysis as a conflictful issue. He will as unlikely discuss it as he would the fact that he ordered a New York cut steak or a *filet mignon.* He knows what he wants and believes that he also knows why he wants it. His typical answer, when asked about his voting intention, may be illustrated by the following example. A young wealthy professional man of an upper-middle-class family whose father was a leading businessman in his community said: "Economically it is better for me to vote Republican. On the other hand, I prefer a more liberal outlook. However, it doesn't make a great deal of difference from the long point of view whether a Republican or Democrat comes in. Things are going well with me and my business and therefore I will vote Republican."

Only the so-called deviant or independent voter shows hesitation, will discuss the pros and cons of his decision, and offers deeper insight into the motivational background of his choice. This does not mean that "proper voting intention"[1] has no unconscious determinants. The fact that a person identifies himself with his group is in itself a motivational factor of which he is not necessarily fully aware; he certainly is not aware of the deeper genetic significance of such an identification. If asked, he may give the simple answer: "I vote Republican because my family always voted so." Only if he is a deviant voter will he feel the need to explain his vote to himself and to others. His deviation, however, may be determined by a large number of coexisting motivations, of which he is only partially aware, such as resentment against his own group, rebellion against authority figures, or the wish to defend himself against an unbearable amount of submissiveness and to show his independence by his deviant vote. Finally he may also be influenced by rational intellectual factors and theoretical doctrines about society and politics. This explains why the deviant and independent voters are the natural objects for the study of unconscious and preconscious motivations.

In general, the deviant voter and the independent voter, like any other, are influenced primarily by two categories of attitudes: (1) attitude toward the person of the candidate and (2) attitude toward the issues involved—both economic and ideologic. These are the voters who are more likely to change their voting intention during the campaign because their intention is determined by a large number of *conflicting* motivations. They are more susceptible to propaganda or conversation; certain external influences reinforce some of their motivations while other influences support the opposite unconscious and preconscious factors. An example is a voter who had the intention to vote for Stevenson, but changed her intention after hearing Stevenson's quip: "Eggheads of the world unite. You have nothing to lose but your yokes." She added: "I can't visualize a President who is capable of making such flippant, witty remarks." This woman, a strong liberal, had obviously an emotional need for a father image to which the personality of the candidate did not live up. This same woman voter was strongly for Wallace. She admired his liberalism and idealism and his championing the cause of the common people. She went to the polls firmly determined to vote for Wallace. At the last minute, when she was already in the booth, she changed her mind. It suddenly dawned upon her: "How can I vote for such an unstable man? He is probably highly neurotic and unreliable." Obviously, her concern with the political issues was outweighed by her attitude toward the person of the candidate.

An example of the fact that interest in the person of the candidate and in the issues together may outweigh family tradition is a young Catholic woman who in the past always voted Democratic mainly because of her family tradition, but who voted for Willkie. When asked about her motivation she said: "I was fed up with the Democrats running my city and I was exposed to their corruption. I also felt that Roosevelt had been in office too long and the change would be good; also I liked Willkie, liked his behavior during the campaign, thought it was more dignified, and I liked him as a person." Obviously the last motive was the decisive one.

A few further examples may illustrate the complexities of the motivational background of voting intention. An upper-class voter who strongly identified himself with intellectuals as a social class voted Democratic. There are two kinds of this type of "out of group" identification: (1) a genuine identification with the intellectual role which is well incorporated within the ego: a person who actually pursues an intellectual occupation such as scientific research and therefore has a genuine feeling of belonging to persons of the same interest and occupation; (2) a kind of pseudo intellectualism: a more or less superficial interest in matters of art, literature, or the sciences rather than real devotion is utilized as a protest against the family. Of course, both motivations, a genuine devotion to intellectual pursuits as well as protest against family attitudes, can be present in the same person. In this observed case, the patient turned toward intellectual pursuits first as a rebellion against his family's attitude but as time went on his interest became more and more genuine; it became an integral part of his ego, and the original rebellious motivation lost significance.

A Jewish professional with overaverage income, of lower class origin, votes Democratic. He explains his voting intention: "I am too much exposed to the selfishness of businessmen. I would not buy a Ford car because Ford was anti-Semitic. Economically it would be better for me to vote Republican, but I vote Democratic. However, I would not vote for Kefauver because I think he is hypocritical in his anti-vice campaign. I do not have enough respect for his sincerity." Without going into details, it is apparent that in this voter's decision different motivations enter his attitude toward the person of the candidate: a rejection of big business and his feeling of being discriminated against as a member of a minority group. This same voter's wife comes from a family who always voted Republican, but she votes "blindly" Democratic. Her father was a tyrant, once successful in business, who even after he lost his fortune identified himself with the psychology of the successful businessman. This woman always protested against her father's tyrannical attitude and developed a strong rebellion against domineering strong male figures.

A young professional voted for a Democratic candidate not because he liked him but because he thinks the Democratic party corresponds more to his social psychology. He votes Democratic even if he does not like the candidate. He thinks Republican policies do not represent the national interest to the same degree as Democratic policies. He believes in progressive legislation, preservation of democratic principles, of national resources, parks, etc. Particularly he does not like the Republican policy of giving away national property to private business. He does not feel, however, that the difference between the two parties is very clear. It is easier for him to think in terms of left and right. He is definitely left from the center. He wants major social reforms and increased government ownership. Although he is afraid of bureaucracy, he would still take the chance of a powerful bureaucratic government for the sake of increased welfare. He is pro-labor although he is quite aware of the deterioration of labor organizations. He firmly believes in equal social opportunity and security for those who are inadequate. His greatest stress is on humanitarianism. He believes that the nonadequate need to be defended. This humanitarian orientation is what he thinks primarily determines his political orientation. Since he has been analyzed he has become less and less leftist, more and more critical and realistic about the actual political issues although his humanitarian orientation has remained as strong as ever.

This patient was the youngest in the family, and his older brother was preferred by mother. He showed extreme sibling rivalry, and his main defense was overcompensation of envy by generosity and humaneness. This sympathy for the weak was further enforced by his attitude toward his father, who was a mild person, often publicly humiliated by mother. During psychoanalytic treatment he often became tearful when he spoke of his father. He felt that he and father were in the same boat, both neglected by mother in favor of the oldest son. Because of this loyalty to his father his original oedipal rivalry evoked severe guilt feelings, particularly because father was so kind to him. In addition the deepest source of his feeling for the handicapped was a serious bodily injury that occurred when he was six years old: he felt at that time that he was in danger of being permanently mutilated.

Another case is a patient who is suffering from a serious neurotic condition, a strong liberal. He intends not to vote for a certain Democratic candidate because after meeting him he felt that they both suffer from the same kind of emotional problem. It turned out that he strongly identified himself with this presidential candidate and felt that he should not become President just as he himself should not become President. His ambitions were connected with a great deal of guilt, and therefore he expected failure and humiliation. Because of his close identification with the candidate he did not want him to run, then be defeated and humiliated.

A psychoanalytic colleague submitted to me the following interesting observation. A young man in his early twenties, a college student, during his treatment became intensely absorbed in a political campaign for the election of an extremely conservative candidate to the United States Senate. This candidate was not popular among the students of the small college town where the patient went to school. The patient idealized him and organized a local political club supporting him. He devoted most of his energies to this political activity. During his treatment fantasies appeared in which he inflamed his fellow students against himself and was mobbed by them. He wallowed in the masochistic enjoyment of his martyrdom. In another fantasy the candidate would hear of the patient's martyrdom and after his election would reward him by appointing him as his personal secretary. Further treatment revealed that the patient closely identified the candidate with his own father. The latter was also conservative and supported this conservative candidate for senator. The therapist concluded that the fantasy of being mobbed by fellow students was the result of guilt resulting from the patient's hostile destructive impulses directed against his sister whom the father preferred. The therapist could reconstruct the patient's early childhood hope of gaining father's favor by standing up for father and his principles and protecting him from an attack by his sister. As a result, father would reject sister and replace her in his affections with the patient. As a further complicating motivation the patient expressed his ambivalence against his father in choosing an unpopular candidate. On the other hand, the fantasy of becoming the candidate's personal secretary reveals his passive submissive desires toward his father which were similar to those of his sister. This example illustrates not only the tendency of voters to identify candidates for high political office with father but also their tendency to identify rival voters with siblings toward whom rivalry existed in childhood.

These examples may suffice to intimate the multifaceted emotional background of voting decisions. While statistically the rational factors, particularly socioeconomic status, may turn out to be the most decisive ones, there is a significant group of voters whose decision is more influenced by emotional factors originating in past family experiences of which they are not conscious but which nevertheless may have a strong influence on their behavior than conscious rational factors. Since in our two-party system the political and economic issues overlap and do not show sharp contrasting differences, one may conclude that the attitude toward the personality of the candidates determined chiefly by irrational emotional and mostly unconscious factors is more decisive than is generally assumed. In the group of undecided voters this motivation should be prevalent. Because in most recent elections the difference of votes between the two parties was not greater than the estimated number of independent or undecided voters, it may be safely concluded that the outcome of elections is to a large degree dependent on the distribution of the vote in this small but strategic group who because of emotional motivations favor one or the other candidate. In other words, whether or not a candidate comes nearer in his public personality to that type of father image which fits into the emotional needs and conflicts of the greater number of flexible (independent and deviant) voters is the decisive factor. Because of the extreme variety of these emotional needs and the difficulties in identifying them without careful individual studies, the gross statistical handling of these factors does not seem feasible.

Although individual attitudes toward political issues are mainly determined by socioeconomic factors, they, too, are influenced by unconscious factors. In *The Authoritarian Personality*[2] Else Frenkel-Brunswik attempted to correlate political orientation with personality structure which in turn she traced back to the structure of the family. She found extreme rightist leanings more common in individuals who come from father-centered families and that the politically unprejudiced persons not inclined toward extreme positions have, as a rule, a close positive relationship to their mother. My own observations only partly confirm this finding. I have found that extreme rightist inclination is often seen in men who tend to identify themselves with a strong father image and at the same time repress all those attitudes which they consider as signs of weakness such as dependence, feminity, indecisiveness. Accordingly, they hate weakness in general and attack the same traits in others which they cannot tolerate in themselves. They often are misogynic. Sympathy with the underdog would threaten to mobilize their awareness of their own weakness, and thus they become intolerant toward minority groups. Conversely, men who come from families with a depreciated, weak father are less apt to repress their own dependent tendencies, particularly if the mother figure is a dominant one. They cannot tolerate strong masculine figures and, being aware of their own weakness, are apt to develop the leaning to unite with their brothers against a dominant male figure. This emotional structure is particularly likely to develop when the mother unconsciously encourages the sons to outdo their father. This family attitude favors the development of collectivist traits and generally a more leftist political orientation. Only methods that would allow a reliable statistical estimation of the relative distribution of such family structures (and corresponding character formation) in a given culture in a given period could make correct prediction of political trends possible.

CHAPTER 17

Independents and Party Identifiers: Characteristics and Behavior in 1952

ROBERT E. AGGER

Just before the national election in 1952, some 22 per cent of the respondents in a national sample survey identified themselves as "independents."[1] In two other sample surveys conducted by the Survey Research Center of the University of Michigan in June, 1952, and September, 1953, self-identified independents comprised 30 and 18 per cent of their respective samples.[2] The Gallup poll has estimated that 20 per cent of the population were independents in 1940 and 29 per cent in 1948.[3] Samuel Eldersveld has indicated that the number of independents is probably larger than self-identification measures have led political analysts and pollsters to believe.[4] Whatever the exact figure may be, and whatever the trend is or may become, the meaning and implications of independence in modern politics deserve to be assessed. The election study of 1952 conducted by the Survey Research Center offers an opportunity to make a start on this assessment.

The importance of party and independent self-identifications in reference to electoral participation was suggested in *The Voter Decides*.[5] A more recent study by the Survey Research Center of the 1954 congressional elections demonstrates even more clearly the importance of party identification in determining the vote.[6] Party identification was more closely related to the vote than any demographic variable. To be sure, party identification is itself related to socioeconomic factors but the differences in degrees of relationship to participation of demographic and identification factors suggests that the second is more than simply a reflection of the first factor. The existence of self-identified independents further suggests that these relationships may not be simple, direct, and one-to-one in character. If political self-identifications are viewed as analytically distinct intervening variables between demographic characteristics and participation, it becomes possible to see more clearly the dynamic relationships between and among identifications, demographic characteristics, other psychological and situational factors (including political environment), and participation.

Regardless of the political, demographic, and psychological causes of independent self-identifications, independents may participate in different ways, to different degrees, or with different goals than party identifiers. A failure to compare independents and party identifiers in terms of their social and psychological characteristics, their political behavior, and their possible effects on politics, would result in at least a partial failure to come to grips with a core interest of political science. As Harold Lasswell and Abraham Kaplan remark: "Identification serves as the mechanism for the creation of the political 'we.' It is this 'we' which lies at the center of political phenomena. Political demands are made in behalf of the egos with which a given ego identifies, and are justified by reference to the resulting 'we.' Politics begins when egos are emotionally bound together in relation to such demands in the name of the identified group."[7]

THE POLITICAL SIGNIFICANCE OF INDEPENDENTS. We are considering a question of fundamental importance for political theory: *Do independents differ significantly from party identifiers in their political behavior?* What functions do independents perform for maintenance of, or changes in, the political system? People argue, partly on the basis of explicit or implicit value premises, that political independence is good, bad, or indifferent. The value premise may stem from a personal code of individual or social ethics, or be in the interest of a particular party or policy. The value premises that shape the following analysis relate to the functioning of a democratic political system. There are a number of puzzling value problems as well as a host of complex questions about the operations of even a "utopian" democracy, but an analysis of certain theoretically relevant characteristics of self-identified independents and party identifiers will illuminate, although certainly not answer fully, certain questions about democratic politics.

There already exists a number of hypotheses, or at least, speculations, about the relationships of particular factors to party identifications. Chains of logic have been developed which frequently depend for their validity not only on untestable value premises, but also on critical, untested assumptions about presumed differences in distributions of demographic characteristics and/or psychological attributes among independents and party identifiers.

An example of this concerns the characteristic of educational level. There are greater proportions of college-educated people among Republican adherents and voters than among Democratic adherents and voters. The explanation offered for this empirical finding is that education, income, and type of profession are highly interrelated, and that the Republican party is more the party of businessmen, professional people, and other high-income groups and the Democratic party, of workers and lower-income groups.

It is sometimes asserted that independents also tend to be highly educated in comparison to Democrats, although whether more or less so than Republicans is less frequently asserted. The "explanation" sometimes offered is based on a proposition that highly educated people tend to place a higher value on independence and/or that more highly educated people stress similarities in, rather than differences between, the two major parties. Another causal notion is sometimes introduced to explain the connection between the presumed education level of independents and their political participation, to wit: the presumably highly educated independents tend to participate to a great extent because of their awareness of the importance of participation. Conversely, it is sometimes argued that independents fail to participate because of their presumed greater awareness of, or stress on, the similarities of, rather than the differences between, the parties on basic issues. A further speculation may be made that the presumably highly educated independents tend to vote as much as party identifiers, but fail to participate as much in other political activities—obviously primary voting, and somewhat less obviously, donating money, urging people to vote for one or another party, and otherwise helping in electoral campaigns.

If, however, independents are presumed to be people who for the most part are poorly educated, then an equally tenuous line of reasoning may be developed involving causal notions of education level and apathy, tendencies to be influenced by mass media, low participation, and the like. Then, on the basis of assumptions about the importance of participation, positions are taken about the value of independence. It would seem that these different interpretative analyses would all profit from comparisons of the actual characteristics and participation levels of independents and party identifiers.

Self-identified independents may function to increase fundamental political consensus by the quality of their psychological participation in politics. Independents might be expected to play a moderating role by having more moderate feelings of crisis than party identifiers. Independents may not expect that important value deprivations or indulgences would follow from the victory of either party to the same degree as party identifiers. Presumably, when the "level of crisis" (as Harold Lasswell has termed these expectations) is high, political consensus is endangered. Yet we have little idea of how to measure political fever, and when to expect a certain level of crisis to disrupt political consensus, either suddenly and violently, or slowly and quietly.

People who are less disposed to view existing political parties as "threatening" to themselves may serve as stabilizing forces in politics to the extent that they do participate. Even should such people tend to be nonparticipant, their very existence as potential activists in the political arena may serve to moderate the behavior of politicians or of potential revolutionaries insofar as they are concerned with issues and/or candidates, and if they are not so apathetic that they are discounted as irrelevant in the political calculus of the important politicians.

Probably an even more important consideration in this context concerns the probable behavior of less "antagonistic" participants in crisis or revolutionary situations. It is possible that whereas in the "normal" electoral situation overt political behavior may be more related to other variables, in the "abnormal" crisis situation expectations of indulgences or deprivations may constitute a more powerful motivational force. Thus, large aggregates of politically interested but relatively nonantagonistic people may constitute a drag on the actions of those bent on destroying the viability of political opposition. It would seem probable that involved people who felt that the opposition would not significantly deprive them if victorious in a national election would tend to resist the appeals of a demagogue or a revolutionary who hurls charges of "treason" or "subversion of our way of life" against one or more of his political opponents in an attempt to rally fearful followers.

On the other hand, "fear" of others may produce beneficial results for some or all concerned. Perceiving the other as a possible depriver or indulger of the self may produce *functional tensions* that lead to personally, socially, or politically adaptive behavior. Instead of an anxiety-ridden aggregate of apathetics or fanatics one might find a creative group of activists bent not on subverting the foundations of a political system but bargaining and forming dynamic coalitions in such a manner that private interest and public welfare become compatible if not synonymous.

Political participation has both psychological and overt behavior dimensions. Psychological participation is probably related to overt involvement but not necessarily in a direct, one-to-one relationship. It is to be expected that there is a correlation between caring and doing, but it was expected that the correlation as well as the magnitude of both aspects of behavior would be different for independents and party identifiers. It was hypothesized that independents would be less participant than party identifiers because the former were thought to be less issue-oriented than the latter. A difference in overt participation was hypothesized also because of the presumed differences in the aforementioned expectations. An expression of opinion about issues should logically constitute more of a disposition to action if it exists with an awareness that the issue is related to the self in an indulgent-deprivational context. In common sense terms, it would seem probable that voting would be more widespread among those who felt that should one or another party or candidate win (or lose), they would personally gain (or suffer) financially, or their country would gain (or suffer), than among those who felt that they (and/or their country) would be as well or as poorly off regardless of which party won an election. Alternatively, overt participation could be more related to a sense of civic duty, participation habits, or social pressures.

The theoretical significance of overt participation is as uncertain as in the case of psychological participation. What is the desirable level of overt participation for the successful functioning of a democratic political system? The recent controversy between the pro- and anti-party responsibility people rests in part on their estimates of the political consequences of increasing ideological-activist type participation. Although this must be suggested tentatively, we would think that fundamental political consensus would be strengthened to the extent that independents participated overtly but with less party-directed hostility than party identifiers.

While the implications of independence in politics are not yet clearly understood, the study of independence requires as clear a conception of the alternative theoretical significances as possible in order to select or devise measures of relevance to the subject. The failure to come to grips with the theoretical problems can be illustrated by the incidental conclusion about independents to be found in the Elmira study, to wit: "The classic 'independent voter' of high interest but low partisanship is a deviant case."[8] Although the classic independent may be a deviant case, the authors of that study have not specifically examined him or his behavior. They reasoned: interest in the election correlated highly with participation, and "since partisanship increases political interest, anything that weakens partisan feelings decreases interest."[9] And presumably self-identification as an independent weakens partisanship.

But political philosophers and theoreticians have been concerned, at least in part, with independents who participated as a result of high interest and low partisanship in the sense that partisan victory was not as important to them as to party identifiers. The latter aspect of political interest, expectations of value indulgences or deprivations as a consequence of party victory or defeat, was not assessed by the Elmira researchers. They believed that "almost all measures of political involvement and participation are highly correlated with one another, and, for analytical purposes, interchangeable."[10] Thus their use of "the simplest measure," interest in the election, permits assumptions about, but precludes assessment of, the degree to which independents, as compared to party identifiers, are of classic character. The following comparisons of independents and party identifiers are intended to illuminate and suggest further

Table 17-1—Relation of National Demographic Characteristics to Party Identification (Percentage)

Characteristic	PARTY IDENTIFICATION Dem	Rep	Ind	Number of Cases
Sex:				
Male	45	45	52	722
Female	55	55	48	822
Age:				
21-34 (18-34)	32	23	34	464
35-44	26	22	24	374
45-54	17	19	19	276
55 and over	25	36	23	422
Religion:				
Protestant	69	86	69	1106
Catholic	26	14	26	343
Race:				
White	89	96	92	1425
Negro	11	4	8	127
Type of community:				
Metropolitan area	25	29	30	430
Towns and cities	59	55	56	894
Rural areas	15	16	14	233
Education:				
Grade school	45	34	35	597
High school	44	46	46	702
College	11	21	19	238
Occupation of head of family:				
Professional and managerial	19	29	27	328
Other white collar	10	14	11	154
Skilled and semiskilled	36	26	34	455
Unskilled	16	10	11	182
Farm operators	13	13	11	171
Housewives	6	8	6	102
Occupation of respondent:				
Professional and managerial	10	18	18	207
Other white collar	10	12	12	161
Skilled and semiskilled	23	15	20	299
Unskilled	13	7	8	145
Farm operators	7	7	6	97
Housewives	37	41	35	548
Trade-union affiliation of head of family:				
Member	31	23	27	435
Nonmember	69	77	73	1113
Income:				
Under $2,000	21	17	14	279
$2,000-2,999	17	14	16	245
$3,000-3,999	25	21	22	356
$4,000-4,999	15	13	19	233
$5,000 and over	22	34	30	414

hypotheses about the causes and consequences of self-identified independence in American politics.

DEMOGRAPHIC CHARACTERISTICS. Selected demographic characteristics of independents and party identifiers in 1952 are presented in Table 17-1.[11] The first frequency distribution indicates not only that there were more male than female independents in 1952, but that there were fewer men than women among both Democrats and Republicans.[12] Independents, as a group, are quite similar to Democrats in their age composition, but somewhat younger than Republicans.[13] They are identical to Democrats on the matter of religious affiliation, and both have more Catholic adherents than do Republicans. Independents resemble Republicans most closely on the matter of educational background. There are fewer people whose education has stopped with grade school and more college-trained people among independents and Republicans than among Democrats. Independents and Republicans have more professional and managerial people, somewhat fewer skilled, semiskilled and unskilled workers, and an insignificantly larger number of other white-collar people than Democrats. Independents number slightly more union members in their ranks than Republicans and equally smaller numbers of union members than Democrats (4 per cent). Finally, independents have fewer people with incomes of less than $2,000 per year than either Republicans or Democrats, fewer people with incomes of $5,000 per year and over than Republicans, and more of such upper-bracket people than Democrats.

Summarizing these comparisons, it is instructive to note that independents resemble Democrats most closely on one item (religion) that is usually a good discriminating item between Democrats and Republicans. On the other relatively good discriminating items (race, type of community, education, occupation of head of family or respondent, trade-union affiliation, and income), independents resemble Republicans most closely, except for race (and there the difference is only 1 per cent), and except for trade-union affiliation, where independents are midway between Republicans and Democrats.

The socioeconomic resemblance of independents to Republicans throws doubt on the hypothesis that independents identify themselves as such simply because of ignorance, concern with and the time involved in making a minimal living, and general lack of interest or apathy frequently associated with marginal existence. The author was surprised by the sex-ratio finding, since he had made one of those apparently logical but speculative assumptions of the type discussed earlier that a large proportion of the independents would be women who so identified themselves because of their home-centered apolitical orientation and because of the presumed cultural value that identification as an independent may have. People less involved politically might have called themselves independents because it has fewer negative connotations than self-designation as disinterested. It appears from these data that if the latter is a factor, it is more of a male than a female phenomenon.

It is still possible, of course, that if a pattern of female independents exists for these reasons, housewives might evidence this more than females working outside of the home. Table 17-1 indicates, however, that even housewives identify themselves somewhat, although insignificantly, more frequently as Democrats or Republicans than as independents.

Independents do seem to be more "cross-pressured" than either Democrats or Republicans. It might be speculated that an independent identification is sometimes an intermediate step for people (particularly Catholics and possibly Negroes) in a transition from Democratic to Republican affiliation, paralleling a rise in educational, income, and social prestige positions.

Turning to an examination of the independent in the South, we see from Table 17-2 that he is apparently a different sort of person than the northern independent. With due regard for the small sample of independents in the South, it appears that they most closely resemble Democrats on the matter of religion, education, occupation (of head and respondent), and income. However, it should be noted that whereas in the North the Democrats were relatively most disadvantaged on these items, the reverse is true in the South. The independent in the South not only resembles the Democrat, he is more frequently a Catholic, college-educated, a professional or manager, and he more frequently has an income of more than $5,000 per year. In the South the independents resemble the Republicans most closely on the items of trade-union affiliation of the head of the family, and race. In the South as well as in the North, a greater proportion of independents were women

Table 17-2—Relation of Demographic Characteristics to Party Identification in the South (Percentage)

Characteristic	PARTY IDENTIFICATION			Number of Cases
	Dem	Rep	Ind	
Sex:				
Male	45	41	40	175
Female	55	59	60	222
Age:				
21-34 (18-34)	29	25	47	122
35-44	27	25	19	101
45-54	16	19	16	64
55 and over	28	30	18	105
Religion:				
Protestant	96	98	88	362
Catholic	4	2	7	16
Jewish			5	3
Race:				
White	82	77	74	318
Negro	18	23	26	81
Type of community:				
Metropolitan area	4	5	13	22
Towns and cities	74	64	74	289
Rural areas	22	31	13	89
Education:				
Grade school	48	67	32	194
High school	38	20	44	143
College	14	13	24	61
Occupation of head of family:				
Professional and managerial	22	13	31	77
Other white collar	10	8	10	33
Skilled and semiskilled	27	24	28	94
Unskilled	17	15	16	59
Farm operators	17	30	9	63
Housewives	7	9	7	27
Occupation of respondent:				
Professional and managerial	9	7	15	35
Other white collar	10	10	10	38
Skilled and semiskilled	19	16	7	59
Unskilled	15	12	8	50
Farm operators	13	14	5	39
Housewives	35	41	54	143
Trade-union affiliation of head of family:				
Member	12	25	24	62
Nonmember	88	75	76	337
Income:				
Under $2,000	35	46	17	131
$2,000-2,999	18	17	22	72
$3,000-3,999	20	17	20	77
$4,000-4,999	11	5	15	41
$5,000 and over	16	15	27	70

as compared to Democrats or Republicans. Thus, the apparent differences between the northern and southern independent become less if each is compared to the relatively more advantaged party identifiers in each place.

However, a special occupational-residence pattern does emerge which differentiates the southern independent from the southern Democrat as well as from the southern Republican. Considerably fewer independents were found in rural areas as compared to both Republicans and Democrats and a disproportionate number of independents lived in metropolitan areas. Whereas independents had proportionately more professional and managerial people in their ranks than did the Democrats (and considerably more than the Republicans), they had considerably fewer farm operators (in terms of both occupation of head of family and occupation of respondent). The data tend to support the contention that Republicanism in the South is generally associated with rural residence, farming, and marginal economic existence.

Self-identification as an independent appears to be associated with a different set of predispositional characteristics. To modify the cross-pressures hypothesis suggested for northern independents, southern independents may be more frequently people who are predisposed by occupation and income to national, if not state Republicanism, but whose metropolitan socio-political environments (and religious affiliation) dictate self-identification as an independent. Republicanism among the poor-white hill folks may stem from a traditional hostility to the wealthy and conservative Democrats, but the impulse to Republicanism among independents (and even among "conservative" Democrats) may reflect an underlying approval of accumulated wealth and conservatism. It would be easier, psychologically, for a person of the latter inclination to call himself an independent in the larger southern cities than in the Democratic towns and countryside.[14] To the extent that southern metropolitan political environments continue to become more Republican in their atmospheres, one can expect a continuation of or increase in the rate of this *political transition process:* from Democratic to Republican through independent identifications.

OVERT PARTICIPATION. The several overt political activities constituting the operational definition of "participation" in the 1952 election include: voting, contributing money, attending political meetings, other work for party or candidates, and trying "to show" people why they should vote for a party or candidate by talking with them. The composite index of participation used herein is based on the following categories: "high participation" includes voting plus one of these other activities; "medium participation" includes voting without other activity, or one of the other activities without voting; and "low participation" includes all others who neither voted nor engaged in any of the other activities.[15]

Table 17-3—Relation of Party Identification to Overt Political Participation (Percentage)

Political Participation	PARTY IDENTIFICATION Democrats	Republicans	Independents
High	24	36	27
Medium	52	52	51
Low	24	12	22
Number of cases	753	438	366

The participation patterns among independents and party identifiers in the same as a whole are presented in Table 17-3.[16]

As Campbell, Gurin, and Miller indicate, the rather surprising inference from these data is that in 1952 "we could not have made a very much better prediction of whether a person would vote or otherwise support his candidate from knowing which party category he put himself in than if we knew nothing about his party identification."[17] Their analysis further shows that if we consider responses to the question about whether they were strong or weak party identifiers, or "closer" to the Republicans or Democrats if an

Table 17-4—Relation of Party Identification to Political Participation* (Percentage)

Political Participation	PARTY IDENTIFICATION† Weak Democrats	Independent Democrats	Independent Republicans	Weak Republicans
High	19	26	32	29
Medium	50	48	46	49
Low	31	26	22	22

*Data from Campbell *et al.*, *The Voter Decides*, Table 7.11, p. 108.

†Weak Democrats and weak Republicans are so designated by responses to the question: "Would you call yourself a strong (R) (D) or a not very strong (R) (D)?" Independent Democrats and independent Republicans are so designated by responses to the question: "Do you think of yourself as closer to the Republican or Democratic party?" An earlier question established the primary self-identification as Republican, Democrat, or independent.

independent, independents closer to the Democratic party are even more highly active than "weak Democrats" and independents closer to the Republican party are somewhat more active than "weak Republicans." The relevant portions of their table are reproduced in Table 17-4.[18]

What are equally interesting are the comparative participation rates on the other overt political activities. Table 17-5 indicates that there are insignificant differences among independents and party identifiers on every activity that would seem to constitute

Table 17-5—Relation of Party Identification to Specific Political Activities (Percentage)

Political Activity	PARTY IDENTIFICATION Democrats	Republicans	Independents
Financial support	3	6	5
Attendance at political meetings, rallies, dinners, etc.	5	10	7
Other political work	2	5	4
Attempted influence by discussion	25	34	26

areas of expected differences. It would have been an apparently logical assumption that even if independents voted and perhaps even attempted verbally to influence others to vote in certain ways as much as did party identifiers, the former would be less active in the other political channels. These data indicate that not only were independents similar to party identifiers on all activity items, but they were more active than Democrats on every item (remembering that the differences and the number of cases were extremely small on all but the attempted influence by discussion item).

The differences were again statistically insignificant but southern independents were slightly less active than southern Republicans in three of the four activities (about equally active on the discussion item), and equally as active or slightly less active than southern Democrats in three of the four activities (insignificantly more active in "other political work"). Lower participation levels of independents in the South is also suggested by the nonparticipation data. Forty-five per cent of the southern independents did not even vote, compared to 37 per cent of the southern Democrats and Republicans, respectively. The comparable figures for independents and party identifiers outside of the South were: 17 per cent nonvoting by independents, compared to 17 per cent nonvoting by

Democrats, and 13 per cent nonvoting by Republicans. Even though southern independents were more highly educated than southern Democrats, their voting rates were identical. Independents were even more highly educated than Republicans in the South, yet the latter voted more than the former. These considerations suggest either that southern and other independents differed on some of the variables to be considered, or that the political environment has much to do with the behavioral resolution of psychological conflict and cross-pressures.

PSYCHOLOGICAL PARTICIPATION. *Attitudes on issues* were significantly related to electoral behavior in 1952.[19] Although the overt participation rates of independents were about as high as those of party identifiers, it was still expected that independents would be less issue-oriented even though more highly candidate-

Table 17-6—Relation of Party Identification to Psychological Participation (Percentage)

	PARTY IDENTIFICATION		
Variable	Democrats	Republicans	Independents
Issue activation:			
High	22	27	29
Medium	62	58	58
Low	16	15	13
High issue activation controlling education:			
Grade school	16	19	12
High school	26	25	30
College	33	50	58
Candidate orientation:*			
High	16	28	24
Medium	36	41	38
Low	48	31	38
High candidate orientation controlling education:			
Grade school	7	12	14
High school	20	32	21
College	30	54	49
Citizen duty:			
High	40	51	49
Medium	43	38	38
Low	17	11	13

*High candidate orientation means three or more personal references; medium means one or two personal references; and low means no personal references made spontaneously during the course of the interview.

oriented or have greater feelings of civic duty to participate than party identifiers. Although the differences are not large, the greater issue activation of independents compared to both Democrats and Republicans tends to disprove the hypothesis (Table 17-6).

Before accepting this interesting and somewhat surprising finding, the possible influence of the higher level of education of the independents in comparison to that of the Democrats needs to be assessed. Possibly the high educational level of independents caused them to be more articulate about issues than Democrats with the difference simply due to education. If the differences in education were removed, comparably educated Democrats might be more highly issue-oriented than independents. Both Democrats and Republicans are compared to independents at grade-school, high-school and college educational levels in reference to high issue activation in Table 17-6.

When education is thus controlled, the differences between the party identifiers and the independents still exist, almost regardless of educational level. The single difference comes not because the independents are more highly educated than Democrats, since at the college and high-school levels independents are more highly activated than both groups of party identifiers, but at the lowest educational level where independents are less highly activated. Controlling on education in this way offers a clue that party identification may make the most difference among the poorly educated. It also suggests that we may be dealing with two rather different types of independents; namely, those who so identify themselves because political disinterest and an independent self-identification may be a more acceptable or prestiged response than refusal of any political label, and those who are more involved in politics, issue-wise at least. The relative proportions of grade-school-, high-school- and college-educated independents should be kept in mind: 35, 46, and 19 per cent, respectively (Table 17-1).

The pattern of independents being more highly issue-activated than party identifiers holds true for the South as well as the rest of the country. The differences are even somewhat greater for southern independents (Table 17-7).

When independents are compared to party identifiers on the degree of internal conflict in the party orientation of their issue attitudes, no significant differences are discovered among Demo-

Table 17-7—Relation of Party Identification to Issue Activation in the South (Percentage)

Issue Activation	PARTY IDENTIFICATION Democrats	Republicans	Independents
High	17	18	26
Medium	61	55	56
Low	22	27	18

crats, Republicans and independents. Southern independents were slightly less conflicted on issue orientation than other independents, and less conflicted on issues than were southern Democrats or Republicans (although insignificantly less conflicted than the latter).

Attitudes toward candidates in 1952 show a pattern of independents being more candidate-oriented than Democrats but less so than Republicans (Table 17-6). Controlling for education presents a different picture than when education was controlled for issue activation. In the latter case the poorly educated independents were less highly issue-activated than poorly educated party identifiers. The reverse relationship is true for extent of candidate orientation. Among lower educated people independents are not less candidate-oriented than are party identifiers: they are in fact slightly more so (Table 17-6).

Among the low candidate-oriented people, independents are fewer in number at both the grade-school and college levels than Republicans or Democrats. Thus we have another clue to the types of independents speculated about in connection with the issue orientation data: one type may be poorly educated and disinterested issue-wise but interested or involved in the electoral process because of his candidate orientation, and another type may be the more highly educated independent who is concerned about both issues and candidates.

Southern independents were as highly candidate-oriented as other independents, and more so than either southern Democrats or Republicans.

Two measures are used to assess the degree to which party identifiers and independents were conflicted or pulled in different directions by their orientations toward the two presidential candidates. Among the voters, independents considered voting for the candidate for whom they did not finally vote some 32 per cent of the time; whereas the comparable figure for Democrats was 24 per cent and for Republicans 11 per cent.[20] On the basis of spontaneous references to the candidates, we find that independents were the most conflicted. This measure of conflict about the candidates serves as a useful check upon the first measure since it can be hypothesized that a self-identified independent might indicate considering voting for the other candidate because this is part of his mental picture of the way an independent is supposed to respond to such a question. The spontaneous personal references measure indicates that there is more at work here than self-images, expectations of others, and conscious role-playing. There seems to be a greater conflict about candidates among independents than was the case on the partisan direction of their issue orientations.

Using the same measures of candidate conflict, we find that southern independents considered voting for the other candidate than for whom they finally voted less frequently than either southern Democrats or Republicans (18 per cent, 33 per cent, and 61 per cent, respectively). Southern independents were less conflicted than other independents, but to a somewhat lesser degree, 18 per cent to 25 per cent, respectively. Using the measure of least conflict based on *pro* and *con* personal references, we find the southern independents more conflicted than southern Democrats and Republicans. So far, then, southern independents differ from independents elsewhere in being somewhat more issue-activated and candidate-oriented, slightly less conflicted on issues, and slightly more conflicted on candidates.

Attitudes towards citizen duty is a more general but theoretically relevant motivational force for political participation. The relationships between a sense of citizen duty and overt political participation in the 1952 election were demonstrated by Campbell, Gurin and Miller.[21] We are interested in comparing independents and party identifiers in terms of citizen duty also because participation with and without such feelings are qualitatively different actions. Psychological participation on the basis of a strong feeling of citizen duty may very well contribute to a stronger fundamental political consensus than participation without such feelings. It may be that the culturally valued pattern of political independence, particularly among higher-educated, middle- and upper-class people, is to have strong feelings of civic duty combined with a belief that party independence is the best path for the responsible citizen.

Using the scale of citizen duty developed by the Survey Research Center, we find that independents scored somewhat higher than Democrats and about the same as Republicans (Table 17-6). Thus we cannot accept the aforementioned hypothesis. In the South independents were less highly citizen duty-oriented than independents elsewhere, just as southern Democrats and Republicans were less highly citizen duty-oriented than Democrats and Republicans elsewhere.

Perceptions of primary group voting behavior are measured by a composite index constructed by the Survey Research Center's researchers on the basis of how the respondents perceived their friends and spouse, or family if unmarried, as having voted (Democratic, Republican, split, nonvoting, or don't know).[22] Presumably, if there were situations where friends and spouse voted in opposite directions, conflicts of loyalties may have had the effect of reducing or eliminating participation on the part of the person caught in the middle. It was initially hypothesized that independents would be more conflicted in this way than party identifiers. In the country as a whole, there were no significant differences among independents and Democrats, although there were differences between independents and Republicans as to the degree to which friends and spouses voted in different directions (Table 17-8). While the

Table 17-8—Relation of Party Identification to Perceived Group Homogeneity on Direction of Vote (Percentage)

Perceived Homogeneity	PARTY IDENTIFICATION		
	Democrats	Republicans	Independents
The national sample	30	51	30
The South	22	28	18
Outside of the South	34	55	33

southern independent is conflicted slightly more than is the southern Democrat, the difference is insignificant. The southern independent is considerably more conflicted by divided primary group voting than is his northern counterpart, with the difference between southern and other Republicans being the greatest in this respect.

Political involvement in the campaign process and outcome can be studied apart from issue and candidate orientations; as a matter of more general entertainment or spectator interest. Although the relatively great involvement of independents on issues and candidates in the 1952 election made it likely that they would be as attentive to the unfolding campaign processes as party identifiers, information on their purported "interest in following the political campaigns," and on their consumption of the mass media (newspapers, radio, television, and magazines) with reference to campaign events was intended to measure this directly and to serve as a partial validity check on their reported issue and candidate involvement.

Independents were midway between the Democrats and Republicans on their interest in following the campaign: more interested than Democrats and less interested than Republicans. They were similarly situated on media consumption.

These items were combined with expressions of how much they cared who won the local, state, and national elections and Guttman scaling techniques were then used. These four items scaled with a relatively high 96.7 per cent coefficient of reproducibility. On the basis of this scale of political involvement, independents are somewhat less involved than Republicans although about as involved as Democrats. The same pattern prevailed for southern independents and party identifiers. The picture of participating, issue- and candidate-oriented independents in 1952 is further elaborated and supported by the findings on these aspects of psychological involvement.

There is finally one aspect of psychological participation that is particularly relevant to our interest in the function of independents for political consensus, the aforementioned *political interests* of independents and party identifiers.[23] Extent of issue orientation, expectations of personal financial consequences stemming from the victory of either party, and expectations of "differences to the country" as a consequence of the election of either party (items taken from the pre-election survey) were combined into a Guttman-type scale of political interests.[24] Independents were at the lowest end of the scale proportionately as much as were party identifiers, but independents were less numerous at the highest end of the scale (Table 17-9).

Whereas the differences between Democrats on the one hand, and Republicans and independents on the other, at the upper end of the political interest scale (scores 1 plus 2) may reflect the rela-

Table 17-9—Relation of Party Identification to Political Interests (Percentage)

Scale Scores on Political Interests	PARTY IDENTIFICATION Democrats	Republicans	Independents
High 1	17	16	10
2	45	34	38
3	34	46	48
Low 4	4	3	4

tively greater economic concern and anxieties of the lower income Democrats, the small difference between independents and both sets of party identifiers at the very top of the political interest scale (score 1) suggests a difference in what might be termed their *partisan antagonistic set.* The political interests of the independent go only so far; they stop short of viewing *the other* as a very significant threat to the country. The reason for this lesser partisan antagonism may stem from realistic perceptions, or be a consequence of playing a role that involves a self-image of such moderation. Whatever the reason, the fact that independents appear to be somewhat less disposed to view the victory of either party as a disaster or a panacea suggests that independents were functioning as at least potential contributors to fundamental political consensus in the way we hypothesized.

In the South, independents also had less partisan antagonism than did party identifiers, although the difference between southern independents and Republicans was smaller than outside of the South. As was expected because of the lower issue orientation of southern Republicans, they had the lowest political interest scores, whereas southern Democrats had the smallest proportion of the lowest scorers. The lesser partisan antagonism of independents in the South and elsewhere is apparently not due to differences in educational achievement (and therefore more accurate perceptions and/or greater sophistication) since independents are less antagonistic at every educational level (grade school, high school, and college).

CONCLUSIONS. The similarity of independents to party identifiers in 1952 is perhaps the most striking finding of the preceding analysis. The similarity extends beyond voting, donating money, working in campaigns, and other overt participation to psychological involvement of various sorts. The lesser feelings of political antagonism on the part of independents is a potentially important difference for political consensus. So too are the regional differences noted between southern and other independents.

Several types of independents have been tentatively delimited. One type may be poorly educated and less concerned about issues than similarly educated party identifiers. Research is needed to establish whether the poorly educated party identifiers so identify themselves as a consequence of their issue orientations or whether their party identifications lead them to become more issue-oriented. Another important question is whether their reported opinions on issues are important to them or simply constitute statements of what they think a party identifier should say.

This type of independent may participate as much as the poorly educated party identifier who is concerned with issues because the former is relatively more candidate-oriented than is the latter. We might hypothesize that poorly educated people are either issue-oriented *or* candidate-oriented but not both. A number of hypotheses to explain this could be developed and tested with larger numbers of cases.

Another type of independent is clearly the highly educated person who is concerned with both issues and candidates. This type of independent may have lesser partisan antagonism. Again, the dynamics of these processes need to be investigated: Do lower political interests cause a person to identify himself as an independent, or do independents have different self-images than party identifiers? It may be that party identifiers exaggerate their expectations of the consequences of partisan victory or it may be that independents minimize their feelings.

To what extent does self-identified independence reflect internal psychological conflicts, socioeconomic-religious cross pressures, or pressures from the political environment? To what extent is the independent-in-transition type on the increase in the United States? Under what socio-political conditions does this type of independent emerge? Under what conditions dooes he become fixated and remain a self-identified independent?

While the study of the political effects or functions of independents must be undertaken by different methods and approaches, the survey method can be used to advantage for the study of many aspects of political independence. National sample surveys along the lines developed by the Survey Research Center should be repeated over time in order to develop trend data on independents as well as for testing some of the above findings and hypotheses with sufficiently large numbers of cases. Complementary community and regional sample surveys along the lines of the Erie County and Elmira studies need to be developed in a comparative setting, with particular attention to diverse political environments, as well as to the political behavior of independents in response to a variety of local political phenomena. The panel method would be particularly appropriate to compare the responses of independents and party identifiers to unfolding partisan activities between and at election time. For the implications of self-identified independence will become clearer only in a more comprehensive set of studies in a broad matrix of political events extending over the range of organized and informal politics.[25]

CHAPTER 18

Analyzing the Social Process Underlying Group Voting Patterns

R. DUNCAN LUCE

This chapter[1] is concerned with the efforts in *Voting*[2] to understand the social process which precedes a voting decision in the American electorate. Particular attention will be paid to the role of verbal imagery in such a process, especially as a precursor to a (partial) mathematical model of the process. Two descriptive images, both drawn largely from *Voting* and to a lesser extent from *The People's Choice*,[3] will be outlined in the barest of terms.

The first of these images, which will be called here the "interaction image," appears implicitly in Chapter 7 of *Voting;* however, it is supplemented and to some degree contradicted by other explanations offered in that book. The central idea has received considerable attention from Lazarsfeld and his colleagues and there have been several attempts to translate it into a formal mathematical system. Its adequacy to account for the data that exist will be questioned, and, in an attempt to show how these explanatory statements might be better unified and made to give a more careful and exact accounting of the data, a more complex outline will be stressed. This will be called the "motivation-interaction image." The word "stress" is used advisedly, for this image—incompatible as it seems to be with the interaction image—lies side by side with it in *Voting*. It was first introduced briefly in *The People's Choice* and it was again given limited emphasis in *Voting;* however, its merits have not gone unrecognized and it has since flowered as the central research idea of the recent book *Personal Influence*.[4]

What seems not to have been fully appreciated, at least in *Voting*, is that the two images are not fully consistent and that the second, which seems to possess greater explanatory power, is probably just as amenable as the first to mathematization as a testable model.

It is difficult to phrase this argument so that the suggested imagery is entirely convincing. In some measure this results from not always having adequate data—either because it was not obtained by the authors or because it was not presented—but at least as important is the fact that whatever image of the social process they may hold, it is never coherently stated in one place. Thus a critic can only attempt to construct it, or reconstruct it, from a mass of statements —some of which are not entirely consistent with others, some of which are allegorical, and some whose role is uncertain (see the Appendix to this chapter for an example).

Of course, it can be contended that no such imagery exists, or, more plausibly, that it is totally irrelevant to the final study, which can be interpreted simply as a collection of data about an important phenomenon. This cannot be the case. The reasons are simple and well known: almost without exception the data are presented as two or three, and occasionally more, dimensional tables with the variation of one discrete variable against another exhibited. For this no preconceptions are needed, although they usually exist: What else determines the variables included in a study and the combinations which are correlated? But, whenever correlations are given a causal interpretation—and in *Voting* that is almost always the case—a portion of the underlying image is exposed. The complete set of explanatory statements forms the (not necessarily complete or consistent) image of the process, and the correlations can only disprove or fail to disprove—which is not the same as confirm —portions of it. Without such an underlying image one can only say that the correlations exist, for a priori, either variable may be independent and the other dependent, or the correlation may be an entirely artificial consequence of each variable depending on a third.[5] With a logical or mathematical model, which in practice is the most precise form one's image of a process may assume, one ideally establishes that a whole collection of correlations are consistent with a relatively few basic hypotheses and some of their consequences.

It is difficult to believe that these well-known, almost trite, observations are still of pertinence in sophisticated social research, yet it is possible to exhibit examples from *Voting* which suggest that they may not always have been kept in mind. One such example is given in the Appendix below.

THE INTERACTION. One of the most reliable and noncontroversial results of the various voting studies is this: there is a relatively high correlation between a person's voting intention (and also his actual vote) and what may be termed social classification—socioeconomic status, religion, and ethnic background. A white Protestant businessman is very likely to vote Republican and to intend to vote Republican throughout the campaign; a negro Catholic laborer is more often than not Democratic. Since voting is an infrequent and transitory event and voting intentions are individual decisions, whereas social classification is a relatively fixed parameter concerning a person's whole relationship to society, few would contend that the former explains the latter. Thus, class and religion tend in some way to account for voting behavior, or each of these variables is a consequence of some more basic underlying variable. The authors and most of their readers accept the first of these as the explanation, that is to say, a basic tenet of the image of the process is that social classification should be a part of the input data which, with whatever other data appear relevant, lead to a prediction of voting behavior.

If the correlation between voting behavior and social classification were perfect and there were no individuals whose social classifications are inconsistent with respect to voting—no so-called "cross-pressured" individuals—then little more would need to be said. But, of course, neither supposition holds: there are white Protestant businessmen who vote Democratic, to say nothing of Catholic businessmen and Protestant laborers. Furthermore, if one admits that understanding differs from predictions—even from perfect prediction—then one may still ask for the mechanisms whereby individuals become identified with social classifications and how the voting integrity of any particular social group is maintained in the short run. (The long-run problem appears to be totally outside the scope of the ideas under discussion.) Presumably, the questions of identification and integrity are intimately tied into the explanations of deviational voting and of voting decisions made by those who live under social cross-pressures. Much, then, of the rest of *Voting* can be viewed as being concerned with this problem, the analysis technique being largely the breakdown of the relationship between two variables according to a third one. For example, the relation between voting intentions and religion may be broken down according to socioeconomic status, or according to the political intentions of an individual's friends, or in terms of the individual's interest in the campaign, etc. Roughly speaking, everything has some effect. The dilemma of the social sciences is not, as some seem to think, a paucity of statistically significant correlations, but, as a glance at the journals shows, an overabundance of moderate but significant ones currently lacking acceptable causal explanations and thus failing to suggest which relationships are basic. The problem is whether some of these correlations can be taken to be basic unexplained effects and the others accounted for in terms of time. Such is the purpose of a model.

The image of the social process which seems to emerge in Chapter 7 of *Voting* says, in the broadest terms, that an individual's interactions with members of his primary groups constitute the basic social mechanism for developing political decisions. There is a tendency for much political discussion to occur within primary groups and this discussion leads, in some unexplained manner, to conformity of viewpoint within such groups. It is suggested that this tendency toward conformity, resulting from politically relatively passive interactions, accounts both for the voting stability of the social classes and for the observed indecision when there are cross-pressures, for then the individual is subject to conflicting viewpoints within his primary groups. There are two major points to this thesis: first, that discussion is the mechanism leading to conformity within primary groups, and, second, that the resulting transmission or diffusion of conformity through chains of overlapping primary groups results in conformity throughout whole social classes.

With respect to the development of conformity in the primary groups, one gradually acquires from Chapter 7 a picture of a politically passive individual "colliding" with members of his primary groups, discussing the campaign with a frequency and intensity that among other things depends inversely on the degree of cross-pressuring (= momentum), and "rebounding" either reinforced or shaken in his views depending on the "initial states" of the two individuals (= molecules). True, I am being facetious in suggesting the molecular model, yet I would insist that this is the flavor left by part of Chapter 6 and by Chapter 7: passive individuals interacting with each other through the medium of political discussion and eventually reaching an equilibrium in which, with high probability, all the members of a given primary group possess the same political opinions. Possibly this image can be suggested by a few quotations:

"Friends transmit the predispositional tendencies of class and religion; in a sense, such predispositions *are* mainly the accumulated influence of like-positioned and hence like-minded associates on each other."[6]

"It is customary to say that what matters for the voter is the social environment *close* to him; and so it does."[7]

"If voters cannot test the appropriateness of their decisions by reference to political consequences, then they are especially likely to be influenced by other, nonpolitical facts—for example, what trusted people around them are doing. As a result, old interests and traditions of class and minority blocs are brought to bear upon the determination of today's vote. In this process the principal agencies are not Machiavellian manipulators, as is commonly supposed when bloc votes are delivered at the polls, but the ordinary family, friends, co-workers, and fellow organization members with whom we are all surrounded. In short, the influences to which voters are most susceptible are opinions of trusted people expressed to one another."[8]

"Those who discuss politics with the opposition are more likely than others subsequently to take on that opposite preference in their own voting."[9]

"Voting change is correlated with the political preferences of family members . . . with opposite political preferences or the absence of known preferences of one's friends . . . [and] of one's co-workers."[10]

"In sum, we have a general finding on implementation. Intentions supported by one's social surroundings are more predictably carried out than are intentions lacking such support."[11]

Without denying that the data establish conformity within many primary groups, we can question the nature of the mechanism effecting the conformity: Is the image of an interacting "molecular" system tending toward equilibrium sufficient?

Suppose, for the moment, that it is, then there still remains the question whether this explains the transmission of homogeneous views throughout one of the social classifications. Clearly, the typical diffusion model familiar from physics is inadequate. Instead we must suppose that society is like a lattice in which each individual has a constrained region of contacts—the individual's primary groups—differing slightly from the region of contacts of those individuals within his region and markedly from the regions of those outside his sphere. The spread of opinion through such a structured society is technically a diffusion problem, but it is unlike the diffusions of classical physics which occur in a continuous homogeneous medium.

The study of diffusion in a discrete structured medium of a suitable sort has been begun in recent years by Rapoport[12] in the context of disease and rumor spread. It may be possible to use, or to adapt, Rapoport's mathematical results to establish, for populations of different sizes with primary groups of known sizes and rates of "infectivity," the amount of primary group conformity needed to achieve a given degree of social class conformity—providing the political integrity of a social class can be developed and sustained in this manner. If his results are not suitable, then the appropriate mathematics must be developed before such an interaction model of the social process can be demonstrated. Without such a demonstration, we do not know to what degree primary group conformity explains conformity within a social class.

More basic than the propagation of conformity throughout a social class is the problem of its creation within a primary group. While no attempts are known that deal with the diffusion problem as such, there have been several papers devoted to possible models of the interaction. These are of two types: a statistical model which does not deal directly with the interaction but assumes that each member of a particular class of people, say those who last reported they would vote Democratic, has a certain fixed probability of changing his intentions. Anderson's model typifies this approach.[13] Alternatively, one may take a more microscopic view and examine the statistical behavior of single individuals, assuming that each has certain propensities to vote Democratic or Republican, that pairs have certain chances of interacting, and that the interaction alters these propensities in fixed ways. Coleman and Bush have discussed such models.[14] It is probably safe to say that to date no startling success has been achieved by these models.

Aside from success, there is the question whether any model of this general type could conceivably be relevant. One objection, though by no means a crucial one, is that such models cannot explain the formation of political opinion; at best they are able to say how one state of political opinion leads into another once the process is under way. One must postulate an initial distribution of political opinion and from there watch how, according to the model, it must change. The social environment determines the individual, and indeed the social environment at a later time, but that leaves open what determines the environment to begin with.

Far more important in my opinion is the assumption that each time an interaction (discussion) occurs the intentions of each of the participants are slightly disturbed. Is this really the way opinions are changed—by small but irregular modifications, much as the energy level of a molecule is altered in the famed "random walks"? One can question whether most interactions serve the function of changing opinion at all. To be sure, some must, but it is possible that the major role of discussion may be to preserve opinion once it is formed. That is to say, group discussion may be a conservative force which prevents small perturbations of opinion from initiating waves of political change which would sweep throughout the whole of a social class to wreak political havoc. However, this does not say that it is the mechanism whereby an equilibrium state of fairly uniform views is developed within a single social classification. Some of the data in *Voting* can be interpreted to support this view. For example, in the Appendix I shall question the interpretation of some data which purport to show that discussion precipitates changes of voting intentions. In addition, the following two quotations are interesting:

"At the height of the campaign, then, political discussion on the grass-roots level apparently consists more of the exchange of mutually agreeable remarks than of controversial ones. The process of clarifying and modifying views with opponents that is assumed to constitute the give-and-take of informal political debate throughout the community is not predominant during the presidential campaign."[15]

"Thus there is relatively little political exchange among the electorate in the sense of open differences of views."[16]

One final point may be made in this connection. Certain of the data raise the question whether primary groups are really *directly* influential in forming individual voting intentions. Specifically, it is shown on page 136 of *Voting* that the parent-offspring voting association is relatively small *provided* the (adult) offspring are separated into homogeneous socioeconomic classes. If this can be accepted at face value, it is psychologically surprising since the parent-offspring relationship is generally considered to have deep and lasting effects on the offspring—of course, it is also known to be a capricious relationship. But more to the point socially is that the result, if it can be accepted naïvely, casts serious doubt upon the whole image of opinion developing from primary group interactions. If, however, discussion actually is the basic mechanism for diffusing political beliefs during the campaign, then these data may merely reveal that little discussion occurs between parent and offspring (perhaps because the parent is dead or lives in another city). The point seems sufficiently crucial to an understanding of the political process that, in a new voting study, conformity within this primary group might be examined by separating those pairs who actually discuss politics from those who do not, as well as by grouping the offspring according to socioeconomic status.

INTEREST AND OPINION LEADERS. Interaction within the primary groups is by no means the only hypothesis offered in *Voting* for the gradual creation of attitudes during the campaign; it is only the one most consistently stressed in Chapter 7. In other chapters at least two other factors are shown to be of importance in the evolution of political opinion; however, it is left somewhat obscure in the book how they tie into the interaction model. One of these is "interest." The authors state: "How do we measure interest? Actually, almost all measures of political involvement and participation are highly correlated with one another and, for analytical purposes, interchangeable. Accordingly, we use here the simplest measure, a direct question asking: 'How much interest would you say you have in this year's election—a great deal, quite a lot, not very much, none at all?' "[17] Some of the assertions involving this individual variable may be considered:

"People who change their vote intention are less interested in the election than the contestants."[18]

"The greater the partisanship, the greater the interest."[19]

"The less cross-pressures between vote and opinion on the issues, the greater the interest."[20]

Often the data give equal support to inverted forms of the above sentences (see the Appendix below), e.g., people who are less interested in the election change their vote intentions more than those who are more interested, etc.

The "interest" variable recurs from time to time throughout the book an dappears to play a significant role in the understanding of the formation of voting intentions:

"the lower the interest the less one votes consistently with his friends."[21]

"Opinion leaders are characterized by (1) greater interest and competence in politics; . . ."[22]

"people who practically never discuss politics with one another do not maintain those qualities (like interest) which lead to stability of the preferences that characterize the social surroundings and group interests."[23]

"Those interested in politics are more likely to know party workers."[24]

"The greater the interest in the election, the sharper the differences between partisans on Position issues like Taft-Hartley and price control."[25]

"The more that people read about and listen to the campaign on the mass media, the more interested they become in the election and the more strongly they come to feel about their candidate."[26]

Again, do not forget the possibility of inverted forms of these sentences.

A second notion which plays a brief role at the end of Chapter 6, but which appears almost nowhere else in *Voting*, is the "opinion leader." At this particular point in the book the authors seem to hold, briefly at least, part of the image which will be discussed in the next section. It also appears in Chapter 16 of *The People's Choice*. Elsewhere in these volumes, however, it tends to be forgotten. An opinion leader is defined in *Voting* as any person who says he feels he is more likely to be asked for his political views than are his acquaintances *or* one who describes himself as being no more or less likely to be asked but says that recently he talked politics with someone. Most of the data reported on opinion leaders, defined in this way, are devoted to trying to characterize them. That is, the distribution and statistical description of opinion leaders in society are social parameters for which the authors desired clarification. They found that:

"Opinion leaders are characterized by (1) greater interest and competence in politics; (2) greater activity in more strategic social locations; and (3) closer representativeness of those they influence.

and (*a*) Within broad strata, opinion leaders are slightly higher in occupational and educational status than others."[27]

It cannot be said that the attempt to locate and to describe opinion leaders met with striking success, quite possibly because of the definition used.

In *Personal Influence* the opinion leader looms large, and far more detailed efforts are made than in either of the voting studies to isolate such people, to characterize their effect on others, and to determine their reactions to their social environment. However, it is unclear how many of these results can be carried over into the voting area, for the areas of leadership investigated were fashions, movies, marketing, and public affairs. It was found that considerable variation, both as to who they are and how they behave, exists among the leaders of these opinion areas. In addition, all the subjects were women who, according to the voting studies, tend to play an extremely passive political role. Nonetheless, the techniques and results of this study are sure to be influential in further attempts to isolate the opinion leaders in a political campaign.

To be sure, variables other than these two—interest and opinion leaders—are examined in *Voting*, but as these strike me of considerable importance, we shall confine our attention to them.

THE MOTIVATION-INTERACTION IMAGE. This section is devoted to sketching an image of the social process related to, but different from, that discussed in the second section of this chapter—an image which may be capable of encompassing not only the data discussed there, but also those involving interest and opinion leaders. It will by no means be possible to establish here that it actually does the job; certain points of view can only be suggested that might be rewarding for future voting research and that could result in the collection of data disproving it if false.

The basic thesis is that at least some people in the society must have motives to reach decisions, that some are able to distinguish among choices and among their purported consequences, and that they have preferences among the consequences. These preferences, in turn, result in decisions. The alternatives to this assumption seem to be two: either to suppose that interactions among passive agents produce a diffusion process which determines decisions, in which case the difficulties (including the dilemma of what initially creates the climate of opinion) mentioned in the second section arise, or to suppose that society as a whole possesses motivations. While the latter view of society and history has been offered in many forms, I find it both unacceptable and useless. Rejection of this view, however, rests on such questions as the source of an over-all social teleology and so on, not on a logical dilemma and on empirical evidence as in the preceding alternative. Its rejection, then, is largely personal and pragmatic.

A model of individual motivation would be relatively transparent in outline if many, or even a relatively few, of the electorate could see how the election would benefit them directly, for then we could assume that they would select the party which in their view was more beneficial. Probably only a few (at least in Elmira) perceive the consequences of a modern national election in such immediate personal terms. For any others who are motivated, an alternative is to suppose that each identifies with certain significant social groups of sufficient size—millions of members in a national election—that the election can be "seen" to alter the fates of these groups, and to suppose that he wishes to select the party benefiting these groups. His reward will be indirect.

The mechanism of class identification is complex and subtle, but presumably the role of various primary groups is crucial. Nonetheless, respondents apparently tend to be accurate, as compared with objective measures, as to their class labels (see page 56 of *Voting*, for example). This topic will be taken here as one which can be measured as a parameter in a voting study. At least equally complex is the question of how these cultural classifications, rather than others such as eye color, are established as social parameters in the first place. Again, this is not a problem here.

It seems reasonable to suppose that the interest variable is a measure of degree of motivation. A person motivated to select a candidate who will benefit the groups with which he identifies himself feels, by definition, that the election is important and so he is "interested"; it is much less clear that an unmotivated person will be "uninterested," for he may be amused and intrigued by the spectacle. Nonetheless, there should be a tendency in that direction.

The motivated person will presumably be "rational" in the sense that he will try to make the choice he is convinced will benefit those groups with which he identifies. This is not to say that he will be rational in any objective sense, but rather that he will tend to expose himself to at least some of the arguments of the campaign, that he will tend to generate his own arguments for a choice, that he will tend to base his choice finally on arguments not readily dislodged by casual contacts with others, and that if he is cross-pressured he will think out the arguments carefully enough not to become a "changer."[28] Schematically, his processes are much like those shown in Figure 18-1. Let it be clear that this diagram does

FIG. 18-1.—Schematic diagram for decision-making by a high-motivation individual.

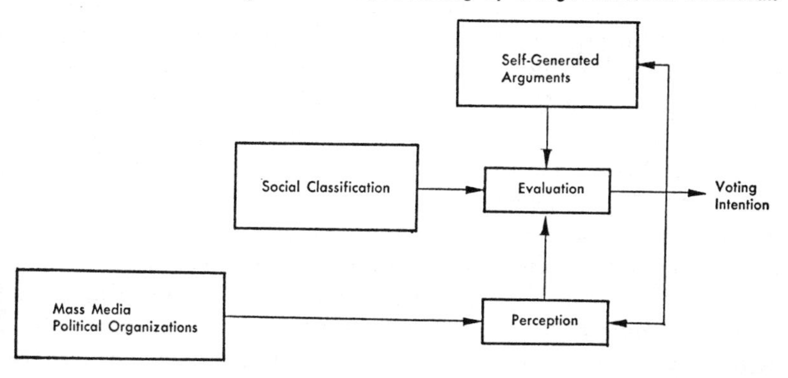

not suppose a singularly intelligent and unbiased mind which weighs alternatives accurately, but rather one which is independent of its associates, that does try to weigh alternatives, and that attempts to reach its own conclusions based on what it considers good reasons. In addition to faulty judgment, we may suppose, as is established in *Voting*, selective perception among the materials available to the individual and, moreover, a feedback from the decision which colors his perceptions even further.

Such highly motivated people are probably much less directly influenced by their primary groups than *Voting* leads one to believe. This is not to say that they will necessarily exhibit a pattern of deviation from the other members of their primary groups, but rather that the influence is not direct. It must not be forgotten that it is highly probable all the members of a given primary group will have the same social classifications and, therefore, will all be subject to the same sorts of "arguments" that a particular voting intention is appropriate and useful for those classes. In addition, such a motivated person may exert a positive impact upon other members of his primary group in the fashion described below.

No doubt, any good measure of motivation will lead to numerous different levels, but, for purposes of exposition, let us simplify the image by supposing that there are only two levels: high and low. The low-motivation person is one of the type discussed in the second section above. He either does not identify strongly with any of the culturally relevant groups or he does not sense that the election will have a deep impact upon his groups; he is unwilling to examine the arguments available or to generate his own; and so he is much more susceptible to those arguments which can be brought to the focus of his attention. With such a passive individual, we would postulate that the main way in which he is brought to focus upon the election at all is by another person who, first, has strong opinions, i.e., high motivation, and, second, who has sufficient motivation to want to influence others. These are the opinion leaders discussed in *The People's Choice* and *Voting*.

At least, this seems to be what is meant by the term in those books. *Personal Influence*, however, tends to rock the boat a bit. "Contrary to our expectations, however, the public affairs leaders . . . are more likely than non-leaders to report personal influence as the more significant component of their recent opinion changes. . . . It is interesting to ask why the public affairs leader, whom we expected to make more use of her greater media exposure in her personal decisions, tends to rely less, not more, on the media than non-leaders. It may be, perhaps, that our sample contains a disproportionately large number of 'local' rather than 'cosmopolitan' leaders, and that the latter—if our data permitted us to examine them separately—would in fact show greater media impact in their decisions. Or, it may be that the effect of the media in public affairs would be more clearly visible if we traced the networks of interpersonal influence further back; in other words, we might find that the next step—that is, the opinion leaders of the opinion leaders—are the ones who form opinions in more direct response to the media. Or, it might be that we would have to go back several steps before we found the link between the interpersonal networks of public affairs opinion and disproportionate mass media effect."[29]

On the question of opinion leaders and interest, the authors have this to say: "Might it be that the leaders are simply the more interested people and that these other factors—life-cycle and the like—are related to leadership only because they are also related to interest?

"Consistently we found that that was not the case . . . a woman's objective position—in the life-cycle, or on the status ladder, or with reference to quantity of social contacts—has a lot to do with whether or not she will be an opinion leader—even when she has a high level of interest.

"It does not mean that opinion leadership is unrelated to interest; as a matter of fact, the two are very strongly related, although not in the specific sense that interest directly bestows opinion leadership. The relationship is much more complicated. First of all, we must repeat, there is a greater interest among leaders than among non-leaders. But, secondly—and this is the important part—it appears that this greater interest results in leadership primarily when one associates with others who also are interested."[30]

Whether these conclusions hold for a national campaign—which is hardly the same as fashions, movies, marketing, or even public affairs—is not clear. Let it be supposed, at least for now, that motivation, of which interest is taken to be the verbal index, is a necessary condition for opinion leadership, though by no means a sufficient one. The real empirical task is to find a usable set of conditions which are sufficient to isolate these leaders.

In any case, our present image of the passive person is that shown in Figure 18-2. It will be noted that there are certain major differences between the two diagrams:

FIG. 18-2.—Schematic diagram for decision-making by a low-motivation individual.

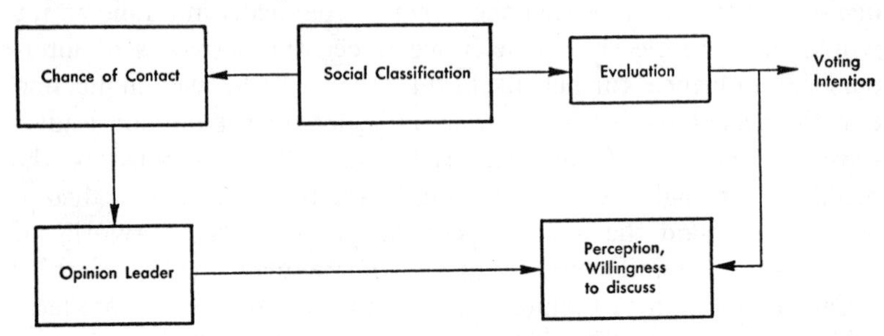

1) The source of information and argumentation for the highly motivated people is largely either social—mass media—or self-generated; for those with low motivation, it is largely personal, the source being the opinion leaders.

2) The source of filtering is almost entirely an individual variable for those with high motivation, but for those with low motivation there is, in addition, the social filtering of whether he has a chance to contact an opinion leader.

3) Those who are highly motivated are subject to all possible arguments insofar as their perceptions will admit them; whereas, those with low motivation may receive only arguments tailored to suit their particular social classification, identifications, etc. This is a consequence of their direct personal sources of information and ideas.

There can be little doubt that this image is too simplified as it stands, but it is sufficient to suggest certain new questions to ask of voting data. Again, let it be emphasized that it differs but little from the two-stage model suggested briefly in *The People's Choice*, where the authors wrote: "This suggests that ideas often flow *from* radio and print *to* the opinion leaders and *from* them to the less active sections of the population."[31] And, as has been noted above, such a conception is primary in *Personal Influence*.

IS THE MOTIVATION-INTERACTION IMAGE SUPERIOR?

There is little point in a more complex image of the social process unless it manages to do some things that a simpler image fails to do. On the other hand, it is nearly impossible to state what an image does or does not do; with a model one can say to what extent it is consistent with data, but an image serves largely to suggest new correlations to examine and new data to collect, and as a complex of "pegs" on which to "hang" the data. Thus, evaluation of the image itself is largely subjective, and evaluation of the impact of an image is largely historical. Nonetheless, certain things can be said.

For one thing, the pure interaction image fails to introduce a source of social "energy," i.e., it fails to say how opinions strong enough to get the interaction and diffusion process under way are ever created. Or as we put it before, how do the political views become established at the beginning of the campaign so as to begin the interaction process? By introducing at least some people who are motivated to make political decisions we both introduce a source of "energy" and, incidentally, a conservative mechanism to reduce the amount of change due to interaction. Of course, one can ask where the individual motivation comes from, but this does not seem to be the task of social theory to answer. It must accept certain psychological facts as given and measurable and from these deduce certain social consequences, even though these psychological facts may, themselves, depend on the social environment. The latter possibility need only be taken into account to the extent of recognizing that in data collection such a factor as motivation may depend, statistically, on socioeconomic status, education, etc.

Second, the pure interaction model as applied to two populations having the same distribution of primary groups will lead, on the average, to the same equilibrium distribution of political opinion. It is doubtful that this conclusion could be sustained empirically; it is very likely that in many cities statistically similar primary group structures exist, but that the distributions of political opinion are quite different. The second image allows this as a possibility since the distributions of opinion leaders throughout the communities may, conceivably, differ appreciably.

Third, the motivation-interaction image and the interaction image both lead to the conclusion of high primary group conformity, but for entirely different reasons. In the interaction image, the reason is that voting intentions are affected by interactions within the primary group and these intentions tend to a uniform statistical equilibrium. It is almost a "second law" of social process. In the motivation-interaction image, the conformity results in large measure from the similarity of social clasification within a primary group, which in turn results in common identifications by the group members, coupled to similar environmental impacts. For example, if one member of a primary group is reached by an opinion leader, possibly by his being in the group, it is more than likely that the others will be reached too. The difference between these two mechanisms of conformity can be illustrated for the parent-offspring primary group. If we restrict our attention to those groups where the parent and offspring do interact with one another at the time of the campaign, but where they are of different socioeconomic status, the interaction image would lead us to believe that conformity would result. The motivational image would, on the contrary, suggest that each would conform to the tendencies of his socioeconomic status, and presumably therefore to most of his *other* primary groups. Thus, there would be very restricted conformity within the parent-offspring group. Which of these hypotheses is true we do not know, but it should be easy enough to determine this empirically. Certainly, the data in *Voting* suggest the latter.

Another prediction suggested by the more complex image (plus a lot of intuition) is that younger voters will conform less well to their social classification than older ones. One reason for arguing this is that some younger people probably fail to identify with their objective socioeconomic class, but rather with the one to which they aspire or expect ultimately to reach. A pure interaction image would, of necessity, fail to make such a distinction.

We could go on to cite other possible advantages, but as with the ones above the conclusions are less than rigorous because we are dealing with images, not models. The main point is that the motivation-interaction image is slightly more rich in possibilities, and thus seems better able to cope with the complexities suggested by the data in *The People's Choice* and *Voting.*

CAN A MODEL BE FORMULATED? A crucial question about any imagery we may produce is whether under any circumstances it would be *possible* to disprove it, and, in particular to disprove it with the methods currently available. To some extent the answer is clearly yes, for in the preceding section we have offered several pairs of conflicting empirical hypotheses which seem to flow from the two images and which could be put to empirical test. But there can be no doubt that our image is far from precisely formulated, and so we can say no more than the hypotheses "seem to flow" from the image; we are in no position to make rigorous deductions. The problems of confirmation and disapproval cannot really come into their own until the image is translated into a more formal statement from which logically correct deductions can be made—until we have a mathematical model. Thus, the question transforms itself into: Can a model be formulated? On this it would be foolish to speculate; it will suffice to point out that if a serious attempt is made then there seem to be four major problems. Briefly, they are:

1) to devise appropriate questions to determine exactly who the opinion leaders are, ultimately leading to a precise definition of them, and to develop ways of ascertaining the motivation of each of the respondents;

2) to ascertain the nature of the political impact of an opinion leader upon someone with whom he interacts and also the impact if any, on himself;

3) to devise ways of determining, or predicting from other data, the statistical space and time structure of these interactions; and

4) to work out mathematics suitable for representing the resulting diffusion process in a structured society.

With respect to the first point, it could be argued that future voting studies should give much more serious attention to the two variables, motivation and opinion leadership. The question, "Are you interested in the election?" gets at motivation to some degree, but it probably should be supplemented by a whole battery of questions exploring the area: Do you feel that the election is important to this or that group, do you think it matters who wins, why do you care, who will benefit from the victory and do you care? etc. It is possible that psychologists who have concerned themselves with personality will have some shrewd ideas as to simple indices of motivation. As to opinion leaders, certainly the definition used in *Voting* is inadequate, and while the methods have been much refined in *Personal Influence*, there still remains the question whether the isolation of these people is as yet satisfactory. Once they are identified, it should not be difficult to find whom among the low motivation people they contact: Is it mostly those within their own primary groups, or do they extend their efforts to larger circles? If so, do they have any influence beyond their own primary groups?

The second problem—the impact of one person on another—seems to encounter extreme difficulties; the problem was raised in both *The People's Choice* and *Voting* but in my opinion it was not resolved in either study. Given a low-motivation person with "consistent" social classifications, he will tend to vote with those classes, but a cross-pressured low-motivation person will vacillate (see the tabulation in note 28 below). The exact nature of the process—which must be known before a model is remotely possible—has not been exposed by these studies: How much contact with opinion leaders is needed to produce what kind of change? Do regular contacts with two Democratic opinion leaders and one Republican amount to the same thing as regular contacts with one Democratic leader? Is regularity of contact important, or will one interaction suffice? Under what conditions? Does the opinion leader have to be a member of one of a person's primary groups to influence him? Does a person not subject to a cross-pressure who is in regular contact with only an opinion leader of the party opposed to his "natural" choice remain as firm as similar people not in contact with such a leader? And so on. Without some such detailed knowledge, it is difficult even to begin thinking about the nature of the assumptions one might build into a model of the process.

In connection with the time and space structure of these interactions, the panel method used in the voting studies does give some statistical information on the time course of the interaction process, but far more detailed knowledge will probably be needed in any formal model of the process. Just how likely is it that a person will be contacted by an opinion leader and what is the chance that politics will be discussed? What is needed is a statistical description of the social filtering discussed in connection with Figure 18-2. Almost no data on these points now exist, and it is not clear that they will soon be forthcoming.

And once all this is done, the following problem must be formulated and solved: Do the assumptions concerning the nature of pairwise interactions plus those about the structure of society—distribution of primary groups, of opinion leaders, of interactions, etc.—account for the observed consistency of voting intentions within the primary groups and do they account at all accurately for the voting integrity of the various social classes? If the answer is Yes, then a number of side problems arise: Do the voting patterns of the social classes change significantly with the size of primary groups (which might be of interest in rural-urban comparisons), with small changes in the probabilities describing interpersonal influence, with changes in the distribution of opinion leaders? etc.

In closing, let those not very familiar with mathematical methods be warned that the program sketched above is surely going to be extremely difficult to carry out; inevitably, the simplest logical consequences needed by social scientists lead to extreme difficulties for those who must work out the deductions. Nonetheless, in voting analysis as elsewhere in science, knowledge that propositions A, B, and C are true is not enough. One must also be concerned with whether the truth of C is a logical consequence of the truth of A and of B.

APPENDIX. The purpose of this appendix is to offer a single, vivid example of the problems of interpreting correlations. The data in *Voting* were analyzed by the authors in a manner consistent with the image given in their Chapter 7 of the voting process as the interaction of politically passive individuals. However, by looking carefully at the questionnaire and by presenting the data in another way, one could offer an alternative explanation which would appear at least as plausible.

Some of the respondents interviewed in October had changed their voting intentions from those they gave in August, others had not. Why? If one believes that political discussion with other people has a major influence upon voting intentions, as the authors apparently do, one would be inclined to examine the correlation between the two successive voting intentions and the occurrence of political discussion just prior to the change. If it is found that discussion with a person of opposite persuasion results in an increased probability of defection to that party, then the hypothesis is not disproved. Such data are given on page 119 of *Voting;* a part of the chart (eliminating the no-discussion and nonvoter entries) is shown in Table 18-1.

Table 18-1—"Voting Changes Are Proportionate to the Type of Discussion Reported"* (Percentage)

Relation between Discussion in October and August Intention	AUGUST TO OCTOBER VOTE CHANGE	
	Stayed Same Party as in August	Changed to Opposite Party
Discussed with person same party as self	88	1
Discussed with person of opposite party	78	13

*From Chart LVII, p. 119, Berelson *et al.*, *Voting*. Data on nondiscussants and nonvoters omitted.

Now, the hypothesis offered in *Voting* is by no means the only one possible, and it may be argued not a very likely one, given their questionnaire. A question asked of each respondent in October and apparently used to construct this table was:

"33. Who was the last person you discussed the election or candidates with? (NOTE RELATIONSHIP) Who was he going to vote for? What did he say about it?"[32]

We must say "apparently used," for there are other possible questions, such as 9, 13, 14, 15, etc., on which the table might have been based, but the sentence on page 119 beginning "About 19 percent talked most recently in October with . . ." strongly suggests that 33 was employed. (It would have been most useful if the questions underlying each table or chart had been indicated.)

It is clear that *all* the discussion *could have* occurred after the changes in voting intentions, for question 33 only asks for the most recent discussion. With this in mind, the same data may be tabulated as in Table 18-2. Thus, the observed correlation equally fails to disprove the intuitively plausible hypothesis that people who change their voting intentions tend as a result of the change to

Table 18-2—People Tend to Discuss Politics Mostly with Those Having the Same Point of View* (Percentage)

August to October Vote Change	RELATION BETWEEN DISCUSSION REPORTED IN OCTOBER AND AUGUST INTENTION	
	Discussed with Person Same Party as Self	Discussed with Person of Opposite Party
Stayed in same party as in August	70	17
Changed to opposite party	20	70

*Adapted from Chart LVII, p. 119, Berelson *et al.*, *Voting*. Data on nondiscussants and nonvoters omitted.

discuss politics with those having their new found faith, an hypothesis not obviously more unreasonable than the contention: "Those who discuss politics with the opposition are more likely than others subsequently to take on that opposite preference in their own voting."[33] Of course, the last hypothesis is not disproved either,[34] but had it been articulated prior to the study, a question aimed at disproving it if false could have been employed.

Still another alternative—and one which may damn the whole panel method—has been suggested by A. J. Brodbeck.[35] The correlations themselves may not represent any true relationship aside from imperfect, or subconsciously distorted, recall. The informants may be "compelled" to remember the past events in what could be considered a consistent pattern, that they suppress discussion-change pairs which they feel would establish them as "irrational" or "irresponsible" or that they found distasteful. Surely, there is some of this; whether it is really important is not clear.

These are important questions of data analysis, but they cannot be allowed to dominate all other considerations. It is not being advocated here that field research be frozen until a nicely articulated image is developed, but only that the resulting correlations cannot be analyzed except in terms of such a system of hypotheses and deductions. Of course, it is the correlations plus past research and hunches which suggest an image, but that does not in any way nullify or abridge the preceding remark. It is true that the correlations can be simply presented without further comment, but they never are, and so it must be kept in mind that the explanations offered do not constitute inescapable conclusions from the data, but only assertions not refuted by it.

When the image is not explicitly stated, but is delicately interwoven into a data-studded and lengthy discourse, it can be difficult to tease out what are hypotheses and what are mere verbal restatements of the tables or correlations. In part this is a trivial consequence of English grammar. For example, in which category—explanation or restatement—does the following sentence fall? "Those who talk with compatible persons remain most firm in their prior convictions; those who cannot recall any discussion of politics in their groups are unstable generally, often receding into nonvoting or neutrality; and those in contact with opposition preferences show it by their heavy rate of defection to that opposition."[36]

If one contends that it is but a statement of the above correlation, then the following phrasing is equally good: Those who remain most firm in their prior convictions talk with compatible persons; those who are unstable, who recede into nonvoting or neutrality, cannot generally recall any discussion of politics in their groups; and those who defect to the opposition show it by their heavy rate of contact with that opposition. Do these both convey the same meaning to the casual reader? Is each really only a recapitulation of a correlation?

CHAPTER 19

Partisan Attitudes and the Presidential Vote

ANGUS CAMPBELL AND DONALD E. STOKES

INTRODUCTION. The primary intention of the study reported in *The Voter Decides*[1] was the "identification and analysis of . . . the psychological variables which intervene between the external events of the voter's world and his ultimate behavior." It attempted to reduce the total complex of "attitudes, expectations, and group loyalties" activated by the countless political stimuli to which the individual citizen is exposed to a limited number of components. These "motivational factors" were assumed to differ qualitatively but to interact dynamically in the determination of individual political behavior.

The variables defined and measured were not systematically derived from existing theory. Political theory deals for the most part with institutional rather than individual behavior and does not provide an applicable conceptual structure. Personality theory might have yielded a classification of motives that could be thought to underlie voter behavior, but it is doubtful if a very substantial proportion of the variance in voting could be accounted for through the use of such variables. Theory depending on variables of social structure also appeared too incomplete for use.

Three considerations guided the choice of intervening variables. The foremost motive was to choose variables which were political in quality. It seemed far more likely that the behavior under investigation is determined in an immediate sense by political attitudes rather than by personality traits or by location in the social structure. Second, variables were wanted which are present in all or most elections since it was hoped to extend the studies beyond the particular election in question. Finally, variables were wanted which would include those varying in strength from one election to another and accounting for the substantial shifts in political behavior that occur from year to year.

These considerations led us to propose six factors which were thought relevant to the individual's decision to vote and to his choice of candidates. They were: (1) Personal identification with one of the political parties; (2) concern with issues of national governmental policy; (3) personal attraction to the presidential candidates; (4) pressure to conform to the political standards of one's primary group associates; (5) a sense of civic obligation to vote; and (6) a sense of personal efficacy in the area of politics. Each of these variables tended to distinguish voters from non-voters, although not equally so. The first three factors—party identification, issue orientation, and candidate orientation—were also found to relate significantly to the choice of candidate. The measurement used for primary group pressure proved the least satisfactory of the six measures proposed. Although it correlated highly with both turnout and party choice, it was so obviously contaminated by projection, selective perception, and other influences that it was not adequate to support conclusions regarding primary group pressure.[2] The present analysis will focus upon the factors related to voting preference. The primary group measure as well as the measures of citizen duty and political efficacy will not be considered further here.

Several refinements of the measures related to preference are introduced in this chapter.[3] The candidate orientation measure has been divided into two variables, orientation to Eisenhower and orientation to Stevenson. The scoring of each is derived from references to the personal characteristics of the candidates made in answer to open-ended questions of the pre-election interview.[4] The issue orientation factor has also been divided into two variables, domestic issue partisanship and foreign issue partisanship. Unlike the previous issue measure, which was derived from answers to questions about specific issues, these variables are scored from issue references volunteered in response to open-ended questions about the parties and the candidates.[5]

Findings reported in *The Voter Decides* indicate that the intervening partisan attitudes are additive in their effect on voting choice. A close inspection of these results and of contingency tables giving the interrelationships of the partisan attitudes suggests that our data can be represented by a rather simple linear model. Accordingly, each of the variables has been given quantitative form and their mutual relationships analyzed by the methods of multiple linear correlation.[6] Despite some inherent limitations[7] the resulting multivariate analysis has proved very useful in pursuing our immediate research objectives.

The work reported here had three ends in view. First of all, we wanted to put to a systematic test the explanatory power of the attitudes in our psychological model. We have assessed the strength of the model and of its parts by observing the capacity of partisan attitudes to explain voting choice across the whole national population. Secondly, we wanted to see whether links could be found between social structure and the motivation of preference. We have probed the influence of demographic characteristics on motivation by examining the relation of partisan attitudes to voting choice in a number of demographic groups. Third, we wanted to see what links could be found between other types of attitudes and behavior and the motivation of preference. We have explored connections of this sort by examining the relation of partisan attitudes to voting choice within groups drawn from the national population on the basis of shared attitudes or like behavior.

RELATION OF PARTISAN ATTITUDES TO PREFERENCE. Findings for the national population[8] testify persuasively to the value of the psychological model studied. The power of the partisan attitudes to explain the choice between presidential candidates is convincing evidence that we have identified a set of variables lying close to preference and exerting a profound influence on this type of choice. The results arrayed in Table 19-1 indicate that the five partisan attitudes together account for about half the variance in preference: a multiple correlation of nearly 0.7 is obtained.[9] The size of this coefficient is the more remarkable in view of the likelihood that errors of measurement have led us to understate the capacity of these partisan attitudes to explain preference. It is of course true that explanation has a purely statistical meaning here and that some ambiguity surrounds the causal relationships involved, particularly those among the several partisan attitudes.[10] But the multiple correlation of the partisan variables with preference is so large that these factors must be conceded a dominant role among attitudes immediately determining the voting choice.

Table 19-1—Relation of Partisan Attitudes to Preference Among All Respondents Expressing a Preference for a Major-Party Candidate (N = 1522)

	Party Identification	Orientation to Eisenhower	Orientation to Stevenson	Domestic Issue Partisanship	Foreign Issue Partisanship
Simple correlation with preference	0.59	0.35	0.23	0.48	0.38
Partial correlation with preference (all other attitudes held fixed)	.42	.16	.12	.23	.20
Standard regression coefficients	.40	.13	.09	.20	.16

Multiple correlation of five partisan attitudes with preference 0.68

If the multiple correlation coefficient of Table 19-1 gives the combined capacity of the partisan attitudes to account for preference, the partial correlation coefficients and standard regression coefficients suggest the relative weight of each factor.[11] The coefficients of partial correlation indicate the correlation of each attitude with preference when the other attitudes are statistically held constant. By inspecting these coefficients we may gauge the capacity of each attitude to explain the variance in preference when the effects of all the other attitudes are removed. The standard regression coefficients give the weights assigned the several attitudes in making a prediction of preference from partisan attitudes that is best in a least-squares sense. By inspecting these coefficients we may learn what weighting of the partisan attitudes minimizes the unexplained variance in preference.[12] If we accept the criteria of importance implicit in these techniques, identification with party is seen as the most important indicator of voting choice. With the other attitudes held fixed, party identification accounts for a sizable part of the remaining variance in preference; in the same circumstances, each of the candidate and issue variables accounts for a much smaller part of the remaining variance in preference.

Likewise, in making a best prediction of preference we would give party identification a greater weight than that assigned each of the other partisan attitudes. Thse coefficients are an eloquent comment on the role of party allegiances in orienting the political behavior of Americans. Not only is the overwhelming majority of our citizens willing to be sorted into a few party categories. This voluntary identification with party is found on the average to be a surer guide to voting choice than are feelings about the personal qualities of either of the candidates or concerns about any of the issues of the day.

In view of the popular interpretations of the 1952 election the slight relative weight of the candidate factors in Table 19-1 may seem surprising. If we are to predict preference across the national population in that year, knowledge of attitudes toward the personal characteristics of Mr. Eisenhower and Mr. Stevenson will be of less help than information on any of the other partisan attitudes measured. This finding may temper some exaggerated estimates of Mr. Eisenhower's impact on American voting patterns. But it cannot prove that the Eisenhower personality did not contribute powerfully to the Republican victory of 1952. This is true because a marked shift of the population on a factor even moderately associated with preference may lead to a considerable over-all change in preference. And even a small shift in the distribution of preference can be of great significance in a two-party system where the parties are fairly well matched. Repeated sampling of the national population indicates that the distribution of party identification has been fairly stable between elections in recent years. If this is so, movements of the population on partisan factors of less influence than party at a given point in time may have been responsible for the changing division of the two-party vote.

An illustration from previous political events may help put in proper perspective the results of our multivariate analysis of voting in 1952. The response to the personality of Dewey in 1948 was a good deal less favorable than the response to the personality of Eisenhower four years later. Let us suppose that the distribution of party identification and the extent of its association with preference were virtually the same in the two election years. Then attitudes toward the Republican candidate as a person could be said to have played the decisive role in the reversal of Republican fortunes even though our studies disclose that party identification was much more highly correlated with preference in 1952. A detailed analysis of the ways in which changes in attitudes enter into changes in the vote must await comparable attitude measurements in successive elections. With these at hand it should be possible to identify with much greater certainty the attitudinal basis of important shifts in the two-party vote.

INFLUENCE OF DEMOGRAPHIC CHARACTERISTICS. Findings for the national population show that the partisan attitudes studied possess together a very great capacity to explain the variance in voting choice. But we have not supposed that complete explanation at the level of attitudes would constitute a complete theory of the motivation of preference, for we have conceived the partisan attitudes as intervening variables which are themselves influenced by a multitude of factors in the voter's world. The search for a fuller theory leads necessarily to variables which are prior to political attitudes in the determination of voting choice. The conceptual possibilities here are vast, encompassing *inter alia* the variables of personality theory and reference group theory as well as a host of variables having to do with particular events of personal history. But in the search for prior variables the greatest popular and scholarly attention has been given the influence of a person's location in the social structure, as described by a variety of sociological or demographic variables. It is to these we now turn.

Investigations of the relation of demographic factors to attitudes have most often treated attitudes as dependent variables and examined their distributions in various demographic groups. In the work reported here we have attempted to bring demographic variables, intervening attitudes, and dependent behavior within the same program of analysis. Demographic factors could be incorporated in a multivariate analysis of partisan attitudes and the vote in several ways. The procedure used would depend on the questions for which answers are sought. If the goal is simply finding what improvement can be made in the prediction of preference we might introduce demographic and attitudinal variables into the same regression equations and assign weights to both types of factors. If the goal is seeing what part of the variance in preference not associated with demographic factors can be accounted for by political attitudes we might examine the correlation of partisan attitudes with residual scores in preference obtained by recording the deviation of observed preference about a preference score predicted from a set of demographic characteristics. If the goal is learning the relative capacity of the several partisan attitudes to explain voting preference in a variety of population groups we can divide the sample on the basis of demographic characteristics and examine the relation of the partisan factors to preference in each group. Although we are carrying forward studies utilizing each of these techniques, the research reported here adopts the third approach. We have divided our sample into a number of demographic groups so that we might compare the motivational patterns found in the several groups.

The set of demographic factors from which we could select variables for the analysis is itself quite large, and the possibilities are still more extensive if the population is divided by combinations of demographic characteristics. Our analysis has not exhausted the list of familiar demographic factors; we have centered our attention on the variables of age, sex, religion, education, ethnic background, income, occupation, and place of residence. A complete report of findings will not be given here. In general, dividing the population by these factors does not disclose marked differences in the relation of partisan attitudes to preference. We do not find, for example, that the factor of candidate orientation is more helpful in explaining the preferences of women than of men, or that party loyalty accounts for a greater proportion of the variance in the preferences of persons of low income than of those of high income, or that the preferences of young people can be more fully explained by their reactions to issues than can those of older people. Illustrative of these similarities are results given in Table 19-2 for nonsouthern voters by level of education. Contrary to what we had anticipated, the relative importance of the several partisan attitudes as a basis for predicting preference is very nearly the same for those whose education ended at the level of grade school, high school, and college. None of the partisan attitudes varies substantially in its relative weight in these three educational groups. The content of the partisan factors may be very different for those of different educational background: the issue references of the college-educated may be directed more specifically to controversial issues of public

Table 19-2—Relation of Partisan Attitudes to Preference Among Nonsouthern Respondents by Level of Education

	Party Identification	Orientation to Eisenhower	Orientation to Stevenson	Domestic Issue Partisanship	Foreign Issue Partisanship	Number of Cases
Simple correlation with preference:						
Grade school	0.62	0.35	0.30	0.54	0.35	313
High school	.64	.38	.28	.53	.39	481
College	.55	.29	.20	.44	.35	160
Partial correlation with preference:						
Grade school	.40	.15	.13	.28	.18	313
High school	.44	.21	.08	.24	.18	481
College	.39	.21	.15	.26	.27	160
Standard regression coefficients:						
Grade school	.39	.12	.10	.25	.14	313
High school	.42	.16	.06	.21	.14	481
College	.36	.17	.12	.23	.22	160

Multiple correlation of five partisan attitudes with preference:

Grade school	0.70
High school	.72
College	.67

policy. But the less informed references of those of less education seem to be equally correlated with the voting decision.

The analysis of demographic groups was not altogether without interesting results. Several of the findings were very suggestive. And a difference of considerable interest emerged when the national population was divided by place of residence. Findings for the four major regions—Northeast, Midwest, Far West, and South—show that each of the regions differs little from the others in the relation of the partisan attitudes to preference. But when respondents are divided according to their place of residence within regions, differences of considerable political importance are found in the results for the South. As may be seen in Table 19-3, party identification in the rural South is highly related to preference, while the candidate and issue factors are not. Traditional allegiance to party, whether Democratic or Republican, continues to be the major correlate of voting choice. In towns of fewer than 2,500 people,

Table 19-3—Relation of Partisan Attitudes to Preference Among Southern Respondents by Population Size of Place of Residence

	Party Identification	Orientation to Eisenhower	Orientation to Stevenson	Domestic Issue Partisanship	Foreign Issue Partisanship	Number of Cases
Simple correlation with preference:						
Cities above 50,000	0.29	0.53	0.27	0.43	0.48	70
Cities 2,500 to 50,000	.43	.32	.12	.46	.43	112
Towns less than 2,500	.55	.19	.20	.44	.35	116
Open country	.63	.07	.13	.25	.40	84
Partial correlation with preference:						
Cities above 50,000	.19	.45	.29	.30	.46	70
Cities 2,500 to 50,000	.26	.10	.06	.22	.18	112
Towns less than 2,500	.46	—.02	.18	.23	.25	116
Open country	.56	.10	.10	—.01	.21	84
Standard regression coefficients:						
Cities above 50,000	.14	.36	.21	.22	.36	70
Cities 2,500 to 50,000	.25	.10	.05	.23	.18	112
Towns less than 2,500	.43	—.01	.14	.20	.20	116
Open country	.57	.08	.08	—.01	.17	84

Multiple correlation of five partisan attitudes with preference:

Cities above 50,000	0.74
Cities 2,500 to 50,000	.57
Cities less than 2,500	.65
Open country	.66

identification with party has less predictive value than in the open country; and in communities of 2,500 to 50,000 its relationship with preference is still smaller. In cities of 50,000 and more population, party identification explains very little of the variance in preference; the proportion of the variance explained is much less than that accounted for in these cities by attitudes toward candidates and issues, particularly toward Eisenhower and foreign affairs. In this, the urban South exhibits a pattern of attitudes exceedingly rare in our data. An inspection of the findings for corresponding areas outside the South indicates that these results are not to be explained in terms of a general urban-rural difference. The pattern of relationship found here between southern attitudes and preference is lent additional interest by the fact that the Eisenhower rebellion in 1952 was strongly urban in character. While Mr. Eisenhower gained support in selected Southern areas outside the cities, studies of voting statistics demonstrate that the principal break in the solid South occurred in the larger urban communities.[13] The urban character of the defection in presidential politics from an historic party commitment is reflected in our attitudinal data for the South in 1952. The coefficients of Table 19-3 describe the motivational basis of a profound change in the politics of the southern region.

Similarities in the findings for various demographic groups suggest that the experiences implied by location in one or another social category are of slight effect on the relation of partisan attitudes to preference. But these similarities might be taken to mean, too, that sorting a national sample on demographic variables is a highly inexact way of dividing people according to common psychological experiences. The political implications of having a given level of income or of doing a certain type of work may be very different in different areas. So may the implications of having a given amount of education, of having reached a given age, or of belonging to a given race, church, or sex. For this reason differences in the motivational patterns of these groups within limited populations may be lost completely when larger populations are studied. This may be illustrated in terms of the regional differences we have already seen. In the social order of the rural South, values—including political values—may be traditionally given to a greater extent than in rural areas elsewhere in the nation. The open country South may approach more nearly the character of a "folk" society. As a result, political choice in the rural South seems to rest on a traditional party allegiance, whereas political choice in rural areas outside the South is more dependent, as it is in urban areas, on current evaluations of personalities and issues. The point is that this difference is seen only when the South is divided separately by place of residence; the difference is lost when place of residence is used to divide the population of the nation as a whole.[14]

The lessening power of demographic factors in larger populations to group people according to common motivational patterns is paralleled by the lessening power of these variables to account directly for the variance in preference as larger populations are investigated. Studies of voting in local areas, most notably the Erie County study, suggest that in a particular locality a significant part of the variance in preference can be explained by a combination of demographic factors. For Erie County in 1940 Lazarsfeld and his associates report a multiple correlation of 0.5 between seven demographic variables and preference.[15] But subsequent work reported by Lazarsfeld[16] and by Janowitz and Miller[17] indicates that correlations of demographic factors with preference tend to be lower as the population sampled becomes larger and less homogeneous. In our studies with the 1952 national sample the present authors have been unable to obtain a correlation higher than 0.39 between as many as eleven demographic variables and voting choice; no linear combination of these variables could be found which accounted for more than 15 per cent of the variance in preference.

The diminishing size of these correlations in more extensive populations presumably is due in part to the fact that relationships observed in a larger population are a blend of those which might be found in its more homogeneous parts. For example, the work of MacRae[18] implies that the relationship between occupation and voting choice in the whole nation would be lower than in its industrial areas since occupation is virtually uncorrelated with the vote in nonindustrial areas. In a similar way, differences in the motivational patterns of demographic groups within homogeneous parts of the population may be distorted or lost when a region or the nation as a whole is studied. If this is true, demographic factors may be of quite limited usefulness in research on the national population of the type reported here unless the sample used is large enough to permit the individual consideration of culturally homogeneous communities within the total.

INFLUENCE WITHIN GROUPS WITH SHARED ATTITUDES. The general absence of difference among the familiar demographic groupings deflected our work in new directions. The largely negative character of these earlier results led us to explore the possibility that something could be learned about the determinants and consequences of various motivational patterns if groups were defined in the population on the basis of shared attitudes or common behavior. In particular, we wondered whether differences might be found in the motivation of preference if the sample were divided according to the manner in which individuals responded to the election or according to when it was that they decided how they would vote. Each of these approaches has led to findings of interest, which will suggest the possibilities of further analysis.

There is in the American electorate wide diversity in the character of response to our presidential politics. We know from data gathered in 1952 that persons differed widely that year in the amount of their interest in the campaign, in the degree of their personal involvement in who would win, and in the extent to which they perceived the election as having important consequences for the country. We have examined the relation of each of these attitudes to the motivation of preference. When this is done, marked differences are found between groups in the extent to which voting choice is associated with partisan attitudes. Table 19-4 gives these

Table 19-4—Relation of Partisan Attitudes to Preference by Degree of Involvement in Election Outcome

	Party Identification	Orientation to Eisenhower	Orientation to Stevenson	Domestic Issue Partisanship	Foreign Issue Partisanship	Number of Cases
Simple correlation with preference:						
Care very much	0.70	0.51	0.31	0.64	0.48	449
Care pretty much	.62	.33	.23	.49	.39	601
Don't care very much	.45	.10	.17	.31	.18	303
Don't care at all	.35	.04	.16	.22	.26	126
Partial correlation with preference:						
Care very much	.45	.26	.12	.34	.23	449
Care pretty much	.43	.18	.14	.22	.24	601
Don't care very much	.42	.10	.14	.19	.11	303
Don't care at all	.35	.02	.06	.16	.29	126
Standard regression coefficients:						
Care very much	.39	.18	.08	.27	.16	449
Care pretty much	.41	.14	.11	.19	.19	601
Don't care very much	.40	.09	.12	.17	.10	303
Don't care at all	.34	.01	.05	.15	.27	126

Multiple correlation of five partisan attitudes with preference:	
Care very much	0.80
Care pretty much	.70
Don't care very much	.53
Don't care at all	.48

differences according to degree of involvement in who would win.[19] The multiple correlation of partisan attitudes with preferences is seen to decline with involvement from 0.8 to 0.48. The partisan factors explain more than 60 per cent of the variance in the preference of those who care very much but less than 25 per cent of the variance in the preference of those who report they care not at all. Among the highly involved, voting choice seems to spring from a relatively consistent set of partisan feelings. But among the slightly involved the pattern is quite different. From the standpoint of attitudes toward parties, candidates, and issues, selection of a candidate among the least involved has more the character of a random choice.

To interpret these findings we need to be clear about the causal link between involvement and partisanship. This problem did not arise in the analysis of demographic groups since membership in a demographic category is not influenced by partisan feeling.[20] But the relation of involvement to the motivation of preference is more ambiguous since partisanship can have a good deal to do with the degree of involvement. Alternative assumptions about the direction of causality will lead to different interpretations. If we assume that a disposition toward involvement at a given level precedes partisan feeling in a causal sense, Table 19-4 shows that people of high involvement develop partisan attitudes strongly influencing preference, whereas people of lesser involvement do so in a lesser degree. On the other hand, if we assume that partisan feeling precedes involvement, Table 19-4 shows that people whose choice is firmly based in partisan attitudes become highly involved. In view of the fact that the partisan attitudes can have various causal relationships among themselves, these alternatives are too simple a statement of what may be at work. But it is likely that Table 19-4 reflects both the tendency of partisanship to heighten involvement and of greater involvement to lead to a voting decision that is rooted in clear partisan feeling.

Just as American voters are spread on a dimension of involvement, so their individual voting decisions are spread on the dimension of time. The electorate as a whole can make up its mind relatively early, as it did in 1952, or relatively late, as it did in 1948. But in each election year there are some who know from the beginning how they mean to vote; some who decide at convention time; some who decide in mid-campaign; and some who decide shortly before the election or on election day. When these groups are drawn from the 1952 sample[21] and their motivational characteristics examined, remarkably sharp differences are found. The character of these can be seen in Table 19-5. To begin with,

Table 19-5—Relation of Partisan Attitudes to Preference by Time of Voting Decision

	Party Identification	Orientation to Eisenhower	Orientation to Stevenson	Domestic Issue Partisanship	Foreign Issue Partisanship	Number of Cases
Simple correlation with preference:						
Knew all along	0.80	0.47	0.22	0.64	0.43	357
Decided at convention time	.67	.38	.30	.53	.43	366
Decided during campaign	.49	.30	.35	.47	.38	238
Decided within two weeks of election	.12	.04	.01	.10	.25	131
Partial correlation with preference:						
Knew all along	.62	.20	.09	.29	.20	357
Decided at convention time	.50	.19	.15	.27	.23	366
Decided during campaign	.32	.22	.19	.22	.18	238
Decided within two weeks of election	.06	—.01	.00	.07	.22	131
Standard regression coefficients:						
Knew all along	.57	.12	.05	.21	.12	357
Decided at convention time	.45	.13	.10	.21	.17	366
Decided during campaign	.30	.18	.17	.21	.16	238
Decided within two weeks of election	.06	—.01	.00	.07	.23	131

Multiple correlation of five partisan attitudes with preference:

Knew all along	0.84
Decided at convention time	.75
Decided during campaign	.64
Decided within two weeks of election	.26

there is between the groups a great disparity in the capacity of the partisan attitudes to account for preference. The proportion of the variance explained by the partisan factors is ten times greater among those who knew all along than among those who decided at the eleventh hour. For the first group the coefficient of multiple correlation reaches 0.84; for the last it descends to 0.26. There are also marked differences in the relative weights of the several factors. In the group of early deciders all the partisan attitudes except attitudes toward Stevenson have relatively high simple correlations with preference; but the partial correlations in this group indicate that party is the one factor whose force unquestionably is independent of the others. In the group deciding at convention time the simple correlations are unevenly lower; the partial correlations indicate that party is not as overriding an independent factor. In the group deciding in mid-campaign, all the simple correlations have declined except that of preference with attitudes toward Stevenson; the partial correlations show that the relationship between preference and party identification is only slightly higher than that between preference and the other factors. In the group deciding at election time, the simple correlations have all but vanished; the partial correlations indicate that concern with foreign affairs alone remains as visibly associated with preference.

From the standpoint of the attitudes in our model the decision of those deciding very late in the campaign has the appearance of a random choice. But this does not mean that last-minute deciders are without partisan feeling. Inspection of the distributions and intercorrelations of the partisan attitudes suggests that this group includes both those of slight partisanship and those of strong and conflicting partisan attitudes. It is likely in each case that a choice is made only when the individual is obliged to perform the socially approved act of voting; in each case the attitudinal conditions of a prior choice are missing. But the psychological context of a late decision may vary with the extent of partisan feeling. Among weak partisans the choice may be governed directly by influences other than those studied here. For example, these people may simply conform to a perceived group norm for voting without developing a consistent set of supporting attitudes. Among strong partisans who are late deciders the choice may still depend on the partisan attitudes. The conflict of partisan feeling which has delayed their choice until late in the campaign may be resolved as election day approaches according to the relative strength of the partisan attitudes at that time.

In reviewing the findings obtained by time of voting decision it should be clear that the relation assumed to hold in the earlier analysis between the variable dividing the sample and the pattern of motivation has now been reversed. The time of decision did not influence the pattern of relationship between partisan factors and preference. The reverse is likely the case: the pattern of motivating attitudes affected the time at which a choice was made. It is hard to read the coefficents of Table 19-5 without sensing the fundamental role of identification with party in fixing the moment of decision and in organizing the other partisan attitudes. The simple correlations of the partisan attitudes with choice in all but a single case are substantially higher among those who knew all along than among those deciding in mid-campaign. Yet the capacity of attitudes toward candidates and issues to explain preference independently of considerations of party loyalty is no greater among the early deciders than among those deciding during the campaign. This contrast raises clearly the question as to whether a strong party attachment does not encourage the development of other partisan attitudes consistent with itself.

CONCLUSIONS. The work reported here has supported prior evidence that attitudes toward the parties, the personal attributes of the candidates, and the issues of foreign and domestic policy have a profound influence on voting choice. Results for the nation as a whole indicate that these attitudes are able to explain a high proportion of the variance in preference. They indicate, too, that by the standard of statistical explanation, identification with party accounts for a larger portion of variance in preference than do attitudes toward the candidates and issues. The partisan attitudes of this analysis are conceived as motivational factors intervening between a wide range of prior influences and a choice of a major-party candidate. To search for effects of antecedent demographic factors we have divided our sample by a number of sociological characteristics and observed the relation of partisan attitudes to preference in each of the resulting demographic categories. Few effects of this sort were found, perhaps in part because membership in one or another demographic category can have very different meanings across the nation. The generally unrewarding character of these results led us to divide the sample on the basis of attitudes and behavior which were likely to bear a closer relationship to the motivation of preference. The use of level of involvement and of time of voting choice in this way has given rise to results of sufficient interest to warrant an extension of the technique in further research.

STATISTICAL NOTE. Risks are taken whenever a mathematical model is fitted to social data. In the research reported here, we have felt that much could be learned by considering preference as a linear function of political attitudes. But a report of this work would be incomplete if the reader's attention were not directed to the several ways in which the data may depart from the assumptions underlying our statistical computations. In the first place, the assumption that the relationships among the variables are linear and additive may not be satisfied. An inspection of contingency tables showing the interrelationships of the variables suggests that the assumption fits the facts fairly well. And this is suggested, too, by the magnitude of some of the coefficients obtained in the analysis. Yet we cannot be sure that a nonlinear model or a linear model with other terms would not have fitted the data more closely and have given somewhat different results.

Secondly, the statistical model requires scored measurements on each of the variables. The candidate and issue variables used in this research are defined in terms of the number of spontaneous references of specified sorts volunteered in answer to open-ended questions. Therefore, a set of scored measurements on each of these variables is available for the analysis. But the variables of party identification and of preference had somewhat artificially to be given quantitative form. A different way of scoring party identification would affect our coefficents, provided the new scores are not obtained from the present ones by only a change of scale or origin. Different ways of scoring preference would not affect the coefficients, since any procedure assigning one value to Republican preference and another to Democratic preference would simply obtain new scores from the present ones by a change of scale or origin.

A special problem, however, is implicit in our measurement of preference. A dichotomous scoring of this variable is in harmony with the political significance of the voting act: in general, one vote for a given candidate is equal in value to another. But this scoring procedure may do violence to psychological realities. It is reasonable to suppose that persons voting for the same candidate do so with very different degrees of certainty or enthusiasm. Indeed, it is probable that our political system forces into two classes an electorate that is distributed at a number of points on an underlying preference variable. If it is the underlying variable and not the manifest behavioral act that is a linear function of partisan attitudes, scoring preference dichotomously results in a nonlinear transformation of the dependent variable which obscures in some degree the linear relationships between preference and the partisan attitudes. This mode of reasoning suggests that the proportion of the variance explained by partisan attitudes would be greater if we could measure gradations in preference more sensitively. It suggests, too, that our method of scoring preference can lead to artificial results. This is true because the proportion of the variance in preference explained will depend in part on the extent to which our respondents are clustered about two points in their true scores on the underlying variable. For any given set of respondents the proportion of the variance in preference explained by the partisan factors will be greater if the group's distribution on the underlying variable is such that the variance of Democratic and Republican voters about their respective means is small relative to the distance between the two means. The proportion of the variance in preference explained will be less if the distribution on the underlying variable is such that the variance of Democratic and Republican voters about their respective means is large relative to the distance between the two means.

The scoring procedures we have chosen lead, of course, to distributions very unlike the multivariate normal, and the departure of the data from this distribution imposes further limitations on the analysis. The departure is of consequence because normality is usually assumed for statistical control of relevant variables. When the association of two variables is examined with other variables constant, the relation will not depend in the normal case on the values at which the other factors are held fixed. But this desirable property is not a property of multivariate distributions generally, and our higher order coefficients should be read with this in mind. If variations in the relation are moderate over the range of values at which other variables might be held fixed, a coefficient of partial correlation can be a valuable statement of the average relationship. But if variations are extreme a partial correlation coefficient can be misleading.

The departure from a multivariate normal distribution is of consequence, too, because the sampling distributions of our several coefficients in other than the multivariate normal case are largely unknown. For this reason the reader has not been treated to a succession of tests of significance assuming normality. A more serious obstacle to the use of common significance tests arises from the complexities of our sample design. Most of these tests assume simple random sampling and are therefore inappropriate for testing statistics computed for a multistage stratified sample. Both these difficulties may be overcome by the use of certain nonparametric tests, but our enthusiasm for extensive significance testing in the early part of our work was diminished by the fact that our approach to the data made impossible a rigorous application of significance tests. In a spirit of frank exploration we have divided the sample into a great number of groups. Working with high-speed computing equipment we have obtained correlation and regression coefficients for more than a hundred groups drawn from the national population on the basis of shared attitudes or shared demographic characteristics. Unless a region of rejection is chosen with more than normal stringency, a statistical search of this magnitude inevitably yields some findings declared significant by statistical tests which are yet the result of chance alone. We may guard against such findings by requiring a consistent pattern in the results for several groups before relying on those for any one. But the confirmation of hypotheses is in some measure uncertain because our approach to the data has made impossible a completely rigorous application of statistical tests.

Some readers may feel that distinguishing Republicans from Democrats by measurements on a set of traits is more properly a problem of discriminatory analysis. If the problem had been reformulated in these terms the mathematics of its solution would not have been very different. Fisher has demonstrated the formal equivalence of linear discriminant analysis and linear regression analysis if the regression problem is one in which the dependent variable is dichotomous, as it is here.[22] In such cases, if the independent variables are expressed as deviates about their respective means, values can be given the dependent variable so that corresponding terms of the regression and discriminant functions differ only by a constant factor. In view of this equivalence we have chosen the familiar methods of correlation and regression as offering a wider range of statistics and as having a customary interpretation more appropriate for an inquiry in which preference is conceived as a dependent variable.

CHAPTER 20

Economic Analysis and Forecasting: Recent Developments in Use of Panel and Other Survey Techniques

FRANCO MODIGLIANI AND F. E. BALDERSTON

INTRODUCTION. Economists have long been interested in determining how households and business enterprises make plans for allocating their resources between current needs and commitments extending into the future. At the beginning of a year a consumer owns some assets, owes some debts, and has an income-earning and consumption history. He looks forward to receiving some amount of income in the year immediately ahead, and he has some idea (though it may not be very clear) of his earnings prospects and his consumption requirements for succeeding years. As the year unfolds, the consumer in question will spend a great part of his income, as he receives it, for day-to-day goods and services that he is "used to"–things that are part of the level of living for people of his age, social background, and family responsibilities. He may, in addition, make a few big commitments–buy a house or an automobile, or take out more insurance. At the end of the year, it may turn out that the sum of all the expenditures was greater, or smaller, than the amount of income received (the consumer saved a negative or positive amount). To what extent did the difference between the amount of income he expected to receive and the amount he actually received, affect the consumer's day-to-day spending and his longer-term commitments? To understand the consumer's actual behavior, are we also required to know what income the consumer expected to receive during that year, and what plans (rough or precise) he made accordingly, or did his actual current consumption depend entirely upon actual current income, so that whether the consumer *expected* (at the beginning of the year) to receive two thousand dollars or twenty thousand dollars of income during that year, his *actual* consumption of, say, four thousand dollars depended strictly on the fact that his *actual* income was, say, five thousand dollars?

Our view of the nature of this decision-making process has considerable bearing on the method whereby an attempt is made to predict, at the beginning of a year, how *all* consumers, as a group, will spend and save during that year. If the only consequential relationship is the one between actual current income and actual current consumption, then it will be possible to incorporate this in a model of the economy as a whole, provided that the character of the relationship can be estimated. A simple example of such a model can be given, where C_t is total consumption expenditure, Y_t, total income, and I_t total investment, all in the year t:

(1) $C_t = a + b\,Y_t$

(2) $I_t = I^*_t$, an amount independent of C_t or Y_t

(3) $C_t + I_t = Y_t$.

To determine what amounts of income (Y_t) and consumption (C_t) there will be in the year t, it is necessary only to estimate I^*_t and the parameters a and b.

The influence of the government sector is missing from the model just given. Forecasts of national income, investment, and consumption expenditure for the early years succeeding World War II were made from a model which did include the influence of government and a probable relation between the amount of investment, I_t, and the amount of income, Y_t. Unfortunately, these forecasts departed grievously from the actual behavior which occurred, as the forecasts implied substantial postwar unemployment when, in fact, postwar employment and income turned out to be high. The chief villain of the piece was the estimated relation between consumption and income which corresponded roughly to equation (1) in our example.

It has been suggested that this approach failed principally because no account was taken of the size of consumer asset-holdings, although other important criticisms were also offered. The consumption-income relationship has also been developed along the line that current consumption will be determined not only by current income but also by the previous peak consumption level or income level. The latter's influence is to establish a standard-of-living referent from which consumers will retreat only with some reluctance.

A host of other potentially important factors needed investigation. First, it is possible that the amount spent out of each dollar of extra income (the slope of the consumption-income relation) might be different for people in different income groups or in different broad occupational categories. Again, the consumer's age—reflecting both his current responsibilities and the probable time interval over which he can expect further earnings before retirement—might have significant influence.

Finally, consumers' income expectations as of the beginning of the year *t* might very well have the effect of altering the sizes of the parameters of the consumption-income relationship that would be relevant for the year *t*. Because most of the statistical work on models of this kind has been done from historical data, there was no possibility of obtaining or utilizing expectations data.

Information concerning these income expectations has been collected in recent years by the Survey Research Center of the University of Michigan, and the expectations data have been used as additional "direct" variables in a consumption forecast.

Faced with all the possible connections between past income and consumption, assets, age, and other variables, economists are in the process of developing models of behavior which will reconcile seeming contradictions in the time series and cross-section data that are available and will permit more cogent methods of representing the behavior of consumers in the aggregate. The behavioral models require that relationships be found between the "given" elements for the consumer—e.g., age, assets at the beginning of the interval, past income and consumption—and the plans he entertains for his remaining life span, *so far as* these bear on his spending-saving decisions for the coming year. The character of these relationships will be explored in detail in a later section of this chapter.

Somewhat analogous problems arise in the understanding and prediction of the actions of business enterprises. A major objective of economists is to provide adequate forecasts of investment activity

—capital outlays. The investment activities of business enterprises—their outlays for new plant and equipment and their additions to inventories—are conceded to have an important influence on the level of national income and employment. Our simple example showed one possible investment equation, which stated that investment for the year *t* was autonomous—i.e., independent of the level of national income. If such were indeed the case, a forecast of national income could be made once the anticipated level of autonomous investment had been determined. For example, the amount of investment in the whole economy might be traceable to the direct and second-order effects of great expansion in a few industries—e.g., the railroads in the late nineteenth century. Study of expansion plans in these industries might then provide the chief basis for an investment forecast. Even if investment were widely distributed over all parts of the industrial scene, it might appear feasible to forecast the total by obtaining statements of planned expenditures from a representative sample of firms.

This is, in fact, what the SEC and McGraw-Hill surveys purport to do, for plant and equipment outlays. The important issue, to the forecaster, then becomes one of estimating what proportion of these statements of anticipations will actually be carried through. Some firms will exceed, and others will fall below, their expected expenditure levels, and the two effects may not cancel each other. Further, increases in inventory holdings may occur for either of two opposite reasons: firms may expect increased business, requiring greater goods-in-process inventories (and, where prices are rising at a rate faster than the cost of holding inventory through time, firms may hold added inventory for the gain to be made); or, firms may produce heavily in anticipation of high rates of sale which do not then materialize—the result being unintended investment in inventories.

Because it is clear that not all investment is autonomous, and because of the difficulties associated with interpreting statements of anticipation as direct evidence of what will in fact be the level of investment expenditure, economists have tried to take into account more determinants and component relationships. As of the beginning of the year *t*, the amount of liquid assets that a firm has on hand will affect the amount of investment expenditure that it can finance comfortably. Also, the total amount of investment expenditure may include a component that depends on the amount of national income that will be generated in the year in question, or on the relation between output and the existing amount of plant. Finally, business enterprises may respond to a favorable or unfavorable "climate" and may, accordingly, undertake large or small amounts of investment *relative to* each possible level of national income in the year *t*.

The plethora of possible relationships suggests once again, that a basis is required for linking the determinants together in a model of planning behavior for the firm. This is needed on its own account for a better understanding of the actions of business enterprises, but a more sensible set of forecasting relationships should also emerge as a consequence.

ANTICIPATIONS, PLANS, AND REALIZATION OF PLANS: THEORY. Statements of anticipation may be taken either as *direct* evidence as to what behavior will in fact occur or, alternatively, they may be incorporated in a model of behavior which includes a number of relationships, the outcome indicated from the model then serving as a predictor. A trivial example of the former type might be to predict total turkey consumption, in pounds, on Thanksgiving Day, by asking each member of a representative sample of the population how much turkey he expected to eat. If it were known (from past comparisons of anticipations against results) that people tend to overestimate their stomach capacity by, say, 50 per cent, and if it were also known that custom absolutely prevented the serving of any main dish other than turkey on Thanksgiving Day, then the forecast volume of turkey consumption would be the weighted sum of anticipations corrected for the consistent upward bias of these anticipations. Where direct predictive use of anticipations is desired, panel surveys can assist materially in the measurement of bias.

The real trouble, of course, is not merely that people's eyes are probably bigger than their stomachs, but that their statements of anticipations are *contingent upon* a great many other things: whether they will feel well on Thanksgiving Day; what numbers of turkeys of various weights will be available in the stores; what price relations will obtain between various sizes of turkeys; what other meats are available for Thanksgiving Day; what strength custom has; etc.

The role of anticipations will now be explored in the decision processes of the consumer and the business enterprise, so as to establish a framework for discussion, in the next two sections, of empirical findings.

The economic agent (consumer or firm) acts in environment over which he exercises only partial control. His actions are guided in two ways: he defines, and evaluates the consequences of, each of a number of *alternative courses of action;* and he chooses among the alternatives by ranking them on a scale that is determined by the character of his *objective.* The latter can be rather narrowly defined (e.g., as dollars of economic profit in the theory of the firm) or it can be a broadly stated criterion which implies merely that the agent can tell when he is "better off" and will push to the point where further improvement (in this relative or ordinal sense) cannot be obtained.

A hypothetical firm is to arrive at a production plan as of time t_0, just before year (1) commences. In this firm's plant the unit cost of materials and labor is $1 for the first 1,000 units, $2 for the second thousand, and so on up to $5 for the fifth thousand, five thousand units being the upper limit of annual output. The cost of holding a unit of output, produced in one year, for sale in the next, is $1, and there is sufficient storage space to accommodate one thousand units at most. The firm sells its output locally to business firms which pay a *price* based, say, on a cost index that is published at the beginning of each year, but how much they will buy depends on their current output. Two possible situations are compared in the following tabulation.

	Situation I	*Situation I'*
Price in year (1), $P(1)$	$3	$3
Price in year (2) $P^e(2)$	$3	$4
Expected sales in year (1), $S^e(1)$ units	2,000	2,000
Inventory held to year (2), $H^e(1)$ units	0	1,000
Output in year (1), $Q^e(1)$ units	2,000	3,000
Expected sales in year (2), $S^e(2)$ units	2,000	5,000
Output in year (2), $Q^e(2)$ units	2,000	4,000
Price in year (3), $P^e(3)$	$1	$1
Inventory held to year (3), $H^e(2)$ units	0	0

Note: Inventory as of t_0 is assumed to be zero.

In this example, the firm's problem is to plan an output level for year (1), $Q^e(1)$. This output plan can be modified during the year if anticipated sales do not correspond with sales as they they unfold. In order to choose $Q^e(1)$ it is necessary not only to anticipate $S^e(1)$ but also to set an expected amount of inventory accumulation of finished goods, $H^e(1)$. How much this should be depends in turn on $P^e(2)$, relative to $P(1)$, on $S^e(2)$, and on $Q^e(2)$. $Q^e(2)$ depends both on $S^e(2)$ and $P^e(2)$ and on $H^e(2)$, which is in turn related to price, sales, and output anticipations in year (3). But these in turn depend not only on data relating to year (3) but on some factors relating to period (4) and so on! The implication is that our firm must have ideas about the whole future in order to do the seemingly simple job of setting an output plan for the year (1). It happens that in both Situation I and Situation I′ the indefinite future is cut off at year (3), for the simple reason that the price anticipation in year (3) is only \$1, a figure too low to justify holding any inventory over from year (2). No sales or output anticipations beyond those of *year* (2) are relevant for the determination of the output plan relating to year (1), *unless* there is a *combination* of expected prices and rates of sale for some more distant future period, say the fifth year, which implies *both* a rate of sale so high that it cannot be satisfied out of the current output of the fifth year, and out of output held over from the fourth, third, and second years. Since output in the first year is expected to be 2,000 units in Situation I, an extra thousand units of output would cost \$3 per unit. The cost of holding a unit in inventory for four periods would be \$4. Thus, a thousand units of output produced in the first year would have to be sold in the fifth year for at least \$7 per unit in order that the firm break even. But at a price of \$7 in the fifth year, the firm would be willing to produce up to its output limit not only in the fifth year but also in the fourth and third years, and it would be willing to produce both the third and the fourth thousand units of output in the second year. Thus, output plans in the first year would be unaffected even by an expected price $P^e(5) = \$7$, unless *sales* expectations in the fifth year were greater than five thousand units *and* unless sales expectations $S^e(4)$, $S^e(3)$, and $S^e(2)$ are too high to permit any carry-over of inventory from those years to year (5). The contingency seems remote. The reader may ask himself whether the answer would be precisely the same for Situation I′.

It seems advisable to identify the parts of the planning procedure in this simple example. The *constraints* on the firm are its production and inventory-holding costs and its output and storage limitations. $P(1)$, the price for the first period, is a known value. Prices for succeeding years are *anticipated* values; note that in this example, these anticipations are stated as mean values with zero variances. In practice, it is often said that the future is uncertain and that, therefore, the more remote an expected price (or other quantity) the larger must be the variance around it. Sales for the first year and for succeeding years are also anticipated values.

The nature of these anticipated values is simply that these are the judgments (based on whatever evidence, from hunch to full-fledged statistical investigation) of the firm as to what the surrounding environment will be like in the relevant time-periods. From these anticipations concerning the environment in which it will have to operate, the firm sets up a plan to attain its objective, subject to the limitations imposed by the constraints. In what does the plan consist? Situations I and I′ both show expected values for output and inventory-holding in years (1) and (2); in our notation, these are:

		Situation I	Situation I′
Year (1):			
$Q^e(1)$	units	2,000	3,000
$H^e(1)$	units	0	1,000
Year (2):			
$Q^e(2)$	units	2,000	4,000
$H^e(2)$	units	0	0

The firm has considered, and rejected, alternative output possibilities for the first year, because, in view of the constraints and the expected values for the environment, expected profit will be maximized by the output and inventory-holding that are indicated above. The set of *all possible* outputs and inventory levels for the first year can be called a *set of moves*, of which, in each move, the output and the inventory-holding are elements. The choices in the two above situations are "best moves" for the first year. Similarly, the output and inventory-holdings for the second year are "best moves," given the conditions in the two situations. A *plan* is a set of "best moves," seen as of time t_0, for the relevant number of time-periods stretching into the future. The "best moves" for the two years are of course interrelated; they had to be determined simultaneously—a plan for the relevant time-span had to be set up—in order that anything could be said. As of t , however, the *only* important thing about the moves for years (2), (3), etc., is their influence in determining what will be the "best move" for the first year. As of the *end* of the first year (if the planning interval is one year) a *new* best move will have to be determined for the second year. The best move for year (2) as seen from t_0, will be the best move later on only if the same anticipations for the environment still hold, and the same constraints are binding. (It could be argued that the firm might ignore small changes in the move for the second year if the potential gain from such changes did not more than offset the cost of making a new plan, but this is a minor emendation.)

As the focus of the planning problem is to determine the best first move, it follows that for this purpose some anticipatory statements about the future environment of the firm will be relevant to the determination of the first move, whereas other anticipations may be irrelevant. For example, the expected price for the third year, $P^e(3)$, is $1. At this price, it cannot pay to hold inventory from any previous period for sale in year (3). Thus, the firm can ignore *sales* expectations, $S^e(3)$, in making a plan as of t_0.

As the firm moves forward from t_0 into the actual events of year (1), the only *certain* element in the picture is $P(1)$, the (pre-established) price for the first year. In accordance with its plan as of t_0, the firm will have made commitments for labor, materials, and other resources to meet the planned output, $Q^e(1)$. Whether *actual* output, $Q^*(1)$, will be equal to $Q^e(1)$ depends, first of all, on the extent to which $S^e(1)$ corresponds with the actual pattern of sales that develops in the course of the period. In addition, $Q^*(1)$ will be affected by any change in the planned amount of inventory-holding for the first year.

There are several alternative methods whereby the firm may relate its performance in year (1) to its plan as of t_0. First, the firm may or may not be able to reopen the plan, that is, change its target output, sales, and inventory-holding levels, during the year. Frequently, no interim change of plan is feasible because of institutional arrangements within the firm causing it to formalize plans only at yearly intervals at budget time, which falls near the end of the fiscal year. Where the plan cannot be reopened, either of two mechanisms may be put into play. *Output* may be held to the terms of the plan, and deviations of actual from anticipated sales will thus be met by altering inventory-holding. That is, $Q^*(1)=Q^e(1)$, and $S^*(1)-S^e(1)=H^e(1)-H^*(1)$. Alternatively, the firm may require that deviations of sales from anticipated levels be met entirely by alteration of current output, inventory being maintained according to the plan. Thus, $H^e(1)=H^*(1)$, and $Q^*(1)-Q^e(1)=S^*(1)-S^e(1)$. In words, shifts in the sales environment from anticipated levels may be transmitted either into changes of output or into changes of inventory. In both cases, the plan that was made at t_0 is only partly *realized.*

Let us, for the moment, assume that the firm does reopen its planning procedure only at yearly intervals. The "best move" for year (2) must be reformulated, as of t_1, the end of the first year, in the light of a new set of environmental expectations. These include $P(2)$—in our example, a certain value as of time t_1—and $S^e(2)$, $P^e(2)$, $S^e(3)$, $P^e(3)$, . . . and so on into the future, to the point where the values of some anticipations are such as to make others irrelevant to the plan and to the best move for year (2). As of t_1, the firm's anticipations of the future will very likely be affected by the extent of deviation of actual from planned values in year (1); in other words, by the *extent of realization of plans.* For example, many businessmen had rather mixed impressions, as of the end of 1945, of what the postwar future might hold; fears were dispelled by the general strength of business activity in 1946, and most firms, in turn, adapted their output and other plans to an optimistic picture of the future. It required singular fixity of opinion (e.g., that of a Sewell Avery) to remain braced for an impending major depression all through one of the greatest expansionary phases that the U. S. economy has ever experienced! For enterprises with somewhat pessimistic expectations in the early postwar period, the *mechanism* whereby the boom made itself felt in their planning was through a continued tendency for $S^*(t)$ to exceed $S^e(t)$ and for actual inventories to be depleted as compared with planned amounts of inventory-holding.

It is of course possible that the firm may have methods of reopening the plan for any period if significant deviation of actualities from plans begins to become apparent. In this case, a prediction as of t_0 of the firm's behavior during year (1) would require not only a knowledge of the firm's anticipations and its plan, as of t_0, but also an independent analysis of the events as they were likely to materialize during year (1) and of the consequent changes in all of the firm's anticipations—for the remainder of year (1) and for succeeding years—as these anticipations would affect the revised output plans upon which the firm would begin to operate *during* year (1). The best move for year (1) would be shifted during the year.

Whether the plan is subject to interim reopening or not, the planning process through time is without an ending. There is no final, once-and-for-all crystallization of *a* plan for the indefinite future; rather, revised views of the future, influenced partly by the positive or negative deviations of actual from planned values for each period, affect the further moves that the firm must choose. This view of the planning process accords reasonably well with economic life; it is hardly feasible to put the future in a permanent strait jacket as of t_0. As a matter of fact, much effort is spent in maintaining flexibility so that the firm may cope with a variety of possible "futures" as they unfold. Its chief interest in viewing the future at any given time is to pick out those elements of the future (so far as it can be anticipated at all) which are unavoidably relevant to the operation of the enterprise in the concrete situation that it faces for the next period ahead.

Our example has been concerned with only one facet of the behavior pattern of the firm: the planning of output and of inventory-holding. Customarily these are short-period planning problems, largely because the adaptability of current output to current sales and the cost of holding inventory both militate against the committing of large amounts of resources to changes in the inventory of finished goods. A much longer look into the future is required in connection with the planning of the firm's capital outlays—its expenditures on plant and equipment. The same basic structure of planning should hold for capital outlays as for production planning, in the sense that anticipations enter into plans, events deviate from anticipations so that plans are only partly realized, and new moves are then determined for future periods on the basis of new anticipations, which are partly formed by the character of deviations of recent events from the past anticipations concerning them. The capital outlay problem does involve additional parameters and requires anticipations concerning the future. For example, the age-distribution of present machinery is relevant to capital outlay planning and not directly relevant to output planning. Also, future prices of capital equipment—such as machine tools—and future technological changes become relevant in the determination of a budget of capital outlays.

The same broad distinctions—between relevant and irrelevant anticipations, moves and best moves, plan and realization of the plan—also enter into an analytical study of consumer behavior. The household is assumed to hold as a long-run objective the maximizing of satisfaction over the life-span of its adult members. As to t_0, the household has an "endowment" of assets, physical and intangible, and may be subject to specific liabilities—e.g., a mortgage on a house, or a promissory note outstanding. The household is also characterized by certain economic-demographic facts: the age and sex of its adult members, the numbers of children and their age and sex, educational background, socioeconomic status, etc. In looking forward into year (1), the family formulates plans (in what degree of precision will be discussed later) concerning expenditure on direct services and on goods which will be entirely used up within the period; concerning acquisition of long-service durable goods (houses, automobiles, television sets, etc.); concerning change in both the size and the composition of its asset-holdings and of its debts. Anticipations enter into the picture: income during year (1) and later years; prices (including interest rates) in year (1) and later years; and possibly, anticipations concerning change in the size of economic-demographic parameters, such as family size. If the postulate of long-run utility maximization is accepted, one of the family's important problems is to mediate between the urgent claims upon income and assets of its needs or desires in each current period, and the prospect of a retirement interval during which current earnings will be low, and for which substantial preparation must be made.

The focus of the problem, once again, is to determine the best first move—the planned amounts of spending, and the planned changes in asset-holdings and debt-commitments—in the first year. The best move for year (1), as determined at t_0, may or may not turn out to be fully realized in the actual event. Spending for items of an ephemeral character (food, medical services, etc.) may differ from the plan because of price changes that were not anticipated, because of illness or other contingencies, or because income turned out to be greater, or smaller, than the anticipated value that entered into the original plan. Deviations of this kind give rise to changes in the best move, as originally planned at t_0, for year (2), when the plan for this year is reformulated either during year (1) or at its end. It is known that households, by and large, engage in considerably less systematic planning of their economic activities than firms do; in particular, specific budget procedures at, say, annual intervals are a rarity. Thus it appears likely that a significant deviation of actual experience from anticipations will bring an immediate response during year (1), the response reflecting not only the current situation but also the revised view of the future which new developments may imply.

Another complication in the study of consumer anticipations, plans, and realizations of plans is that the family may actually alter its *objective*. If the thirty-six-year-old head of a family unexpectedly gains a position of significant executive responsibility after some years of work at a much lower rate of pay, a new level of living becomes an immediate possibility and, perhaps, a social requirement, for the family. More gradually, the desired level of living during a retirement interval becomes subject to shift, and the family may change its savings objective accordingly. Thus, the economic-demographic parameters of the family—we have just referred to "socioeconomic group," which is one of these—are subject to shift. No less important, though not always recognized, is the fact that as the family lives through year (1), a small shift occurs in the expected length of the retirement interval. This happens for two reasons: morbidity tables themselves are subject to obsolescence as medical advances lengthen the average number of further years of life; but also, within the perspective of a given morbidity table, a thirty-seven-year-old man has a slightly greater chance of living to, say, age seventy-five than does a thirty-six-year-old man. Thus, as the family moves through its life cycle, the probable length of the retirement interval increases as the living adult members of the family grow older. To the extent that a family saves through the purchase of government bonds rather than through accumulation of annuities or pension rights, the proportion of the principal value of each dollar of savings which can be devoted to each year of retirement slowly falls. For a family which had no Social Security, annuities, or pensions, the *target value* of total savings as of the date of retirement would slowly rise during the working life of its adult members, if the objective was to maintain a given level of living during retirement.

ANTICIPATIONS, PLANS, AND REALIZATION OF PLANS: EMPIRICAL EVIDENCE. *Business enterprises.* We recall that investigation of the anticipations and plans of economic agents has two purposes: first, to increase our general understanding of social, and specifically economic, phenomena; and second, to provide a basis for forecasts of actual individual and group behavior, as these forecasts of the behavior of the whole are economy and of its parts are germane to the policy decisions of individual economic agents and of government at all levels.

The investment plans of business enterprises have proved to be a fairly reliable *direct* indicator of the total amount of plant and equipment expenditure that firms will undertake in the period immediately ahead. One-year forecasts from these direct statements of investment plans have ranged, in error, from 2 per cent to 10 per cent. These forecasts have been made without a "theory" of the relationships between plans, as revealed by statements, and the other factors which may influence actual events. Part of the "success" of a forecast may be due to cancellation of errors: firms which spent more than they planned to on plant and equipment may be matched by others which spent less than planned. In fact, such canceling is important, according to the best evidence now available. Forecasting a total, under these circumstances, leaves the forecaster in a state of perennial embarrassment that the errors may fail to compensate in a particular period. For 1949, it was found, a sample group of firms had the following rather disturbing record: about a quarter of the firms came within 20 per cent of their plans; almost a third of the firms spent more than twice as much, or less than half as much, as they had planned. Better interpretation of anticipations data becomes possible if the reasons for deviations from plans are better understood. A number of studies have been and are being devoted to this purpose.

The first notable result of these studies is that deviation from plans is much more marked in terms of *money* spent than in terms of the physical programs carried through. Many firms seem to set rather definite goals of physical expansion; these goals are held to even though prices of capital equipment (and of new buildings) may change unexpectedly. Second, there is greater correspondence between plans and realization for large firms than for small ones, mainly because large firms have more formalized capital budgeting procedures but also because they are less likely to be forced to change plans (and to be able to change them quickly) in response to unanticipated changes in sales or in working capital position. Large firms are also characterized by the fact that, even though spending plans for the many subparts or divisions of the firm, and for the many specific investment projects, are subject to wide error, some of these errors tend to cancel out when the total investment spending of the large firm is added up.

A seasonal factor—the crowding of largely unanticipated expenditures for minor items into the fourth quarter of each year—also causes deviation of actual from planned expenditures. There is a good possibility of applying correction factors to the consistently understated planned values of fourth quarter investment spending. Again, this seasonality factor is more characteristic of small than of large firms, as the latter are the more likely to set up contingency allowances for the minor items.

A large *percentage* discrepancy between anticipated and actual expenditures may reflect a change that is both *absolutely* small (in dollars) and small in relation to the existing plant and equipment of the individual firm. Measurement of the discrepancies against gross fixed assets showed, in the 1949-50 study of Friend and Bronfenbrenner,[1] that only 7 per cent of cases involved discrepancies amounting to more than 10 per cent of gross fixed assets, while about 70 per cent of the discrepancies amounted to less than 4 per cent of existing fixed plant.

Each year's investment brings about relatively small increases in the existing capital plant of most firms, and these findings merely emphasize the fact that *deviations* of actual from expected investment spending are a still smaller fraction of existing capital.

Firms involved in *major* investment programs (measured as a percentage of the firm's existing gross fixed assets) make anticipatory statements with less error than do those spending only minor amounts in comparison with their existing plant. Equipment expenditures (machine tools, etc.) are anticipated about equally well in the major and the minor programs, but the accuracy of anticipations for expenditure on *plant* (buildings, etc.) is markedly greater for major than for minor programs.

Furthermore, the *urgency* of plant and equipment needs apparently affects the degree of downward deviation of actual from anticipated expenditure. "Urgent" programs for the year 1949 were those made by firms which had done very little spending on plant and equipment in the years 1946-48 and might therefore be expected to "need" expansion more.

The comments above are concerned with attempts to measure some differences in the objective circumstances facing firms which were able to anticipate, with varying degrees of accuracy, what they would spend on plant and equipment for the year 1949. A group of the reporting firms was also requested, after the end of 1949, to indicate what major factors explained the difference between actual and anticipated expenditure. A change in the sales outlook was the single most important reason given (for 12 per cent of those firms which spent *more* than anticipated, and for 23 per cent of those firms which spent *less* than anticipated). Thus, it appears, the plan, as based on a sales anticipation, was subject to alteration during the period if the anticipation proved not to be correct in the actual event. The second most frequently mentioned principal factor for firms which spent less than anticipated was an unanticipated change (presumably a decline) in net earnings after taxes. The second most important factor leading to an *excess* of actual over anticipated expenditure was the plant and equipment cost situation; in the recession year of 1949, some costs dropped. This factor was closely followed by the plant and equipment supply situation (availability, rather than price) and by net earnings after taxes. Most anticipations, not surprisingly, seem to be based on the price and supply conditions which obtain at the time of planning.

Anticipations of plant and equipment expenditure, therefore, can be summed up as having a significant direct relation to the actual behavior of firms. But the extent of realization of plans by individual firms depends on two things. First, the actual events, as they unfold, may differ from the expectations entering into the original plan and thus impede or facilitate the realization of the moves of that plan, in the sense that the timing may be altered for the given set of moves, although the program itself remains unaltered except for being slowed down or speeded up. Second, the realization of the original plan may cease to be a relevant issue for the firm because, in the light of new anticipations about the environment (both the present year, as it unfolds, and revised ideas about the future on the basis of new evidence), the magnitude as well as the timing of the old plan must be changed, including the first move.

These considerations, therefore, lead us back to an examination of the determinants of the original investment decision, and the determinants of a revised decision. Roughly speaking, plant and equipment expenditure can be considered either *nonexpansionary* or *expansionary* in character. Replacement of worn-out equipment and investment based on cost-cutting and modernization considerations would be examples of the nonexpansionary type, while an increase of total capacity to produce–say, a whole new plant–would be an example of the second type. Differences will become apparent, for these two types of investment program, in the character of responses to a change of expectations. The firm having an expansionary program was found, in a study by Jean Bronfenbrenner,[2] to react quite sensitively to a difference between anticipated and actual sales. If actual sales turn out to be significantly lower than the sales volume anticipated at the time when a capacity expansion was formulated, doubt would be cast upon the profit possibilities from expanded capacity in the year of the investment; but more important, the sales anticipations for the more distant future probably tend to be revised downward from the figures that entered into the original plan. Thus, the original plan is reformulated in the light of a changed view of the future. The extent of realization of the original expansion plan is an index of the firm's reaction to a change in the whole constellation of anticipations concerning the future environment.

Similarly, if a firm already planning an expansion finds that actual sales are substantially *greater* than anticipated, the original plan may be reformulated upward to reflect changed anticipations about years (2), (3), and the more remote future.

The firm which plans to spend for nonexpansionary or cost-cutting reasons tends to react quite differently to lower actual than anticipated sales, in that the need for the improved facilities may be doubly emphasized by the adverse development. Within fairly broad limits of downward deviation of actual from anticipated sales, the nonexpansionary plan was found to remain unaffected, partly because equipment replacement plans tend to depend on the *level* of sales, which is not much affected by a discrepancy between actual and anticipated sales, but also because smaller actual than anticipated sales may imply declining market share for the company, and a decline in market share would argue for an *increase* in replacement and modernization expenditure.

The same differences in response tend to hold when the expansionary and the nonexpansionary firms face unanticipated reductions in earnings. Unless the earnings drop is so severe as to impair the solvency of the firm and render it incapable of doing anything, a fall in actual earnings below anticipated levels should be a reinforcing signal for cost-cutting expenditure, whereas a comparable earnings drop would probably cast doubt on the desirability of a capacity expansion.

For each broad type of investment decision, then, prediction of actual spending rates will become more accurate as we are able to take into account not only the investment plans which are formulated (at time t_0) upon some anticipations of sales, earnings, etc., for the first and succeeding years, but also the character of responses to disappointment (favorable or unfavorable) of these anticipations, as shown in the degree of realization of the original investment plans.

The problems of observation clearly imply a need for panel techniques, and such progress as has been made – for example, the Friend-Bronfenbrenner study[3] of 1949-50 investment plans and realizations, and the separate Bronfenbrenner monograph[4]–has required panel applications. At t_0 it is necessary to know the firm's plan and the anticipations which entered into the formulation of that plan. At the end of year (1), it is necessary to know, for the same firm, what the actual investment and the actual course of anticipated variables (sales, earnings, etc.) were for year (1), and what the planned levels and the new anticipations are for year (2). The anticipations can become more and more a part of a broader explanation of what happens, and thus of a more sophisticated prediction of what may happen in the future. In the forecasting of general business volume (Gross National Product estimates), for example, the anticipated amounts of investment spending are really *contingent* statements in the minds of executives who have sales and earnings anticipations about the coming year. The forecaster may be able to combine these statements of anticipated investment and find that their effect (through a more general model of interaction) will be to produce sales rates in most industries which differ from the sales anticipations upon which investment plans were based. In order to do this, it will have been necessary, first, to correct for any known systematic bias in the investment plans, such as the understatement bias of the small firms. Experience with the realization functions for firms, *by types of investment program*, may then permit the forecaster to predict what will be the responses to disappointed expectations as the year progresses, and hence to predict what actual volume of investment will be generated in the business sector.

Direct use of investment anticipations already provides more reliable estimates of actual investment than does a straight projection of past values. Firms are able partially to anticipate changes of direction in the economic environment. What the new method may do is to permit a prediction in which the compensating errors and the reinforcing errors of anticipations are taken account of, and thus to provide a still better basis for obtaining quantitative estimates of changes in business activity.

Consumer behavior. Interest in the facts of consumer behavior goes back to the budget studies of the German statistician Engel, but the measurement of consumer anticipations is a quite recent development. During World War II a group of government employees gained experience with the application of survey techniques to the administration of War Bond selling campaigns. A number of members of this group formed the nucleus of the Survey Research Center at the University of Michigan.

In co-operation with, and through the financial support of, the Federal Reserve System Board of Governors, the Survey Research Center has gathered information from a probability sample on consumer-spending anticipations. Statements of anticipations, and a variety of facts about income and assets, have been obtained from respondents, and estimates for the U. S. consuming public have then been computed. As a descriptive tool—for providing information on income savings, assets, and some types of past expenditure—the Survey Research Center approach has proved invaluable. A recent evaluation of consumer survey statistics[5] reports the finding that this aspect of the Survey Research Center's work should be continued and improved.

Direct anticipations have been obtained for such things as: intentions to buy automobiles, houses, major appliances, or furniture. The Center also collects information on consumer *attitudes*. The attitude most directly connected with buying intentions is the consumer's evaluation of durable goods markets: "Is this a good time to buy?" Another is whether consumers expected a rise or a decline in the prices of "the things you buy" during the coming year. In addition, consumers were asked to evaluate their own financial situation and to make anticipatory statements about expected changes in their incomes.

Buying intentions and attitudinal data have been used to make evaluations, published at intervals in the *Federal Reserve Bulletin*, of the future strength or weakness of consumer demand in the important durable goods markets. These evaluations, based on the perceptions that consumers had of their own economic situation and on their expectations about prices and other factors, have been assessed as valuable indicators of turning points in aggregate consumer markets demand for the postwar years.[6] On the other hand, comparison of planned and actual purchases for *individual* items, such as automobiles, did not yield as satisfactory results.

The surveys have not, with a few exceptions, involved extensive reinterviewing of respondents to obtain comparisons, for individual families, between what they planned to do and what they actually did. A few Survey Research Center reinterview programs and some other panel information indicate that highly variable proportions of anticipated purchases are actually carried through. The *aggregate* prediction may be fairly successful, but this masks the fact that a great many families expressing intentions to buy do not do so, and that some families expressing the intention not to buy actually do buy. As an example, about 12 per cent of a sample group expressed the intention, at the beginning of 1952, of buying a new or used automobile during that year. Fifty-six per cent of this group actually did buy, according to reinterview information obtained at the end of the year; whereas of the 87 per cent who did not expect to buy, 15 per cent actually did.[7]

There was some degree of association between intentions to buy and actual purchases, as indicated by the difference between the 56 per cent figure and the 15 per cent figure in the two groups of respondents. Even so, because the number of those expressing intentions not to buy was far greater than the number of those planning to do so, about two-thirds of actual automobile purchases in 1952 turned out to be made by families expressing intentions *not* to buy. This fact makes the aggregate prediction ambiguous unless, in repeated cases, there turned out to be considerable stability in the proportions of those reversing their positions in the course of the year. No basis presently exists for supposing that such stability of reversals characterizes intentions to buy.

Some light is thrown on this problem by two recent studies which had the purpose of ascertaining the extent to which consumers are able to forecast their own action, for various types of purchases.[8] Katona and Mueller attempted to measure the degree of deliberateness with which purchase decisions are made, and then to relate this to income, education, and other characteristics of buyers, as well as to certain characteristics of the product. It was found that many purchases, even of high-priced items, were made with only a few days' forethought and with a minimum of circumspectness and careful comparison. Buyers with the lowest incomes and the smallest amount of education exhibited the least degree of deliberation. There was substantially less deliberation shown in the purchasing of sports shirts than in the purchasing of important durable items. The Katona-Mueller results throw some light on the extent to which "intentions to buy" statements can be representative of actual purchases that are made; it appears that consumers have concrete "plans" to a far smaller degree than do business organizations which set up budgetary controls for their capital expenditures.

There has been one significant attempt to discover whether, in the setting of numerous variables in which families do their deciding, the purchase intentions and attitudinal variables were needed as an integral part of the explanation of actual behavior.[9] Klein and Lansing attempted to find statistical relationships which would predict the proportion of buyers of durable goods in the population. They considered three classes of variables—financial, demographic, and attitudinal—as candidates for inclusion in a predictive equation. Their conclusion was that some variables in each of the three classes are needed to provide the best possible prediction from the survey and reinterview data (for the year 1952 only) which were at their disposal. This work can really be taken as a series of tests of hypothesis about interactions between the kinds of variables already mentioned, and it points up the need for more panel information about other years, as there is considerable question about the stability of the relationships that were found to hold for 1952.

Klein and Lansing were interested in "average" behavior over a representative group of households, and they had to adopt a practic of scoring attitudinal variables in order to introduce them into the quantitative relation. Intentions to buy were the most important attitudinal variable, and the "feeling of financial well-being" was also significant. Price expectations of consumers proved not to have a stable relation to purchases—anticipation of higher prices might lead either to heavier buying or to postponement of purchase. The chief financial variable that proved useful was income-lagged-one-year; liquid assets at the beginning of the year had no discernible effect on decisions to buy. The demographic variables—age, marital status, and geographical region—all turned out to be important.

The work of Klein and Lansing points to the need for multivariate explanation of decisions to purchase durable goods. Prediction of total purchases of individual durable items in any year may remain hazardous even with these additional elements of explanation, because the behavior of consuming units is subject to so many kinds of random disturbance.

When attention turns to the amount of spending by the individual household on all nondurable items as a group, or on all durable items as a group, we should expect that somewhat more stability may inhere in the underlying relationships, once these are better understood. The behavior of consuming households, as an aggregate, should also be subject to better prediction on the basis of a good model of the individual spending unit's mode of behavior.

The earliest Keynesian formulation—that the proportion of an individual's total income spent on consumption goods should fall as his income rises—has received some empirical support in the numerous studies that have been undertaken, but in order to improve the explanatory power and empirical validity of this approach, efforts have been made to incorporate both economic and demographic variables in a model of the consumer's planning behavior.[10]

Arguing that "the rate of consumption in any given period is a facet of a plan which extends over the balance of the individual's life, while the income accruing within the same period is but one element which contributes to the shaping of such a plan,"[11] Modigliani and Blumberg develop the hypothesis that the consumer's objective is to adjust his consumption in each year (defined as spending on nondurable items only) so that an extra dollar of his resources will make a proportional contribution to the satisfaction to be gained, not only in the current year, but in all further years of his expected life. The hypothesis implies that preparing for the future (taking the interest rate and the curve of expected future income into account) is an important element in decisions concerning present spending on nondurable items.

There is considerable empirical evidence that, at each level of current income, families whose incomes are higher than last year's spend less, and families whose incomes are lower than last year's spend more, than do families of that income group whose incomes are unchanged from the previous year. The effects seen in these "cross-section" data are usually traced to habit-persistence, but the model just referred to accords equally well with the data. If the income change has been regarded as transitory by the family, then it should be true that the preceding consumption pattern would remain largely undisturbed—that is, savings should change in the same direction and roughly by the same amount that income did. If, on the other hand, the income change was indicative of long-run improvement or deterioration in the position of the family, then the adjustment comes in the form of a change in the target-level of life savings and life consumption. Other empirical findings on the consumption behavior of families in different parts of the income distribution, and at different ages, are also reviewed and found to be consistent with the model.

Unfortunately, no full-scale test has yet been made of the reaction pattern, over time, of households to changes in expected income, actual income, and the demographic variables (such as age and socioeconomic status). Thus there is no conclusive basis on which to accept or reject the ideas that have been advanced here. It is hoped that in due course such tests will be made, to measure the relations between consumer anticipations, plans, and the realization of plans. Prediction of behavioral responses to the emerging economic environment of each year will then become much more feasible.

INFERENCES FOR THE STUDY OF VOTING BEHAVIOR. Voting behavior may constitute, at best, only a partial analogue to the kinds of response to the economic environment that have been discussed above. It will be our purpose to explore some implications of the present framework for prediction of voting behavior, but the present authors embark on this with a hesitancy similar to that of the plumber who was asked how he would repair a break in the penstocks at Hoover Dam; he said, "I know it's only water, but you fellows have got a lot more of it!"

When people are asked, some time before an election, to state their preferences for one candidate as against another, or to indicate how they would vote if the election were held today, or to specify how they expect to vote, the opinion pollster can utilize these responses in any of a number of ways. Assuming that he has constructed a representative sample of the population at large, he may make a predictive statement of any of the following forms:

(1) X per cent of the population as of today *prefer* Mr. Doe, Y per cent prefer Mr. Smith, and $(100-X-Y)$ per cent are uncommitted or refused to respond. These percentages, at the 1 per cent confidence level, fall within the following percentage ranges (a table of such ranges would then follow).

Or (2) X per cent of the population *will vote for* Mr. Doe, Y per cent will vote for Mr. Smith, and $(100-X-Y)$ are uncommitted or refused to respond. (Again, confidence intervals would be specified.)

Or (3) Mr. Doe will win, and Mr. Smith will lose.

The differences between these three types of alternative statements are of course well known to political scientists. Those concerned with opinion surveys have been sorely tempted to adopt alternative (3) and predict how the election would come out. (If a quota sample that is not a strict probability sample has served as the basis for the investigation, the opinion surveyor must, of course, omit, or make arbitrary estimates of, the confidence interval around his prediction.)

As our example of automobile purchase intentions showed, it would be desirable in a more fully developed statement of prediction to include, for the *X* and *Y* preference classes, *(a)* the percentage of those who would, in fact, vote according to their present preferences; *(b)* the percentage of those who would switch; and *(c)* the percentage of those who would not vote at all. Similar apportionment of the uncommitted and the refusals between the three classes would then be necessary before any predictive statement concerning the outcome of the election, subject to some level of confidence, could be made.

Apportionment along the lines suggested could not be made solely from the information available from a sample survey unless other knowledge permitted the forecaster to apply estimated rates of stability of preferences, according to, say, income, education level, previous voting history, or other items for which respondents gave information at the time of the survey.

It is the authors' understanding that panel surveys, to collect information of the types required, have already been undertaken on a considerable scale. If these yield consistent and sensible relationships that explain the deviations of actual voting behavior from the anticipations of voters, correction factors may already be available with which to modify the results of a sample survey of anticipations.

We have seen that the anticipations of business enterprises and of consumers have some direct predictive quality, even in the absence of a full behavioral model into which the statements of anticipations can be introduced. Businessmen's short-period estimates of their future investment expenditure were the most reliable of these, and consumers' anticipations as to the purchase of particular durable goods were the least reliable. The degree of reliability of anticipations hinged, essentially, on three things: (*a*) the size, formality, and degree of articulateness of the organization; *(b)* the necessity for planning toward an objective (and the stability of the objective); and *(c)* the stability of the external environment whose characteristics, so far as they are foreseen, enter into the plans of the organization.

Improvements on the direct predictive power of anticipatory statements were thought to be feasible because the anticipations were only contingent statements: the organization would respond to the environment in such and such a way *if* the environment, in the future period, turned out to have certain characteristics. A "realization function," which would tell how the organization (firm or consumer) would respond to a future environment differing from the one expressed in the original anticipations and the original plan, based on those anticipations, is a device for summing up all of the systematic response characteristics of an organization having a given type of objective. The realization function would be used in the broader context of interaction between all economic units in the whole economy, and a solution of the prediction problem would involve simultaneous estimation of all of the relevant economic variables.

This analytical framework has been in process of development for a long time, and as yet there remains considerable doubt among economists as to the particulars. How much analogy is there between a framework, thus conceived, and the ideas of the political scientist concerning the structure of the system in which voting decisions are made?

The framework of economic decision-making required that any deviations of the "actual" future, as it unfolded, from the situation anticipated in the original plan would produce a systematic response in the form of a new course of action to be followed by the organization in question. At first sight, it might appear that similar considerations would enter into voting behavior. Some voting groups might be sensitive to changes in the economic environment, others to changes in the programs advocated by the candidates, etc. If the observer had a means of estimating the responses of voters to such changes, *and* a means of making independent estimates of the economic environment or the programs, as they would in fact develop, he might be able to improve on the kind of prediction which could be made directly from statements of anticipation. It is to be doubted, however, whether much more is known by the observer than by the lay public about either of these things.

There appears also to be some difference between the kind of action implied in voting behavior and the kind implied in business investment expenditure or consumer expenditure and saving. In models of such behavior, it will be recalled, care was taken to show what changes in the future situation would produce changes from the course of action implied by the plan. In some instances, a particular variable could take on a whole range of possible values without affecting the plan for the coming period; in these cases, the anticipation of the values of such variables was said to be an *irrelevant* anticipation.

For most voters, it might be suggested, the direct impress of the outcome of the election upon other actions which the voter will take, is very small, if not zero. The decision on which way (or whether) to vote may therefore fall outside the area of planned action–in the sense in which anticipation of the future, plans about a course of action, and realization of those plans are all connected together. Thus, the voter's statement of anticipation, as of October, concerning which way he will vote in November may not have to bear the same kind of content as the businessman's statement of anticipation about the amount of investment expenditure he will undertake next year. If the future fails to match the businessman's expectations about it, he will perforce make adjustments in a whole scheme of action. Prediction of his behavior involves prediction about some systematic responses that the environment will require of him, and some systematic impact that he will have (when added to the actions of others) on the environment. Prediction of the voter's behavior may have more the character of a statement as to the number of flies which will land on a piece of flypaper–the variables are the number of flies that happen to be flying, the wind velocity, the size, flavor, stickiness of the flypaper, etc.

In summary, panel techniques may prove extremely useful in the study of factors affecting voting decisions, but the models that economists are beginning to use to link together anticipations, plans, and the realization of plans have a very doubtful bearing on decision-making behavior in the political context. We leave this question in the hands of the political scientists.

CHAPTER 21

Some Psychodynamic Aspects of Voting Behavior

RICHARD E. RENNEKER, M.D.

This chapter is based on a review of the clinical records of forty-two patients in psychoanalytic psychotherapy or psychoanalysis during the elections of 1948, 1952, and 1956. The review covered the two-month periods preceding and following the election dates. Clinical histories frequently included a lifelong presidential voting record. No attempt will be made to present these data statistically since the major emphasis will be devoted to the multidetermined nature of psychological influences upon political choice, candidate preference, and voting behavior. Focus is fixed upon the importance of understanding the individual conscious and unconscious emotional motivations for political behavior and the different combinations of intensities of the basic psychological factors involved.

I make practically no attempt to deal with the voting realities of geographical distribution, socioeconomic factors, basic election issues, and the like. They have been adequately dealt with elsewhere in this book. This is a presentation of the psychodynamics of voting behavior as seen by a psychoanalyst from his privileged seat at the edge of the patient's unconscious.

There was *always* some sort of meaningful relationship between the voting history of the patient and of the *dominant* parent. The most expected finding was that party-fixated parents generally tended to influence their offspring toward the same party orientation. The effect of religion did not appear to be nearly as important a factor in these patients' material as the governing emotional influence of the significant parent. It has been commonly noted in voting studies that socioeconomic status, religious affiliation, urban vs. rural residence all allow for fairly reliable predictions regarding the percentage of Democrats vs. Republicans in each group. The clinical data indicated that the various external pressures associated with each of these variables were important in molding the cultural values of the individuals, but that party choice seemed transmitted more by *identification* with the parents. This was more true for sons than daughters, since the primary political figure from childhood seemed almost without exception to be the father.

THE POSITIVE FATHER AND THE SON AS VOTER. Father's party preference and pet political opinions were found to be part of the pattern of *primary identification* [see Chapter 14 above] within the core of the male patient. This political frame of reference became something which the patient subsequently treated in one or all of the following ways:

1) Blind perpetuation as a symptomatic manifestation of failure of maturation.

2) Total rejection as a symptomatic manifestation of neurotic rebellion against father with acceptance of a completely different set of beliefs.

3) Confrontation and testing of various portions with the facts of changing reality of the self and the external world. This was part of the natural process of differentiation of the self and usually resulted in an *individualistic* set of political ideas which were different than father's but still in the same philosophical or party direction.

The latter could be disrupted and either one of the previous two instituted or vice versa.

Example 1: A thirty-three-year-old Protestant lawyer with a long history of sexual impotency, work inhibitions, and feelings of inadequacy faithfully followed and echoed his strong father's unswerving political convictions. The working through of the unresolved paternal conflicts was accompanied by a continued challenging of the old political concepts during the pre-election months. It progressed to a temporary decision to vote for the opposite party. This was given up in favor of return to the primary party which best reflected the actual values of his current life. He was, however, no longer a "follower" but assumed a postelection course of activity aimed at helping to institute some "progressive changes" within the local party. His political activities were for the first time experienced with enthusiasm. Passive, noncritical voting compliance was thus a symptomatic manifestation of his inability to compete with and to complete separation of himself from the powerful father.

Example 2: A twenty-two-year-old medical student with disturbing periods of depression, sporadic anxiety, and hypochondriasis had gotten himself deeply involved in communist causes and party-line activities. This was quite disturbing to his staunchly Republican physician father who worried greatly about the possible negative social and professional consequences of such behavior. The symptoms were most centrally related to guilt over conflictful hostile destructive impulses directed toward father. His communistic activities not only provided other targets as substitutes for father, but also managed to "hurt" him through worry. Guilt was neutralized by the pain of social ostracism which came to him because of a need to talk about his activities.

Diminution of rage against father within therapy was followed by a de-emphasis of his "radical" orientations. The fortunate establishment of a really functioning relationship with the male parent was accompanied by a comfortable acceptance of certain of father's candidate preferences and a shift into the company of "independent" voters.

Example 3: A forty-three-year-old chemical engineer came for therapy because of a chronic depressive reaction of five years' duration. His wife complained of a gradual personality change in him from a light-hearted, easy-going, understanding fellow into a serious, worrisome, and authoritative man. He had been relatively inactive politically with no definite party affiliation, but with the change came much self-recrimination about his past "shirking of social responsibilities." He became deeply committed to one party, and in the election months spent more time in political work than with his family. Analysis revealed that the chain of events was precipitated by the man's unresolved guilt over the sudden death of father, whose character traits were unconsciously assumed by the patient as a means of magically attempting to neutralize guilt by undoing father's death. Father was still living in a sense—through the son.

There were a small number of instances in which death of the father *freed* the son to express or to develop his own political beliefs.

Example 4: A forty-seven-year-old university instructor had never completed his partially carried through individualization from the primary father identification. He lived in a stage of arrested, half-hearted revolution against the parental figure. This was beautifully expressed through his voting record. He prided himself upon his thorough knowledge regarding party stands on basic issues, records of the candidates, and so on. He had always functioned as an independent voter. We discussed his voting performance in six previous national elections. On three occasions his carefully thought out presidential choice was at variance with his father's, so he voted without mishap. The other three times his candidate turned out also to be father's pick. He failed to vote each time because of varying, unconsciously supplied interferences on election day. His intellectual integrity demanded that he vote for the father-shared candidate, but his semiactive, unconsciously perpetuated adolescent defiance of father was so strong that solution to the conflict each time was an "unfortunate" or "accidental" occurrence which prevented voting. We had opportunity to see this pattern because of a "strange" association which flitted across his mind during father's funeral. He felt a sense of sad relief and was suddenly conscious of the thought that now he could vote for any candidate. This remained puzzling until it was recalled in therapy because it had never occurred to him that he wasn't free to vote for whomever he selected.

There seemed to be a tendency for first voting young men to deviate from father's established political preferences. The passively compliant, deeply identified, party-line son was the chief exception, otherwise the male first voter at least seriously considered divergent voting. Our culture has set twenty-one as the age when "now you are a man." This seems more linked to assumption of the right to vote than to anything else. The initial vote is therefore an initiation rite which formally recognizes the former youth as a man. It is something to be approached with great seriousness since voting choice is expected by the young man to be evaluated by his elders and peers for evidence of wisdom and independent thinking. He has been in the shadow of a parent for many years and a vote *with* father has to be instinctively explained and defended to others. A vote different from father's is like a declaration of manhood and stands distinct and separate from this parent.

The first vote did not seem to provide any consistent basis for predicting subsequent voting behavior. This appeared to be more dependent on the eventual degree of resolution achieved in the working through of the father-connected conflicts.

I had the impression that return to the general direction of father's party or political philosophy was determined by whether the basic father-son relationship had been positive or negative. History of positive relationship in the formative childhood years was correlated with change or shift towards father, whereas negative relationship always seemed to produce political divergence.

A pattern for those with positive father associations was the following:

1) Primary identification with father's masculine frame of reference, including political attitudes if these were strongly felt and verbalized.

2) An early manhood phase of rejection of father's political convictions as part of the process of prematurely declaring total independence and separation from the male parent before it actually existed. This phase was by-passed by some in the political area because it was enacted in another part of his life (i.e., choice of profession, girl, etc.). It usually involves a selected area of rejection of father's values as a sort of battlefield upon which the battle for independence takes place. The political area can easily be selected if time for self-differentation coincides with an election year and the "first vote."

3) Resolution of the unconscious conflicts impinging upon father, accompanied by development of the self into functioning manhood, allows a swing backwards in which many of the values previously unconsciously rejected because of their father contamination, are now reintegrated within consciousness. This is right because the nucleus of the developed man always remains his identification with the positive, strong portion of the loving father. Father's political ideas are logical extensions of his value systems, thus it would follow that some of them would make sense within the son's personality which is founded upon the father's. These political values have been exposed to a shakedown cruise within himself and have been joined by new shipmates. They have been accepted as belonging to the crew, although originally held suspect because of the feeling that they represented another ship. Father's

values of all kinds have been critically examined, subjected to various tests, and some have been discarded as nonfunctional within the son's world. The rest finally secure the son's seal of approval and thus become indefinably merged with the self. They are no longer "father's values" but are now the son's values. The final product is a combination of some new, acquired values of the son plus some old ones learned from the father. "Sowing one's wild oats" is the shakedown cruise in which he reacts away from learned parental frames of reference in a too sudden and too far search for identity apart from father. The "wild oats" can be expressed in sexual, behavioral, and political areas.

There is another way in which the positive father identification reasserts itself in later life. We know that human beings when placed in difficult conflict situations which they seem unable to solve, tend to react with regressive manifestations. Regression as a reaction to such a situation is movement backwards in time to some past relationship or to some method of past adaptation, associated with feelings of security. The strong, dominant, loving father was obviously often the source of such security orientations, therefore such troubled times often result in regressive activation of unconscious need for re-establishment of the old parent-son relationship in which father could seemingly solve any problem or ward off any threat. These are the moments in a man's life when he deeply appreciates help from his boss, a friend (etc.). It has political significance because *the presidential candidate is commonly regarded by the unconscious as a father substitute* (e.g., Washington as the "father" of his country). This means that people displace onto him needs and hopes which were originally connected with the positive father or the quest for an ideal parent.

It is easy to see that there will always be a varied number of individually and temporarily dislocated people who will make a presidential candidate the focus of their regressive needs for protection and help. They can be drawn outside of party lines by the particular personality characteristics, physical appearance, and behavior of one candidate. He might remind the person unconsciously of his longed for dead father—no longer there to help him in his hour of need. The resemblance might be confined to a single physical feature. The candidate, consciously or unconsciously, endeavors *to act the part* of a strong, gentle, loving, interested, understanding, friendly, helpful father. After all, he kisses babies, puts in appearances at athletic contests, stumbles over rocky river beds to the accompaniment of clicking shutters. He smiles on all voters and looks properly strong and serious when discussing the acute problems of his times. He makes a point of understanding all groups, professions, and the like. His family clusters around him admiringly or else smiles reassuringly into the camera of the people. We must get the message of "this is a contented family." The children should appear properly clean-cut and secure. The wife has to be lost in love, deep admiration, and obvious compliance to her master. Her faith must be unswerving, so that she and the family become living proof of his infallible ability to meet and banish all obstacles. The depreciating, hostile behavior of Stevenson's wife during his two campaigns was the decisive factor in several patients' decisions not to vote for him although they otherwise felt that he perfectly represented their opinions. In each instance they were products of a matriarchally dominated family in which father was a mere figurehead for the proclamation of mother's policies. These men could not buy Adlai because he did not represent to them the sort of a man who could give security to their regressive needs.

The sights and sounds of the strong father have become essential equipment for presidential candidates since the crash of 1929. Roosevelt's voice, electrifying mannerisms, and decisive actions generated such belief in his basic strength as to make most forget his physical incapacity. He was thus a fine figure for preserving hope in millions throughout the depression years. They were able to postpone hopelessness through regressive retreat to a feeling of almost total reliance upon the confident, strong voice which came into their homes with the story of what he was doing for them and what they must do to help. The concept of fireside talks was psychologically brilliant since it conveyed the essence of a calm, wise father speaking to his family. The only Republican candidate who was a worthy opponent on the level of father representation was Willkie. The war revitalized Roosevelt's political career since it seemed impossible to take a chance on someone else who couldn't conceivably be as strong father-wise. His gradual physical deterioration was massively denied by millions because its recognition was the signal for collective irrational anxiety such as the child feels when he thinks about the possible death of the key parent.

He was mourned as a father, and his passing reactivated unresolved oedipals all over the country. After Roosevelt, Truman was like a man seen through the wrong end of a telescope. He was said to look like the average man on the street because people, for a long time, couldn't really see him as a distinct person. They kept looking at him through the afterimage of Roosevelt. The feeling was like that of a family which loses the respected, loved father—no one can take his place. A new man starts coming around regularly but no one takes him seriously for awhile because "he isn't daddy." New events may gradually bring him into positive focus and so blur the memory of father. Truman imperceptibly emerged as the cocky, confident fighter who wouldn't back down for anyone. There was much critical press comment over his violent attacks upon the critics of his daughter, but more people felt vaguely reassured and pleased by them than otherwise. He was like a living demonstration of the Americanism: "My father can lick any father on the block." His courageous, jut-jawed campaign against the personally unconvincing Dewey pulled in the legions of those who would rather have a strong father figure in their corner just in case. Eisenhower by the same token never really had any competition from Stevenson. Potentially explosive and dangerous times seem to call for an unequivocally strong presidential personality. For some reason the opposite seems to hold (e.g., Coolidge and Hoover) in times of unthreatened peace.

NONPOLITICAL PARENTS AND VOTING BEHAVIOR OF THE SONS. Those patients who came from families in which there was practically no political emphasis or interest during their childhood years tended to develop strong convictions about politics. They seemed to act out fantasies of what their parents should have been like in order to be saved the repeated social embarrassments suffered through mother and father's inert social behavior. It was also part of their defense against the partially nonfunctioning primary identification with these same parents.

There were other patients who represented the modern counterpart of such socially disinterested parents. They were the uninvolved, with long histories of disinterest and avoidance of what was outside of themselves. They were often nonvoters and generally unreachable with information about pertinent issues since they simply didn't try to understand. Some were the hugely narcissistic characters who frequently manage to go through life without sensing or meeting the needs of anyone other than themselves. For such a man life was with himself. He voted only because there seemed to be some immediate personal gain involved in the act.

Example 5: A middle-aged businessman temporarily trapped in therapy by his internist's frightening predictions about the outcome of a malignant essential hypertension admitted he had never voted. He didn't have the time. There was never time for anything but the pursuit of his own goals. People came into focus only as obstacles standing between himself and what he wanted. His wife and children were perpetually involved in the service of *his* needs. He thus taught them selfishness, interpersonal blindness, and one-way communication. Politics simply never entered the home because nothing was allowed to exist there except what was in his head at the moment. He was the mirror image of a father who had lived an identical life. His philosophy was anchored in the idea that childhood had been governed by the needs of his father, thus he was entitled to get his as an adult.

A few nonvoters were deeply disturbed people whose life was spent on the brink of a psychotic break. They were the lonely ones who had pulled in their senses so that only the most literal aspects of the reality of their immediate environment filtered through to perception. Psychic energy was spent either in intrapsychic ruminations or in constant defensive attempts aimed at deceiving others and at times themselves.

Example 6: One man had cast his ballot in five elections without being able to remember for whom he had voted. It didn't matter really. The important fact was that he *had* gone into the voting booth; what happened then was not important because he either carelessly checked a few boxes or gravely handed in an unmarked ballot. He let everyone in his world in on his "social act" but sagely refrained from identifying his choice. He waited until the results were obvious and simply took credit for picking winners. His reputation was that of never having voted for a losing candidate. This pseudo personality expended all of his energies in an effort to prevent others from recognizing the vacuum within.

THE NEGATIVE FATHER AND THE SON AS VOTER. Negative fathers with identifiable political views seemed to produce a variety of disturbed voting behavior in their sons. The term negative father is used here to denote a parent who contributed little to his son other than the repeated frustrations of his needs for love, dependency, and a masculine frame of reference. He usually used the boy for his own needs or ignored him. He often was crushing in his competitiveness or else totally discouraged it. He engendered pain, fear, hostility, and destructive impulses in his son. These were defended against in the offspring by various defensive intrapsychic maneuvers. The common denominator in the sons of these fathers was a peculiar sort of ambivalence. Ambivalence is ordinarily thought of as a mixture of opposing feelings struggling for dominance, but here the feeling was almost pure hatred camouflaged, with varying degrees of success, from the self and others. These patients were sometimes the superidealists whose hostility had been converted into a reaction formation of emotionless, pure theorizing. They all seemed possessed of the perpetual dream of finding a good, loving father. Their relationships with men, however, were disruptive ones since the unconscious hostility constantly interfered. They leaned occasionally toward paranoid defenses.

Father's political preferences were, of course, rejected, as was the image of father. Islands of father identification were disturbing parts of the personality since they inevitably represented nonfunctioning elements. Political campaigns, during late adolescence, usually represented a perfect opportunity for verbalizing in one more area their disagreement with everything that father stood for. The basic principle was to be sure what this *was*, and then to take the opposite viewpoint. Father was a Democrat, then be a Republican. Father was against an issue, then be for it. Many had histories of dipping into communism because it represented the antithesis of the parents' conservatism. The only factor which silenced the loud sounds of their constant identification of areas of disagreement was continuing fear of the father. This diverted the process into nonverbal channels within the home (i.e., passive resistance) or into external channels of rebellion (i.e., antisocial acting out, or involvement in the youth communist movements).

There was a startling repetition in the case notes of these men. They did not really speak *for* a candidate but always *against* one.

Consciously this was not so to them, since in their minds they were vigorous forces working towards the election of a carefully chosen candidate. Records of their comments about candidates disclosed that they spent much more time and energy in attacking the other candidate than in extolling the virtues of their own. They seemed to specialize in first identifying the black characteristics of one party or candidate which had to be avoided or defeated at all costs. These were overdrawn and overemotionalized. There were dire predictions of national disaster if so and so was elected. The issues had to be clear-cut and opposing. They doctored them to become so in their minds. It was a dedicated struggle to defeat an evil force which was threatening the nation with a period of being used. The men pictured as behind the candidate were political prototypes of the hated father. The candidate was sometimes also so depicted, particularly if there was some real theory to distort into evidence —otherwise he was thought of as a well-meaning but hopelessly impotent front man for the evil power behind the throne. I noticed that this latter version seemed to be found in men whose fathers were impotent, passive characters dominated by strong, masculine protest women. It is easy to see the reduplication of this real-life family situation in their fantasied version of an evil force behind the hapless candidate.

This is a description of an extreme reaction but it of course existed also in benign forms wherein emphasis was still on *defeating* a candidate rather than on *electing* one. Enthusiastic sounds *for* a candidate seemed to be rationalizing activity to cover up the real source of their efforts—to work *against* and defeat a despised and hated parental surrogate. It boiled down to a choice of evils, because when pushed several revealed that they wouldn't be a bit surprised to see their man turn out badly. This is understandable since their experiences with father figures had generally been repeated episodes of unrealistic hope of finding the ideal parent substitute, which inevitably had culminated in feelings of bitterness and frustration.

They were susceptible to good father propaganda, but were especially sensitive to bad father information or rumors. The first step for such a one was to construct a case *against a candidate* or a party, then to construct a case *for the remaining side*. Both steps could be riddled with irrational distortions of the facts essential to the building of "airtight" cases *for* and *against*.

Example 7: A political scientist, who was a superpurist, reached the ultimate in this type of voting behavior. He set himself the professional task of identifying the negative qualities of *both* candidates. In order to do this he had decided not to vote and thus to avoid emotional blindness in the service of defending his choice against himself. This was a neat maneuver which freed him from the necessity of going through the motions of being *for* something. It also allowed free rein to his critical, hostile feelings unconsciously directed toward father figures. He was ostensibly operating in the interests of science, in fact, people admired him for greater purity of investigative method, therefore people—including himself—didn't dream that his real satisfaction came from the exercise of his hostility.

WOMEN VOTERS. There isn't too much to be said here, since the female patients shared the political views of their husbands, or if unmarried, their fathers. They displayed a ready capacity for giving up father's views in favor of the husband's. Although, as patients, they were inevitably part of a disturbed, conflictful marriage, political disagreement somehow did not occur in *these* marital relationships. A few of them passively belonged to the League of Women Voters only because a friend, husband, or neighbor had talked them into it.

The women with strong political convictions and activities were the following:

1) *Masculine protest women.* These were like the sons of negative fathers since they specialized in the *against* technique. Unconscious gratification was derived through depreciation of the rival candidate. Father was either a defeated shell of a man, or a rigid, narcissistic character who encouraged daughter to seek security through masculine identification. One woman persisted in the fantasy that Roosevelt's really important decisions had actually been made by his wife. Mother tended to be the prototype of daughter or else a masochistic woman whose fate the patient was attempting to avoid through identification with the aggressor (father). Hostility toward father was a common factor. These women were of course competitive with their husbands and dominated the relationship. They said that there was no marital disagreement about

choice of candidate, but one did worry that her husband had secretly changed his vote without her knowledge.

2) *Father seekers.* These were the ones, for the most part single, who were bound to spinsterhood, or to frigid, masochistic marriages by unresolved incestuous conflicts. They reacted strongly to the candidates in terms of the positive father image. The candidate of choice (selected by the husband) was aggrandized by them into somebody with a heart as big as a barrel, wisdom greater than that possessed by the high lama of Shangri-la, and so on ad infinitum. They wished to help him in the same fashion that they had worked to please father. Some of them were the best doorbell pushers in their precinct. They operated strictly in terms of *for* their candidate and *not against* the other one. I can easily imagine that they effectively convinced other women by the sheer purity and intensity of their love for the candidate (father). They must have rekindled hope in the breasts of women who had almost given up finding a good father. Their sincerity was possible because they identified the candidate with the overidealized father memories.

3) *Identity seekers.* These were the pseudo-political interest women whose seemingly intense dedication covered up feelings of worthlessness, of nothingness, or the like. Such a woman's activity might be an imitation of her husband's, necessary because she came to life only through imitating his enthusiasm. She could very well have had no political interests or voting record prior to marriage. She might have been single and deeply involved in the middle of party headquarters, but she was really there to suck in the excitement and dedication of others. Her work was an ego transfusion which brought her to life—temporarily. One such woman worked endlessly throughout a campaign and then didn't bother to vote since outcome of the election was not the point of her endeavors. She simply told her fellow workers that a vote had been cast.

DEPTH INTERVIEWS. Voting surveys have been aimed at securing information as to *how* a sample population is going to vote. This can be further broken down into statistical descriptions of the *how* of various cultural groups and subgroups. Predictions based on such *hows* have a fairly high degree of constancy but are static and completely miss the decisive fluctuations which determine the outcome of an election. The voting studies discussed in this book attempted to get at the *why* of voting choice primarily through tackling it on the level of the voter's *conscious explanation.* This chapter has presented many examples of the irrational unconscious element in voting behavior. It is therefore immediately obvious that unless one knows the deeper dynamics of the voting act in terms of its function and meaning within the total personality, the conscious explanation can never be separated from the rationalization. The *why* was also sometimes confused with *what* happened, for example, the tendency of sons of Republican fathers to vote Republican.

I do not believe that we are yet at a place in the development of depth psychology where it will be easy to set up predictive studies of behavior. We have spent most of our energies explaining why something occurred in the past or present. Prediction of the future has had to take a back seat because we haven't been ready. It is time to begin.

Voting behavior would be a fine place to start since it culminates in a single act executed at a time agreed upon in advance. The act, though based upon complex factors, narrows itself down to the selection of one element from each of a few units of two possible choices (i.e., Democrat vs. Republican; candidate vs. candidate). One difficulty is our inability to observe the act itself, thus we are left with no means of controlling for voter falsification in the reporting of voting choices.

The predictive study should be small and thorough, being based in depth interviewing aimed at eliciting adequate personal information for the understanding of the personality development, the neurosis, and the current dynamics. Special effort can be made to get more details in the areas critical to an understanding of the emotional background of voting behavior. These would stress the points touched upon in this paper: personality characteristics of each parent, nature of voter relationship with parents (past and present), with spouse, longitudinal voting histories on all, their pet political convictions, and the voter's description of the personality of each candidate.

The sample for interviewing could be selected from those who indicate indecision regarding their future voting act. Psychoanalytic evaluation of the depth interview data would allow for understanding of the individual's psychodynamics of voting. The data can be used in several different ways. The unconscious meaning of the act in his life at that time can be grasped by the voter. Predictions can be made regarding party and candidate. The psychoanalytic bases for the predictions must, however, be made explicit.

SUMMARY. The following points were extracted from a review of the psychotherapeutic notes of forty-two patients in psychoanalytic psychotherapy or psychoanalysis.

1) The positive father with political convictions has decided influence upon his son's subsequent voting behavior. This tends eventually to resemble a contemporary, individualized version of father's.

2) The negative father with political convictions can produce strongly divergent political views in his son who seems to work more *against* a candidate than *for* one.

3) Nonpolitical parents seemed to produce politically conscious sons.

4) Nonvoters were deeply narcissistic characters or semiwithdrawn, precariously balanced patients.

5) Women were in political agreement with their husbands.

6) These neurotic patients in psychiatric treatment seemed for the largest part to have intense feelings about voting behavior. They also tended to make up their minds early and to carry their decision into the final vote.

CHAPTER 22

The Principles of Permanence and Change: Electioneering and Psychotherapy Compared

ARTHUR J. BRODBECK

Ours is a time of transition. At an accelerated pace, we are moving from society as we have known it to what has come to be envisaged as "mass society."[1] During this transitional period, the problems and principles relating to permanence and tradition, on the one hand, and change and experimentation, on the other, is bound to grip the imagination of alert individuals and groups within every level and area of our social order. The contemporary American nostalgia for the twenties probably has many roots in a wish for a similar sense of devil-may-care openness and adventurousness which characterized that decade and which has paled in the wake of staggering world events since then.[2] Interest in "the conservative mind" probably also grows out of a wish to slow down, to put mental brakes upon social forces moving at too fast a clip toward no one quite knows what. For Americans, the problem is doubly intense. Our ideologies have always welcomed change; it is built into most of our social order and our individual personalities. Yet, our American scene keeps getting redefined by us in such quick and breath-taking succession that it evokes a certain intellectual dizziness. Too rapid change often produces apathy and boredom and many other signs of unutilizable and paralyzing anxiety.[3]

Empirical studies of voting patterns have a prepossessing role to play in the articulation of abstract principles governing permanence and change, especially if they carefully define the outstanding features of the historical period and social context in which they are conducted.[4] They provide the kind of recorded history that goes beyond mere anecdotal reports and haphazard intuitions of participants in the making of history toward reporting that is more precise, objective and detached. They provide the possibilities of a history that is not merely an art and which provides the kind of data against which hypotheses can be less intuitively tested.

But change and permanence may be measured in terms of shorter slices of time than that in terms of which we ordinarily think of history. Smaller time "baselines" can be selected. Every political campaign can be looked upon as mobilizing forces for change in some respects and mobilizing counterforces for the resistance to change, for the maintenance of the *status quo*. The time "baseline" may be, during an on-going campaign, the state of political power resulting from the previous campaign, and everything occurring from then up until the present campaign gets started can be used as the "unit" in terms of which change is defined. The area of interest may be similarly limited entirely to one merely of primitive power. Thus, the interest in permanence and change may be focused on whether the party in power maintains power or whether it is displaced from power, and the factors that have contributed to the result. The voting studies of the Columbia and Michigan groups confine themselves mostly, but not entirely, to an analysis of permanence or change in these most primitive terms of shifts in or maintenance of power offices. And the time 'baseline" in terms of which change is defined, is usually a rather short one.

Such investigations can be both enlarged and refined. It is seldom that a party "out of power" advocates a radical across-the-board policy of changes when challenging the policy of the party "in power." Some of the values and practices of those "in power" is usually partially incorporated into the counter-policy of those inciting the voter to change the power positions of the parties. Even when a party remains in power, policy may be changed through the campaign. Every campaign mobilizes internal conflicts within a party and brings internal strains into prominence, sometimes leading to extensive policy changes from within, helped along by pressures upon the party from competing parties. Thus, we may make our analysis in terms of policy issues—i.e., on education, taxes, racial segregation, etc.—rather than in the cruder terms of power changes alone. In such a case, the correlation between change measured in terms of pure total power outcomes and in terms of policy modifications on a selected number of issues becomes itself an interesting empirical problem. The voter's ego may be split by identifying with a party power while simultaneously feeling strongly sympathetic about a limited issue in the "plank" of the opposing party. One thinks, of course, of the race prejudice issue in the Democratic party and the impact of this upon the non-Southern voter.

Because the voting studies coming from the Columbia and Michigan groups do not explicitly organize their findings around a self-conscious "baseline" in terms of which they measure change or permanence brought about by an election, it is difficult to say just what their time "baseline" is. But, in general, it is rather a short one. It could be enlarged in further studies so that the voter could be followed by panel technique through several elections, and particularly followed through the puzzling and still relatively unstudied "in-between" periods from campaign to campaign.

When the study of political campaigns is approached with such problems in mind, the observer is led to look upon the events transpiring at election times, and events related to them, in terms of *a science of social engineering*. In the contest for power, one party seizes the public confidence more than another. The stand taken and communicated by the winning candidate (and those allied with him) has had a more over-all effective impact upon those willing to go to the polls. The majority of the electorate has been led to support change or to reject it, or has been led to support change on some matters and reject it on other matters. Each political campaign can be described in terms of the forces and counterforces advocating change and resisting it among and within the contesting parties. The outcome can be described in terms of which party on which issues has succeeded in moving the greater number of voters toward willingness to accept change or to resist it, and the processes by which success is achieved. Given such an analysis, one has the necessary materials to study processes of successful and unsuccessful social engineering involving special groups or individuals going to the polls. Since the materials are those relating to an election, the resulting body of knowledge may be labeled *a science of electioneering*.

The success of such an analysis depends upon further refinements. One important refinement relates to the most meaningful definition of the voting act itself. The voting response can be a *total act* of the personality or it can be *a partial involvement.* A sign of the times seems to be the trend toward not losing one's own identity when one participates politically through the voting act. The Michigan study, which covers an election in which "It's time for a change!" was itself a passionately debated issue, appears to have produced such a hefty number of non-party identifiers or "independents" that attention was called to this phenomenon more than in the Columbia studies covering previous elections. When voting is a total act, one "buys" and incorporates the candidate and party or "rejects" and expels the competing party and candidate with the whole personality, with a total investment in the decision. When it is a partial act, something is held in reserve, and the voting response is not seen as "completing" the self through a secondary political identification with candidate or party. Some part of the self is held back and closed off in the voting performance and felt to be incompletely realized in it. Criticism toward the self and the supported party or candidate enters into the very act of support through the vote. Appreciation for the political object in opposition to the act, rather than antagonism toward it, becomes an element in the total voting response.

Behind a partial act of voting, a mechanism of *constriction of identification* sometimes appears to operate, an inability to expand the personality so as to include any secondary identifications in the definition of the self. A voter so constricted never talks about "*my* party" but remains a political "lone wolf." The emotions are held back to form a style of participation which might be called "emotional quietism." The rule is simple: Never feel or show "heat" or emotions about anything and avoid those who do. When the voting decision is total and complete, the whole personality is likely to suffer from reverses of the candidate and party and, on the other hand, to glow from successes, as if the voter himself were a direct target of the reverses and successes. When it is partial, the candidate and party remain "an object" toward which any great subjective involvement is blocked or controlled so that they can be "shut out" or "tuned in" in a way that occasions little internal crisis of the personality. Excitement during any phase of the voting act is likely to intensify it for those for whom it is a total act, whereas it weakens it for those for whom it is a partial act.

Because voting can be a total or partial act of the personality, the units in terms of which the voter can be moved to accept change or permanence becomes more difficult to select. The probability is that, where voting is a total act, permanence or change will be accepted by the voter in terms of global identifications with a party or candidate. When a partial act, voting for acceptance of permanence or change is likely to be more focussed on issues than on party or candidate. Furthermore, there may be a very different type of focus on issues when voting is a full as compared to a partial act. Attention to the exciting issues, and the most ambiguous ones, may be the mark distinguishing those for whom full political participation is accomplished in the act of voting. But, on the contrary, the focus may be on issues on which there is more clarity and general consensus for those who make voting a partial act of the personality, and a withdrawal may operate, both in attention and feeling, toward the more highly charged emotional issues.

Unless, therefore, we ascertain whether voting has been a partial or complete act of political participation, and adjust our units of measurement accordingly, we will not be able to state clearly what the social engineering effects of a political campaign has actually been, toward the end of accomplishing acceptance of permanence or change. Two voters with different levels of involvement may both vote for the same party, but what they have accepted in marking the ballot (and what they have rejected) may be remarkably dissimilar. Their actions, while superficially similar, are actually different in meaning.[5]

The analysis of permanence and change in terms of social engineering principles requires still another refinement. The Michigan study demonstrates that panel technique needs to be extended to include the aftermath of the voting decision. What are the effects of *experiencing* a policy of change or the rejection of change for which one has voted *after* it has been put into practice? In short, the problem is whether we need to *enlarge* the definition of the voting act, *even though we may be interested in using only the smallest meaningful unit.*

When voting is a total act of the self, there is a greater likelihood that the voter will stick to the identification through thick and thin, that the identification will be maintained even when it hurts or is puzzling. For such a person, the act is more or less complete when the ballot has been marked and favorable returns are announced. As voting becomes more a partial act of the self, it is probable that there is less relaxation after the ballot is marked and the returns are announced. The point of relaxation may theoretically come anywhere after election eve, and for some it may never come. The voting act, for such people, is not consummated by the announcement of the returns. Labelling oneself "an independent" could have the significance that the returns on election eve are not the event that signalizes the time for relaxation. The voting act is complete only when something happens *after* the party is in power.

The gnawing anxiety, often expressed in terms of feelings of loneliness, that seems to go hand in hand with those disposed toward "emotional quietism" probably reflects the absence of relaxation which such a style of life creates. One of my acquaintances who voted a second-term for Eisenhower appears never to have relaxed over that decision and at various points in the second administration reported memories going back to the time of decision, the day of actually going to the polls. As far as she could remember, there was no such memory fixation during the first Eisenhower administration which she had also voted into office and she had felt completely relaxed about her decision right after the returns were announced. Her first vote was as "a Republican," whereas her second was as "an independent." Her deeply loved father was a Republican and had died between the two elections, and she had come under the influence of a "Democratic" suitor. It thus appears that the point at which the voting act concludes cannot be arbitrarily determined, and panel technique extended beyond election eve and prior to the start of a campaign is needed to help define the beginning and conclusion of a voting act. For some, the voting response becomes part of the self and completes the total voting act only after a considerable period of time has elapsed since its occurrence.

PSYCHOTHERAPY AS SOCIAL ENGINEERING. A science of electioneering, after such appropriate refinements have been satisfactorily introduced into it, becomes one of the family of the social-engineering sciences. Contributions toward discovering general principles of permanence or change can come from any one of the family of such sciences, since presumably *some* of the processes operating within any one of them to produce permanence or change are similar to those operating in others. The differences are a matter many times of the specific context in which the processes appear.

The study of electioneering is still so descriptive and rudimentary in current development that it is natural to turn to any one of the other social engineering sciences for "hunches" about the best way to state hypotheses and discover abstract laws governing permanence and change in further electioneering studies. The most highly developed social engineering science is, of course, psychotherapy. And psychoanalysis is the most highly developed theory and technique produced by the practitioners of psychotherapy. This essay is an attempt to make some preliminary abstract and concrete suggestions about how the science of electioneering might be able to utilize materials coming from the science of psychotherapy. More incidentally, it attempts to depict how psychotherapy can be studied in a very special way so as to extract the materials by which a new outlook on *both* social engineering sciences might develop.

Like a political campaign, psychotherapy mobilizes forces within the personality for *both* permanence and change. Should a marriage be maintained or broken? Should the patient continue in a profession or change it? Should the patient concentrate on continuing an education under economic hardships or should the patient leave college and go into a promisingly lucrative business arrangement? These are all policy questions and are the counterparts in psychotherapy to conflicting policies in a campaign with respect to foreign relations or with respect to cutting taxation demands upon the electorate.

However, a classical view of psychotherapy is that, unlike electioneering, the therapist does not advocate any policy at all to the patient. Instead, the patient "projects" policies onto the therapist, attributing at some times one alternative and at others still another alternative. This may be true, but the candidates for power are still there in reality. The marital mate who does *not* want a divorce and the "third person" who *wants* the divorce so as to marry the patient are contenders for power, for a vote. The reactions of either "party" may be "projected" onto the therapist as the patient tries to make up his mind which way to "vote." But the fact remains that the patient is working (through the symbolic agency of the therapist) to decide the result of a *real* power struggle, not just a fantasied one.

If the therapist does behave in the "classical" tradition of suggesting in no way his stand on the policy question, he still helps the patient exposed to the campaign to face the problem *in special ways* which he judges will help the patient solve the problem in a reasonably "rational" manner. *What* he chooses to confront the patient with about the way in which the patient's personality enters into the decision, the interpretations he uses, and what he chooses to ignore about the patient's personality investment may all inadvertently and sometimes unconsciously play a role in how the "patient-voter" decides ultimately to resolve an issue about maintaining a marriage or dissolving it and starting another. However, even though he concentrates on only some of the "issues" involved to the exclusion of others, he is usually increasing by psychoanalytic procedure the amount of rationality going into the decision more than if the patient were not to go through "the campaign" with him. Yet, the final decision may rest on more left-over "unconscious" and "unanalyzed" material than the therapist prefers to think exists and which is less than ideal in terms of theory. Such a result, I believe, is inevitable since the therapist *as a person* has preferences about policy which, although he may not *express*, come out indirectly in terms of what issues he chooses to concentrate upon through confrontation and interpretation. His values influence his "intuitions" about the patient.

There is perhaps more of a "myth" about the "value-free" psychoanalyst than a reality. Loaded words are used in speaking to the patient which give away the therapist's values about where his sympathies in the campaign rest, what *he* would be inclined to do, how *he* feels about the patient's plight. There is strong reason to believe that there are as great gaps between psychoanalytic theory and practice on this question of "values" as there is in every other attempt to apply theory. Some psychoanalysts are notoriously "active." They take "sides" and express them vigorously with respect to the cultural conflicts in which the patient is caught. They tend to coerce and pressure the patient toward "voting" one way rather than another. Sometimes, this may go hand in hand with a great willingness to modify the stand taken on policy when further material is associatively produced by the patient, and the "stand" is expressed only as a way of producing important material. Others, and luckily the rarer if not almost non-existent case, very quickly and openly take a stand against which nothing the patient may say is really considered, except to "rationalize" it away as "resistance." Such a therapist usually harbors deep-seated sadistic tendencies and tends to be "a power personality." He is usually likely to be a "trouble-maker" among his professional colleagues. The campaign he conducts is with a ballot on which there is only one possible choice and the patient may from time to time vote either "yes" or "no." A basic alternative is never provided. The patient is made to mould himself in the therapist's image, rather than allowed to become a person in his own right. I suspect that there is a human tendency among all therapists to move toward this kind of "power coercion" whenever the issues which the patient presents touch too much on their own residual neuroses.

But the point I want most to emphasize is that sometimes with some therapists (and with almost *all* therapists with respect to *some* patients) the power struggle is not only "symbolically" present and carried over from the events outside of the therapy room so as to distort a purely objective relationship. Theory to the contrary notwithstanding, it may be directly present in the therapy room *as a reality*. Far from seeing this departure from "value-freeness" as a disgrace to the psychiatrist, I want rather to emphasize that it *is* a reality of possibly beneficial or harmful effect and makes it possible to analyze the electioneering in psychotherapy in quite different ways than those implied by so-called "blank screen" theory. Furthermore, my point is that it may be present in all sorts of ways.

And even when it is *not* directly there, psychotherapy may *still* be scrutinized in terms of forces mobilized for permanence or change in terms of symbolic displacements from "outside" persons onto the therapist's person. Additionally, the way the patient works toward "a vote" (intra-psychically and in relationship to the "campaign" such outside persons conduct) can be studied in parallel ways to those used in an election. My impression is that *both* types of analysis could be performed for *any* therapist-patient pairing. Both symbolic and direct power struggles would be present, although the way the two are quantitatively and qualitatively correlated would have to become an empirical area of investigation in its own right.

These remarks are made in order to establish the reasonableness of the idea of studying psychotherapy in terms that are similar to the way in which election campaigns are studied. The emphasis has been that there is a great deal of "electioneering" that goes on in psychotherapy, although many times unhonored by theory and overlooked by therapists. My major purpose, however, is to show the reverse relationship—i.e., that there is a great deal of "psychotherapy" in electioneering. It has been necessary to establish the first point in order to move on to the second one, and I do not want to dwell on finer and finer details of the possible parallels between electioneering and therapy. Rather, I would like, with this background, to turn to the manner in which principles coming out of psychotherapy may be useful in conducting electioneering studies, so as to arrive at better and better ways of studying processes of permanence and change through the voting decisions that result from political campaigns.

The full survey of how knowledge coming out of the study of psychotherapy could be put to use in the study of change and permanence in voting decisions is much too scopeful an endeavor at this beginning stage of the development of the social engineering sciences. What I should like to do is to indicate, by an example or two, the type of hypotheses and approach that might be worth investigation, when the view is taken that what we know of processes of change in psychotherapy can be made transferable in some meaningful sense to the study of change in voting patterns.

One of the most stimulating concepts regarding change in psychotherapy developed in this country within psychoanalysis is Franz Alexander's concept of "a corrective emotional experience."[6] The idea behind the concept is that the patient has come to both expect and provoke certain reactions from others which reinforce a neurotic, unsatisfying behavior pattern for him or her and/or others integrated with the patient in actual life. The therapist breaks this pattern by refusing to be "provoked" into showing it and shakes the patient up by giving him or her an actual experience of "something" contrary to expectation. An experience of this type produces considerable internal stress and, if followed up correctly, produces amazing amounts of insight into the self and simultaneous shifts in social reactions toward the therapist.

It is not unlikely that such "corrective emotional experiences" take place in situations of every-day living that are not explicitly designed to be therapeutic. It is not unlikely either that many shifts during a political campaign may be due to such experiences. Dr. Alexander's concept could be used to study the dramatic highlights of a campaign, where a part of the total electorate have their expectations rather dramatically raised or dashed. A political candidate, during the course of a campaign, may rise or fall in terms of the expectation system which his followers have of him or which those opposed to him hold. The situation may be brought about deliberately by his party or by an opposing party. It can occur inadvertently. At such dramatic moments of crisis, it would be expected that a higher proportion of the electorate would begin to experience internal stress. During such moments, too, the emotional basis for one's political loyalties may surge to the surface of awareness, producing ripe conditions for a rather full insight into the political self of the individual voter. Depending upon the public resolution of the crisis situation[7] of the political candidate, the insight into the self may go to rather elaborate lengths or severely neurotic defenses may develop instead. Furthermore, the insights may not only pertain to the emotional basis for one's political identifications, but may extend to one's own politically tinged activities in the home, school, church, business, or other community institutions. Similarly, the neurotic defense against growing insight may lead to modifications of one's behavior in community institutions in which one participates and be along the lines of strengthening particular defenses against growing insight. At the simplest level, the manner in which one argues politics in these institutions may shift toward greater intellectual dishonesty, a greater readiness to use arguments (with one's fellows) involving emotional blackmail, and even perhaps toward an increase of masochistic tendencies in political discussions (in which one cannot argue any more for the self). One's own behavior may duplicate, totally unconsciously, the "wrong-doing" with which the political candidate is charged within one's dealings with certain types of people in the community environment; or a noble act of a political candidate may, equally unconsciously, be duplicated in similar ways, although perhaps with different types of "others" in the social environment.

The impact of these dramatic moments of a political campaign upon all of the voting public may be heavy indeed. Studies of the voting public hardly begin to suggest the costs and gains of political struggles among parties and candidates upon all other institutions of the nation through the individual and selective impact they have upon each group of members of the voting public whose emotional basis for commitments and antagonisms is stirred up by the crisis situation. We will begin to realize the potent tool psychoanalytic theory offers for applied social research only when we begin to make "dynamic" studies of this kind, even in a very limited way.[8]

"SELECTIVE INATTENTION" AND POLITICS. There is another contemporary development within psychoanalytic thinking which has some bearing upon the ways in which processes of permanence and change may be studied in relationship to voting practices. It comes from the writings of Harry Stack Sullivan,[9] who is often spoken of as the "American Freud." Sullivan felt less impressed with the repression concept than many other American psychiatrists as he focussed on a phenomenon which he titled "selective inattention." During his many years of observation of patients undergoing psychotherapy, he was impressed instead with the way in which neurotic individuals seemed to learn techniques by which they refused to profit from significant experiences, even when these experiences were repeatedly present in their life histories. Some aspect of their internal and/or external environment went unnoticed in such a singularly predictable fashion that it seemed as though the lack of noticing was almost a form of contempt for some part of the process of living amounting to a kind of planned polity. Yet, what went unnoticed was frequently relevant to the goals which such neurotic individuals pursued, so that the price paid for such selective inattention patterns was a partial or complete failure to gratify the motives and reach outcomes important to the person. It took considerable skill for Sullivan to bring such unnoticed aspects of the experiences of the patient to his full focus of attention, since they were present in the associations of the patient only in very disguised and fragmented forms. The contempt for such unnoticed aspects of experience seems to well from the capacity these aspects of experiences had acquired to arouse intense anxiety, or a threat to the self-esteem of the patient.

Let me give a hypothetical example. Two men develop a professional friendship in which intimate intellectual collaboration is involved. One of the two may have mild psychopathic tendencies covered over by immense skill in performing as a highly moral person. Over the years, it develops that the psychopathic person in the pair repeatedly profits from his association with his partner. He is recommended for special awards and consultancies, for special lectures and for contributions to publications by his professional associate. All the skills of the latter are patiently taught to the former. Yet, puzzlingly enough, while the psychopathic partner of the pair benefits from every professional association of his partner, he in turn finds that hostility or indifference is directed toward him from most significant associations that the psychopathic person develops. Furthermore, the psychopathic partner refuses to communicate or share the special skills he has developed with his associate, giving all sorts of plausible reasons for the one-sided withholding process within the relationship.

Out of this situation the non-psychopathic member develops a growing jealousy of his partner's other associations. Both of them begin to accept and define this jealousy as unreasonable. The more giving member of the pair never links up this sense of jealousy with the pattern of hostility that greets him from most major associations his partner forms. Furthermore, just enough occasions on which his partner strategically utters words of praise for him directly or in the presence of other people make the feelings of suspiciousness that his partner may be creating hostile feelings toward him in the minds of significant others seem almost a trifle paranoid. Yet, there are also small discoveries made now and again during the course of the relationship in which some of the unfavorable things said about him by his partner to others comes to his attention. The strategy of the psychopathic person in the pair remains, however, selectively inattended to by the associate. It may touch, perhaps, too deeply on certain specious ideals by which his own life-history anxieties have been irrealistically mastered. He cannot bring himself to believe he could extend an intimate professional friendship toward anyone who was two-faced and essentially hostile. Every bit of evidence and explanation judiciously fed by the psychopathic member to his associate who maintains a state of selective inattention toward the divide and conquer strategy and damaging impulses in operation in the relationship is quickly used by the associate to buttress the perceptual patterns that maintain the continuance of the relationship. He never "catches on" to the game.

The example serves to point to the essential features of such neurotic patterns that Sullivan had an uncanny ability to depict and describe in devastating detail. First, *the goals of the individual are not being fully realized.* Selective inattention, while it does help to maintain self-esteem, also blocks the gains for which the professional association was formed. Secondly, *there is no learning going on for the person.* The associate does not bring each repeated bit of evidence of the damaging tendencies of his psychopathic partner to bear on the next bit of evidence, so that a repeated pattern in the relationship becomes articulate for him, nor does the associate link up his anxiety over this evidence with past-life experiences in other relationships that have threatened his self-esteem by a recognition of his gullibility to people who enjoy the process of duping.

Sullivan, in his therapeutic practice, centered his attention, therefore, upon these selective inattentive patterns among his patients, and tried to modify them through his particular therapeutic practices.[10] A point of his, especially useful for application to studies of voting patterns, was the constant attempt to keep the self-esteem of the patient fairly high (and anxiety low) throughout therapy because he felt that, *when the patient felt secure, the selective inattention patterns would become more obvious.* Sullivan considered, therefore, the ability to make others feel comfortable, esteemed, respected and so on a primary skill of all therapeutic activity. Without that skill, a therapist, no matter how intellectually agile and intuitive, no matter how highly developed his "third ear," could not really assist the patient toward any greater personality integration of social realities. The patient's fantasies could perhaps be substituted for the realities, and the neurosis strengthened or modified so the person could "get by" with selective inattention more skillfully, and sometimes more aggressively (with lesser pain for the self, but greater pain for others exposed to the patient's "autistic" maneuvers or vice versa) but it would still be there.[11]

The concept of "selective inattention," it will perhaps be noticed, is a way of dealing with the somewhat 19th-Centuryish concept of "irrationality." I have, in other context, defined "irrationality" as an inability to continue to learn how to actualize one's values in better and better ways. By better, I mean, of course, *more skillful*, but in addition, there is the factor of doing so *without damaging others or the self for the continuing growth and development of all.* The person who selectively inattends behaves irrationally, in the two senses in which I am using that term. Depending upon how limited in scope or how extensive the inattention may be, the irrationality can become fairly damaging to those who become integrated into social networks of relationships and exposed to it. In a sense, then, irrationality is bound to be incompatible with democratic conditions, since *autocratic contempt* for some of the factors involved in an interpersonal situation are part and parcel of the maintenance of it.[12]

One need only glance at the chapter on social perception in the Elmira study conducted by the Columbia researchers, or at any chapter of the Michigan study on the Eisenhower-Stevenson elections, to see at once how much selective perception goes on during a political campaign. A position is frequently ascribed to a party or candidate, with whom a voter is identified, which is not the true position of that party or candidate. The position of an opposing party may be severely distorted. The inconsistencies among the leaders of a party may be glossed over so that it appears that all of the leaders share a common position. It takes but a brief review of the voting findings, therefore, to surmise that Sullivan's "selective inattention" concept—and his explanations of how that phenomenon comes to exist and how it can be modified—has an enormous potential for understanding the principles of permanence and change underlying voting processes.[13]

There is some tendency in our American society to look upon people in power, or people who attempt to occupy positions of power, as people with evil, non-democratic intentions. The idea that power ennobles—i.e., brings out the best aspects of the personality of all involved in the power situation—has seldom been scrutinized for the conditions under which it might hypothetically and actually be a fair statement to make about events. We are much more willing to believe that power corrupts, and absolute power corrupts absolutely. Yet, such an outlook may affect the very situation it is meant to protect the self against. The science of electioneering could perhaps take on an added dignity by suffusing into it some of the study of the same basic principles which govern the science of psychotherapy. There is no reason why a candidate and his party should not function, in a democratic society, in a way calculated to reduce the selective inattention to issues among its supporters as well as among its non-supporters. Of course, a candidate is always "ego-involved" in an election, but so, too, is a therapist emotionally invested in the treatment of a patient. The idea that a therapist remains "a blank screen" is often a bit of propaganda which therapists circulate among themselves, and their patients and the public to raise their own morale—often containing, furthermore, a high amount of selective inattention. *Yet, it is the therapist's very subjectivity*, as Theodor Reik attempted to document in his not altogether well-defined concept of "the third ear"[14] *which often is most useful to the patient and to therapeutic activity.* Sullivan referred to this "subjectivity" with the term "participant observation." The impact upon the therapist, brought about by the patient's unwitting activities, *is quite like that upon any other person in the patient's environment*—with the exception that the therapist is skilled at recognizing the impact, the sources of its occurrence, the purposes behind it, and the possibility of maximizing the capacities of the patient to recognize it in source and outcome and to modify it when it violates the patient's, therapist's or society's basic values.

In short, then, what I want to emphasize is that a political candidate in American society stands upon a platform of *common democratic aims* with an opposing candidate. Yet, as long as that candidate reinforces selective inattention among his supporters or non-supporters, he *undermines democracy*. A political candidate can learn techniques for the science of electioneering which will reduce patterns of inattention among his supporters or non-supporters, and he can learn a good many of them from the skilled psychotherapist. In doing so, he is creatively engaged in discovering ingenious democratic practices.[15]

There is, of course, the matter of "resistance." Democracy is often made synonymous with letting people raise their hands and voices and check names on a ballot. Yet, when people ballot without thinking about issues and the records of candidates first, we are reminded of the spectacle of hand-raising in totalitarian countries that make hollow mockeries of balloting practices. I think, in this connection, of progressive education which often converted "permissiveness" into a total disregard of the responsibility of presenting immature minds with the *opposing* facts and views, and other alternatives, to their already formed interests, beliefs, and attitudes. Education tended to pander to ignorance rather than service democracy, since selective inattention processes were reinforced by an often mistaken policy of neglect which used the high-sounding slogan of "permissiveness." A somewhat similar view of politics is often articulated; politicians are seen as engaged in pandering to parochial pressure groups and small-minded interest groups with narrow investments. (Politics as a "give-away" show.) The electorate is not looked upon as an audience whose selective inattention processes can be changed. (Professor Lazarsfeld's collaborative studies on "cross-pressure" show how much *they can be changed* in every-day conversation, although his analysis is not quite as deep as that which is needed.[16] Yet, a high regard for democracy depends upon the use of campaigns for (a) educating this public and (b) the handling of "resistances" which appear as selective inattention patterns among the voters. Political leaders have not expended half the ingenuity they might toward weakening selective inattention patterns among their supporters or nonsupporters as they have upon strengthening and using these selective inattention factors.[17]

There is, however, another issue pertinent to studies of selective inattention processes occurring during elections, both *among* the electorate as well as *through* campaign activities. Americans have acquired a notorious reputation for their formidable ability to store up great masses of facts within themselves about anything that interests them deeply. Yet, one often hears that a political campaign must recognize the "realities" which turn out to be that people cannot keep "all the political facts" in mind and think on anything but the most primitive levels. Selective inattention is, therefore, something that cannot be eradicated from political campaign policies nor from the people according to those who hold this view. There are, of course, powerful arguments for this position.

One way of discussing it is to look at the same issue when it concerns psychotherapy. A staggering amount of communication goes on between a patient and therapist during a psychoanalysis. Yet, part of communication theory tells us that it is humanly impossible to store up all the information that one receives. There is always "loss." And since there is loss, presumably because of the limited "receiving" properties of the human organism and the way it is structured, there is thus the continued possibility for selective inattention. Selective inattention becomes a *necessary* part of all human communication.

On the other hand, Freud has repeatedly shown us that what we forget, don't listen to, hear incorrectly, etc. is determined by our emotional conflicts. Forgetting is motivated. Distortions are in the service of neurotic defenses. Certain patterns of deafness are unconsciously set in motion through hysterical personality organization. Any psychoanalyst can give you a good dozen detailed examples of complex motivational factors behind the loss of information. Thus, selective inattention is bound to be due to the contemptuous censorship or "repression" of part of the processes of life, whether sexual, or political, or what not.[18]

At the present time, communication theory is still not well enough developed to allow us to settle questions of this sort. It would not be too optimistic to expect that gradually there will be found techniques of thinking about events in which the limited human capacity to absorb information is reconciled with the need to avoid selective inattention. The kind of "map" one has of one's social environment may make it more humanly possible to absorb more information than was hitherto thought possible, or at least, if the "map" is comprehensive enough, it may assist the thinker to not neglect huge areas of information toward which selective inattention might otherwise operate. At present, the theory of cognitive processes is an area of behavioral science which is just beginning to develop in America after a long period in which it was wrongly felt to be incompatible with our predominant behavioristic approach toward psychological problems.[19] One is reminded of the great contribution Freud made in this regard. He demonstrated empirically how huge reservoirs of information are stored in "the unconscious" and can be brought to awareness when conditions are appropriate. He says, in essence, that *most* information is *never* irretrievably lost.

Pessimism, then, about the potential of the electorate to receive a full array of the relevant information regarding political campaigns may be more defensive than is necessary. When interested, Americans do store up mountains of information in any area of concern. (And the voting studies show the large-scale apathy among the electorate, which is perhaps a more important limiting condition than the capacity to absorb facts, one much more amenable to change, and one coming out of the "boredom" induced by politicians who do not believe in the ability of the electorate to be influenced by anything other than Madison Avenue techniques of suasion.) Secondly, we have not been as inventive about teaching people how to think as we could be and as our age requires as all institutions and decisions grow infinitely more complex than they once were. We have not yet taught people how to rise to the occasion of a movement toward a "mass society" by offering them appropriate new cognitive tools.[20]

A more specific application of the concept of "selective inattention" may be useful to introduce at this point in this discussion. Sullivan felt that, as the individual's security was increased, his selective inattention systems became more obvious to an observer if he is skilled at recognizing them. The implication for the study of political campaigns is rather striking. The prediction would be that, as the followers and leaders of a political party began to feel more certain of their acceptance and election by the majority of voters (and the "polls" often function to both stir up and allay political anxiety about victory so that they might be used as an objective index), the party members would begin to manifest *more obviously* those parts of the political issues to which they are not predisposed to pay attention because of the arousal of anxiety if they did. One thinks, immediately, of the enormous confidence Thomas Dewey and his followers had in his election. The sudden swing away from Dewey during the campaign of the late forties has never been fully explained by a penetrating analysis. The selective inattention concept provides a way of conducting such a depth analysis of an especially puzzling campaign. But it can be utilized for both sides of any political campaign during various stages of the campaign in which there is movement toward greater self-confidence in acceptance by the majority of voters.[21] As that self-confidence intensifies and reaches the required level of assurance, one would begin to see manifested more obviously, other things being equal, those parts of the election issues which had hitherto been selectively inattended to by the party members and leaders. Of course, "rationalizations" will also appear as to why they are of no importance, but at least *signs of awareness* of issues embarrassing to the party will begin to become publicly demonstrable, allowing one to understand how the processes of selective inattention follow the same laws in political campaigns as they do during the course of psychotherapy. Research study could follow the course of attention to issues as a function of the relative security of the political participants, in which especial attention may be paid to whether these were first introduced by the opposing party at very distant points in time to their eventual public discussion or whether as an immediate dramatic "challenge" to a party membership becoming too secure in the public's affections.

SOME CONCLUDING CONSIDERATIONS. Two parallel processes occurring during electioneering and psychotherapy have been briefly sketched for possible research study. There are hundreds of others that might have been chosen. There are, furthermore, internal controversies, still unresolved, within psychoanalytic theories of therapy, regarding which of a variety of "models" (a) most adequately describes how psychoanalytic cures actually occur in practice and (b) whether the "shifts" in personality produced by a therapist working in terms of one therapeutic model rather than another may result in different types and areas of personality modification with different degrees of stability afterwards. One doesn't need to look at recent developments within psychoanalytic practices, but when surveying the first generation of psychoanalytic thinking, one finds highly developed differences in the thinking of Rank, Ferenczi, Adler, Jung, and Rado[22] regarding how psychoanalytic types of theories can best be applied to personality difficulties. Scientific issues involved in this controversy may just as easily be studied simultaneously in research on political processes as in research on psychotherapy directly.

As a matter of fact, one could schematize the issues involved in these diverse views of psychotherapeutic processes *in political terms.* Does the practitioner adhering to one therapeutic model, the "active" therapy of Ferenczi perhaps, exert *more power* over the patient than the practitioner adhering to more classical conceptions? Is power over the patient exercised *more subtly* by the therapist predisposed toward silence than the wildly intuitive therapist who verbalizes "insights" on slim evidence and without waiting for insight to first develop from within the patient? The translation of existing models of therapy into political terms is in no sense a purely academic exercise.[23] For the psychotherapist can be quite reasonably seen as having the goal of *trying to exercise power for the recognition and examination of unconscious impulses which have been kept political prisoners without adequate trial by jury*. There is, too, a kind of "political education" occurring in psychotherapy, for much of it consists in trying to make the patient become a more effective person socially in getting what he wants from life. The therapist who encourages sadistic and masochistic "acting out" is encouraging power techniques discerningly different from the therapist who inculcates the idea that needs should be socially satisfied only in terms of recognizing the needs of others with whom one is socially integrated rather than wholly imposing oneself upon the environment. One often hears among psychotherapists and their patients the expression: "It's *his* problem!" The expression is used frequently as a defense against "social feeling" and an encouragement of a false sense of "insularity" toward another with whom one is socially integrated and whose states of emotions ordinarily impinge on the self. But the expression is used for many other purposes by different therapists and patients undergoing a socio-political education in the process of realizing their demands upon the environment, and it is used many times inconsistently with several meanings. A fuller awareness of the fact that political education in a functional sense (ways of exercising power) occurs within psychotherapy would help to clarify and sharpen therapeutic practices involving the integration of the patient's needs with those of the environment. The testing of hypotheses regarding processes of permanence and change (formulated with respect to psychotherapy) within an actual political context like voting, might help, not only to clarify electioneering practices, but also to clarify psychotherapeutic ones.[24] Furthermore, the prevailing pessimism about inducing processes of change toward greater and more effective democratic relationships might be confronted with realistic grounds for optimism by such an interchange in studies of electioneering and psychotherapy. There is bound to be, and has been, a growing modification of psychoanalytic practices by new knowledge about techniques coming from the social sciences. (Think of the great modifications occurring in the interpretation of dreams as we learn more about personality functioning during exposure to the fantasies of the mass-media). The psychotherapist increasingly needs to be an expert on value maladies in the culture as well as upon effective techniques by which a patient's values may be effectively attained within the culture in which the patient and therapist must operate.

The testing and use of therapeutic principles regarding permanence and change within political campaigns, however, must always proceed with a certain amount of concern with the differences in context. Many times, voting studies are concerned with mass psychology and the group as a unit. In this connection, the great innovation for those with such interests is the development of group psychotherapy, which may well be a rather crucial intermediate area in which advance will be made toward the full application of psychoanalytic knowledge to institutional patterns and practices. Many traditional concepts, never under question within the practice of individual psychotherapy, have been undergoing rather extensive modifications as psychoanalysts begin to engage in the practice of group psychotherapy. The careful description of the modifications in behavior and thought of the psychoanalyst who practices individual psychotherapy as he moves into group psychotherapy would be an invaluable addition to our knowledge of influence and decision processes. We need also to carefully describe the activities of the patient who moves from one type of psychotherapy into the other type, or who engages in both simultaneously. The trend toward group psychotherapy is part of the trend toward applied psychoanalysis in the social sciences.[25]

Psychoanalysis rests upon the idea of giving the censored, the weak, the contemptible aspects of the personality greater respect and a just hearing. It, thus, in its way, embodies the idea of "a free forum" in which the self-images of the participants are challenged and tested against one another. Ideally, psychoanalytic practices thus are fully consonant with democratic principles. Yet, there are those who fear the full application of psychoanalytic principles to the analysis and operation of institutions. There is the growing fear of "the manipulator." But, psychoanalysis is itself concerned with this problem, and Freud himself first pin-pointed the issue in his concept of "counter-transference." There is, at present, no one therapeutic issue which more concerns psychoanalytic practitioners than the inadvertent way in which the analyst may exploit "the free forum" for non-democratic purposes (to impose his image of the self and the world, and his values about them, upon the patient without a maximum participation of the patient, and the therapist's unwillingness to give the perspectives of the patient a full, rational examination to a point where he will alter his own views). There is, thus, within psychoanalysis, some principles governing processes of "manipulation" or "counter-transference" which themselves can be applied to the study of political campaigns and which serve to check and balance the exploitation of psychoanalytic principles regarding permanence and change for non-democratic purposes.[26]

Briefly summarizing, this essay has attempted to suggest how processes of permanence and change might be investigated within political campaigns by transferring some useful concepts relating to such processes that have been formulated with respect to psychotherapy. Electioneering and psychotherapy are both viewed as social engineering sciences for which adequate principles of permanence and change are a cornerstone. Since they are both social engineering sciences, too, there is bound to be a sharpening of research study in both areas of concern by testing principles arising within one context within the other. Although no specific research designs are proposed, there is implicit, throughout the discussion, many hypotheses which all lend themselves to conventional testing methods developed within the social sciences. The essay is, however, mostly meant to be programmatic, outlining by general example a type of interaction between social scientists interested in both electioneering and psychotherapeutic practices and policies which has fruitful possibilities for the future development of sounder philosophies of permanence and change.

Notes and References

NOTES TO CHAPTER 1

1. The preparation of this chapter was supported in part by a grant from the Social Science Research Committee of the University of Chicago, whose assistance is gratefully acknowledged.

2. Historical and bibliographical accounts are contained in: S. M. Lipset, "Political Sociology: 1945-1955," in Hans Zetterberg (ed.), *Sociology in the United States of America* (Paris: UNESCO, 1956); G. Dupeux, "Electoral Behaviour," *Current Sociology*, (1954-55), 318-44; and S. M. Lipset and Others, "The Psychology of Voting," in Gardner Lindzey (ed.), *Handbook of Social Psychology* (2 vols.; Reading, Mass.: Addison-Wesley, 1954).

3. S. A. Rice, *Quantitative Methods in Politics* (New York: Knopf, 1928).

4. P. F. Lazarsfeld, B. R. Berelson, and Hazel Gaudet, *The People's Choice* (2d ed.; New York: Columbia University Press, 1948). All references in this chapter are to the second edition.

5. B. R. Berelson, P. F. Lazarsfeld, and W. N. McPhee, *Voting* (Chicago: University of Chicago Press, 1954).

6. Angus Campbell, Gerald Gurin, and W. E. Miller, *The Voter Decides* (Evanston, Ill.: Row, Peterson, 1954).

7. S. A. Rice, *Farmers and Workers in American Politics* (New York: Columbia University Press, 1924); W. F. Ogburn and Delvin Peterson, "Political Thought of Social Classes," *Political Science Quarterly*, XXXI (1916), 300-17; and W. F. Ogburn and Inez Goltra, "How Women Vote," *ibid.*, XXXIV (1919), 413-33.

8. It is interesting to note that more recent monographs employing the same approach no longer require such an extensive argument for the utility of an empirical political science. See, for example, V. O. Key, Jr., *Southern Politics* (New York: Knopf, 1949).

9. In a personal communication, Dr. Rice indicates that his excursion into the quantitative study of politics was sparked by Giddings' suggestion that he attempt to understand the failure of the farmer-labor movement, in which Rice had once been very active, by undertaking research on voting statistics. The attention given his *Farmers and Workers in American Politics* led a publisher to suggest that he write a book illustrating how the method could be applied to research on a variety of political problems. Hence *Quantitative Methods in Politics!* Dr. Rice further states that this book was written quickly, in the space of three weeks, by weaving together the substance of previously published articles with research that he had ready to be published.

10. This gap in treatment of the history of voting behavior research is certainly a glaring deficiency in coverage. Any complete coverage would necessarily have to consider the notable contributions of such work to our understanding of voting behavior. My only excuse for the partial coverage offered is to characterize this chapter as an attempt to cover a particular type of tradition.

11. An example characteristic of the period is the classic article by Louis L. Thurstone, "Attitudes Can Be Measured," *American Journal of Sociology*, XXXIII (1928), 529-54, published while Rice was writing *Quantitative Methods in Politics.*

12. The first assessment of the possibilities of this technique was made by Claude Robinson in his doctoral dissertation, *Straw Votes* (New York: Columbia University Press, 1932).

13. Compare, for example, the treat-

ment of this field in Gardner and Lois Murphy's *Experimental Social Psychology* (New York: Harper, 1931) with the second edition published in 1937 (in collaboration with T. M. Newcomb).

14. In the third edition of *Politics, Parties, and Pressure Groups* (New York: Crowell, 1952), p. 565, V. O. Key, Jr., finds that voting behavior is still a poorly studied phenomenon. He states: "A striking characteristic of the study of politics in the United States is the relatively small amount of effort devoted to the careful analysis of voting behavior. . . ."

15. Rice, *Quantitative Methods in Politics*, pp. 318-19.

16. The information contained in this section was obtained from personal interviews with Dr. Lazarsfeld, the senior author.

17. P. F. Lazarsfeld, *Jugend und Beruf* (Jena: G. Fischer, 1931).

18. Panel studies of consumer purchases had been conducted before this time. However, the research organizations involved primarily employed the panel because of its lower costs compared to repeated surveys with different samples. As is true nowadays, they did not take advantage of its strategic ability to measure change.

19. A point which is not mentioned in the final report.

20. In an interview, Dr. Lazarsfeld stated that the analysis of the Erie County data was once laid aside for a year because of the disappointment of the analysts with their first excursions into tabulations.

21. Although the importance of religion as a point of cleavage in the electorate was known by those close to the practice of politics, the high correlation between religious preference and socioeconomic status led some to consider the relationship largely a reflection of the latter. Dr. Lazarsfeld related that George Gallup expressed disbelief when he told him of his finding that this factor was independently related to voting behavior. Gallup later was able to verify this finding by reanalyzing some of his earlier polls. Rice also mentions (*op. cit.*) that political journalists give great weight to religion and ethnicity, but related to me that he suspected that when socioeconomic status was held constant religious preference would wash out. The role of religion as a point of cleavage in the American electorate is still novel enough to account for much of the popularity of the analysis of American politics by S. A. Lubell, *op. cit.*

22. See H. H. Hyman, *Survey Design and Analysis* (Glencoe, Ill.: The Free Press, 1955).

23. V. O. Key, Jr., using the same kinds of data in his *Southern Politics*, was confronted with the same sort of limitation on his analysis. While he was able to give adequate analysis to the rural areas of the South, his treatment of urban areas, with their greater class differentiation, has been less definitive.

24. It should be noted that, before the publication of *The People's Choice*, T. M. Newcomb's *Personality and Social Change* (New York: The Dryden Press, 1943) had reported on an elaborate panel study of the formation of political attitudes among Bennington College students extending over several years. Lazarsfeld and his associates were not aware, however, of Newcomb's work.

25. The name Office of Radio Research was later changed to Bureau of Applied Social Research, a change signifying corresponding shifts in emphasis and closer attention to more basic research interests.

26. See, for example, the three volumes of collected research papers published by the Office of Radio Research: P. F. Lazarsfeld (ed.), *Radio and the Printed Page* (New York: Duell, Sloan & Pearce, 1940); P. F. Lazarsfeld and F. N. Stanton (eds.), *Radio Research*, 1941 (Duell . . ., 1941);

and, by the same editors, *Radio Research, 1942-43* (Duell . . ., 1944).

27. These instructions have recently been published for the first time. See Hazel Gaudet, "A Model for Assessing Changes in Voting Intention," in P. F. Lazarsfeld and Morris Rosenberg (eds.), *The Language of Social Research* (Glencoe, Ill.: The Free Press, 1955).

28. The type of analysis envisaged here is shown in Chapter 12 of *Voting* in the analysis of the mutual interaction between the image of Truman and the salience of class issues over the period June to October, 1948.

29. Some of the background information on *The Voter Decides* is based on a short personal interview with Angus Campbell. Unfortunately, because of the pressure of time, it was not possible to obtain as detailed an account as might be desired.

30. See, for example, the statement by Rensis Likert, "The Sample Interview Survey as a Tool of Research," in Daniel Lerner and H. D. Lasswell (eds.), *The Policy Sciences* (Stanford, Calif.: Stanford University Press, 1951).

31. Angus Campbell and R. L. Kahn, *The People Elect a President* (Ann Arbor, Mich.: Survey Research Center, 1952); and Frederick Mosteller and Others, *The Pre-Election Polls of 1948* (New York: Social Science Research Council, 1949).

32. It will be found almost universally that attitudes of this sort will predict behavior better than any other variables. Thus, if one were interested in predicting how many families were going to move over a short-term period, the best predictor would be their intentions concerning moving; next best would be their satisfaction with their present dwellings; and least predictive would be some measure of the amount of space and facilities within their present dwellings, taken in conjunction with the housing needs generated by family composition. This occurs because these variables have an implicit time relationship. Family composition generates certain housing needs which are either met or not met by the dwelling unit. Dissatisfaction results in the latter contingency, ordinarily leading to an intention to move. Intentions are closest in time to the behavior and hence most closely predictive of moving. See P. H. Rossi, *Why Families Move* (Glencoe, Ill.: The Free Press, 1956).

33. Angus Campbell and D. E. Stokes have undertaken an analysis of the different patterns of motivation in various subgroups of the population. See Chapter 19 below.

34. The term "factorial" has been borrowed from the agricultural experimental designs employed to test the effects of simultaneously varied sets of variables.

35. Elihu Katz and P. F. Lazarsfeld, *Personal Influence* (Glencoe, Ill.: The Free Press, 1955).

36. Several studies, not considered here, have actually employed similar designs: T. M. Newcomb's classic study at Bennington College (*op. cit.*) followed a class of students throughout their college career, examining changes in political attitudes. A study of married students in a housing project (Leon Festinger, Stanley Schacter, and Kurt Back, *Social Pressures in Informal Groups* [New York: Harper, 1950]) related friendship patterning to consensus on opinions and the flow of rumors.

NOTES TO CHAPTER 2

1. R. E. Horton, R. E. Mainer, and H. H. Remmers, "Youth and the 1952 Election," *Purdue Opinion Panel Report*, No. 33, Jan., 1953.

2. P. F. Lazarsfeld, B. R. Berelson, and Hazel Gaudet, *The People's Choice* (2d ed.; New York: Columbia University Press, 1948).

3. *Ibid.*, p. 141.
4. *Ibid.*, p. 141.
5. *Ibid.*, p. 143.
6. *Ibid.*, p. 142.
7. The fact that the results from our teen-age sample predicted the Eisenhower popular vote more accurately than did the results of polling agencies —Gallup, Roper, Crosley, etc.—polling adults leads me to an interesting speculation. The climate of opinion of McCarthyism prevalent at the time may, in considerable part at least, have been responsible for the difference in accuracy. Adults may have been more wary in revealing their political ideology, particularly if they were Democrats (consider the slogan "twenty years of treason" and the application of the concepts of guilt by association and kinship), than were the teen-agers in a completely anonymous school situation in which they were certain that no one who could identify them with their opinions would see the results.
8. See T. D. Peterson, "The Relationship Between Certain Attitudes of Parents and Children," *Further Studies in Attitudes, Series II* ("Studies in Higher Education," Vol. XXXI, No. 4; Lafayette, Ind.: Purdue University, 1936), pp. 127-44; and H. H. Remmers and L. D. Whisler, *Further Studies in Attitudes, Series III* (*ibid.*, Vol. XXXIV; 1938), pp. 114-25.
9. Naomi Weltman and H. H. Remmers, "Pupils', Parents', and Teachers' Attitudes – Similarities and Differences," *Further Studies in Attitudes, Series IX* (*ibid.*, Vol. LVI; 1946), pp. 1-52.
10. "What the U. S. Thinks about Its Schools," *Life*, Oct. 16, 1950, pp. 11-12.
11. H. H. Remmers, A. J. Drucker, and R. B. Kirk, "Youth Looks Toward the Future of Education," *Purdue Opinion Panel Report*, No. 29, May, 1951.
12. R. B. Kirk, "American High School Students Evaluate Their Public School System," *Further Studies in Attitudes, Series XIX* ("Studies in Higher Education," Vol. LXXXI; Lafayette, Ind.: Purdue University, 1953), p. 35.
13. Robert Louis Stevenson, "Crabbed Age and Youth," *Virginibus Puerisque* (Everyman's Library; London: Dent, 1925), p. 38.
14. M. S. Myers, "The Latent Role of Religious Orientation," *Further Studies in Attitudes, Series XIX* ("Studies in Higher Education," Vol. LXXVIII; Lafayette, Ind.: Purdue University, 1951), pp. 61-94. See also H. H. Remmers and Others, "Some Personality Aspects and Religious Values of High School Youth," *Purdue Opinion Panel Report*, No. 28, March, 1951.
15. Louis Guttman, "The Cornell Technique for Scale and Intensity Analysis," *Educational and Psychological Measurement*, VII (1947), 247-79.
16. Myers, *op. cit.*, p. 91.
17. A. J. Drucker and H. H. Remmers, "Citizenship Attitudes of Graduated Seniors at Purdue University, U. S. College Graduates, and High School Pupils," *Journal of Educational Psychology*, XLII (1951), 231-35. See also H. H. Remmers, A. J. Drucker, and Ben Shimberg, "The Citizenship Attitudes of High School Youth," *Purdue Opinion Panel Report*, No. 22, May, 1949.
18. C. R. Pace, "What Kind of Citizens Have Our College Graduates Become?" *Journal of General Education*, III (1949), 197-202.
19. *Ibid.*, p. 202.
20. Drucker and Remmers, *op. cit.*
21. *Life*, *op. cit.*
22. R. E. Mainer, *Attitude Change in Intergroup Education Programs* ("Studies in Higher Education," Vol. LXXXIII; Lafayette, Ind.: Purdue University, 1954), pp. 40-41.
23. H. H. Remmers, R. E. Horton, and Sverre Lysgaard, "Teen-age Personality in Our Culture," *Purdue Opinion Panel Report*, No. 32, May, 1952.

REFERENCES TO CHAPTER 3

1. Anderson, T. W. "Probability Models for Analyzing Time Changes in Attitudes," in P. F. Lazarsfeld (ed.), *Mathematical Thinking in the Social Sciences*. Glencoe, Ill.: The Free Press, 1954.

2. Berelson, B. R., P. F. Lazarsfeld, and W. N. McPhee, *Voting*. Chicago: University of Chicago Press, 1954.

3. Hovland, C. I., A. A. Lumsdaine, and F. D. Sheffield. *Experiments on Mass Communication*. Princeton: Princeton University Press, 1949.

4. Kendall, Patricia. *Conflict and Mood*. Glencoe, Ill.: The Free Press, 1954.

5. Maccoby, Eleanor E. "Pitfalls in the Analysis of Panel Data: A Research Note on Some Technical Aspects of *Voting*," *American Journal of Sociology*, LXI (1956), 359-62.

NOTES TO CHAPTER 4

1. I am indebted to Samuel A. Stouffer, John W. and Matilda Riley, and Charles Drekmeier for a number of stimulating suggestions.

2. B. R. Berelson, P. F. Lazarsfeld, and W. N. McPhee, *Voting* (Chicago: University of Chicago Press, 1954).

3. The concept of the economy used here is fully discussed in Talcott Parsons and N. J. Smelser, *Economy and Society* (Glencoe, Ill.: The Free Press, 1956). The parallel concept of the polity has not previously been discussed in print, except sketchily in the above publication. Unfortunately limitations of space make it impossible to present it here, also, except in very sketchy form. A brief discussion of these and related concepts in formal theoretical terms appears in the Technical Note appended to this chapter.

4. The reader will note that these are the variables introduced above.

5. The paradigm for this boundary-interchange of the economy (with the household in the empirically primary case) is set forth in Parsons and Smelser, *op. cit.*, chap. 2. Cf. especially fig. 5, p. 11. A simplified version of the general interchange paradigm is presented in the Technical Note.

6. In technical analytical terms I conceive the public in this sense as an aspect of the integrative subsystem of the society. See Parsons and Smelser, *op. cit.*, pp. 51-70 and fig. 4, p. 68.

7. There is not, of course, at any given time a wide range of alternatives, but if the analysis of the direction of party orientation given later in this chapter is correct, it is highly important, and a wide range would be incompatible with effective political integration.

8. This is by no means to say either that "business" has taken a consistently laissez-faire attitude—on many occasions it has sought help from government. But clearly the *main* trend is the one stated.

9. This is a type of intervention characteristic of the right. Cf. footnote 41 below.

10. Of course realistically neither the worker nor the voter *could* be self-sufficient. The argument is analytical, not a discussion of concrete alternatives.

11. The necessity for the operation of nonrational mechanisms may be further illustrated as follows: I have emphasized that the focusing of the decision of the electorate on two candidates forces a very high level of the generalization of support. A voter cannot, in effect, decide on highly concrete grounds, using his vote as a specific means to a specific end. However important such specific considerations may be for a given voter, the *effect* of his vote must be to contribute to the pool of general support for the candidate and party, and he cannot fail to be aware that on some level he is thrown, with respect to this pool, together with strange bedfellows who

have quite different specific ends in view than his.

At the same time, to judge rationally in terms of the welfare of the country" is an intellectual task of a very high level of complexity and difficulty. Since even the most competent technical experts in such matters, political and social scientists, are far from being agreed on the better direction in a given case, how can the average voter have a competent and well-grounded opinion? This is a classic type of situation in which nonrational psychological mechanisms can be expected to operate. The voter is faced with problems to which a rational solution in the usual sense is impossible; he must fall back on mechanisms that are psychologically possible for him. But at the same time there must be some type of regulation of these mechanisms lest voters' behavior prove to be too unsettling to the society.

12. Berelson, Lazarsfeld, and McPhee, *op. cit.*, chap. 1, especially propositions stated on pp. 33-34.

13. *Ibid.*, p. 33, proposition 6.

14. *Ibid.*, pp. 148-49.

15. *Ibid.*, pp. 27, 34.

16. *Ibid.*, chap., 6, especially p. 116.

17. Some technical aspects of this deduction are discussed in the Technical Note.

18. Berelson, Lazarfeld, and McPhee, *op. cit.*, p. 33.

19. Clear insight into this problem is shown by Berelson, Lazarsfeld, and McPhee, *op. cit.*, chap. 4, with special reference to the functioning of position.

20. *Ibid.*, pp. 184-85.

21. It is interesting to note the systematic attempts of totalitarian governments to destroy the solidary groupings that mediate between individual and state.

22. There is a possible confusion in classifying religion as a "style" issue, if the distinction between it and position issues is meant to be more than a rather *ad hoc* empirical one. Religious groups constitute bases of solidarity just as do "economic" or local groups. They can become, especially in a system of denominational pluralism like the American, the focus of highly specific position issues. But for reasons having to do with the integration of the society, there are strong pressures against making religion an *explicit* focus of political controversy. It hence tends to become one of the things nearly everyone is "in favor of" with careful avoidance of mentioning the differences of interest between different denominational groups.

23. Berelson, Lazarsfeld, and McPhee, *op. cit.*, especially chap. 9, summarized on p. 212.

24. *Ibid.*, chap. 4.

25. Cf. especially P. F. Lazarsfeld, B. R. Berelson, and Hazel Gaudet, *The People's Choice* (2d ed.; New York: Columbia University Press, 1948), Introduction.

26. Berelson, Lazarsfeld, and McPhee, *op. cit.*, pp. 262-72, in connection with the "Fair Deal Rally."

27. This problem is discussed at greater length in the two essays on naziism in Talcott Parsons, *Essays in Sociological Theory* (2d ed.; Glencoe, Ill.: The Free Press, 1954).

28. These terms were used by Emile Durkheim in *Suicide* (Glencoe, Ill.: The Free Press, 1951), but can be generalized to include modes of reaction to strain in other fields. A third type of response illustrated by Eisenhower's special popularity will be commented on briefly later in this chapter.

29. Berelson, Lazarsfeld, and McPhee, *op. cit.*, pp. 116-17.

30. See Talcott Parsons, "McCarthyism and American Social Tensions," *Yale Review*, Winter, 1955. Reprinted under the title "Social Strains in America," chap. 5, in Daniel Bell (ed.), *The New American Right* (New York: Criterion Books, 1955). See also the other essays in that volume.

31. This and other cross-pressure situations are discussed in S. A. Lubell,

The Future of American Politics (New York: Harper, 1952).

32. See S. A. Stouffer, *Communism, Conformity, and Civil Liberties* (New York: Doubleday, 1955) for some evidence on these points. See also Bell, *op. cit.*

33. On the historical and analytical associations of McCarthyism and Populism, see E. A. Shils, *The Torment of Secrecy* (Glencoe, Ill.: The Free Press, 1956).

34. Three types of evidence may be cited in favor of this interpretation. The first is the unusual amount of ballot-splitting of 1956 which led to the selection of a slightly Democratic Congress in the same election that produced a Republican landslide for the presidency. This strongly suggests that it is not conservatism in the party sense which alone accounts for the result. The second point is the unusual margin by which the vote of the sexes differed; when other factors are held constant, there was something like a 5 per cent excess of women's votes for Eisenhower. Generally speaking, political attitudes of women tend to be more conservative than those of men, for good sociological reasons. [See S. A. Stouffer, *op. cit.*, for evidence that women's attitudes toward radicalism or nonconformity are markedly more conservative than are those of men.] But the difference was, particularly in the second Eisenhower election, substantially greater than normal. Finally, the third bit of evidence is the magnitude of the shift to Eisenhower occasioned by the international crises over Egypt and Hungary. It is authoritatively estimated that about 5 per cent of Eisenhower's vote was attributable to this shift. Hence if the international situation had been calm and if women had divided in the same ratio as men, there is a probability that Stevenson would have been elected by a small margin.

The Republican slogan of "Peace and Prosperity" expresses well the basis of the Eisenhower appeal. [In Durkheim's terms this may be said to be an "altruistic" pattern of response; a flight into identification with a national symbol relatively independent of party.] It seems to rest above all in a need to find a base of security through national solidarity in a world felt to be full of uncertainties and threats. There seems to have been a general feeling that with "Ike" in the White House things would be safer than otherwise.

35. Berelson, Lazarsfeld, and McPhee, *op. cit.*, pp. 34, 252. By political is clearly meant party bases.

36. *Ibid.*, p. 117.

37. *Ibid.*, pp. 116-17.

38. *Ibid.*, p. 251. The studies point out that the mass media are not as directly influential in getting the voter to change his political allegiance as is commonly supposed. Voters generally select campaign materials to confirm the position they hold regarding candidates and issues.

39. This is in accord with the theory of the junction of ritual advanced by Emile Durkheim in *The Elementary Forms of the Religious Life* (Glencoe, Ill.: The Free Press, 1947).

40. Berelson, Lazarsfeld, and McPhee, *op. cit.*, pp. 129, 251.

41. This seems to be the most reasonable interpretation of the British-French intervention in Egypt in the fall of 1956 and indeed also, in one aspect at least, of the Soviet intervention in Hungary.

42. Berelson, Lazarsfeld, and McPhee, *op. cit.*, p. 87.

43. *Ibid.*, pp. 206-12.

44. The "gateway" theory thus, rightly in my opinion, throws strong doubt on the depth of the wisdom of the anonymous Republican pundit of early 1954 who is reported as having said, "We could stay in office indefinitely just by running against Joe Stalin and Dean Acheson."

45. Cf. Berelson, Lazarsfeld, and McPhee, *op. cit.*, pp. 207-9.

46. The administration of Theodore Roosevelt cannot be considered to have been a "typical" Republican administration in these terms.

47. Presented in Parsons and Smelser, *op. cit.*

48. It is of course extremely important to be clear about the sense in which I am and am not advancing a claim to a deductive anticipation of the findings of *Voting* and other studies. As I have stated it above, "it was possible to identify four main areas in which to look for mechanisms relevant to these functional requirements." Given the "gross structural facts" of the American political system, ascertainment of which does not require technical research procedures, in terms of such a "functional" model it is possible to deduce that there must be mechanisms that operate in each of these areas, and that they must operate within certain limits if the degree of stability of the system which has historically obtained is to be accounted for. In addition to these and various other sociological considerations I have postulated certain simple psychological assumptions about the limitations of rational decision-making by the individual and the kinds of psychological mechanisms that can be expected to operate where rational decision-making is impossible.

This, however, is very different from deducing the *specific* findings of the empirical research. Of course this has not been done. I have only provided certain "theoretical boxes" into which these findings can be fitted and have tested the goodness of fit in a broad way. One of the main reasons why I could not possibly have deduced the specific findings is that they must in the nature of the case be functions of whole ranges of factors not considered in my model. The model itself is necessarily abstract and deals with only part of the specifically political aspects of the concrete phenomena.

49. See Talcott Parsons and E. A. Shils, *Toward a General Theory of Action* (Cambridge, Mass.: Harvard University Press, 1951).

50. Talcott Parsons, R. F. Bales, and E. A. Shils, *Working Papers in the Theory of Action* (Glencoe, Ill.: The Free Press, 1953). See especially chaps. 3 and 5.

51. R. F. Bales, *Interaction Process Analysis* (Reading, Mass.: Addison-Wesley, 1950).

52. Parsons, Bales, and Shils, *op. cit.*, chap. 3.

53. See Parsons and Smelser, *op. cit.*

54. Cf. Parsons, Bales, and Shils, *op. cit.*, chap. 5, pp. 264 ff.

55. Parsons and Smelser, *op. cit.*, fig. 4, p. 68.

56. For the detailed argument see Parsons and Smelser, *op. cit.*

57. Parsons and Smelser, *op. cit.*, chap. 3.

NOTES TO CHAPTER 5

1. See Eli Ginzberg and Others, *Occupational Choice* (New York: Columbia University Press, 1951); P. H. Rossi, *Why Families Move* (Glencoe, Ill.: The Free Press, 1955); and W. J. Goode, *After Divorce* (Glencoe, Ill.: The Free Press, 1956). The *International Journal of Social Psychiatry* also contains many interesting articles within this area of concern.

2. A good deal of the sociological research on this problem has come from the students of Robert K. Merton at Columbia University, especially in the publications of Philip Selznick. See Professor Merton's *Social Theory and Social Structure* (rev. ed.; Glencoe, Ill.: The Free Press, 1957). See also C. Northcote Parkinson, *Parkinson's Law* (New York: Houghton Mifflin, 1957), for a novel approach to the "irrational" in sociological organization.

3. Sigmund Freud used the term "intention" in his *Three Contributions to the Theory of Sex* (4th ed.; Baltimore, Md.: Williams & Wilkins, 1930) pri-

marily to refer to "aims" rather than "objects" of sexual choice. But "aim" is a kind of division of an object (erotic zone) as well as a preferred form of sexual activity in Freud's scheme.

4. See the yearly symposia, *Current Theory and Research in Motivation* (Lincoln, Neb.: University of Nebraska Press, 1953-57). Of especial interest is D. C. McClelland, *Studies in Motivation* (New York: Appleton-Century-Crofts, 1955) which attempts to survey the varying views systematically. A very original and stimulating discussion of motivational theory is contained in James Olds, *The Growth and Structure of Motives* (Glencoe, Ill.: The Free Press, 1956).

5. There is, apparently, no "fixed" amount of energy (no "scarcity of resources") that needs to be husbanded. Fatigue seems more and more to be a matter of emotional and value conflicts rather than the depletion of "available" physiological energy.

6. Josephine Hilgard, I believe, has conducted a survey of the reactions of physicists to the behavioral sciences and finds that they conceive of psychoanalysis as one of the most important developments within social science. It is not the "physicalism," however, which impresses them so much but the bold speculations within psychoanalytic theory.

7. An unusually interesting example of such a study, among many lesser ones, is contained in E. C. Tolman, *Drives Toward War* (New York: Appleton-Century, 1942).

8. A somewhat advanced discussion of aggressive behavior is to be found in Lydia Jackson, *Aggression and Its Interpretation* (London: Methuen, 1954). Dr. Jackson attempts to show, by a review of theory and empirical research, that aggressive activity is often constructive and in the interests of self and social growth and creativity.

9. It is not meant to deny that social values arise out of and gratify biological needs and that they require biological skills for their attainment, only that social values act to complicate simple biological activities relating to sexual aggression. See D. P. Ausubel, *Theory and Problems of Adolescent Development* (New York: Grune & Stratton, 1954) for a discussion of how various cultures "complicate" sexual activity by special value systems. See also Herbert Marcuse, *Eros and Civilization* (Boston: Beacon Press, 1955), for a provocative discussion of this issue.

10. The writings of Harold D. Lasswell contain an attempt to work out a usable set of value categories for such purposes. Professor Lasswell's contribution in Richard Christie and Marie Jahoda (eds.), *Studies in the Scope and Method of the Authoritarian Personality* (Glencoe, Ill.: The Free Press, 1954) contains a good delineation and discussion of this scheme. More recently, his "The Normative Import of the Behavioral Sciences," *Ethics*, LXVII (April, 1957), contains a more general outline of value analysis and a highly systematic presentation of his views on the place of normative issues in social science.

11. Even the universal biologically rooted "Oedipus complex" may take a different form depending on what the parents value in each other. The Oedipal rivalry of one son toward his father may be a money-making one if those are the terms in which his father was primarily valued by his mother. With another son and another father, rivalry may be confined to getting more deference from others than father received or being brighter than father, if the father was valued by the mother in these quite different value terms. Oedipal rivalry may thus be quite circumscribed value-wise rather than general in nature. It can be complicated, too, by the ambivalence of the mother toward what she values in her husband and by the son's misperception of the mother's ambivalence toward certain

values which the father represents. See Leo Rangell, "The Role of the Parent in the Oedipus Complex," *Bulletin of the Menninger Clinic*, XIX (1955), 9-15, for some initial considerations of the varying forms in which an Oedipus complex becomes manifested, depending on the "properties" of the parents involved.

12. Elihu Katz and P. F. Lazarsfeld, *Personal Influence* (Glencoe, Ill.: The Free Press, 1955).

13. The literature on learning theory is vast. R. R. Sears and Others, *Patterns of Child Rearing* (Evanston, Ill.: Row, Peterson, 1957) contains one of the most recent and thoughtful attempts to study social learning. See also J. W. M. Whiting and I. R. Child, *Child Training and Personality* (New Haven, Conn.: Yale University Press, 1953). An outline of the basic conflictful issues on which learning psychologists are at work may be found in E. R. Hilgard, *Theories of Learning* (2d ed.; New York: Appleton-Century-Crofts, 1956).

14. Howard V. Perlmutter has begun studies at the Massachusetts Institute of Technology's Center for International Studies in which the neurotic personality of the "xenophile" or "outgroup identifier" is seen to be similar to the "authoritarian" personality who lines up heavily with ingroup authority. See A. J. Brodbeck and H. V. Perlmutter, "Self-Dislike as a Determinant of Marked Ingroup-Outgroup Preferences," *Journal of Psychology*, XXXVIII (1954), 271-80. An application of this type of analysis to problems of prejudice is to be found in Louis Schneider and A. J. Brodbeck, "Some Notes on Moral Paradoxes in Race Relations," *Phylon* (Second Quarter, 1955).

15. See M. B. Smith, J. S. Bruner, and R. W. White, *Opinions and Personality* (New York: Wiley, 1956), for a "depth" analysis of the relationship between political opinion and behavior and personality processes. More studies of this sort are needed to supplement demographic sociological ones. H. D. Lasswell's "Current Studies of the Decision Process: Automation versus Creativity," *Western Political Quarterly*, VIII (1955), 381-99, deals with suggestions for studying, at deeper levels, the kinds of processes to which attention is drawn in this chapter.

16. See Eleanor E. Maccoby, R. E. Matthews, and A. S. Morton, "Youth and Political Change," *Public Opinion Quarterly*, XVIII (1954), 23-29. Professor Philip Nogee and his associates at Boston University report, in a personal communication, findings at great variance with those of Dr. Maccoby, although both studies contain subjects from approximately the same geographical area around Boston.

17. See M. L. Hoffman, "Conformity as a Defense Mechanism and a Form of Resistance to Genuine Group Influence," *Journal of Personality*, XXV (June, 1957), for some particularly pertinent data on this problem.

18. Fred I. Greenstein has begun some study of children's political perspectives at the Yale Political Science Department which promises to clarify the issues discussed in this chapter during the late childhood years of socialization of political attitudes. Professor Lasswell and myself are preparing a manuscript in which parent-child interactions are studied during infancy for the predispositions established at that time toward power and other values entering into adult roles such as voting within election campaigns.

18. Russell Lynes, *A Surfeit of Honey* (New York: Harper, 1957) contains some subtle and entertaining thinking about changed processes of social influence as traditional class structures break down and as "Upper Bohemians," like earthworms, play a crucial and influential role in cultivating the cultural topsoil.

20. What often appears to be "magical" influence in terms of social intent

or impact may often turn out, on deeper analysis, to be quite rational. Anthropologists often challenge medical knowledge by reporting "cures" (of what are conventionally considered purely medical disease entities) by social rituals, the social participation in which involves much "magical thinking" that seems, however, to work much as a placebo does in our culture. Psychoanalytic theory was once widely felt to consist of little but magical thinking. When an explanation does not appear to fit in with our established but inadequate scientific laws, or when we have no explanation for certain phenomena, it is indeed easy to ascribe "magical thinking" to an innovation in thinking, thereby magically protecting one's own scientific status. Pertinent references for the study of magical thinking are: J. W. Woodard, *Intellectual Realism and Culture Change* (Minneapolis, Minn.: The Sociological Press, 1935); B. L. Whorf, *Language, Thought, and Reality* (New York: Wiley, 1956); Clyde Kluckhohn, *Navaho Witchcraft* (Cambridge, Mass.: Peabody Museum, 1944); and Vance Packard, *The Hidden Persuaders* (New York: McKay, 1957). Solomon Asch has, in his *Social Psychology* (New York: Prentice-Hall, 1952), attempted to show the rational elements in what is often taken to be social influence of a "magical" character.

21. Ernest R. Hilgard and O. H. Mowrer have been two of the outstanding theorists in developing a theory of social learning involving a "self" concept. Within the psychoanalytic movement, Harry Stack Sullivan, among others, has introduced elaborate modifications of psychoanalytic ideas to accommodate a "self" concept. W. V. Silverberg, *Childhood Experience and Personal Destiny* (New York: Springer, 1952) contains an attempt to integrate the "self" concept with libido theory. José Ortega y Gassett, *Man and People* (New York: Norton, 1957) contains some highly creative and unconventional thinking about the "self," social learning, and social organization somewhat in the George Herbert Mead and George Simmol traditions combined. A learning theory of "identification" phenomena without a "self" concept seems to induce internal theoretical contradictions.

22. See Gustav Bergmann, *The Metaphysics of Logical Positivism* (New York: Longmans, 1954).

23. The best single example of this approach is in Rollo May, *The Meaning of Anxiety* (New York: The Ronald Press, 1950). An interesting forerunner in the gestalt tradition is Prescott Lecky's *Self-Consistency: A Theory of Personality* (New York: Island Press, 1945). G. W. Allport's *Becoming* (New Haven, Conn.: Yale University Press, 1955) attempts to place the "self" concept among contemporary issues in psychology.

24. Lewin's experiments on "group atmospheres" lent great support to the progressive education movement. Certain "excesses" in the enthusiasm for progressive education are coming belatedly to light. See A. J. Brodbeck, "Education as Psychotherapy," *Confluence*, VI (Spring, 1957). See also the research study of Isidore Bogen, "Pupil-Teacher Rapport and the Teacher's Awareness of Status Structures within the Group," *Journal of Educational Sociology*, XXVIII (1954), 104-14.

NOTES TO CHAPTER 6

1. Alfred Cobban quoted in B. R. Berelson, P. F. Lazarfeld, and W. N. McPhee, *Voting* (Chicago: University of Chicago Press, 1954), p. 323.

2. The findings listed in *Voting* are exceptions.

3. An example of the logical positivist's distrust of ethical language is

contained in Richard Robinson, "The Emotive Theory of Ethics," *Proceedings of the Aristotelian Society*, Supp. Vol. XXII (1948), 79-106. The formulation of a political policy free of ethical stresses has been attempted in T. D. Weldon, *States and Morals* (New York: McGraw-Hill, 1947) and also in his *The Vocabulary of Politics* (Penguin Books, 1954). But, in general, positivists have ventured only tentatively into the field of political theory. When they have their commitment to the idea of two worlds, preference and reality remains firm.

4. See Frederick Mosteller and Others, *The Pre-Election Polls of 1948* (New York: Social Science Research Council, 1949) for an intensive discussion of the internal problems. M. B. Parten, *Surveys, Polls, and Samples* (New York: Harper, 1950) contains a description of procedures in this field.

5. The argument is complicated, but so familiar that it does not warrant discussion here. From the time of G. E. Moore, *Principia Ethica* (London: Cambridge University Press, 1903) to Gilbert Ryle, *Concept of Mind* (New York: Barnes & Noble, 1950), however, the central idea is not much changed: ethical formulations, it is argued, cannot offer as proof nonethical premises or terms.

6. See Berelson, Lazarfeld, and McPhee, *op. cit.*, pp. 333-47, for an interesting table of results listing the frequency with which "findings or generalizations" appear in various contemporary studies.

7. John Locke, *Two Treatises on Civil Government* (Everyman's Library; London: Dent, 1949), p. 161.

8. *Ibid.*, p. 183.

9. This is especially apparent in *The Social Contract,* but *Emile* is also an elaboration of the essential rationality of man and the damage which that quality suffers in civilization. *Nouvelle Heloise* depicts a pattern of moral relations which is not in any essential way in conflict with the theory of rational man. For a discussion of recent pessimism over Rousseau's influence, see J. L. Talmon, *The Rise of Totalitarian Democracy* (Boston: Beacon Press, 1952).

10. Adam Smith, *The Theory of Moral Sentiments* (London: H. G. Bohn, 1853).

11. Henry Sidgwick quoted in Harry K. Girvetz, *From Wealth to Welfare* (Stanford, Calif.: Stanford University Press, 1950), pp. 15-16.

12. *The Writings of Thomas Paine,* ed. M. D. Conway (New York: G. P. Putnam's, 1894), I, 68.

13. Berelson, Lazarfeld, and McPhee, *op. cit.*, p. 227.

14. Angus Campbell, Gerald Gurin, and W. E. Miller, *The Voter Decides* (Evanston, Ill.: Row, Peterson, 1954).

15. Berelson, Lazarfeld, and McPhee, *op. cit.*, p. 220.

16. *Ibid.*, chap. 11.

17. *Ibid.*, p. 309.

18. Unlike the authors of *Voting,* I am treating interest as if it were a political principle. I see no logical reason why a view of the political structure as an instrument of advancing self-interest is not principled.

19. Berelson, Lazarfeld, and McPhee, *op. cit.*, p. 321.

20. The illustration is oddly out of character with the data presented. There is little in the volume, for example, that would justify characterizing "sociable man" as nonpartisan and flexible. He seems rather to emerge as disinterested, but rigid in whatever political ideas he does possess. The editors do not, however, suggest that the pleasing illustration is literally representative of the data. The illustration may instead be a monument to a liberal publication budget and the belief that *pictorial* images are more informative than words.

21. See Harold J. Laski, *Authority in the Modern State* (New Haven, Conn.: Yale University Press, 1919); *The Foundations of Sovereignty and*

Other Essays (New York: Harcourt, Brace, 1921); *A Grammar of Politics* (2d ed.; New Haven, Conn.: Yale University Press, 1931); and *The State in Theory and Practice* (New York: Viking, 1935). For contrasting views of pluralism see G. H. Sabine, "Pluralism: A Point of View," *American Political Science Review*, XVII (1923), 49 ff.; M. P. Follett, *The New State* (New York: Longmans, 1918); W. Y. Elliott, *The Pragmatic Revolt in Politics* (New York: Macmillan, 1928); and G. D. H. Cole, *Guild Socialism Re-stated* (London: L. Parsons, 1920).

22. Although theories of party function and efficacy vary, the main body of writings upon this subject argue that the party is valuable in at least two senses: (1) as the machinery by which elections are won, and (2) as the device by which institutions of government are brought into consonance with popular feeling. The following works differ in emphasis, but are representative: M. Ostrogorski, *Democracy and the Organization of Political Parties* (2 vols.; London: Macmillan, 1902); American Political Science Association, *Toward a More Responsible Two-Party System* (New York: Rinehart, 1950); Peter H. Odegard and E. A. Helms, *American Politics* (New York: Harper, 1938); and V. O. Key, Jr., *Politics, Parties, and Pressure Groups* (3d ed.; New York: Crowell, 1952).

23. This is a perennial and troubling problem of sociology. The point at which a concept, useful in field work and analysis, moves over into the area of real groups is most uncertain. The conflict about the existence of social and economic classes is relevant—and it has not been solved yet. However, the problem of when social groups should have legal status is even more complicated. For a discussion see: A. W. Kornhauser, "Analysis of 'Class Structure' of Contemporary American Society," in G. S. Hartmann and T. M. Newcomb (eds.), *Industrial Conflict* (New York: The Dryden Press, 1939), chap. 11; and R. M. MacIver and Charles Page, *Society: An Introductory Analysis* (New York: Rinehart, 1949), chaps. 10-14.

24. The nineteenth century experience of France is a striking parallel. The statutes against any form of subordinate association were weakened by the simple reality of the existence of such associations. Eventually French law came to tolerate the associations, and such groups as trade unions and corporations came to have a legal status. Tonnie's discussion of the difference between "community" *(Gemeinschaft)* and "association" *(Gesellschaft)* is also relevant. See Léon Duguit, *Les transformations du droit public* (Paris: A. Colin, 1913); Francis Coker, "The Technique of the Pluralistic State," *American Political Science Review*, XXIV (1930), 186-213; and Hsiao, Kung-Chuan, *Political Pluralism* (New York: Harcourt, Brace, 1927).

25. Judge Learned Hand quoted in Berelson, Lazarsfeld, and McPhee, *op. cit.*, p. 312.

26. See Lindsay Rogers, *The Pollsters* (New York: Knopf, 1949), chap. 8, for a lucid and critical treatment of this argument. See also Thomas Bailey, *The Man in the Street* (New York: Macmillan, 1949) for a sympathetic presentation of the view.

27. Walter Bagehot, *Physics and Politics* (New York: Knopf, 1949), p. xv.

28. Samuel Stouffer, *Communism, Conformity, and Civil Liberties* (New York: Doubleday, 1955).

29. John C. Calhoun, *A Disquisition on Government* (New York: Political Science Classics, 1947).

30. Berelson, Lazarsfeld, and McPhee, *op cit.*, p. 73.

31. Walter Lippmann, *The Public Philosophy* (Boston: Little, Brown, 1955).

32. *Ibid.*, p. 19.

33. *Ibid.*, pp. 65-67.

34. Berelson, Lazarsfeld, and McPhee, *op. cit.*, p. 312. Italics in original.

NOTES TO CHAPTER 7

1. B. R. Berelson, P. F. Lazarsfeld, and W. N. McPhee, *Voting* (Chicago: University of Chicago Press, 1954), p. 311.

2. P. F. Lazarsfeld, B. R. Berelson, and Hazel Gaudet, *The People's Choice* (2d ed.; New York: Columbia University Press, 1948), p. 4.

3. *Ibid.*, p. 3, footnotes 1 and 2.

4. Gerhard Tintner, *Econometrics* (New York: Wiley, 1952), p. 255.

5. T. W. Anderson, "Probability Models for Analyzing Time Changes in Attitudes," in P. F. Lazarsfeld (ed.), *Mathematical Thinking in the Social Sciences* (Glencoe, Ill.: The Free Press, 1954).

6. *Ibid.*, p. 18.

7. *Ibid.*, p. 60.

8. *Ibid.*, p. 27.

9. C. E. Shannon and Warren Weaver, *The Mathematical Theory of Communication* (Urbana, Ill.: University of Illinois Press, 1949).

10. *Ibid.*, p. 95.

11. *Ibid.*, p. 96.

12. Elihu Katz and P. F. Lazarsfeld, *Personal Influence* (Glencoe, Ill.: The Free Press, 1955), p. 167.

13. *Ibid.*, p. 169.

14. "How Television Changes Strangers into Customers," a survey conducted by the National Broadcasting Company, New York, 1954. See also Katz and Lazarsfeld, *op. cit.*

15. Berelson, Lazarsfeld, and McPhee, *op. cit.*, p. 282.

16. Norbert Wiener, *The Human Use of Human Beings* (Anchor Books; New York: Doubleday, 1954), p. 61. See also Norbert Wiener, *Cybernetics* (New York: Wiley, 1948), chap. 4, for a discussion of feed-back mechanism, the device which, both in humans and machines, may act to guide activity toward a desired goal.

17. The Advertising Research Foundation recently announced the formulation of a research program to investigate consumer decision-making. From the brief outline that has been made available, it is not clear that a panel study is part of the plan.

18. Lazarsfeld, Berelson, and Gaudet, *op. cit.*, p. xiv.

19. *Printers' Ink* (Jan. 6, 1956), p. 43. The writer of the article states, "the institutional campaign is not designed to sell products as such. . . ."

20. From research conducted by the Public Opinion Index For Industry, Opinion Research Corporation, Princeton, New Jersey.

21. Clark Hull, *Principles of Behavior* (New York: Appleton-Century, 1943), chap. 16.

22. Mark Abrams in Foreword to R. S. Milne and H. C. Mackenzie, *Straight Fight* (London: The Hansard Society, 1954), p. 6.

NOTES TO CHAPTER 8

1. These studies are listed in tabular form together with findings or generalizations relevant to the discussion in this chapter in B. R. Berelson, P. F. Lazarsfeld, and W. N. McPhee, *Voting* (Chicago: University of Chicago Press, 1954), pp. 331-35.

2. Eleanor E. Maccoby, "Youth and Political Change," *Public Opinion Quarterly*, XVIII (1954), 23-29.

3. At this point, it may be remarked that such a generalization is not new. That people who associate with one another tend to behave and believe alike has been discovered many times in socio-psychological research, and has appeared in the literature under many different titles: accommodation, value homophily, conformity to group norms, cohesiveness and pressures toward uniformity of opinion, and so

on. True as this assertion may be, it in no way detracts from the importance of the finding in studies of voting.

4. For a discussion of this proposition see G. C. Homans, *The Human Group* (New York: Harcourt, 1950). Recent empirical studies bearing on the proposition are reviewed in H. W. Riecken and G. C. Homans, "Psychological Aspects of Social Structure," in Gardner Lindzey (ed.), *Handbook of Social Psychology* (2 vols.; Reading, Mass.: Addison-Wesley, 1954).

5. For a summary of the relevant theoretical views and empirical research of this group, see Dorwin Cartwright and Alvin Zander (eds.), *Group Dynamics* (Evanston, Ill.: Row, Peterson, 1953), chaps. 7, 8, 15-17.

6. Obviously the explanation offered is not the only tenable one. The available data do not permit ruling out the alternative explanation that homogeneity of opinion in a primary group is the result of common or homogeneous experiences to which its members are exposed. Similarly, it is possible to argue that homogeneity in some primary groups is the result of self-selection; i.e., that those with similar opinions tend to associate. Data bearing on the first alternative will be presented later in the chapter, and the role of self-selection will also be discussed further. The chief reason for preferring an explanation in terms of group norms, even though *unequivocal* data are not available in the area of political opinion, is that there is good support for this position from socio-psychological experiments on opinion formation and group norms.

7. From unpublished research of Herbert McClosky and Harold Dahlgren conducted through the Laboratory for Research in Social Relations, University of Minnesota. The findings reported in this chapter were contained in a personal communication from Professor McClosky, 1956.

8. Maccoby, *op. cit.*, p. 28.

9. *Ibid.*, p. 29.

10. *Ibid.*, p. 29. Italics supplied.

11. A. J. Brodbeck and H. V. Perlmutter, "Self-Dislike as a Determinant of Marked Ingroup-Outgroup Preferences," *Journal of Psychology*, XXXVIII (1954), 271-80.

12. McClosky and Dahlgren, *op. cit.*

13. R. K. Merton and Alice Kitt, "Contributions to the Theory of Reference Group Behavior," in R. K. Merton and P. F. Lazarsfeld (eds.), *Continuities in Social Research* (Glencoe, Ill.: The Free Press, 1950).

14. Maccoby, *op. cit.*, p. 35.

15. T. M. Newcomb, *Personality and Social Change* (New York: The Dryden Press, 1943).

16. A later study of the same college community by S. W. Bloom suggests that political issues had lost their earlier importance. In 1951 he found no relationship between politico-economic conservatism and sociometric position in the college community. (S. W. Bloom, "Some Patterned Effects of Membership in a College Community: A Continuity in the Social Research of T. M. Newcomb," a paper delivered at the annual meeting of the Eastern Sociological Society, 1953.)

17. McClosky and Dahlgren, *op. cit.*

18. P. F. Lazarsfeld and R. K. Merton, "Friendship as Social Process: A Substantive and Methodological Analysis," in Morroe Berger, Theodore Abel, and C. H. Page (eds.), *Freedom and Control in Modern Society* (New York: Van Nostrand, 1954).

19. Berelson, Lazarsfeld, and McPhee, *op. cit.*, p. 106.

20. D. H. Baxter, "Interpersonal Contact and Exposure to Mass Media during a Presidential Campaign," (unpublished Ph.D. dissertation, Faculty of Political Science, Columbia University, 1951).

21. Berelson, Lazarsfeld, and McPhee, *op. cit.*, p. 106.

22. May Brodbeck, "The Role of Small Groups in Mediating the Effects of Propaganda," *Journal of Abnormal and Social Psychology*, LI (1956), 166-70.

23. A similar finding was obtained in a field study of a social movement: see Leon Festinger, H. W. Riecken, and Stanley Schacter, *When Prophecy Fails* (Minneapolis, Minn.: University of Minnesota Press, 1956). When some of the members whose faith had been shaken by the failure of a prophecy had an opportunity to discuss their opinions with other members, they tended to regain their earlier convictions. Those who had no such opportunity tended to lose their faith altogether.

24. This last factor is outside the scope of the present discussion, since it depends on an evaluation both of the individual's chances of acceptance in new groups, and his risk in leaving old ones. It may well depend primarily on what goals or rewards the various groups mediate or control, and thus, in the final analysis, on what the individual's motives are.

25. Leon Festinger, "An Analysis of Compliant Behavior," in Muzafer Sherif and M. O. Wilson (eds.), *Group Relations at the Crossroads* (New York: Harper, 1953).

26. Berelson, Lazarsfeld, and McPhee, *op. cit.*, p. 27.

NOTES TO CHAPTER 11

1. Owing to the pressure of time, this account was written solely by the present author, but the work of the 1951 and 1955 Bristol surveys was carried out jointly with Mr. H. C. Mackenzie of Bristol University. Many of the views expressed are taken from a joint stock of ideas to which Mr. Mackenzie contributed equally.

2. R. S. Milne and H. C. Mackenzie, *Straight Fight* (London: The Hansard Society, 1954), pp. 128 ff.

3. P. F. Lazarsfeld, B. R. Berelson, and Hazel Gaudet, *The People's Choice* (2d ed.; New York: Columbia University Press, 1948), pp. 28 ff.

4. R. S. Milne and H. C. Mackenzie, *Marginal Seat, 1955* (London: The Hansard Society, in press).

5. So have most other British sample surveys.

6. See P. Campbell, D. Donnison, and A. Potter, "Voting Behaviour in Droylsden, 1951," *The Manchester School*, Vol. XX, no. 1, pp. 62-64.

7. See David Butler, *The British General Election of 1955* (London: Macmillan, 1955), p. 206.

8. The Labour party also considered this point. The committee which it set up on the question, with Mr. Harold Wilson as chairman, placed the chief blame on organization. This view is not confirmed for Bristol North-East by the 1955 survey.

9. Angus Campbell, Gerald Gurin, and W. E. Miller, *The Voter Decides* (Evanston, Ill.; Row, Peterson, 1954), pp. 136 ff.

10. R. T. McKenzie, *British Political Parties* (London: Heinemann, 1955).

11. Maurice Duverger, *Les partis politiques* (Paris: A. Colin, 1951).

12. In 1955 the authors' labors were substantially lightened by a generous grant from the Ford Foundation. The publication of the 1951 survey was eventually made possible by grants from Columbia University, Bristol University, and the London Press Exchange.

13. See Mark Benney and Phyllis Geiss, "Social Class and Politics in Greenwich," *British Journal of Sociology*, I (1950), 310-27. A fuller account of the survey is in Mark Benney, A. P. Gray, and R. H. Pear, *How People Vote* (New York: The Humanities Press, 1956).

14. D. B. Truman reported in John P. White, *The Role of Public Opinion*

Polls in the Study of Political Parties (Ann Arbor: University of Michigan, 1955), a report prepared for the Stockholm meeting.

15. The large number of electors in old people's homes and in mental institutions.

16. In Milne and Mackenzie, *Straight Fight*, pp. 146-47, it was suggested that "socially homogeneous groups," say trade unionists, might be studied with advantage. But this kind of study would be supplementary to constituency studies and not be a substitute for them. In any case, the cost of collecting a sample of trade unionists would be extremely high.

17. B. R. Berelson, P. F. Lazarsfeld, and W. N. McPhee, *Voting* (Chicago: University of Chicago Press, 1954), pp. 209 ff.

18. *Ibid.*, chap. 14, p. 305.

19. Milne and Mackenzie, *op. cit.*, pp. 138 ff.

20. Max Beloff, "Counting the Votes," *The Fortnightly*, 179 (Jan. 1953), 3-9.

NOTES TO CHAPTER 12

1. B. R. Berelson, P. F. Lazarsfeld, and W. N. McPhee, *Voting* (Chicago: University of Chicago Press, 1954); R. S. Milne and H. C. Mackenzie, *Straight Fight* (London: The Hansard Society, 1954); and Angus Campbell, Gerald Gurin, and W. E. Miller, *The Voter Decides* (Evanston, Ill.: Row, Peterson, 1954).

2. In a separate article, the authors have discussed the role of television but qualify their data in stating that they had "no clear evidence" on how it affected the voting. Cf. Angus Campbell and Others, "Television and the Elections," *Scientific American*, 188 (1953), 46-48.

3. Milne and Mackenzie, *op. cit.*, pp. 96 ff.

4. Berelson, Lazarsfeld, and McPhee, *op. cit.*, p. 248.

5. In Erie County, Ohio (1940), roughly one half were pre-campaign deciders. Cf. P. F. Lazarsfeld, B. R. Berelson, and Hazel Gaudet, *The People's Choice* (2d ed.; New York: Columbia University Press, 1948), p. 53. According to a "Gallup" poll before nomination day, 84 per cent of the British electorate were already decided. Cited by R. B. McCallum and A. Readman, *The British General Election of 1945* (London: Oxford University Press, 1947), p. 201. British figures seem to hover around the 80 per cent mark, with American figures, perhaps because of the more protracted campaign period, on the whole closer to two-thirds.

6. Best known among these are the famous "rum, Romanism, and rebellion" phrase so successfully used during the 1884 contest; and Charles Evans Hughes's alienation of Hiram Johnson, which lost him California and, consequently, the election.

7. There are important differences between the Elmira and Bristol studies. But our basic interest here is in the logic of their approach, not in a detailed methodological evaluation.

8. Berelson, Lazarsfeld, and McPhee, *op cit.*, pp. 246 ff.

9. Milne and Mackenzie, *op. cit.*, p. 104.

10. Namely, "attitudes, perceptions, and group loyalties which mediate between the external environmental facts and the individual response." Campbell, Gurin, and Miller, *op. cit.*, pp. 7 ff.

11. D. B. Truman, "Political Behavior and Voting," in Frederick Mosteller and Others, *The Pre-Election Polls of 1948* (New York: Social Science Research Council, 1949), p. 225.

12. Milne and Mackenzie, *op. cit.*, p. 26.

13. D. E. Butler, *The Electoral System in Britain 1918-1951* (Oxford: The Clarendon Press, 1953), p. 201.

14. Milne and Mackenzie, *op. cit.*, p. 121.

15. Campbell, Gurin, and Miller, *op. cit.*, p. 12.

16. Berelson, Lazarsfeld, and McPhee, *op. cit.*, p. 264 n.

17. Campbell, Gurin, and Miller, *op. cit.*, p. 184.

18. Cf. S. A. Lubbell, *The Future of American Politics* (New York: Harper, 1951); Louis Harris, *Is There a Republican Majority?* (New York: Harper, 1954); and Richard Hofstadter, "The Pseudo-Conservative Revolt," *The American Scholar*, Winter 1955, pp. 9-27.

19. As far as the campaign is concerned, Stevenson, if anyone, gained more in personal appeal than Eisenhower. Cf. Harris, *op. cit.*, pp. 52 ff.; and *The Influence of Television on the 1952 Election* by the Oxford Research Associates, Oxford, Ohio, Dec. 1954.

20. Apparently such an analysis was conducted, but results have not yet come to our attention.

21. H. H. Hyman and P. B. Sheatsley, "The Political Appeal of President Eisenhower," *Public Opinion Quarterly*, XVIII (Winter 1953-54), 459.

22. Berelson, Lazarsfeld, and McPhee, *op. cit.*, p. 235. Italics supplied.

23. Elihu Katz and P. F. Lazarsfeld, *Personal Influence* (Glencoe, Ill.: The Free Press, 1955), p. 185. Also J. T. Klapper, *The Effects of Mass Media* (New York: Columbia University, Bureau of Applied Social Research, 1949).

24. Berelson, Lazarsfeld, and McPhee, *op. cit.*, p. 61.

25. Harris, *op. cit.*, chap. 7, shows that women as a group gave a larger majority to Eisenhower than did men and that, especially, the wives of union members voted contrary to their husbands.

26. Berelson, Lazarsfeld, and McPhee, *op. cit.*, report this "unexpected" finding: "More people showed signs of exposure than claimed to be paying 'attention.' "

27. "Political Participation and the Television Audience," paper read by the authors at the annual meeting of the American Sociological Society, Washington, D. C., 1955.

28. Cf. G. D. Wiebe, "Responses to the Televised Kefauver Hearings," *Public Opinion Quarterly*, XVI (Summer 1952), 179-200, for a discussion of the phenomenon of "social impotence."

29. R. H. Rovere and A. M. Schlesinger, Jr., *The General and the President* (New York: Farrar, Strauss, and Young, 1951), and Kurt and G. E. Lang, "The Unique Perspective of Television and Its Effect," *American Sociological Review*, XVIII (Feb. 1953), 3-12.

30. Gabriel Tarde referred to this phenomenon of contagion in his *L'opinion et la foule* (Paris: F. Alcan, 1901).

NOTES TO CHAPTER 13

1. P. F. Lazarsfeld has written an article (based on a study of children) here relevant: "Why Is So Little Known about the Effects of TV and What Can Be Done about It?" *Public Opinion Quarterly*, XIX (Fall 1955), 243-51.

2. P. F. Lazarsfeld, B. R. Berelson, and Hazel Gaudet, *The People's Choice* (2d ed.; New York: Columbia University Press, 1948).

3. Note particularly the works of H. F. Gosnell, *Machine Politics* (Chicago: University of Chicago Press, 1937) and *Grass Roots Politics* (Washington, D. C.: American Council on Public Affairs, 1942). See also the various French studies of political geography such as François Goguel-Nyegaard, *Géographie des élections françaises de 1870 à 1951* (Paris: A. Colin, 1954).

4. Lazarsfeld, Berelson, and Gaudet, *op. cit.*, p. xxvii.

5. B. R. Berelson, P. F. Lazarsfeld, and W. N. McPhee, *Voting* (Chicago: University of Chicago Press, 1954),

chap. 8. Angus Campbell, Gerald Gurin, and W. E. Miller, *The Voter Decides* (Evanston, Ill.: Row, Peterson, 1954) chose the opposite alternative of explicitly narrowing its field to eliminate attention to the campaign. It is a limited study. What is outside the average voter is simply disregarded.

6. The full report was mimeographed: Douglas Waples and B. R. Berelson, *Public Communications and Public Opinion* (Chicago: University of Chicago Press, 1941).

7. Lazarsfeld, Berelson, and Gaudet, *op. cit.*, p. 101.

8. Berelson, Lazarsfeld, and McPhee, *op. cit.*, pp. 235-40; chaps. 9 and 10.

9. Campbell, Gurin, and Miller, *op. cit.*, pp. 30-32.

10. Angus Campbell and Others, "Television and the Elections," *Scientific American*, 188 (May 1953), 46-48.

11. In *Personal Influence* (Glencoe, Ill.: The Free Press, 1955), p. 3, Elihu Katz and P. F. Lazarsfeld say that the 1940 Erie County study "indicated that the effect of the mass media was small as compared to the role of personal influences." This is an interpretation too strong for the data to sustain. The data certainly showed the action of personal influence, but the interview responses in voter surveys do not permit the separation of personal and mass-media influence and thus a comparison of their relative weight.

12. Cf. C. R. Carpenter, "Psychological Research Using Television," *American Psychologist*, X (1955), 608. "The majority of research conducted on the sound motion picture, a first cousin of television . . . has been on the character of stimulus materials. This research has been limited largely to the field of learning. However, almost with monotonous repetition these studies have yielded small or non-significant differences. Much less emphasis has been given to research on the determinants of responses related to the subjects or reactors; these have in most experiments been considered 'intervening' variables. There are accumulating results which point to the characteristics of subjects as being most forceful in determining reactions to or 'effects' of the communication stimuli. This trend of results leads to hypotheses which conceptualize communication stimuli as acting like releasor-organizer mechanisms."

13. Cf. E. S. Bogardus, "Television and the Political Conventions, *Sociology and Social Research*, XXXVII (1952), 115-21.

14. H. A. Simon and Frederick Stern, "The Effect of Television upon Voting Behavior in Iowa in the 1952 Presidential Election," *American Political Science Review*, XLIX (1955), 470-77.

15. *The Influence of Television on the 1952 Election* by the Oxford Research Associates, Oxford, Ohio, Dec. 1954.

16. Kurt and G. E. Lang, "Television Personality and Politics," *Public Opinion Quarterly*, XX (Spring 1956), and "The Inferential Structure of Political Communications," *ibid.*, XIX (Summer 1955).

17. The study was made possible by an unrestricted research grant from the Ford Foundation.

18. On this point see the definitive article on television personality by Kurt and G. E. Lang, *op. cit.*

19. What has been called the evaluative factor was clearly dominant in the ratings. The traits with a highly evaluative character (i.e., good or bad) were rated with the highest degree of consensus. Where the evaluative element was more ambiguous the rating was less uniform. Eisenhower supporters asserted he had the good traits and denied that he had the bad. Their choice of candidate controlled their image more than it followed from it. To that extent the variance for which TV exposure could account is substantially reduced.

20. This assumes something that voting studies have not yet proved, i.e.,

that interest causes increased partisanship rather than interest being derivative from partisanship. The voting studies have shown a correlation between these two variables, but not which way the causality goes. It could go either way or both ways at once. Interest and partisanship, as a matter of fact, are very likely mutually reinforcing, each causing the other. Our assumption here is that interest is not entirely derivative.

21. This chapter, substantially in its present form, was written before the 1956 election.

REFERENCES TO CHAPTER 14

1. Berelson, B. R., P. F. Lazarsfeld, and W. N. McPhee. *Voting*. Chicago: University of Chicago Press, 1954.

2. Campbell, Angus, Gerald Gurin, and W. E. Miller. *The Voter Decides*. Evanston, Ill.: Row, Peterson, 1954.

3. de Grazia, Sebastian. "A Note on the Psychological Position of the Chief Executive," *Psychiatry*, VIII (1945), 267-72.

4. Fairbairn, W. R. D. *An Object-Relations Theory of the Personality*. New York: Basic Books, 1954.

5. Gorer, Geoffrey. *The American People: A Study in National Character*. New York: Norton, 1948.

6. Hoffer, Eric. *The True Believer*. New York: Harper, 1951.

7. Lazarsfeld, R. F., B. R. Berelson, and Hazel Gaudet. *The People's Choice*. 2d ed. New York: Columbia University Press, 1948.

8. Orlansky, Harold. "Reactions to the Death of President Roosevelt," *Journal of Social Psychology*, XXVI (1947), 235-66.

9. Sullivan, Harry Stack. *The Interpersonal Theory of Psychiatry*, ed. Helen S. Perry and Mary L. Gawel. New York: Norton, 1953.

10. von Hayek, F. A. *The Counter-Revolution of Science*. Glencoe, Ill.: The Free Press, 1952.

NOTES TO CHAPTER 15

1. P. F. Lazarsfeld, B. R. Berelson, and Hazel Gaudet, *The People's Choice* (2d ed., New York: Columbia University Press, 1948).

2. A basic contribution of *The People's Choice* was, of course, its development of a technique for observation of at least short segments of the time dimension of decision, and its authors manifest an awareness of the significance of this factor not common among electoral sociologists.

3. The similarity between two such maps drawn with the same class intervals in the distribution of counties depends somewhat on the elections chosen for comparison. Since most counties tend to fluctuate in unison, the comparison of elections at which the division of the entire state's vote is approximately the same maximizes the similarities of the county-by-county pattern.

4. Thus, the Republican county of Jefferson in the southeast is surrounded by Democratic territory. In the first decades of the nineteenth century the county seat, Madison, was the metropolis of the state and a flourishing river trading center. The county was peopled, the local histories say, by the "educated" and "upper strata of society" from Philadelphia and Baltimore, some of whom built magnificent residences that still stand as monuments to the erstwhile glory of Madison. Long since the river trade virtually disappeared. Dreams of metropolitan grandeur came no longer to haunt the county's declining population. Yet so firmly did the old Whig traders fix the political tradition that the county ranked low in Democratic strength even after 1900.

5. A word of caution is in order about both the maps and the scatter-diagram. The maps convey an erroneous impression in that they make no allowance for differences in population density. The significance of a metro-

politan center in the entire picture is thus minimized. Similarly, one dot on the diagram may represent a rural county of small population; another a densely populated metropolitan county. Moreover, differentials in behavior within subgroups of the population of large counties are concealed by this sort of analysis.

6. If one plots on the map of Indiana clusters of underground railroad stations and points at which Union authorities had difficulties in drafting troops, he separates, on the whole, Republican and Democratic counties. Whether the sort of animosities associated with such long-past events project themselves far through time in lending strength to political groupings, perhaps unbeknownst to succeeding generations, raises an interesting question.

7. Some evidence pointing in this direction has been presented by George Belknap and Angus Campbell, "Political Party Identification and Attitudes Toward Foreign Policy," *Public Opinion Quarterly*, XV (1951-52), 601-23.

8. See S. J. Eldersveld, "The Independent Vote: Measurement, Characteristics, and Implications for Party Strategy," *American Political Science Review*, XLVI (1952), 732-53.

9. How one converts this kind of proposition into a problem susceptible of neat empirical testing presents another question.

10. This factor may partially explain the frustration that almost invariably accompanies attempts to identify party characteristics by correlation of votes with demographic characteristics. One element of the variance unexplained by such analysis may lie in variables in the behavior of "political" man, such as persistence of partisan attachment, which may be quite independent of the so-called determinants.

11. Obviously the manifestation of a secular trend in particular counties depends to some extent on the terminal points chosen for identifying them. Further, it would be erroneous to suppose that all areas moving in a secular manner either begin that movement at the same time or proceed at the same rate.

12. The mean LaFollette percentage of the total vote in the fifteen counties was 9.0; in all counties the mean was 4.8.

13. The great upswing in Democratic strength in Indiana from 1920 to 1936 may have represented principally Democratic success in recruiting new voters rather than in the conversion of erstwhile Republicans. With 1920 as 100, the total presidential vote, the Republican vote, and the Democratic vote from 1920 to 1936 were as follows:

	Total	*Republican*	*Democratic*
1920	100.0	100.0	100.0
1924	100.8	100.9	96.3
1928	112.5	121.8	110.0
1932	124.7	97.2	168.6
1936	130.7	99.3	182.8

Apart from their temporary expansion in 1928, the Republicans only about held their own from 1920 to 1936, while the Democrats almost doubled their vote. These figures do not prove that the Democrats had greater success in winning new voters. Yet from what is known of the stability of voting attachments, the figures strongly suggest that such an interpretation provides at least a partial explanation.

14. One should cover himself against the possibility that the apparent secular trend of the fifteen counties is not a secular divergence from the movement of the state but a cyclical fluctuation with a wider amplitude than the cyclical movement of the state as a whole.

15. The fifteen counties were Blackford (near Muncie), Clark (which falls within the Louisville metropolitan district), Delaware (Muncie), Elkhart (Elkhart), Howard (Kokomo),

Knox (Vincennes), Lake (Gary), LaPorte (Michigan City), Madison (Anderson), Porter (adjacent to Lake), Starke (in northeastern Indiana, the home of Henry Schricker, important Indiana Democratic leader), St. Joseph (South Bend), Vanderburgh (Evansville), Vermillion (a marginal coal mining county), Vigo (Terre Haute). The range of the 1920 Democratic percentages was from 21.3 (Lake) to 51.0 (Clark). The 1948 range was from 36.7 (Porter) to 61.0 (Clark). Of the fifteen counties, eleven were over 50 per cent Democratic in 1948; only one was over 50 per cent Democratic in 1920.

16. For example, Marion (Indianapolis) and Allen (Fort Wayne).

17. Those counties containing cities of over 25,000 and with less than 10 per cent Roman Catholic population were Delaware, Elkhart, Howard, Madison, Marion, Vigo, Wayne. Those with over 15 per cent Catholic population were Lake, LaPorte, St. Joseph.

18. Completely rural counties with under 5 per cent Catholic population *and* under 5 per cent of their population foreign-born or of foreign or mixed parentage were Brown, Carroll, Crawford, Hendricks, Orange, Owen, Parke, Scott, Switzerland. The other group consisted of rural counties with over 10 per cent Catholic population *and* over 10 per cent foreign-born or of foreign or mixed parentage. These were Benton, Pulaski, Starke, Franklin, Spencer. It scarcely need be said that the available census data provide no satisfactory differentiation of counties according to the national origin of their population.

19. This is the thesis of Louis Bean, *How to Predict Elections* (New York: Knopf, 1948), pp. 93-99.

20. The possibility should not be excluded that a series of "peculiar" elections may have cumulative effects productive of a secular growth of one party.

21. The counties compared were drawn from those counties with 20-29.0 per cent urban population in 1930 and with no cities of over 10,000. The differentiation of Catholic and non-Catholic counties was based on the percentage of the 1930 total population reported as Roman Catholic by the Census of Religious Bodies of 1936. The counties under 2 per cent Catholic were: Boone, Clay, Fulton, Greene, Hamilton, Hancock, Johnson, Kosciusko, Morgan, Putnam, Wells. Those over 12 per cent Catholic were Daviess, Decatur, Dubois, Perry, Porter, Warrick. It scarcely needs be said that the data on religious composition are not very reliable.

22. Which, of course, points to one of the great advantages of the sample survey over the analysis of election returns.

23. The phenomenon of departure and return to party suggests the question whether the pattern of party division among the counties of the state could be regarded as something of an equilibrium which may be disturbed by the impact of particular campaigns yet tends to restore itself when the next campaign comes along. To test the notion the county-by-county Republican percentage in 1916 was regarded as the "normal" pattern. A rank order correlation was made with succeeding elections with the following results: 1920, 0.862; 1924, 0.775; 1928, 0.634; 1932, 0.754. Through 1928 the correlations steadily declined. Each election marked a further departure from the 1916 pattern. The 1928 election showed the sharpest deviation as the crosscurrents of that campaign played havoc with past voting patterns. Yet in 1932, the counties moved back toward their pre-existing ranking.

24. Tests of the index of political predisposition of the Erie County study of 1940 against national samples in the elections of 1944 and 1948 illustrate the problem. (See Lazarsfeld, Berelson, and Gaudet, *op. cit.,* pp. xv-xviii; and Morris Janowitz and W.

E. Miller, "The Index of Political Predisposition in the 1948 Election," *Journal of Politics*, XIV [1952], 710-27.) An index descriptive of the association between particular social characteristics and political preference among the electors of a particular locality at a particular election did not fit so well national samples at other elections. To round out the theory of the determinism of social characteristics, it would be necessary to devise a scheme to account for the shifting political significance of these characteristics. If they do change in significance, no index in terms of particular characteristics could be expected to have much predictive value save under conditions of a highly stable politics or over the relatively short run.

25. For a statement of other directions of development, see B. R. Berelson, "Democratic Theory and Public Opinion," *Public Opinion Quarterly*, XVI (1952), 313-30.

26. It should be noted for the record that this essay was completed essentially in its present form in June, 1953. It, therefore, does not take into account the theoretical advances by Berelson, Lazarsfeld, and McPhee in their *Voting* (Chicago: University of Chicago Press, 1954). Moreover, since the essay was drafted Mr. Munger has completed an intensive analysis of Indiana politics reported in *Two-Party Politics in the State of Indiana* (MS dissertation, Harvard University, 1955). Full utilization of his detailed findings would permit considerable refinement of the factual data underlying the argument.

NOTES TO CHAPTER 16

1. This expression is used by B. R. Berelson, P. F. Lazarsfeld, and W. N. McPhee in Chapter 13 of *Voting* (Chicago: University of Chicago Press, 1954). They designate "proper" voting intention as one which corresponds to the prevailing voting intention of the social stratum to which the voter belongs.

2. T. W. Adorno, Else Frenkel-Brunswik, D. J. Levinson, and R. N. Sanford, *The Authoritarian Personality* (New York: Harper, 1950), chap. 13.

NOTES TO CHAPTER 17

1. Angus Campbell, Gerald Gurin, and W. E. Miller, *The Voter Decides* (Evanston, Ill.: Row, Peterson, 1954), Table 7.2, p. 94.

2. *Ibid.*, p. 94.

3. These figures were cited in S. J. Eldersveld, "The Independent Voter," *American Political Science Review*, XLVI (1952), 732-53.

4. *Ibid.*

5. Campbell, Gurin, and Miller, *op. cit.*

6. See *Group Differences in Attitudes and Votes: A Study of the 1954 Congressional Election* (Ann Arbor: Survey Research Center, Institute for Social Research, University of Michigan, Oct. 1955, mimeographed), p. 164.

7. Harold Lasswell and Abraham Kaplan, *Power and Society* (New Haven: Yale University Press, 1950), pp. 11-12.

8. B. R. Berelson, P. F. Lazarsfeld, and W. N. McPhee, *Voting* (Chicago: University of Chicago Press, 1954), p. 27.

9. *Ibid.*, p. 27.

10. *Ibid.*, p. 24.

11. Although the numbers of cases are sometimes too small for assessing statistical significance with much meaning, when differences are reported as "significant" or "insignificant" the test used is chi-square, and the level of significance is 5 per cent. The data on southern independents are intended to be only suggestive since there were only 62 southern indepen-

dents in contrast to 304 other independents in the sample.

12. See also Campbell, Gurin, and Miller, *op. cit.*, Table 10.7, p. 155. A similar finding was also reported by Eldersveld, *op. cit.*, p. 751, from the data of the Survey Research Center's 1948 national survey. Eldersveld used a combination measure of independence based on ticket splitting and past party voting.

13. Hereinafter independents will be compared to Republicans and Democrats separately. Combining Democrats and Republicans in a single category of party identifiers would run the risk of hiding the differences between independents and the two sets of party identifiers that go in different directions, or reduce the differences between independents and either Democrats or Republicans.

14. Donald S. Strong has found that in the 1952 election upper-income groups in larger southern cities were deserting the Democratic party. "The Presidential Election in the South, 1952," *The Journal of Politics*, XVII (1955), 343-89. We have found that whereas Republican identifiers are found proportionately more frequently in rural areas in the South, they are already relatively as numerous as Democratic identifiers in metropolitan areas in the South (Table 17-2).

15. Campbell, Gurin, and Miller, *op. cit.*, chap. 3, pp. 28-40, contains detailed discussion of participation and interest. Their participation index differs in slight detail from the index used in Tables 17-3 and 17-4. Respondents who had participated in some way but who did not vote were included in the "low" participation category in our tables but in the "medium" category in their tables.

16. See Campbell, Gurin, and Miller, *op. cit.*, Table 7.11, p. 108 and pp. 107-10.

17. *Ibid.*, p. 108.

18. *Ibid.*, Table 7.11, p. 108.

19. *Ibid.*, chap. 8, pp. 112-35.

20. See Campbell, Gurin and Miller, *op. cit.*, Table 10.4, p. 151.

21. *Ibid.*, Appendix B, pp. 194-99.

22. *Ibid.*, Appendix C, pp. 199-206.

23. Harold Lasswell and Abraham Kaplan define an interest as a pattern of demands and its supporting expectations. *Power and Society* (New Haven: Yale University Press, 1950), p. 23. Political interests plus political identifications constitute political *perspectives*. *Op. cit.*, p. 25. Concern with the theoretical importance of expectations for behavior has been stressed by psychologists under the label of ego-involvement. Political interests defined in this way are conceptually and analytically distinct from the more traditional view of interest as attention to political events as reflected in either media consumption or as evidenced by responses to questions about "how interested are you in the campaign?" The extent to which political interest and political attention are related is an empirical question.

24. The coefficient of reproducibility for the scale of political interests was a high 96.3 per cent. The range of error for individual items was 3 to 5 per cent. This scale is used for exploratory purposes and as a matter of convenience instead of discussing the relationships of each of the items to party identification. For a scale to be used as an indication of unidimensionality, it should contain a larger number of items. Further research is indicated for the development of sufficiently valid and reliable scales of political interest.

25. The analysis in this chapter is based on data from a national sample survey conducted by the Survey Research Center, University of Michigan, under the sponsorship of the Political Behavior Committee of the Social Science Research Council. The analysis was made possible by the writer's participation in the 1954 summer seminar on Political Behavior Research held at the Survey Research Center under a

grant from the Social Science Research Council. While the author is grateful to the center and the committee for access to the data, neither group bears any responsibility for the analysis.

NOTES TO CHAPTER 18

1. This work was supported in part by the Behavioral Models Project, Bureau of Applied Social Research, Columbia University, through funds extended by the Office of Naval Research. Reproduction in whole or in part is permitted for any purpose by the United States Government. An earlier draft was read by Professors A. J. Brodbeck, H. H. Hyman, P. F. Lazarsfeld, and Mr. Herbert Menzel. Their comments and criticisms were of considerable value to me.

2. B. R. Berelson, P. F. Lazarsfeld, and W. N. McPhee, *Voting* (Chicago: University of Chicago Press, 1954).

3. P. F. Lazarsfeld, B. R. Berelson, and Hazel Gaudet, *The People's Choice* (2d ed.; New York: Columbia University Press, 1948).

4. Elihu Katz and P. F. Lazarsfeld, *Personal Influence* (Glencoe, Ill.: The Free Press, 1955).

5. For an extensive discussion of these problems see Patricia Kendall and P. F. Lazarsfeld, "Problems of Survey Analysis," in R. K. Merton and P. F. Lazarsfeld (eds.), *Continuities in the Social Sciences* (Glencoe, Ill.: The Free Press, 1950), pp. 133-96; and H. A. Simon, "Spurious Correlation: A Causal Interpretation," *Journal of the American Statistical Association*, XLIX (1954), 467-79.

6. Berelson, Lazarsfeld, and McPhee, *op. cit.*, p. 96. Italics in original.

7. *Ibid.*, p. 98. Italics in original.

8. *Ibid.*, p. 115.

9. *Ibid.*, p. 119.

10. *Ibid.*, p. 148.

11. *Ibid.*, p. 283.

12. Anatol Rapoport in a series of papers on random nets appearing in the *Bulletin of Mathematical Biophysics*, beginning in 1948.

13. T. W. Anderson, "Probability Models for Analyzing Time Changes in Attitudes," in P. F. Lazarsfeld (ed.), *Mathematical Thinking in the Social Sciences* (Glencoe, Ill.: The Free Press, 1954), pp. 17-66.

14. James Coleman, "Formalization of McPhee's Model," and R. R. Bush, "A Suggested Stochastic Interaction Model for Panel Studies," Dartmouth Seminar on Social Process, Columbia University, 1954. [Processed.]

15. Berelson, Lazarsfeld, and McPhee, *op. cit.*, p. 106.

16. *Ibid.*, p. 106.

17. *Ibid.*, p. 24.

18. *Ibid.*, p. 33.

19. *Ibid.*, p. 34.

20. *Ibid.*, p. 34.

21. *Ibid.*, p. 107.

22. *Ibid.*, p. 117.

23. *Ibid.*, p. 139.

24. *Ibid.*, p. 180.

25. *Ibid.*, p. 213.

26. *Ibid.*, p. 246.

27. *Ibid.*, p. 117.

28. In this connection, percentage data on who make up the constants and who the changers from *The People's Choice* (page 68) are interesting:

	Constants	*One-party changers*	*Two-party changers*
Two or more cross-pressures and less interest	13	29	51
Two or more cross-pressures and great interest	8	9	13
No or one cross-pressure and less interest	44	48	31
No or one cross-pressure and great interest	35	14	5

29. Katz and Lazarsfeld, *op. cit.*, pp. 318-19.

30. *Ibid.*, p. 326.

31. Lazarsfeld, Berelson, and Gaudet, *op. cit.*, p. 151. Italics in original.

32. Berelson, Lazarsfeld, and McPhee, *op. cit.*, p. 361.

33. *Ibid.*, p. 119.

34. However, an argument which favors our alternative hypothesis—and, indeed, the hypothesis that all, or most, of the discussions occurred after conversion took place—is the nearly perfect symmetry of Table 18-2. This table is consistent with the view that whether or not a person has changed voting intentions, there is a 70 percent chance that he will talk politics with someone of the same party affiliation as he currently holds and an approximately 20 per cent chance he will discuss politics with someone of the opposite persuasion.

35. Personal communication.

36. Berelson, Lazarsfeld, and McPhee, *op. ct.*, p. 120.

NOTES TO CHAPTER 19

1. Angus Campbell, Gerald Gurin, and W. E. Miller, *The Voter Decides* (Evanston, Ill.: Row, Peterson, 1954).

2. See Appendix C of *The Voter Decides* for a discussion of the problems involved in interpreting the meaning of primary group homogeneity.

3. The authors wish to acknowledge the important contributions of Dr. Leslie Kish, Director of the Sampling Section of the Survey Research Center, to the development of the analysis which is presented in this chapter.

4. Scores on each candidate variable were obtained by subtracting the number of negative references to personal characteristics of a candidate from the number of positive references. For example, an individual who commented favorably three times and unfavorably once on personal attributes of Mr. Eisenhower would be scored two in the Republican direction on orientation to Eisenhower.

5. Scores on each issue variable were obtained by subtracting the number of pro-Republican and anti-Democratic issue references from the number of anti-Republican and pro-Democratic issue references. For example, a person who made one pro-Republican and one anti-Democratic reference to domestic issues but three pro-Democratic and two anti-Republican references to domestic issues would be scored three in the Democratic direction on domestic issue partisanship.

6. The five categories of party identification—strong Republican, weak Republican, independent, weak Democrat, and strong Democrat—were scored zero, one, two, three, and four respectively. Preference for Eisenhower was scored zero; preference for Stevenson one.

7. Several of these are discussed in the Statistical Note appended to this chapter.

8. We are considering respondents in our sample who voted for Eisenhower or Stevenson or who did not vote but told us which of the major-party candidates they preferred.

9. In the course of our discussion we will often speak of the proportion of the variance in preference explained in a statistical sense by one or more of the partisan attitudes. This is equivalent to speaking of the correlation of preference with these attitudes since the proportion of the variance explained is the square of the correlation coefficient.

10. A really satisfactory unraveling of the causal relationships among the partisan attitudes must await successive attitude measurements on the same persons over time.

11. The use of standard regression coefficients removes the effect of certain differences in scales and distributions by treating variation in terms of standard deviations.

12. The reader will note that corresponding partial correlation and standard regression coefficients are roughly of equal size in the results re-

ported in this chapter. Nonetheless, the two measures of relationship are conceptually distinct and both sets of coefficients are given.

13. See, for example, Donald S. Strong, "The Presidential Election in the South, 1952," *Journal of Politics,* XVII (1955), 343-89.

14. A detailed review of this problem would raise a number of questions about the way in which demographic circumstances are associated with political attitudes and motives. We have treated demographic characteristics as independent variables in this analysis largely as a matter of convenience. The fact is that the ways in which these attributes are linked to motivation are complicated and obscure and are doubtless subject to great variation. A careful specification of these relationships is a problem of theory which goes beyond the present analysis.

15. P. F. Lazarsfeld, B. R. Berelson, and Hazel Gaudet, *The People's Choice* (2d ed.; New York: Columbia University Press, 1948), p. 25.

16. *Ibid.*, p. 25.

17. Morris Janowitz and W. E. Miller, "The Index of Political Predisposition in the 1948 Election," *Journal of Politics,* XIV (1952), 710-27.

18. Duncan MacRae, Jr., "Occupations and the Congressional Vote, 1940-1950," *American Sociological Review,* XX (1955), 332-40.

19. This measure was based on answers to the pre-election question "Generally speaking, would you say you personally care a good deal which party wins the presidential election this fall, or that you don't care very much which party wins?"

20. In some cases this may not be true. For example, occupation or even church preference could be affected by partisan belief.

21. The report of time of voting decision was obtained from the post-election question "How long before the election did you decide that you were going to vote the way you did?"

22. R. A. Fisher, "The Statistical Utilization of Multiple Measurements," *Annals of Eugenics,* VIII (1938), 377.

NOTES TO CHAPTER 20

1. Erwin Friend and Jean Bronfenbrenner, "Plant and Equipment Programs and Their Realization," in *Short-Term Economic Forecasting* ("Studies in Income and Wealth," Vol. XVII, National Bureau of Economic Research [Princeton, N. J.: Princeton University Press, 1955]), pp. 53-98.

2. Jean Bronfenbrenner, unpublished manuscript.

3. Friend and Bronfenbrenner, *op. cit.*

4. Bronfenbrenner, *op. cit.*

5. Report of Consultant Committee on Consumer Survey Statistics, *Consumer Survey Statistics* (Washington, D. C.: Federal Reserve System Board of Governors, July, 1953).

6. *Ibid.*, pp. 37-45.

7. *Ibid.*, p. 62. The percentages of those expecting to buy and expecting not to buy do not add precisely to one hundred, presumably because of refusals to answer and because of rounding errors.

8. George Katona and Eva Mueller, "A Study of Purchase Decisions," in Lincoln Clark (ed.), *Consumer Behavior* (New York: New York University Press, 1954; and R. Ferber, "The Role of Planning in Consumer Purchases of Durable Goods," *American Economic Review,* XLIV (1954), 854-74.

9. L. R. Klein and J. B. Lansing, "Decisions to Purchase Consumer Durable Goods," *Journal of Marketing,* XX (Oct., 1955), 109-32.

10. Franco Modigliani and Richard Blumberg, "Utility Analysis and the Consumption Function: An Interpretation of Cross-Section Data," in K. K. Kurihara (ed.), *Post-Keynesian Eco-*

nomics (New Brunswick, N. J.: Rutgers University Press, 1954), pp. 388-436.

11. *Ibid.*, p. 392.

NOTES TO CHAPTER 22

1. See "The Theory of Mass Society" by Daniel Bell in *Commentary*, (July, 1956) for a comprehensive and evaluative discussion of sociological thinking about this concept.

2. The current rash of "adult" Westerns in the mass-media may reflect a wish to simplify contemporary complex problems by placing them in the traditional black-and-white framework of the good guy-bad guy cowboy story.

3. It has long been known that a certain amount of anxiety often facilitates social learning. The research of Allison Davis is particularly pertinent. See "Socialization and Adolescent Personality" in the *Forty-Third Yearbook of the National Society for the Study of Education*, Part I, pp. 198-216, and "The Ego and Status-Anxiety" in *The State of the Social Sciences*, edited by Leonard D. White, (University of Chicago Press, 1956).

4. The choice of locations for election studies should be reviewed by those attempting further studies. It is surprising to me that sociologists have not converged upon Los Angeles as they once did upon Chicago. The sociological studies of Chicago were conducted during a time in which that city represented an extreme case of a problem more mildly experienced in many other American cities. Los Angeles now represents an extreme case of a city moving towards mass society at an unprecedented rate. Furthermore, I am told by marketing experts that a commodity which sells well in Los Angeles is likely, within several months to a year's time, to begin selling well in other major American cities, so that in at least some areas, trends discoverable in Los Angeles are predictive of coming trends elsewhere. There is some reason to believe that voting patterns in Los Angeles are much different than those depicted in the Columbia and Michigan studies in many details and that voting patterns of Los Angeles may be predictive of changes in voting patterns in large Eastern and Middle-Western cities.

5. It may well be that the primary personality problem induced by a rapid movement toward mass society is to find techniques whereby one remains committed emotionally to secondary groups (has a sense of belonging) but continues to be critically detached (so that the needed flexibility to meet complex changing conditions continues to operate).

6. Alexander, F. and French, T. M., et al. *Psychoanalytic Therapy: Principles and Applications* (Ronald Press, New York, 1946).

7. A crisis situation may result when one candidate suddenly appears in a very favorable light which was not anticipated. People frequently have internal stress mobilized by sudden success as well as by sudden failure. A sudden success for one side has, in a competitive society, many repercussions in the personality of organizations of the member of the other side, depending upon the absence or presence of neurotic involvement.

8. Robert Lindner's *The Fifty Minute Hour* contains a psychoanalysis of two political extremists in which the neurotic investments and the ramifications of them in the behavior of the patient in "non-political" institutions is sketched in amazingly arresting ways. G. Almond's studies of different types of personality factors behind communist membership in different European and American settings is well worth reading. (*Appeals of Communism*, Princeton University Press, 1954.) However, studies of po-

litical extremists may frequently act as a defense against deciphering the neurotic investments of those with more conventional political identifications in which a more subtle interplay between personality and political identifications may operate. *Personality and Political Crises*, edited by Alfred H. Stanton and Stewart E. Perry (Free Press, Glencoe, Ill., 1951) is well worth reviewing in terms of impact analysis.

9. With the exception of *Conceptions of Modern Psychiatry* (1940, William Allanson White, Psychiatric Foundation, Washington, D.C.) most of the volumes of Sullivan's writings were published posthumously from his lecture notes and transcripts. See *The Interpersonal Theory of Psychiatry* (1953) and *Clinical Studies in Psychiatry* (1956) (both published by W. W. Norton, N. Y.).

10. These practices are outlined in his book, *The Clinical Interview* (W. W. Norton, N. Y., 1954). Patrick Mullahy has been a particularly important person is the exposition and clarification of Sullivan's theories. See especially *The Contributions of Harry Stack Sullivan* (Hermitage, N. Y., 1952) edited by him.

11. The puzzling "transference" cures often, but not always, seem to be reducible to therapeutic reinforcement of neurotic patterns not fully understood by either participant.

12. Richard J. Bonier and Milton Rokeach have begun some fascinating research studies on dogmatism and time perspective. They find the dogmatic (selectively inattentive) person tends to orient himself toward the future without adequate regard for the present—a type of "magical thinking" perhaps in which there is no continuity concepts to bridge the gap between the present and the future. The technique, if applied to the voter and the voting process, promises much by way of enlightenment about irrational processes underlying voting behavior. Loyalty to a party may remain even when there is no present justification for it; it is maintained perhaps by projecting happy unrealistic images of the future into party identifications. Dogmatism about political issues would be expected to rapidly harden so as to "defend" the "magical" time perspective. The phenomena of "unrealistic" (purely sentimental) "hope" is very widespread in America. Another research study of high potential toward understanding voting processes is Herbert C. Kelman's "Three Processes of Acceptance of Social Influence: Compliance, Identification, and Internalization" (Paper read at APA meetings, Chicago, 1956)

13. *The New American Right* (Criterion, N. Y., 1955) edited by Daniel Bell, highlights many processes of selective inattention related to Republican victories at the ballot boxes, during the last decade. The essays of Richard Hofstadter on "Pseudo-Conservatives" and Talcott Parsons on "Social Strains in America" are among the best examples of the application of psychoanalytic principles, sometimes seemingly unwittingly used, to studies of political campaigns, although the hypotheses that result are still in need of rigorous research substantiation by the types of methods that the voting volumes represent.

14. Theodor Reik, *The Third Ear*, Farrar, Straus (1948). Many people believe that Reik did not take into account sufficiently the checking of "third ear" messages (impact of the patient upon the analyst's emotions) against other types of unconfirming or confirming evidence. Thus, a wildly intuitive psychoanalyst might be led to make many errors of judgment, if he were inadvertently engaged in a marked "countertransference" relationship.

15. See Harold D. Lasswell's *The Decision Process: Seven Categories of Functional Analysis* (1956, Bureau of Government Research, University of

Maryland, College Park, Maryland) which provides intellectual tools for the development of ingenious political processes to further democratic atmospheres of influence. See also George Simmel's *Conflict* (1955, published by the Free Press and translated by Kurt H. Wolff).

16. There appears to be only a small impact upon the voter made by the mass-media in the empirical studies completed thus far. The process of mass-media influence, however, may be more subtle than the models used by behavioral scientists to design research studies presuppose. As pointed out by David Riesman, I believe, the plays, novels and films about politicians tend to depict them in rather intensely and repeatedly unfavorable terms. Such exposures may lead the voter, who is heavily exposed to the dramatic products of the mass-media to "discount" all political messages of any *real* politician using the mass-media as a base of potential influence, whereas those sparingly exposed may be more affected. Furthermore, political apathy may be greater among the heavily exposed mass-media audience than among the more lightly exposed. A serious dramatic film, play or novel about the triumph of a politician with an admirable personality and set of values may do more to raise interest in a political campaign and weaken apathy than any other single stimulus. The favorable use of dramatic mass-media agencies toward arousing political interest is still an untried experiment.

17. I am reminded here of the delightful film, "Miracle on 34th Street" in which a policy of commercial altruism at Xmas time had enormous "cash value" for Macy's much to the surprise of a hard-bitten store manager who wanted Santa Claus to peddle toy surpluses. One suspects that a candidate in the next national election, who appealed to humanitarian motives by emphasizing the need for reform of educational institutions or legal institutions, might catch the imagination and fire the thoughtfulness of huge masses of the public. Arthur Koestler's *Reflections on Hanging* (Macmillan, 1957) is probably the beginning of a whole series of similar volumes which could lead to political campaign issues.

18. A general hypothesis of some utility for the study of the voter's perceptions is the following: The more secure the individual, the more he will adequately observe the "facts" impinging upon him; the more self-esteem the individual has, the more adequately he will "interpret" the facts. Security refers to expectations of being able to satisfy one's needs; self-esteem refers to one's own evaluation of the self as being "worthy" of required satisfactions. One can increase people's security without increasing their self-esteem. The opposite state is a little more difficult to produce, but is hypothetically possible. The technique of "false praise" may produce such a result, where the actions expected to follow praise are withheld or shown in half-hearted fashion.

19. Any careful study of John B. Watson's writings regarding cognitive processes could not fail to impress one with the rather strategic importance they occupy within his system. Watson had a knack for stating complex ideas with deceptive simplicity, and if one does not read him with the proper appreciation for the complexity of his ideas, it might appear that his program of behaviorism wiped out interest in the study of thought processes. Some of Watson's specific ideas about thinking still appear novel and in need of the kind of testing which he advocated. Watson's views about psychoanalysis are also somewhat misunderstood. He appears to have "mellowed" toward analytic theory over the years.

20. The work in progress at Har-

vard University, under the direction of Jerome S. Bruner, is a great stride forward. See *A Study of Thinking* (1956, John Wiley and Sons, N. Y.). See also the thoughtful volume which, comprehensively summarizes research on cognition, Vinacke, *The Psychology of Thinking* (McGraw Hill, N. Y.). The research of Harry F. Harlow on "learning sets" attempts to relate "insight" and "trial and error" learning to each other. A good summary of Professor Harlow's conclusions is to be found in the chapter on "Thinking" which he prepared for *The Theoretical Foundations of Psychology* (D. Van Nostrand, N. Y., 1951) edited by H. Helson. See also I. A. Richards' *Speculative Instruments* (University of Chicago, 1955) for some ingenious ideas about the education of the public.

21. The victory of the opposing party often produces highly neurotic reactions among the members of the defeated party. In discussions with people at this stage of a campaign, one frequently hears suicidal fantasies verbalized, paranoid thoughts expressed bordering on paranoid breaks, alcoholic sprees contemplated, and many other types of autistic reactions not infrequently set into motion by psychotherapy itself.

22. See Ruth L. Munroe's *Schools of Psychoanalytic Thought* (Dryden, N. Y., 1955) and William Healy, Augusts T. Bronner and Anna May Bowers, *The Structure and Meaning of Psychoanalysis* (Alfred A. Knopf, N. Y., 1949). *Twenty Years of Psychoanalysis* edited by Franz Alexander and Helen Ross (W. W. Norton, N. Y., 1953) is an interesting attempt to up-date issues. Harold D. Lasswell's "Impact of Psychoanalytic Thinking on the Social Sciences" in *The State of the Social Sciences* (University of Chicago Press, 1956) edited by Leonard D. White, outlines some of the controversial issues within psychoanalysis. The author is currently engaged in a research project directed by Franz Alexander in which psychoanalytic therapy is being observed through one-way screens in an attempt to state as objectively as possible the therapeutic agents within psychoanalytic practice.

23. August B. Hollingshead and Fredrick C. Redlich's *Social Class and Mental Illness* (Wiley, N. Y., 1958) shows the political issues in the practice of psychotherapy in another way than is under discussion here. In a study comparable to those of the voting books, the volume depicts how different types of psychotherapeutic attention and respect is given in a sharply discriminating way to members of the community who become mentally ill according to their socioeconomic positions. The findings of this study are all the more astounding since they were not anticipated or desired by the members of the psychiatric profession who were surveyed.

24. The valuable *Language of Politics* by Harold D. Lasswell, Nathan Leites and Associates, suggests many ways in which the communications between patient and therapist might be scrutinized so as to discover the way in which political and power impulses are expressed within therapy.

25. *The Psychology of Economics* by Walter A. Weiss Ropf is an arresting excursion into the psychoanalysis of economic thought. *Personality and Organization* by Chris Argyris (Harper, N. Y., 1957) although not specifically psychoanalytically oriented, is a study of human relations in institutional settings. *Character and Social Structure* by Hans Gerth and C. Wright Mills (Harcourt, Brace, N. Y., 1953) outlines a model of social-historical change which deserves study. Karl Mannheim's *Essays on Sociology and Social Psychology* (Routledge and Kegan Paul, London, 1953) are, of course, masterful exercises in interdisciplinary thinking

as to the application of psychological issues to sociological problems. The interesting experimental psychoanalytic practices of Don Jackson at Palo Alto, in which all members of an institution (the family) are treated group fashion, are found to add to an increase in understanding of better applications of psychoanalysis. See also George Bach's *Intensive Group Psychotherapy* (Ronald Press, N. Y., 1954).

26. For a particularly interesting recent discussion, see Allen Wheelis, "The Vocational Hazards of Psychoanalysis", *The International Journal of Psychoanalysis*, Vol. XXXVII, Parts II-III, 1956, P. 1-14. For "countertransference" under extreme conditions, see Richard E. Renneker, "Counter Transference Reactions to Cancer", *Psychosomatic Medicine*, Vol. XIX, No. 5, Sept.-Oct. 1957, pp. 409-418. See also "The Feeling of Superiority: An Occupational Hazard in the Practice of Psychotherapy" by Judd Marmor in *The American Journal of Psychiatry*, Vol. 110, No. 5, Nov. 1953.

The Contributors

Robert E. Agger is Assistant Professor of Political Science, University of North Carolina.

Franz Alexander, M.D., is Director of the Institute for Psychosomatic Research at Mount Sinai Hospital, Los Angeles, California.

F. E. Balderston is Assistant Professor of Business Administration, University of California, Berkeley.

Herbert Blumer is Chairman of the Department of Sociology and Social Institutions, University of California, Berkeley.

Angus Campbell is Director of the Survey Research Center and Professor of Psychology and Sociology, University of Michigan.

Leslie A. Fiedler is Chairman of the Department of English, Montana State University.

Ray Hyman is Assistant Professor of Social Psychology, Harvard University.

V. O. Key, Jr., is Associate Professor of Political Science, Harvard University.

Gladys Engel Lang was formerly associated with Carleton University, Ottawa.

Kurt Lang is on the staff of the Canadian Broadcasting Corporation.

R. Duncan Luce was formerly an Assistant Professor of Mathematical Statistics and Sociology, Columbia University, and is now an Instructor at Harvard University.

Eleanor E. Maccoby is Research Associate in the Laboratory of Human Development, Harvard University.

R. S. Milne, formerly of the Department of Economics, University of Bristol, is Professor of Political Science, Victoria University, Wellington, New Zealand.

Franco Modigliani is Professor of Economics and Industrial Administration, Graduate School of Industrial Administration, Carnegie Institute of Technology.

Frank Munger is a graduate student in the Department of Political Science, Harvard University.

Talcott Parsons is Chairman of the Department of Social Relations, Harvard University.

Ithiel de Sola Pool is Director of the Research Program in International Communications, Center for International Studies and Associate Professor of Political Science, Masachusetts Institute of Technology.

H. H. Remmers is Director of the Division of Educational Reference and Professor of Psychology and Education, Purdue University.

Richard E. Renneker, M.D., is Associate Director of the Institute for Psychosomatic Research, Mount Sinai Hospital, Los Angeles, California.

Henry W. Riecken is Associate Professor of Sociology, University of Minnesota.

Irving Roshwalb is Vice-President and Technical Director, Audits and Surveys Company, Inc., New York, N. Y.

Peter H. Rossi is Assistant Professor of Sociology, University of Chicago.

Donald E. Stokes is associated with the Survey Research Center, University of Michigan, as a fellow of the Social Science Research Council.

C. W. Wahl, M.D., is Assistant Professor of Psychiatry, University of California and Consultant in Psychiatry at the Sepulveda Veteran's Administration Hospital, Los Angeles.

Index